COGNITIVE SCIENCE, COMPUTATIONAL INTELLIGENCE, AND DATA

T0296830

COGNITIVE SCIENCE, COMPUTATIONAL INTELLIGENCE, AND DATA ANALYTICS

Methods and Applications With Python

VIKAS KHARE

School of Technology, Management and Engineering, NMIMS, Indore, Madhya Pradesh, India;
Bureau of Energy Efficiency, India

SANJEET KUMAR DWIVEDI

Senior Consultant at Wind Energy Business RDT Engineers, Denmark; Curtin University, Perth, Australia

MONICA BHATIA

School of Business Management, NMIMS, Indore, Madhya Pradesh, India

Morgan Kaufmann is an imprint of Elsevier
50 Hampshire Street, 5th Floor, Cambridge, MA 02139, United States

Copyright © 2024 Elsevier Inc. All rights are reserved, including those for text and data mining, AI training, and similar technologies.

Publisher's note: Elsevier takes a neutral position with respect to territorial disputes or jurisdictional claims in its published content, including in maps and institutional affiliations.

No part of this publication may be reproduced or transmitted in any form or by any means, electronic or mechanical, including photocopying, recording, or any information storage and retrieval system, without permission in writing from the publisher. Details on how to seek permission, further information about the Publisher's permissions policies and our arrangements with organizations such as the Copyright Clearance Center and the Copyright Licensing Agency, can be found at our website: www.elsevier.com/permissions.

This book and the individual contributions contained in it are protected under copyright by the Publisher (other than as may be noted herein).

Notices
Knowledge and best practice in this field are constantly changing. As new research and experience broaden our understanding, changes in research methods, professional practices, or medical treatment may become necessary.

Practitioners and researchers must always rely on their own experience and knowledge in evaluating and using any information, methods, compounds, or experiments described herein. In using such information or methods they should be mindful of their own safety and the safety of others, including parties for whom they have a professional responsibility.

To the fullest extent of the law, neither the Publisher nor the authors, contributors, or editors, assume any liability for any injury and/or damage to persons or property as a matter of products liability, negligence or otherwise, or from any use or operation of any methods, products, instructions, or ideas contained in the material herein.

ISBN: 978-0-443-16078-3

For Information on all Morgan Kaufmann publications
visit our website at https://www.elsevier.com/books-and-journals

Publisher: Mara Conner
Acquisitions Editor: Chris Katsaropoulos
Editorial Project Manager: Vaishali Panwar
Production Project Manager: Jayadivya Saiprasad
Cover Designer: Matthew Limbert

Typeset by MPS Limited, Chennai, India

Contents

6. Data analysis applications and methodology

Foreword

In the ever-evolving landscape of science and technology, the confluence of cognitive science, computational intelligence, and data analysis has emerged as a powerful and transformative force. This interdisciplinary fusion has not only deepened our understanding of human cognition but also unlocked unprecedented possibilities in machine learning, artificial intelligence, and data-driven decision-making.

"Cognitive Science, Computational Intelligence, and Data Analytics" is a comprehensive exploration of this dynamic intersection, offering readers a unique journey through the realms of cognitive science, computational intelligence techniques, and the practical application of Python for data analysis. This book is designed to serve as a guiding light for students, researchers, and practitioners seeking to harness the symbiotic relationship between these fields to advance their knowledge and problem-solving capabilities.

As we embark on this intellectual voyage, we will delve into the core principles of cognitive science, unveiling the mysteries of human thought processes, perception, learning, and memory. We will then transition seamlessly into the world of computational intelligence, where algorithms inspired by nature and the human brain are employed to solve complex problems, optimize processes, and enhance decision-making.

Throughout this journey, Python will be our trusty companion, providing the toolkit necessary for data acquisition, manipulation, visualization, and modeling. Python's versatility and simplicity make it an ideal choice for both beginners and experts in the field, and our hands-on approach will ensure that you not only understand the theoretical foundations but also gain practical experience in applying these concepts to real-world scenarios.

You will have gained a holistic understanding of cognitive science, computational intelligence, and data analysis, as well as the proficiency to apply these concepts using Python. Whether you are a student eager to explore the cutting edge of interdisciplinary science, a researcher seeking to leverage computational intelligence for innovative solutions, or a data analyst aiming to expand your toolkit, this book will equip you with the knowledge and skills to thrive in the rapidly evolving landscape of cognitive science, computational intelligence, and data analysis.

So, without further ado, let us embark on this exciting journey into the realms of the mind, algorithms, and data-driven insights. Together, we will unravel the mysteries of cognitive science, harness the power of computational intelligence, and wield the capabilities of Python to transform the way we perceive and analyze the world around us.

Pradip Chande[1,2,3,4]

[1]*M.P. State Electronics Development Corporation, Bhopal, Madhya Pradesh, India*
[2]*IIM Indore, Madhya Pradesh, India*
[3]*MANIT, Bhopal, Madhya Pradesh, India*
[4]*SGSITS, Indore, Madhya Pradesh, India*

Overview of the book

"Cognitive Science, Computational Intelligence, and Data Analytics" is a comprehensive guide that illuminates the fascinating synergy between three distinct yet interconnected fields: cognitive science, computational intelligence, and data analysis. This book serves as a roadmap for readers who wish to explore the intricate web of human cognition, artificial intelligence (AI), and data-driven insights, all while harnessing the versatility of the Python programming language.

This book is divided into the six chapters.

Chapter 1 discusses the foundation of analytics. Analysis is a very important tool to measure the different attributes of any type of real-life problems. This chapter enlightens the basic concept of descriptive, diagnostic, prescriptive, and predictive analytics askey components of analytics. This chapter also elaborates emerging areas of analytics in the form of data analysis, web analysis, business analytics, and big data analysis. This chapter also includes different aspects of value chain analysis with their features. The chapter concludes with the case study on performance of Mumbai Indians in the Indian Premier League as well as value chain analysis of Starbucks.

Chapter 2 talks about the foundation of cognitive science. An example that exemplifies this is the challenge of recalling a phone number afterward. To comprehend this process, one approach would involve examining behavior through direct or naturalistic observation. Within this chapter, the fundamental concepts of cognitive science

are explored, encompassing the understanding of the brain, sensory motor information, language, and linguistics. This exploration encompasses the concepts of psycholinguistics and creative linguistics. Additionally, the chapter delves into the theory of information processing and the notion of short-term memory. Moreover, the chapter presents case studies that revolve around the aforementioned topics of brain and sensory motor information, language and linguistic knowledge, information processing, and the concept of short-term memory.

Chapter 3 presents data theory and data taxonomy. This chapter explores the concepts of data as a whole, different views of data, measurement and scaling, and various types of scales. Understanding the taxonomy of data and the different types of scales is essential for selecting appropriate analytical techniques, designing data collection instruments, and interpreting results accurately. It forms the foundation for organizing and classifying data, enabling researchers and analysts to make informed decisions and draw meaningful insights. This chapter encompasses the understanding of data as a whole, different views of data, measurement and scaling concepts, and various types of scales. These concepts are crucial for analyzing and interpreting data accurately, facilitating effective decision-making and insights generation in various fields.

Chapter 4 descibes multivariate data analytics and cognitive analytics. This chapter explores key methodologies such as factor analysis, principal component analysis, regression analysis, logistic analysis, and multivariate analysis, and their applications in understanding and analyzing multivariate data. Factor analysis is employed to identify latent variables that explain the correlations among observed variables, facilitating dimensionality reduction and a deeper understanding of underlying constructs. Principal component analysis transforms correlated variables into uncorrelated principal components, enabling dimensionality reduction and visualization of complex datasets. Regression analysis examines the relationship between dependent and independent variables, allowing for predictions and insights into causality. Logistic analysis focuses on modeling binary outcomes or categorical variables, aiding in predicting probabilities and classification. Multivariate analysis encompasses a range of techniques for examining multiple variables and their relationships simultaneously, offering holistic perspectives and uncovering intricate patterns.

Chapter 5 explores the applications of AI and machine learning (ML) in data analysis, focusing on key aspects such as knowledge representation, the AI cycle, and the intersection of cognitive science with AI. Knowledge representation plays a crucial role in data analysis, as it involves organizing and structuring information in a way that can be processed by AI algorithms. Various techniques, including semantic networks, ontologies, and probabilistic models, are employed to represent knowledge effectively. These representations serve as the foundation for AI and ML algorithms to reason, learn, and make informed decisions based on the available data. The AI cycle, consisting of data acquisition, preprocessing, modeling, evaluation, and deployment, forms a systematic framework for implementing AI and ML in data analysis. Data acquisition involves gathering relevant datasets, while preprocessing techniques, such as data cleaning, normalization, and feature selection, ensure data quality and readiness for analysis. Modeling encompasses the development and training of AI and ML models using appropriate algorithms and techniques. Evaluation is crucial to assess the model's performance and refine it, if necessary.

Chapter 6 reviews data analysis application and methodology. The chapter focuses on the application of data mining methodologies and AI in object detection. It introduces two popular data mining methodologies: CRISP-DM and SEMMA. CRISP-DM stands for Cross-Industry Standard Process for Data Mining, while SEMMA stands for Sample, Explore, Modify, Model, and Assess. Both methodologies provide a structured approach to data mining projects, with CRISP-DM being more widely used in industry. The chapter then explores the application of AI in object detection. Object detection is a critical task in computer vision, with numerous applications in fields such as surveillance, autonomous vehicles, and robotics. The chapter discusses the use of convolutional neural networks for object detection, with a focus on the popular YOLO (You Only Look Once) algorithm.

1

Foundation of analytics

Abbreviations

KBytes	kilobytes
MBytes	megabytes
TBytes	terrabytes
PBytes	petabytes
NCSS	Number Cruncher Statistical Systems
JMP	John's Macintosh Project
BI	business intelligence
KPI	key performance indicator
CTA	call to action
HTML	hyper text markup language
API	application programming interfaces
XML	extensible markup language
HTTP	hypertext transfer protocol
URL	uniform resource locator
CPU	central processing unit
IPL	Indian Premier League
MI	Mumbai Indians
RCB	Royal Challengers Bangalore
BCCI	Board of Control for Cricket in India
ICC	International Cricket Council
GDP	gross domestic product
KDD	knowledge discovery in database

1.1 Introduction

In the current landscape, researchers are heavily focused on various cutting-edge fields such as Artificial Intelligence (AI), Machine Learning, Cloud Computing, Blockchain, Augmented Reality, and the Internet of Things. All of these domains rely on the crucial process of data evaluation and analytics. Analytics serves as the transformative process that converts conventional information into intelligent data, which can then be utilized in diverse decision-making processes, as illustrated in Fig. 1.1.

Analytics is a scientific method for identifying and expressing the significant patterns that may be identified through the data. Analytics is the combination of math, statistics, programming language, and general assessment based on the human perception. Fig. 1.2

Cognitive Science, Computational Intelligence, and Data Analytics
DOI: https://doi.org/10.1016/B978-0-443-16078-3.00004-6
© 2024 Elsevier Inc. All rights are reserved, including those for text and data mining, AI training, and similar technologies.

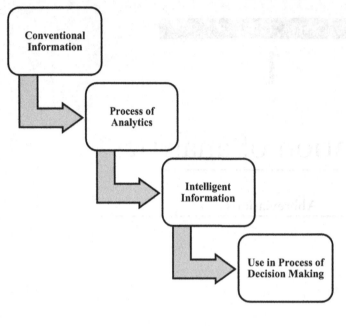

FIGURE 1.1 Process of analytics.

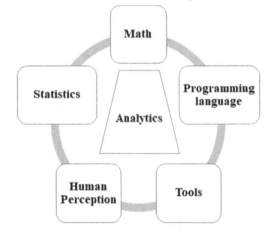

FIGURE 1.2 Key components of analytics.

shows the key components of the analytics. In analytics, to define the problem statement, it is necessary to convert it into the mathematical equation and the objective function. Mathematical equations show different parameters, which directly or indirectly affect the process of analytics. Regression analysis is a highly effective mathematical technique used for interpreting datasets. It encompasses both single regression and multiregression methods. Statistics plays a vital role in the realm of analytics, as it classifies the analytics process based on various attributes, providing valuable insights into the given dataset.

For the example, applying statistical analysis to the temperature data for the month of January in a specific city, we find that the mean, minimum, and maximum temperatures are recorded as 12°C, 1°C, and 17°C, respectively. These values indicate that the city experiences winter during January. While this may seem like ordinary information, the XYZ textile industry can leverage it as intelligent data. Consequently, during the month of January, the XYZ textile industry can strategically market and sell woolen clothes in the city, capitalizing on the seasonal demand. Programming languages and a variety of tools are essential components of analytics. Analyzing data using traditional mathematical and statistical methods can be challenging, particularly when dealing with large volumes of data measured in KBytes, MBytes, TBytes, or PBytes. In such cases, specific programming languages and data analysis tools play a vital role in effectively analyzing the given dataset.

Python and R are two programming languages commonly employed for data analysis. These languages offer extensive capabilities for processing and interpreting data. Additionally, there are several tools available that facilitate data analytics, such as NCSS, JMP, Power BI, and RapidMiner. These tools provide advanced functionalities and features that aid in the analysis and exploration of datasets.

In organizations, decisions are often made relying on a given dataset, but this approach doesn't always yield fruitful results since data itself can be rigid while human perception is flexible. When making decisions based on a dataset, it's crucial to consider that data collection is carried out by human beings, and it's improbable for data collection to be 100% accurate. To illustrate this point, let's consider an example where we want to measure the temperature of New York City. We assign this task to 20 students in a specific class, and each student measures the temperature at different locations throughout the city. However, all these measurements are collectively considered as the temperature of New York City. In this scenario, it becomes challenging to determine the accuracy of the dataset. Therefore, it is important to explore ways to ascertain the accuracy of such datasets.

In the present day, human perception plays a crucial role in data evaluation and the ultimate decision-making process. This integration of human perception and data assessment involves the field of cognitive science. Cognitive science is an interdisciplinary field that combines insights from linguistics, psychology, neurology, philosophy, AI, and anthropology. Its purpose is to delve into the workings of the mind and its various functions. Through cognitive science, researchers explore the characteristics, functions, and processes involved in cognition. Lots of researchers are already works on the field of data analysis.

Sun et al. describe significance of analytics in the field of chemical and biological process of manufacturing. In this article, various higher order data types in manufacturing processes are discussed, along with their possible applications. The use of tensorial data analytics in industrial processes is then discussed from a few angles, with a focus on multilinear substructure learning issues. Mazanec et al. describe importance of big data analysis in the tourism industry. In order to clear up certain misconceptions, the author reviews recent research, primarily in the area of tourism design, and points out the theoretical components that are obscured by strongly information big data analytical methodologies. Quin et al. analyze the role of data analytics in the machine learning process. Using developments in statistical learning theory over the past 20 years and the financial success of top big data businesses, we introduce the current direction of progress in machine learning and AI in this study. The features of process manufacturing systems are then covered, and a brief history of data analytics research and development over the previous three decades is given. Marquez et al. describe diagnosis of qualitative management through data analytics. The technique focuses on identifying and quantifying links between internal and external measures that enable the transition from effective performance management from performance measurement. It has been put to the test as a case study methodology utilizing actual data from the balanced scorecard of a top manufacturing business for two full years. Thagard et al. describe different aspects of COVID-19 through cognitive science. The adoption of theories concerning the origins and prognoses of disease by scientists, which are based on explanatory coherence, can be explained by cognitive models. Motivated inference, in which conclusions are affected by personal goals that contribute to emotional coherence, is used to explain irrational departures from sound reasoning. Well-known psychological and neurological factors can also influence decisions regarding COVID-19. By altering beliefs and enhancing behaviors that come from intention-action gaps, cognitive science offers guidance on how to enhance human behavior in pandemics. Emily et al. describe different prospectus of cognitive science with the interaction between man and mind. Even while socially interactive robots are becoming more common, our knowledge of the brain mechanisms behind these interactions is still quite restricted. The cognitive and brain sciences can significantly advance this effort's theory and methodology. Botvinick et al. describes the role of cognitive science in the field of AI. Rapid advancements in AI shine a new light on a persistent issue: how can we effectively develop AI to maximize its advantages for humanity? It will be a fascinating task for cognitive science as a whole, as well as for AI research, to provide a satisfying and timely response to this topic.

This chapter is classified into the seven sections. Section 1.1 is Introduction, and Section 1.2 is the concepts of analytics. Emerging areas of analytics and value chain in analytics are described in Sections 1.3 and 1.4, respectively. Conclusion is in Section 1.5, and further chapters will end with case study and exercise in Sections 1.6 and 1.7, respectively.

1.2 Concepts of analytics

Analytics is a scientific approach that aims to identify and reveal significant patterns present within data. It involves the transformation of raw and unprocessed data into actionable knowledge, enabling improved decision-making. To interpret and extract meaningful insights from data, analytics leverages the utilization of statistics, computer programming, and operations research. Its value becomes particularly evident in domains where vast quantities of data or information are collected. Analytics grants us access to crucial information that would otherwise remain hidden within the vast sea of data. It is a valuable tool that can be utilized by managers, leaders, and individuals across various fields, especially in today's data-driven world. Analytics serves as a powerful forge, generating valuable information that has long been regarded as a potent weapon. It revolutionizes nearly every industry where extensive amounts of data are amassed, including business, science, sports, healthcare, and numerous others. Fig. 1.3 shows the type of analytics, and there are four types of analytics. Following are the description of the different types of the analytical processes:

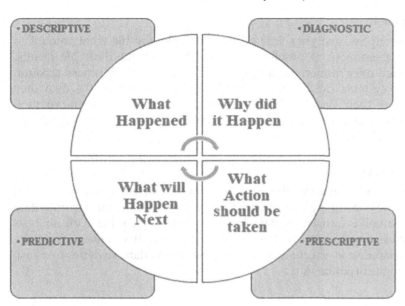

FIGURE 1.3 Types of analytics.

1.2.1 Descriptive analytics

Descriptive analytics is a branch of analytics that focuses on describing and summarizing historical data to gain insights and understand patterns, trends, and characteristics of a given dataset. Its primary objective is to provide a comprehensive overview and understanding of past events and occurrences. In descriptive analytics, data is examined and analyzed to answer questions such as *"What happened?"* and *"What is the current state?."* Businesses use descriptive analytics to assess how well they are performing and whether they are on track to meet their objectives in many areas of the business. Business executives and financial experts monitor basic financial measures generated by descriptive analytics, like the growth in quarterly sales and expenses. Marketing teams utilize descriptive analytics to analyze indicators like conversion rates and the amount of social media followers to track the effectiveness of the campaigns.

1.2.1.1 Five steps in descriptive analytics

Determining the metrics, you want to output is typically the first step in applying descriptive analytics and presenting them in the proper format is the final step. The procedures to generate your own descriptive analytics are listed below:

1.2.1.1.1 State business metrics

The meaning of Metrics, is to identify number of attributes, which directly or indirectly effect the system. Identifying the attribute, are the first step to analyze the problem statement. For instance, a business that is focused on growth may measure quarterly revenue growth, while its accounts receivable department might keep track of different attributes like days' sales outstanding and others that show how long it takes to recover money from consumers.

1.2.1.1.2 Identify data required

In the next step of descriptive analytics, it is necessary to identify the what amount of data is required for the assessment of problem statement to reach the desirable results. The data may be dispersed over numerous programs and files at same business account. Businesses that use ERP systems can already have the majority or all of the data they require in the databases of their systems. Some indicators might also need information from outside sources, like social media platforms, e-commerce websites, and databases used for industry benchmarking.

1.2.1.1.3 Extract and prepare data

Extracting, integrating, and preparing the data for analysis when it originates from numerous sources is a time-consuming but essential process to develop the accurate data set. This process could involve translating data into a format compatible with analysis tools as well as data cleansing to remove the discrepancies and inaccuracies from the given data set. Data preparation is a technique used by advanced data analytics to assist, prepare, shape, and arrange corporate data.

1.2.1.1.4 Analyze data

Businesses can apply descriptive analytics using a range of technologies, including spreadsheets and business intelligence (BI) software. Applying elementary arithmetic computations to one or more parameters is a common step in descriptive analytics. Sales managers might, for instance, keep tabs on the typical revenue per sale or the quarterly revenue from new clients. Financial measures like gross profit margin, or the proportion of gross profit to sales, may be monitored by executives and financial experts.

1.2.1.1.5 Present data

Stakeholders are frequently more likely to grasp data when it is presented in visually appealing ways like pie charts, bar charts, and line graphs. However, certain individuals, such as financial experts, might prefer information to be presented in the form of statistics and tables.

1.2.1.2 Use case of descriptive analytics

Reports: Descriptive analytics is used to provide the primary financial indicators found in a company's financial statements. Descriptive analytics are often used in other typical reports to emphasize specific areas of business performance.

Visualizations: To convert the data set into the graphical representation is called the data visualization. Metrics can be more effectively communicated to a larger audience by being displayed in charts and other graphic forms.

Dashboards: It is a tool that executives, managers, and other staff members can use to monitor progress and organize their daily workload. Dashboards offer a selection of KPIs and other crucial data that are catered to the needs of each individual. To help people quickly digest the information, it may be presented as charts or through the other visualizations approach.

1.2.1.3 *Advantages of descriptive analytics*

There are several benefits to descriptive analytics. It can be carried out using commonly available instruments and doesn't necessitate a thorough understanding of analytical or statistical approaches. It can respond to a lot of the frequently asked inquiries regarding how well a company is doing, like whether or not sales last quarter met targets. This assists the company in identifying areas that require improvement.

1.2.1.4 *Disadvantages of descriptive analytics*

Descriptive analytics' main flaw is that it merely recounts what has occurred without seeking to understand its causes or foresee what will happen later. Additionally, it is typically restricted to relatively straightforward analyses that focus on the interactions between two or three variables.

Python program and their outcome for descriptive analytics:

```
Program:
import pandas as pd

# Create a sample dataset
data = {'Name': ['John', 'Jane', 'Mike', 'Emily', 'David'],
    'Age': [25, 30, 35, 28, 32],
    'Salary': [50000, 60000, 75000, 55000, 70000]}
df = pd.DataFrame(data)

# Display basic statistics of the dataset
print("Descriptive Statistics:")
print(df.describe())

# Calculate mean salary
mean_salary = df['Salary'].mean()
print("\nMean Salary:", mean_salary)

# Calculate median age
median_age = df['Age'].median()
print("Median Age:", median_age)

# Calculate mode of names
mode_names = df['Name'].mode()
print("Mode Names:", mode_names.to_list())

# Identify the youngest and oldest individuals
youngest_person = df.loc[df['Age'].idxmin()]
oldest_person = df.loc[df['Age'].idxmax()]
print("\nYoungest Person:")
print(youngest_person)
print("\nOldest Person:")
print(oldest_person)
```

(cont'd)

Outcome:
Descriptive Statistics:

	Age	Salary
count	5.000000	5.000000
mean	30.000000	62000.000000
std	3.807887	10368.220677
min	25.000000	50000.000000
25%	28.000000	55000.000000
50%	30.000000	60000.000000
75%	32.000000	70000.000000
max	35.000000	75000.000000

Mean Salary: 62000.0
Median Age: 30.0
Mode Names: ['David', 'Emily', 'Jane', 'John', 'Mike']

Youngest Person:
Name   John
Age   25
Salary 50000
Name: 0, dtype: object

Oldest Person:
Name   Mike
Age   35
Salary 75000
Name: 2, dtype: object

In this program, after performing the basic descriptive analytics steps such as displaying the dataset statistics, calculating mean salary, median age, and mode of names, it also identifies the youngest and oldest individuals in the dataset using the idxmin() and idxmax() functions.

1.2.2 Diagnostic analytics

Diagnostic analysis provides an explanation for why something occurred or "why did it happen." By using methods like data discovery, drill-down, and correlations to go deeper into the data and pinpoint the underlying causes of events and behaviors, it advances descriptive analytics.

With compare to the descriptive analytics, in diagnostic analysis, past data to be used for the assessment. For instance, a fashion company can experience an unexpected increase in profits. The business can create and evaluate several theories regarding why that occurred by utilizing diagnostic analytics. One of their apparel lines may have been featured on a Netflix series or pushed by a famous influencer. They can determine the most likely reason for the profit rise by gathering and evaluating new data, which will then drive their future strategy.

1.2.2.1 Use case of diagnostic analytics

Diagnostic analytics provides a wide range of potential applications, much like descriptive analytics, which also emphasizes retrospective data. Almost all disciplines and sectors use it in some capacity. Diagnostics analytics, for instance, can be applied by:

- *Sales teams*: To determine why a company's profits are dropping or growing.
- *Marketing teams*: To figure out why a website has seen a traffic increase.
- *Information technology*: To diagnose technical problems within a company's digital infrastructure.
- *Human resource*: To understand the factors contributing to why employees may leave a company.
- *Big pharma*: To evaluate the effectiveness of different drugs.
- *Hospitals*: To understand why patients are admitted for particular ailments.

1.2.2.2 Advantages of diagnostic analytics

- Provide more detailed insights by digging deeper into the data than you can with just descriptive analytics.
- Using concrete evidence from the past to create (and test) hypotheses is possible with diagnostic analytics.
- Information about, whether data points are merely correlated or whether they clearly show cause and effect by comparing input and output data.
- If outliers and anomalies represent important discoveries or are simply the result of inaccurate data by identifying them.
- Knowing what caused previous events allows to avoid costly mistakes in the future or, on the other hand, repeat behaviors that resulted in unanticipated favorable outcomes.

1.2.2.3 Disadvantages of diagnostic analytics

Diagnostic analytics' primary flaw is its reliance solely on historical data. This has a number of secondary effects, such as:

- Limitations on its ability to predict potential future events that are necessary.
- A requirement to add more sources to your analysis, such as current data and historical data from third parties.
- Compared to descriptive analytics, it takes more effort and more sophisticated knowledge.
- Correlation and causation are frequently confused, which can have expensive consequences.

Python program and their outcome for diagnostic analytics:

```
Program:
import pandas as pd

# Create a sample dataset
data = {'Name': ['John', 'Jane', 'Mike', 'Emily', 'David'],
    'Age': [25, 30, 35, 28, 32],
    'Salary': [50000, 60000, 75000, 55000, 70000]}
df = pd.DataFrame(data)

# Calculate correlation between age and salary
correlation = df['Age'].corr(df['Salary'])
print("Correlation between Age and Salary:", correlation)

# Identify individuals with above-average salary
average_salary = df['Salary'].mean()

above_average_salary = df[df['Salary'] > average_salary]
print("\nIndividuals with Above-Average Salary:")
print(above_average_salary)

# Calculate age range
age_range = df['Age'].max() - df['Age'].min()
print("\nAge Range:", age_range)

# Calculate salary range
salary_range = df['Salary'].max() - df['Salary'].min()
print("Salary Range:", salary_range)

Outcome:
Correlation between Age and Salary: 0.9814845636467362

Individuals with Above-Average Salary:
   Name Age Salary
2  Mike  35  75000
4  David 32  70000

Age Range: 10
Salary Range: 25000
```

In this program, after importing the pandas library and creating a sample dataset, it demonstrates diagnostic analytics by performing the following operations:

Calculates the correlation between age and salary using the corr() function.

Identifies individuals with above-average salary by comparing each salary value to the mean salary.

Calculates the age range by finding the difference between the maximum and minimum age values in the dataset.

Calculates the salary range by finding the difference between the maximum and minimum salary values in the dataset.

1.2.3 Predictive analytics

The question "What is likely to happen in the future?" is answered by predictive analytics. This area of advanced analytics makes predictions by combining information from descriptive and diagnostic analytics with sophisticated predictive modeling, machine learning, and deep learning approaches. The use of statistical and modeling approaches to forecast future results and performance is known as predictive analytics. With predictive analytics, data patterns in the past and present are examined to see if they are likely to recur. This enables companies and investors to change where they allocate their resources in order to profit from potential future occurrences. Additionally, operational savings and risk reduction can be increased through predictive analysis. A type of technology called predictive analytics generates forecasts regarding some future unknowns. It uses a variety of methodologies, including AI, data mining, machine learning, modeling, and statistics to arrive at these conclusions. Big data and data science are frequently linked with predictive analytics. The amount of data that exists in transactional databases, equipment log files, pictures, video, sensors, and other data sources nowadays is overwhelming for businesses. Data scientists employ deep learning and machine learning algorithms to detect patterns and forecast future events in order to obtain insights from this data. These consist of support vector machines, decision trees, neural networks, and both linear and nonlinear regression.

1.2.3.1 *Use cases of predictive analytics*

Banking: Machine learning and quantitative methods are used by the financial sector to forecast credit risk and identify fraud.

Healthcare: To identify and coordinate the care of patients with chronic illnesses, healthcare organizations use predictive analytics.

Human resources: To find and hire personnel, analyze labor markets, and forecast an employee's performance level, HR teams apply predictive analytics.

Marketing and sales: Cross-sell tactics and marketing initiatives throughout the client lifecycle can both benefit from predictive analytics.

Retail: Predictive analytics is a tool used by retailers to manage seasonal inventories, anticipate sales, and identify product recommendations.

Supply chain: Predictive analytics is used by businesses to improve inventory management, helping to fulfill demand while reducing inventories.

1.2.3.2 *Advantages of predictive analytics*

The possibility to develop more effective marketing, sales, and customer service plans is one of the key advantages of adopting predictive modeling. Additional advantages that businesses may have from employing predictive modeling are listed below:

- Improving one's knowledge of competition
- Using techniques to acquire a competitive edge
- Enhancing current goods or services
- Recognizing customer requirements
- Recognizing an industry's or business's target market
- Reducing the cost, effort, and time spent on outcome estimation

- Predicting external elements that can have an impact on output or process
- Recognizing monetary hazards
- Inventory or resource management methods forecasting
- Recognizing upcoming trends
- Preparing churn or workforce analyses

1.2.3.3 Disadvantages of predictive analytics

A business that wants to use data-driven decision-making must have access to significant relevant data from a variety of activities, and massive data sets can occasionally be difficult to find. Even if a business has enough data, critics contend that computers and algorithms fail to take into account factors that could affect client purchase patterns when predicting human behavior, such as changing weather, moods, and relationships.

Python program and their outcome for predictive analytics:

```python
import pandas as pd
from sklearn.linear_model import LinearRegression

# Create a sample dataset
data = {'YearsExperience': [1, 2, 3, 4, 5],
    'Salary': [45000, 50000, 60000, 70000, 80000]}
df = pd.DataFrame(data)

# Separate the features (YearsExperience) and target variable (Salary)
X = df[['YearsExperience']]
y = df['Salary']

# Create and train the linear regression model
model = LinearRegression()
model.fit(X, y)

# Predict the salary for a given years of experience
years_of_experience = 6
predicted_salary = model.predict([[years_of_experience]])
print("Predicted Salary for {} years of experience: ${:,.2f}".format(years_of_experience,
predicted_salary[0]))
```

Outcome:
Predicted Salary for 6 years of experience: $88,000.00

In this program, after importing the necessary libraries and creating a sample dataset, it demonstrates predictive analytics by performing the following operations:

Separates the features (YearsExperience) and target variable (Salary) from the dataset.

Creates and trains a linear regression model using the LinearRegression() class from scikit-learn.

Predicts the salary for a given number of years of experience using the trained model.

1.2.4 Prescriptive analytics

Using prescriptive analytics, we can determine "what course of action to pursue." In order to assess the effects of potential actions and choose the optimal course of action in a scenario, this cutting-edge type of analytics uses very sophisticated tools and methodologies. It builds on findings from descriptive, diagnostic, and predictive analytics.

1.2.4.1 Use case of prescriptive analytics

In banking: Ever had your bank text you to alert you to possibly fraudulent charges? Humans don't typically carry out this process. It is supervised by sophisticated AI technology. These AIs analyses, forecast, and prescribe based on previous charges.

In retail: There's one form of prescriptive analytics so commonplace, likely seen it without even realizing it. It is, of course, Amazon's recommendation engine. Everything see on Amazon's homepage comes from buying and browsing patterns.

In healthcare: The prescriptive model of decision making is often used by hospitals and large healthcare networks. They're used to improve patient outcomes. Historical data and predictive models are analyzed to determine the cost-effectiveness of certain medical procedures. They can even determine which patients have the highest risk of readmission or relapse.

In education: Public schools and universities have a more challenging time utilizing prescriptive analysis. But the online education space is way ahead of the curve. Online education marketing is projected to reach $350 billion by 2025 globally.

In travel: Airline companies are often masters of prescriptive analytics. This is why there is such a dramatic variance in the cost of air travel. AI systems are always analyzing variables such as weather, customer demand, time of year, and even gasoline prices. The resulting data affects ticket prices on a day-by-day basis.

1.2.4.2 Advantages of prescriptive analytics

Effortlessly map the path to success: Prescriptive analytic models are made to combine operations and data to create a roadmap that outlines what to do and how to accomplish it correctly the first time. BI is taken over by AI, which applies simulated behaviors to a scenario to generate the procedures required to prevent failure or succeed.

Inform real-time and long-term business operations: Decision-makers can evaluate anticipated and real-time data concurrently to make choices that will promote long-term success and growth. By providing detailed advice, this facilitates decision-making.

Spend less time thinking and more time doing: Your team can focus more on creating the ideal solutions because of the quick turnaround of data analysis and outcome prediction. In a fraction of the time, AI can filter and process data more effectively than your staff of data engineers.

Reduce human error or bias: Predictive analytics offers an even more thorough and accurate kind of data collection and analysis than descriptive analytics, predictive analytics, or even individual users due to more sophisticated algorithms and machine learning processes.

1.2.4.3 Disadvantages of prescriptive analytics

- Only effective with valid input
- Not as reliable for long-term decisions
- Not all prescriptive analytics providers are legit

Python program and their outcome for predictive analytics:

```python
from pulp import *

# Create a linear programming problem
prob = LpProblem("Prescriptive Analytics Problem", LpMaximize)

# Define decision variables
x = LpVariable("x", lowBound=0)
y = LpVariable("y", lowBound=0)

# Set the objective function
prob += 2*x + 3*y

# Add constraints
prob += x + y <= 10
prob += 2*x + 5*y <= 15

# Solve the problem
prob.solve()

# Get the optimal solution
optimal_x = value(x)
optimal_y = value(y)
optimal_value = value(prob.objective)

# Print the optimal solution and objective value
print("Optimal Solution:")
print("x =", optimal_x)
print("y =", optimal_y)
print("Optimal Value =", optimal_value)
```

1.3 Emerging areas of analytics

Nowadays analysis is not only a part of statistics, but it can be used in the form of data analysis, business analytics, and web analysis. Quantitative and qualitative analysis of different attributes of a particular problem statement is the part of data analysis, further in which we can utilize the outcome of data analysis in the business prospectus is the part of business analytics. Following are the detailed discussion about the Emerging Areas of analytics:

1.3.1 Data analysis

The process of cleaning, transforming, and modeling data in order to find relevant information for business decision-making is known as data analysis. Extracting useful information from the raw information and making decisions based on that analysis are the goals of data analysis. Every time we make a decision in daily life, as a simple example of data analysis, we consider what happened previously or what would happen if we make that particular choice. This is nothing more than evaluating the past or the future and making choices in light of it. For that, we assemble our past experiences or our future aspirations, so all that is data analysis. Today, data analysis refers to the same process an analyst uses for commercial goals.

1.3.1.1 Process of data analysis

The process of data analysis is nothing more than the collection of data using the right software or tool that enables you to study the data and identify patterns in it. Get to final conclusions or make decisions based on such information and data. Fig. 1.4 shows the process of data analysis.

Data analysis consists of the following phases:

Data requirement: It is necessary to first consider why wish to perform this data analysis. The only thing left to accomplish is to determine why data analysis is being done. It must identify what to analyze and how to measure it at this phase, as well as why looking into the matter and the methods will employ to conduct this analysis.

Data collection: It will have a clear notion of what to measure and what are the findings should be after gathering the requirements. It's now time to gather data based on the specifications. After gathering data, keep in mind that it needs to be structured or processed for analysis. It must keep a diary detailing the sources and dates of data gathering as you gather information from various sources.

FIGURE 1.4 Process of data analysis.

Python program for data collection:

```python
import csv

def collect_data():
    data = []
    while True:
        name = input("Enter your name (or 'quit' to exit): ")
        if name.lower() == "quit":
            break

        age = input("Enter your age: ")
        email = input("Enter your email: ")
        data.append([name, age, email])

    return data

def save_data(data, filename):
    with open(filename, "w", newline="") as file:
        writer = csv.writer(file)
        writer.writerow(["Name", "Age", "Email"])
        writer.writerows(data)
    print("Data saved successfully!")

def main():
    data = collect_data()
    filename = input("Enter the filename to save the data: ")
    save_data(data, filename)
if __name__ == "__main__":
    main()
```

Outcome:
Enter your name (or 'quit' to exit): vikas
Enter your age: 39
Enter your email: vikaskharekhare@gmail.com
Enter your name (or 'quit' to exit): quit
Enter the filename to save the data:

In this program, the collect_data function prompts the user to enter their name, age, and email. The inputs are stored in a list called data. The loop continues until the user enters "quit" as the name.

The save_data function takes the collected data and the desired filename as parameters. It opens a CSV file in write mode and uses the csv.writer module to write the data to the file. The first row of the CSV file contains the column headers ("Name," "Age," "Email"). The function prints a success message after saving the data.

The main function is the entry point of the program. It calls the collect_data function to gather user information and prompts for the desired filename. Then it calls the save_data function to save the collected data to a CSV file.

Data cleaning: Now that the data has been gathered, it may not be pertinent to analysis or usable, so it needs to be cleansed. The data that is gathered could have duplicate records, blank spaces, or mistakes. Data should be error-free and thoroughly cleansed. Data cleaning must come before analysis since it will make analysis' results more likely to match expectations.

Python program for data cleaning:

```python
import pandas as pd

def clean_data(data):
    # Remove duplicates
    data = data.drop_duplicates()

    # Remove missing values
    data = data.dropna()

    # Convert data types if needed
    data['Age'] = data['Age'].astype(int)

    # Remove outliers
    data = remove_outliers(data, 'Age')

    # Normalize data
    data['Income'] = (data['Income'] - data['Income'].mean()) / data['Income'].std()

    return data

def remove_outliers(data, column):
    Q1 = data[column].quantile(0.25)
    Q3 = data[column].quantile(0.75)
    IQR = Q3 - Q1
    lower_bound = Q1 - 1.5 * IQR
    upper_bound = Q3 + 1.5 * IQR
    data = data[(data[column] >= lower_bound) & (data[column] <= upper_bound)]
    return data

def main():
    # Read data from a CSV file
    data = pd.read_csv('data.csv')

    # Perform data cleaning
    cleaned_data = clean_data(data)

    # Display the cleaned data
    print(cleaned_data)

if __name__ == "__main__":
    main()
```

(cont'd)

In this example, we use the pandas library to handle the data cleaning tasks. Here's a breakdown of the data cleaning steps:

clean_data function: This function takes the raw data as input and performs various cleaning operations. Here are the steps included:

Removing duplicates: We use the drop_duplicates method to remove any duplicate rows from the dataset.

Removing missing values: The dropna method is used to remove rows containing missing values.

Converting data types: We convert the "Age" column to integer type using the astype method.

Removing outliers: We define the remove_outliers function to remove outliers from a specific column using the IQR (interquartile range) method.

Normalizing data: We normalize the "Income" column by subtracting the mean and dividing by the standard deviation.

remove_outliers function: This function takes a DataFrame and a column name as input. It calculates the lower and upper bounds for outliers using the IQR method and filters the DataFrame to include only the rows within the specified range.

Main function: The entry point of the program reads the raw data from a CSV file using pd.read_csv. Then, it calls the clean_data function to perform the data cleaning operations. Finally, it displays the cleaned data using print.

Data assessment: The collected, processed, and cleaned data is now ready for analysis. As work with the data, might discover that already have all the details require or that need to gather more information. Use data analysis software and tools to comprehend, evaluate, and come to conclusions based on the requirements throughout this phase.

Data interpretation: It's now time to evaluate findings after data analysis. Data analysis can be expressed or communicated verbally, visually, or both, such as in a table or chart. After that, choose the best line of action using the outcomes of data analysis method.

Data visualization: Probably encounter data visualization frequently in your daily life; it frequently takes the form of graphs and charts. In other terms, data presented graphically for quicker processing and understanding by the human brain. To find undiscovered facts and patterns, data visualization is frequently employed. It can uncover relevant information by examining relationships and contrasting datasets. Table 1.1 shows the Python library for data analysis with the parameters of data processing, data cleaning, and data visualization.

TABLE 1.1 Python library for data analysis.

Parameter of data analysis	Categorization	Python library
Data processing	Text data	NLTK, Spacy
	Audio and musical data	Librosa and Essentia
	Image data	Pillow
	Advanced array operation	Numpy (Numerical Python)
	Linear algebra, integration, optimization, and statistics	SciPy
	Series data (1 dimensional) DataFrame (2 dimensional)	Pandas
	Image data	Scikit Learn
	Deep learning data	PyTorch
	Deep learning data	TensorFlow
Data cleaning	Join, merge, concatenate, or duplicate DataFrame	Pandas
	Missing values with the mode or median on a column-by-column basis	Datacleaner
	Reading data with missing and poorly scaled values	Dora
	Time zone conversion; automatic string formatting and parsing; support for pytz	Arrow
	Eliminating personally identifiable information (PII) from free text	Scrubadub
	Number formatting, headers, and column alignment by the decimal	Tabulate
	Handling missing values	Missingno
	Modify the data set	Modin
	To take bad Unicode and useless characters and turn them into relevant and readable text data	Ftfy
	Handle missing values, convert categorical variables into numerical values	Dabl
	Remove missing, inconsistent, or otherwise irregular values in your dataset	Imblearn
Data visualization	Two-dimensional diagrams and graphs	Matplotlib
	Visualizing statistical models heat maps and other types of visualizations	Seaborn
	Interactive and scalable visualizations	Bokeh
	Animation and crosstalk integration	Plotly
	Oriented and nonoriented graphs	pydot

Python program for data visualization:

```python
import matplotlib.pyplot as plt

def visualize_data(x_values, y_values):
    plt.plot(x_values, y_values)
    plt.title('Data Visualization')
    plt.xlabel('X-axis')
    plt.ylabel('Y-axis')
    plt.show()

def main():
    # Sample data
    x = [1, 2, 3, 4, 5]
    y = [2, 4, 6, 8, 10]

    # Visualize the data
    visualize_data(x, y)

if __name__ == "__main__":
    main()
```

Outcome:

Data Visualization

(cont'd)

In this example, we use the matplotlib library to create a simple line plot. Here's a breakdown of the program:

Visualize data function: This function takes two lists (*x*_values and *y*_values) as input. It plots the data points using the plot function from matplotlib. We set the title, *x*-axis label, and *y*-axis label using title, xlabel, and ylabel functions, respectively. Finally, plt.show() displays the plot.

Main function: The entry point of the program defines sample data (*x* and *y*) that we want to visualize. It then calls the visualize_data function, passing the data lists as arguments.

1.3.2 Business analytics

Business analytics is a subset of BI and a data management solution that focuses on the use of methodologies like data mining, predictive analytics, and statistical analysis to analyze data, turn it into information, spot trends, predict outcomes, and ultimately make better, data-driven business decisions. The fundamentals of business analytics are typically divided into three categories: descriptive analytics, predictive analytics, and prescriptive analytics. Descriptive analytics analysis historical data to determine how a unit may respond to a set of variables; predictive analytics examines historical data to determine the likelihood of specific future outcomes; and prescriptive analytics combines descriptive analytics, which provides insight into what happened, with predictive analytics, which provides insight into what might happen in the future.

1.3.2.1 Common component of business analytics

Data aggregation: It is the process of gathering, organizing, and cleaning up data so it can be evaluated. Analytics require a strong data management strategy and a current data warehouse.

Data mining: Data mining sifts through sizable databases, analyzes data from various perspectives, and discovers trends, patterns, and linkages that were not before recognized.

Big data analytics: To analyze enormous amounts of structured and unstructured data in databases, data warehouses, and Hadoop systems, big data analytics uses cutting-edge techniques including data mining, predictive analytics, and machine learning.

Text mining: For both qualitative and quantitative research, text mining examines unstructured text data sets like documents, emails, social media posts, blog comments, call center scripts, and other text-based sources.

Forecasting and predictive analytics: Forecasting makes predictions about future events using historical data, while predictive analytics calculates the possibility that these predictions will come true using cutting-edge methods.

Data narrative and visualization: Data visualizations, such as graphs and charts, offer a simple means of understanding and expressing trends, outliers, and patterns in data. These visualizations can be connected to give a more comprehensive data story and assist in making decisions.

1.3.3 Web analytics and web scrapping

The gathering, monitoring, and evaluation of website data is referred to as web analytics. The emphasis is on developing metrics based on your organizational and user goals and using website data to assess the accomplishment or otherwise of those objectives, inform strategy, and enhance user experience. Web analytics are essential to the company's success. It can utilize these insights to better understand to the website visitors and enhance their experience there. For instance, it might concentrate on making website more mobile-friendly if find that the majority of visitors to your site are doing so via a mobile device.

1.3.3.1 Use case of web analytics

Page views: Page views represent the total amount of times a page on website has been visited. A page view is recorded whenever a browser loads a page from the website. Therefore, if a user visits a page on website and then reloads it in their browser, that counts as two views. A user would be considered to have viewed three pages of website if they first viewed one, then another, and then came back to the first.

Unique Page views: The total number of unique Page views is the sum of all user sessions during which a page was viewed. Therefore, unique Page views would only count one Page views if a user viewed it twice (or more) in a single session.

Sessions: A session is a collection of activities that happen on website over a specific period of time, such as page views, CTA clicks, and events. The length of a session varies depending on the web analytics tool. For instance, sessions in the traffic tracking tools from Hub Spot and Google Analytics are set to 30 minutes. If a user becomes active after 30 minutes of inactivity, when the clock strikes midnight, or if they enter via one traffic source, depart, and then return via another, their session expires and a new one begins for them.

Returning visitors: The quantity of people who have previously visited on the website is referred to as returning visitors (or users). This indicator is not included in all online analytics platforms, but some do, including Google Analytics. It may check behaviors in Google Analytics audience reports to see the proportion of new and returning visitors to the website. It can get a good idea of how well you're keeping visitors and how successful are at bringing in net new visitors at the top of the funnel by examining both metrics for new and returning visitors.

Bounce rate: The percentage of visitors to website that leave after only reading one page is known as the "bounce rate." Bounce rate can be seen as a site-wide or page-level measure. The percentage of sessions that began on a page and did not navigate to another page on the website is known as bounce rate at the page level. Bounce rates of 40% or less are typically seen as favorable, those of 40%–70% as normal, and those of 70% or more as high.

Web scrapping: Web scraping is a computerized technique for gathering copious volumes of data from websites. The majority of this data is unstructured in HTML format and is transformed into structured data in a database or spreadsheet so that it can be used in multiple applications. To collect data from websites, web scraping can be done in a variety of methods. These include leveraging specific APIs, online services, or even writing your own code from scratch for web scraping. It may access the structured data on many huge websites, including Google, Twitter, Facebook, Stack Overflow, and others, using their APIs. Fig. 1.5 shows the different Python library for web scrapping.

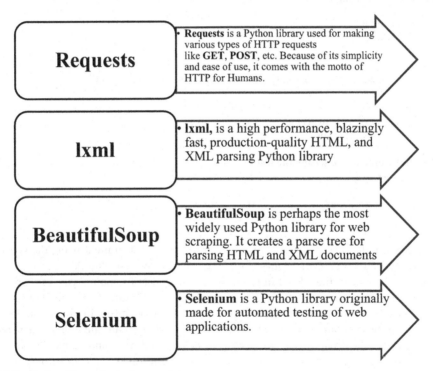

FIGURE 1.5   Python library for web scrapping.

Python program for web scrapping:

```python
import requests
from bs4 import BeautifulSoup

def scrape_website(url):
    # Send a GET request to the URL
    response = requests.get(url)

    # Check if the request was successful
    if response.status_code == 200:
        # Create a BeautifulSoup object from the HTML content
        soup = BeautifulSoup(response.content, 'html.parser')

        # Find and extract specific data from the HTML
        # Here's an example of extracting the titles of all <h1> tags
        titles = soup.find_all('h1')

        for title in titles:
            print(title.text)

    else:
        print("Failed to scrape the website. Status code:", response.status_code)

def main():
    # URL of the website to scrape
    url = "https://example.com"

    # Call the function to scrape the website
    scrape_website(url)

if __name__ == "__main__":
    main()
```

In this example, we use the requests library to send an HTTP GET request to a specified URL and the BeautifulSoup library to parse and extract data from the HTML content of the website. Here's a breakdown of the program:

scrape_website function: This function takes a URL as input. It sends a GET request to the URL using the requests.get function and checks if the request was successful. If the request was successful (status code 200), it creates a BeautifulSoup object from the HTML content using the specified parser (in this case, "html.parser").

Using BeautifulSoup, you can find and extract specific data from the HTML structure of the website. In the example provided, we find all the <h1> tags using soup.find_all('h1') and then iterate over them to print their text content (title.text).

Main function: The entry point of the program defines the URL of the website you want to scrape and calls the scrape_website function, passing the URL as an argument.

1.3.4 Big data analysis

Using cutting-edge analytical methods on very large, diversified big data sets that comprise structured, semistructured, and unstructured data from many sources and range in size from terabytes to zettabytes is known as big data analytics. Big data describes data sets that are too big or intricate for conventional data-processing application software to handle. While data with more fields have more statistical power, they may also have a higher false discovery rate than data with fewer fields.

Three distinguishing characteristics can be used to deconstruct the phrase. The three V's volume, velocity, and variety are crucial to comprehending how big data may be measured and how dissimilar it is from traditional data. Fig. 1.6 shows the three V's concept of big data analysis.

Volume: The size of the data sets that an organization has gathered for analysis and processing is referred to as the volume of data. These data sets are regularly observed in today's technology pushing on the higher size of bytes, such as terabytes and petabytes. In contrast to traditional storage and processing capabilities, the increased volume of data typically necessitates distinct and diverse processing technologies. Simply said, the magnitude of the data sets within big data makes it impossible to compute them using a standard laptop or desktop CPU. So in that case different big data tools can be used for the analysis of such type of large data set.

Velocity: Data velocity refers to the speed in which data is generated, distributed, and collected. The velocity rate depends on a number of variables, including the number of sensors present on IOT-enabled devices and the number of internet users. High data velocity is produced at such a rate that it necessitates particular processing methods. The faster the data can be collected and processed, the more valuable it will be, and the longer it will last, the higher the velocity rate. But the systems that are employed to analyze the data must also be capable. A user has more flexibility to obtain answers through queries, reports, and dashboards the more quickly they can process information into their data and analytics platform.

Variety: Structured, unstructured, and semistructured data that is compiled from various sources is referred to as "variety of big data." Data is now available in a variety of

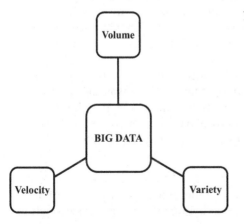

FIGURE 1.6 Three V's concept of big data.

formats, including emails, PDFs, photographs, videos, audios, social media posts, and much more, as opposed to the past when it could only be gathered through databases and spreadsheets. One of the key components of large data is variety. Traditional data types are ideally suited to relational databases since they are structured. As big data has grown in popularity, new unstructured data kinds have emerged. To derive meaning and support for metadata, some semi and unstructured data types require further preprocessing.

1.3.4.1 Key big data analytics technologies and tools

Processes for big data analytics involve a wide variety of tools and technologies. The following technologies and techniques are frequently used to support big data analytics processes:

HADOOP: Hadoop is an Apache open-source platform used to store, process, and analyze extraordinarily large volumes of data. Hadoop is written in Java not in an online analytical processing. Facebook, Yahoo, Google, Twitter, LinkedIn, and many other sites use it.

HBASE: Built on Hadoop, HBase is an open source database with sorted map data. It is scalable horizontally and column-oriented. It is based on the Big Table from Google. It has a number of tables that store data in a key-value manner. Sparse data sets, which are frequently encountered in big data use cases, are ideally suited for HBase. HBase has APIs that make it possible to create in almost any programming language. It offers random real-time read/write access to data in the Hadoop File System and is a component of the Hadoop ecosystem.

HIVE: Hive is a data warehouse system used for structured data analysis. It is constructed on top of Hadoop. Facebook was the one who created it. Hive offers the ability to read, write, and manage huge datasets that are stored in distributed storage. It executes HQL (Hive query language) queries, which are SQL-like queries that are internally translated to Map Reduce jobs. It may avoid the need for the difficult Map Reduce program writing process by using Hive. Hive supports User Defined Functions, Data Manipulation Language, and Data Definition Language.

SQOOP: Sqoop is a command-line interface application for transferring data between relational databases and Hadoop. It allows free-form SQL queries or incremental loads of a single table, as well as saved jobs that can be executed repeatedly to import database updates made since the previous import. Data may be migrated from MySQL, PostgreSQL, Oracle, SQL Server, and DB2 into HDFS/hive/Hbase using Sqoop, and vice versa.

SPARK: Apache Spark is an open-source cluster computing framework. Its primary purpose is to handle the real-time generated data. Hadoop Map Reduce was the foundation upon which Spark was developed. Unlike competing methods like Hadoop's Map Reduce, which writes and reads data to and from computer hard drives, it was optimized to run in memory. As a result, Spark processes the data far more quickly than other options.

1.3.4.2 Use case of big data analysis

Customer acquisition and retention: Companies' marketing initiatives can benefit from consumer data so they can take advantage of trends and improve customer satisfaction.

Personalization tools for services like Spotify, Netflix, and Amazon, for instance, can enhance user loyalty and experiences.

Targeted ads: Users can benefit from engaging targeted ad campaigns that are both small-scale and broad-based when personalization data from sources like prior purchases, interaction patterns, and product page viewing histories is used.

Product development: Big data analytics can offer information on product feasibility, development choices, progress tracking, and how to improve products to better serve customers.

Price optimization: In order to increase profits, retailers may choose pricing models that model and utilize data from various data sources.

Supply chain and channel analytics: Predictive analytical models can assist with proactive restocking, B2B supplier networks, inventory management, route improvements, and delivery delay notice.

Risk management: Effective risk management techniques can be developed using big data analytics to find new dangers in data trends.

Improved decision-making: Businesses may make quicker and better decisions with the help of the insights business users derive from pertinent data.

1.3.4.3 *Advantages of big data analysis*

The following are some advantages of big data analytics:

* Quickly processing huge data sets from various sources, in a wide range of formats and types.
* Making quick, more informed decisions for strategic planning that will help and advance the supply chain, operations, and other strategic decision-making sectors.
* Cost savings that may be brought about by improved and new business processes.
* Improved marketing insights and data for product development might result from a greater understanding of client needs, behavior, and sentiment.
* Improved, more educated risk management techniques that make use of massive data samples.

1.3.4.4 *Disadvantages of big data analysis*

Despite the wide-reaching benefits that come with using big data analytics, its use also comes with challenges:

Accessibility of data: Storage and processing become more difficult as data volume increases. To enable use by data scientists and analysts with less experience, big data must be appropriately kept and preserved.

Data quality maintenance: Data quality management for big data necessitates a substantial amount of time, effort, and resources to maintain due to the large volumes of data coming in from many sources and in various forms.

Data security: The complexity of big data systems presents unique security challenges. Properly addressing security concerns within such a complicated big data ecosystem can be a complex undertaking.

Choosing the right tools: Organizations must learn how to choose the best tool that complements users' needs and infrastructure from the wide range of big data analytics tools and platforms that are readily available on the market.

1.4 Value chain analysis

The numerous business operations and procedures involved in producing a good or providing a service are defined by a value chain. It includes all phases of the lifecycle of a product, from conception to creation to distribution. Value chain analysis is a method for visually examining a company's operations to determine how the company might gain a competitive edge. A company can better understand how it provides value by using value chain analysis, which also enables it to determine how much it can charge for a good or service while still making a profit. To put it another way, if they are managed effectively, the value received should outweigh the costs of managing them, which means that customers should return to the business and engage in free and willing exchanges. Value chain analysis is a conceptual idea of value-added in the form of a value chain that was developed in the 1980s by Michael Porter. Fig. 1.7 shows the basic concept of value chain analysis.

The majority of businesses do hundreds or even thousands of activities in order to transform inputs into outputs. These can be broadly categorized as primary or supporting activities that are necessary for all businesses to perform in one way or another.

1.4.1 Component of value chain analysis

Primary activities are those that go directly into the creation of a product or the execution of a service, including:

Inbound logistics: Activities related to receiving, warehousing, and inventory management of source materials and components.

Operations: Activities related to turning raw materials and components into a finished product.

Outbound logistics: Activities related to distribution, including packaging, sorting, and shipping.

Marketing and sales: Activities related to the marketing and sale of a product or service, including promotion, advertising, and pricing strategy.

After-sales services: Activities that take place after a sale has been finalized, including installation, training, quality assurance, repair, and customer service.

Secondary activities help primary activities become more efficient effectively creating a competitive advantage and are broken down into:

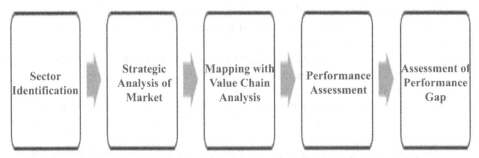

FIGURE 1.7   Step by step process of value chain analysis.

Procurement: Activities related to the sourcing of raw materials, components, equipment, and services.

Technological development: Activities related to research and development, including product design, market research, and process development.

Human resources management: Activities related to the recruitment, hiring, training, development, retention, and compensation of employees.

Infrastructure: Activities related to the company's overhead and management, including financing and planning.

1.4.2 How to conduct value chain analysis?

Identify value chain activities: Understanding all of the direct and indirect processes that go into the production of your goods or service is the first step in carrying out a value chain analysis. It's crucial to carry out this approach for each of your company's products or services when anyone sell a variety of them.

Determine the cost and value of activities: Once the primary and secondary activities have been identified, the next step is to determine the value that each activity adds to the process, along with the costs involved. When considering the value produced by an activity, consider how each one improves the happiness or enjoyment of the end user. How does it add value to my company? For instance, does using a particular material make a product more luxurious or durable for the user? Does adding a specific feature improve the likelihood that your business will experience network effects and grow?

Identify opportunities for competitive advantage: It can assess with value chain using the perspective of whatever competitive advantage are attempting to acquire once you've assembled it and comprehend the cost and value involved with each step. For instance, if cutting costs is main priority, it should assess every link in value chain from that perspective. Which procedures might be more effective? Exist any that could be deleted or outsourced in order to drastically cut expenses but still produce little value? In a similar vein, which links in your value chain have the best possibility to fulfill core goal of product differentiation? Would the added value outweigh the expenditure of more money?

1.4.3 Value chain with data analytics

A value chain framework can be used to analyze the business of gathering and utilizing all forms of data, including personal, machine, and system generated data. This new data value chain entails a number of distinct steps, including:

Generation: Recording and capturing data

Collection: Collecting data, validating, and storing it

Analytics: Processing and analyzing the data to generate new insights and knowledge

Exchange: Putting the outputs to use, whether internally or by trading them on a conventional value chain, several businesses would usually specialize in a small number of activities before trading inputs and outputs with other businesses. Value was produced at each stage along the way, from raw material inputs to finished goods and services. The organization that gathers the data is very likely to keep it throughout the steps to generate the output itself, while buying in specialized supporting services, due to the nature of

TABLE 1.2   Parameters of value chain analysis.

Personal	Volunteered Private Identified	Inferred Public Pseudonymised
Nonpersonal	Anonymous	Machine data
Timeliness	Instant/live	Historic
Format	Structured	Unstructured

data, which results in a closely integrated value chain. Table 1.2 shows the parameters of value chain analysis. The causes of this and its ramifications for those involved in the value chain as well as policymakers are examined in this research. One important property of data is that, as it moves up the value chain, it is frequently difficult to assign a concrete value to a single piece of data. Following are the parameters of the value chain analysis.

Personal data: Anything relating to a recognized or identifiable individual is considered personal data and can be either public or private. Companies have traditionally gathered sensitive personal data, including name, address, and frequently bank information. Health information is another type of private personal information. Companies and organizations who collect this data have a responsibility to retain it securely and to make sure it is only used for the purposes for which it was collected.

Volunteered: Data and content that have been voluntarily disclosed by the data source, such as social network posts, private information provided to service providers like banks, uploaded photos, measurements from linked devices, etc.

Observed: Data that is passively gathered about a person's environment or actions (with or without the subject being aware that they are being watched) and may include the location or sharing device used, the amount of time needed to complete a task, other services used, etc.

Inferred: These are fresh insights developed by the examination and processing of collected and voluntary data; as such, they cannot be regarded as primary facts and rely on probabilities, correlations, predictions, etc.

There is a lot of data which is machine or system generated which is clearly nonpersonal, e.g., engine performance data, transport ticket machine sales, energy usage data, stock price and transaction data, blockchain records, etc. Data relating to individuals but which is fully anonymized is also considered to be nonpersonal, e.g., blockchain ledgers.

Nonpersonal data: There is a tone of data that is generated by machines or systems but is obviously nonpersonal, such as engine performance data, sales from automated ticket vending machines for public transportation, energy usage data, stock price and transaction data, blockchain records, etc. Nonpersonal data includes information about specific people that has been completely anonymized, such as blockchain ledgers.

Timeliness: There is a tone of data that is generated by machines or systems but is obviously nonpersonal, such as engine performance data, sales from automated ticket vending machines for public transportation, energy usage data, stock price and transaction data, blockchain records, etc. Nonpersonal data includes information about specific people that has been completely anonymized, such as blockchain ledgers.

Structure: Whether or not the data is structured is another factor that influences its worth. Clearly defined data types are grouped into searchable fields with a pattern that makes them simple to query. Examples of structured data include a database of customer information or a set of readings from a specific sensor. On the other side, unstructured data includes information in formats that are more difficult to organize and search, such as audio, video, and social network postings.

Relevance: Frequently, the data lacks understanding. Machine learning is frequently used to analyze unstructured data. It has the potential to be extremely effective and shockingly accurate, but it is by no means perfect. To train a computer, some understanding of the trends is required (correlation or causality concerns).

Volume: Some firms find it impossible to keep up with the unstructured data volume growth rates. As a result, using and protecting the data is difficult.

Quality: There must be enough checks in place to validate the source data and its accuracy because a sizable amount of unstructured data is captured at the source but is still unverified. This fact could be lost in the processing and usage of the data later on.

Usability: Businesses will need to devise a means to find, extract, organize, and store the data in order for it to be useful. To record information that does not fit the mold, one must create a whole new sort of database, and businesses are working with companies that are creating software and services to address this problem. Fig. 1.8 shows the framework of value chain analysis.

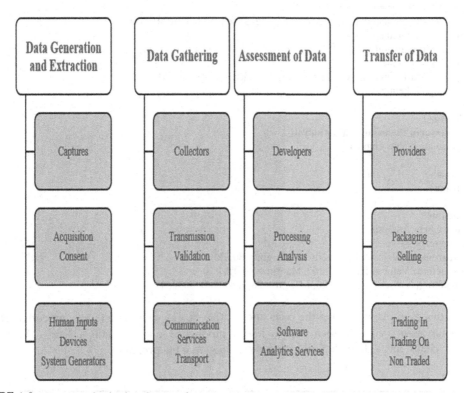

FIGURE 1.8   Framework of value chain analysis.

Python program for the value chain analysis:

```python
def calculate_value_chain():
    # Define the costs and revenues for each stage of the value chain
    procurement_cost = 5000
    production_cost = 10000
    marketing_cost = 3000
    sales_revenue = 25000
    # Calculate the value-added and margin for each stage
    value_added_procurement = sales_revenue - procurement_cost
    margin_procurement = value_added_procurement / sales_revenue * 100

    value_added_production = sales_revenue - (procurement_cost + production_cost)
    margin_production = value_added_production / sales_revenue * 100

    value_added_marketing = sales_revenue - (procurement_cost + production_cost + marketing_cost)

    margin_marketing = value_added_marketing / sales_revenue * 100

    # Print the results
    print("Value Chain Analysis:")
    print("=====================")
    print(f"Procurement: Value Added = {value_added_procurement}, Margin = {margin_procurement}%")
    print(f"Production: Value Added = {value_added_production}, Margin = {margin_production}%")
    print(f"Marketing: Value Added = {value_added_marketing}, Margin = {margin_marketing}%")

def main():
    # Perform the value chain analysis
    calculate_value_chain()

if __name__ == "__main__":
    main()
```

Outcome:
Value Chain Analysis:
=====================
Procurement: Value Added = 20000, Margin = 80.0%
Production: Value Added = 10000, Margin = 40.0%
Marketing: Value Added = 7000, Margin = 28.000000000000004%

In this example, we define the costs and revenues associated with each stage of the value chain for a hypothetical company. The stages considered are procurement, production, and marketing. Here's a breakdown of the program:

<hr>

(cont'd)

Calculate value chain function: This function calculates the value-added and margin for each stage of the value chain based on the defined costs and revenues. The value-added is calculated as the difference between the sales revenue and the cumulative costs up to that stage. The margin is calculated as the value-added divided by the sales revenue, multiplied by 100 to get a percentage.

Main function: The entry point of the program calls the calculate value chain function to perform the value chain analysis.

<hr>

1.5 Conclusion

The future of analytics is promising for a number of reasons. A career in business analytics is lucrative and provides many prospects for both professional and personal growth. A few of the inherent skills required to be a data analytics specialist are big data. It's also essential to have the capacity to assess business situations and come up with original solutions. Big data's extensive use ensures future growth in demand, higher earnings, and a high level of employment. By gathering a sizable amount of data, broadening business models, igniting creative processes, and fostering the overall growth and development of a company, analytics has the power to drastically alter the current business environment. This confirms why the future potential of analytics in all over the world offers excellent career opportunities.

1.6 Case study

1.6.1 Analytics in performance of Mumbai Indians in the IPL

This case study taken from the Research Paper "V. Khare, Performance assessment of Mumbai Indians and Royal Challengers Bangalore in Indian Premier League by computational data analysis," International Journal of Data Science, July 2023.

Eight clubs from eight different cities compete in the professional Twenty20 cricket tournament known as the Indian Premier League (IPL) in India. The league was established in 2007 by the BCCI (Board of Control for Cricket in India). Every year, between March and May, it takes place, and it has a special spot in the ICC Future Tours Program. The IPL, the most well-known cricket league in the world, has the sixth-highest average attendance of any sports league in 2014. In 2010, the IPL became the first sporting event in history to stream live on YouTube. The IPL's brand value in 2019 was 475 billion (US$6.7

TABLE 1.3 Role of analytics in the assessment of MI performance in IPL.

Case study domain	Analytics
Data collection	Cricbuzz, Website of Mumbai Indians, Wikipedia
Attribute selection	Captain, salary, individual batting performance, individual bowling performance, performance of MI team
Data assessment	NCSS tool, KDD process
Relationship between different parameters	Regression analysis
Result assessment	Data visualization, Michaelis–Menten curve

billion), according to Duff & Phelps. The BCCI estimates that the 2015 IPL season increased India's GDP by 11.5 billion rupees (US$160 million). There have been 13 seasons of the IPL competition. The United Arab Emirates hosted games for the 2020 season as a result of the COVID-19 outbreak. Table 1.3 shows the role of analytics in the assessment of MI performance in IPL.

The Mumbai Indians (MI) are a cricket franchise team for the IPL that is based in Mumbai, Maharashtra. The squad is owned by Reliance Industries, the largest conglomerate in India, through its 2008-founded 100% subsidiary India Win Sports. The team has played its home matches at Mumbai's 33,108-seat Wankhede Stadium ever since it was founded. The MI were the first IPL team to have a brand worth more than $100 million in 2017. The first step of the data analysis is the collection of data and in this project collects the data of year-wise salaries of MI in the span of 2008–20. The data of year-wise salary of individual players of MI, year-wise win% of MI also collect the data of batting and bowling performance of MI. After the collection of data, data assessment is done through the NCSS tool. NCSS tool is used to the descriptive and regression based analysis of the data. Mean maximum value, minimum value, range, standard deviation, standard error, skewness, kurotisis, F-test, and T-test value of all the parameters are assessed in this analysis. Analysis of data is also done through the different types of graphical analysis. The equation of the straight line relating year-wise MI salaries (Millions) and Years is estimated as: MI (Millions) = (−94784.2494) + (47.3326) years using the 14 observations in this dataset. The estimated value of MI (Millions) when years is zero, is −94784.2494 with a standard error of 7160.2166. The slope, the estimated change in MI (Millions) per unit change in years, is 47.3326 with a standard error of 3.5543. The year-wise relationship between salaries of MI and win% of MI is years = 2002.90413352717 + 0.0186286938224725 × salaries of MI + 1.51634173330256 × Win% of MI. Estimated nonlinear-regression model of win% of MI is given by (1045.9274405185) × (Win% of MI)/(((0.514810315548479) + (Win% of MI)).

1.6.1.1 Data analysis based on knowledge discovery in database process

Data analysis is the process of reviewing, cleansing, transforming, and modeling data with the aim of finding useful knowledge, informing conclusions, and assisting decision-making is known as data analysis. Data analysis has many aspects and methods, encompassing a wide range of techniques under various names and being used in a number of industry, research, and social science domains. Data analysis is essential in today's business world because it helps companies make more scientific decisions and run more efficiently. In data analysis knowledge discovery in databases, also known as knowledge extraction from databases, is the nontrivial extraction of implicit, previously unknown, and potentially useful information from database data. Fig. 1.9 shows the process of data assessment.

1.6.1.1.1 Steps involved in knowledge discovery in database process

Data cleaning: Data cleaning is the process of removal of irrelevant data of MI.

Data integration: Data integration is the process of heterogeneous data from different sources such as the official website of MI, Wikipedia, and that data combined in a common source of data.

Data selection: Data selection is characterized as the process of determining and retrieving data from the data collection that is important to the study. For the example, in this process year-wise salary of MI team, batting and bowling.

Data transformation: The process of transforming data into the appropriate form needed by mining procedures is known as data transformation.

Data mining: Data mining is described as the use of clever techniques to extract patterns that may be useful.

Pattern evaluation: Pattern evaluation is characterized as the process of identifying strictly increasing trends that reflect information based on predetermined criteria.

Knowledge representation: Information representation is a technique for representing data mining results using visualization software.

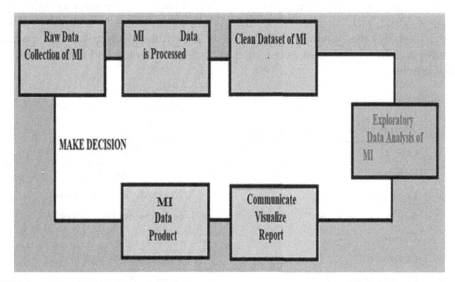

FIGURE 1.9   Process of data assessment.

1.6.1.2 Data collection of Mumbai Indians

The MI are an IPL franchise cricket team based in Mumbai, Maharashtra. Reliance Industries, India's largest conglomerate, owns the team through its 100% subsidiary India Win Sports, which was established in 2008. Table 1.4 shows the general information about the team of MI. Since its inception, the team has played its home ground at Mumbai's Wankhede Stadium, which seats 33,108 people. In 2017, the MI became the first franchise in the IPL to surpass the $100 million mark in brand value. For the fourth year in a row, the MI' brand value is expected to be about 809 crores (roughly $115 million), the highest of all IPL franchises. After defeating Royal Challengers Bangalore by 31 runs in the final, MI won the 2011 Champions League Twenty20. The team completed the double by winning its first IPL title in 2013, beating Chennai Super Kings by 23 runs in the final, and then defeating Rajasthan Royals by 33 runs in the Champions League Twenty20 final the following year. They became the third team to win more than one IPL title on May 24, 2015, when they defeated the Chennai Super Kings by 41 runs in the final. They became the first team to win three IPL titles on May 21, 2017, when they defeated the Rising Pune Supergiant by one run in a thrilling final. With 239 million viewers between the first and second seasons of the IPL, the MI were the most watched team on television. The first season ended with a net loss of INR 16 Crore after revenue of 69 Crore and expenditure of 85 Crore, and the owners planned to break even in the 2009 season.

Table 1.5 shows the captains of MI in the span of 2008—20. One of the best cricketers in the history of cricket, Sachin Tendulkar led the team from 2008 to 2011 and his captaincy MI reached the final in 2010. Table 1.6 shows the year-wise investment on the MI team by the franchise. Table 1.7 shows the year-wise performance of the MI team with the parameters of total matches, number of win and loss, win%, and position of team in the IPL. Table 1.8 shows the comprehensive details of salaries of individual players in the span of 2008—20. Table 1.9 shows the batting performance of individual players of MI team with parameters of span of individual player, number of matches, number of innings, total runs, average, strike rate, number of centuries and half centuries, and number of 4's and 6's. Table 1.10 shows the bowling performance of individual players with the parameters of number of matches, number of overs, total wicket, and average and economy rate of the individual bowler.

TABLE 1.4 Mumbai Indians team information.

City	Mumbai, Maharashtra, India
Founded	January 24, 2008
Home ground	Wankhede Stadium, Mumbai
Second home ground	Brabourne Stadium, Mumbai
IPL wins	5
CLT20 wins	2 (2011, 2013)
Official website	Mumbaiindians.com

TABLE 1.5 Captains of Mumbai Indians.

Year	Captain of MI
2008	Sachin Tendulkar
2009	Sachin Tendulkar
2010	Sachin Tendulkar
2011	Sachin Tendulkar
2012	Harbhajan Singh
2013	Rohit Sharma
2014	Rohit Sharma
2015	Rohit Sharma
2016	Rohit Sharma
2017	Rohit Sharma
2018	Rohit Sharma
2019	Rohit Sharma
2020	Rohit Sharma
2021	Rohit Sharma

TABLE 1.6 Year-wise salaries of Mumbai Indians Team.

Year	MI (Millions)
2008	247
2009	251.6
2010	265.14
2011	420.82
2012	536.53
2013	559.82
2014	600
2015	594.95
2016	655.95
2017	626.45
2018	742
2019	784
2020	845

TABLE 1.7 Performance of Mumbai Indians.

Year	Total	Win	Loss	No result	Win%	Position	Stage
2008	14	7	7	0	50%	5	League stage
2009	14	5	9	1	35.71%	7	League stage
2010	16	11	5	0	68.75%	2	Runner up
2011	16	10	6	0	62.5%	3	Play off
2012	17	10	7	0	58.8%	4	Play off
2013	19	13	6	0	68.42%	1	Champion
2014	15	7	8	0	46.67%	4	Play off
2015	16	10	6	0	62.5%	1	Champion
2016	14	7	7	0	50%	5	League stage
2017	17	12	5	0	70.58%	1	Champion
2018	14	6	8	0	42.85%	5	League stage
2019	16	11	5	0	68.75%	1	Champion
2020	16	11	5	0	68.75%	1	Champion

1.6.1.3 Data assessment of MI Win%

The assessment of MI Win% is done through the NCSS statistical tool. In the data collection process Table 1.11 shows the year-wise Win% of MI player in Millions. Fig. 1.10 shows the graphical representation of year-wise MI Win%. According to the Fig. 1.10, it is find out win% in the year of 2013, 2015, 2017, 2019, and 2020 is maximum.

Based on the data of year-wise win% of the MI team in IPL is defined by the equation of the straight line relating MI Win% and Years is estimated as:

$$\text{Mumbai Indians Win\%} = (-18.7653) + (0.0096)\text{Years}$$

using the 13 observations in this dataset. According to the Table 1.12, the y-intercept, the estimated value of MI win% when years is zero, is −18.7653 with a standard error of 17.2547. The slope, the estimated change in MI Win% per unit change in Years, is 0.0096 with a standard error of 0.0086. The value of R-Squared, the proportion of the variation in MI Win% that can be accounted for by variation in Years, is 0.1026. The correlation between MI Win% and Years is 0.3202. A significance test that the slope is zero resulted in a t-value of 1.1212. The significance level of this t-test is 0.2861. Since $0.2861 > 0.0500$, the hypothesis that the slope is zero is not rejected. The estimated slope is 0.0096. The lower limit of the 95% confidence interval for the slope is −0.0093 and the upper limit is 0.0285. The estimated intercept is −18.7653. The lower limit of the 95% confidence interval for the intercept is −56.7426 and the upper limit is 19.2121.

The Tables 1.12 and 1.13 shows the least-squares estimates of the intercept and slope followed by the corresponding standard errors, confidence intervals, and hypothesis tests.

TABLE 1.8 List of Mumbai Indians player (2008–20) with their salary in rupees.

Player	2008	2009	2010	2011	2012	2013	2014	2015	2016	2017	2018	2019	2020
A. Chavan	8×10^5												
A. Dananjaya											5×10^6		
A. Finch								3.2×10^7	3.2×10^7				
A. Milne											$7.5 \times 10 \times 106$	$7.5 \times 10 \times 106$	
A. Mithun								$3.00 \times 10^6 \times 106$	$3.00 \times 10^6 \times 106$				
A. Murtaza			8.00×10^5	$2.00 \times 10^6 \times 106$									
A.P. Singh													$8.00 \times 10^6 \times 106$
A. Nayar	$1.20 \times 10^6 \times 106$	$1.20 \times 10^6 \times 106$	$1.20 \times 10^6 \times 106$										
A. Nehra	1.60×10^7												
A. Nel	$1.20 \times 10^6 \times 106$												
A. Nechim					$3.00 \times 10^6 \times 106$	$3.00 \times 10^6 \times 106$							
A. Prince	7.03×10^6												
A. Rahane	1.20×10^6	1.20×10^6											
A. Gunaratne										3.00×10^6			
A. Hales								1.00×10^7	1.00×10^7				
A. Symonds				3.91×10^7									
A. Tare			6.00×10^5		1.00×10^6	1.00×10^6	1.20×10^7	1.60×10^7	1.60×10^7	1.60×10^7	2.00×10^6	2.00×10^6	2.00×10^6
A. Wankade					1.00×10^6	1.00×10^6	1.00×10^6	1.00×10^6	1.00×10^6				
A. Nechim			6.00×10^5	3.00×10^6									
A. Tare													
A. Blizzard				9.20×10^5	1.01×10^6	1.07×10^6		3.00×10^6	3.00×10^6				

(Continued)

TABLE 1.8 (Continued)

Player	2008	2009	2010	2011	2012	2013	2014	2015	2016	2017	2018	2019	2020
A. Rayadu			1.20×10^6	3.00×10^6	3.00×10^6	3.00×10^6	4.00×10^7	4.00×10^7	4.00×10^7	4.00×10^7			
A. Singh					1.00×10^6	1.00×10^6							
A. Roy											2.00×10^6	2.00×10^6	2.00×10^6
A. Wankhede													
A. Zoseph												7.50×10^6	
A. Patel						1.00×10^6							
B. Cutting											2.20×10^7	2.20×10^7	
B. Dunk							2.00×10^6						
B. Hendricks												7.50×10^6	
B. Hilfahaus								5.00×10^6	5.00×10^6				
B. Saran												3.40×10^7	
C. Lynn													2.00×10^7
C. Mckay				5.06×10^6	5.53×10^6								
C. Anderson							4.50×10^7	4.50×10^7	4.50×10^7				
C. Gautam							2.00×10^6						
C. Munro								5.00×10^6	5.00×10^6				
C. Nanda		1.20×10^6											
C. Mdan													
D. Bravo	6.02×10^6	7.37×10^6	6.94×10^6										
D. Ukhdeshm													2.00×10^6
D. Fernando	6.02×10^6	7.37×10^6	6.94×10^6	4.60×10^6		2.00×10^6							
D. Kulkarni	1.20×10^6	1.20×10^6	1.20×10^6	2.00×10^6									7.50×10^6
D. Smith	2.01×10^6				5.03×10^6	5.33×10^6							
D. Thornely	1.20×10^6												
D. Jacobs				8.74×10^6	9.55×10^6								

D. Kartik				4.10×10^7	4.10×10^7							
D. Smith												
D. Puniya									1.00×10^6			
E. Lewis										3.80×10^7	3.80×10^7	
G. Bhiman	8.00×10^5											
G. Maxwell					5.33×10^7							
G. Napier		1.47×10^6	1.39×10^6									
H. Gibbs				2.51×10^6								
H.A. Singh		3.40×10^7	3.40×10^7	5.98×10^7	5.98×10^7		5.50×10^7	9.50×10^7	8.00×10^7			
H. Pandaya							1.00×10^6	1.00×10^6	1.00×10^6	1.10×10^8	1.10×10^8	1.10×10^8
I. Kishan										6.20×10^7	6.20×10^7	6.20×10^7
I. Malhotra			6.00×10^5				1.00×10^6	1.00×10^6				
J. Behendorff										1.50×10^7	1.50×10^7	
J. Duminy										1.00×10^7		
J. Buttler									3.80×10^7			
J. Franklin				5.03×10^6	5.33×10^6		1.00×10^6	1.00×10^6				
J. Hazlewood						5.00×10^6	5.00×10^6	5.00×10^6				
J.P. Duminy		4.67×10^7	4.40×10^7									
J. Shah		1.20×10^6			3.00×10^6							
J. Suchith							1.00×10^6		1.00×10^6			
J. Oram					2.66×10^6							
J. Saxena					1.00×10^6	1.00×10^6						
J. Bumrah					1.00×10^6	1.20×10^7	1.20×10^7	1.20×10^7	1.20×10^7	7.00×10^7	7.00×10^7	7.00×10^7
J. Khan					1.00×10^6							
J. Petinson												
J. Shah												1.00×10^7

(Continued)

TABLE 1.8 (Continued)

Player	2008	2009	2010	2011	2012	2013	2014	2015	2016	2017	2018	2019	2020
J. Yadav												5.00×10^6	5.00×10^6
J. Sharma										1.00×10^6			
K. Gowtham										2.00×10^7			
K. Khejroliya										1.00×10^6			
K. Mills		7.37×10^6											
K. Pandya										2.00×10^7	8.80×10^7	8.80×10^7	8.80×10^7
K. Pollard			3.47×10^7	4.10×10^6	4.52×10^7	4.79×10^7	7.50×10^7	9.50×10^7	9.50×10^7	9.50×10^7	5.40×10^7	5.40×10^7	5.40×10^7
K. Sontokie							3.00×10^6						
K. Yadav					1.00×10^6	1.00×10^6							
Karn Sharma										3.20×10^7			
L. Malinga	1.41×10^7	1.72×10^7	1.62×10^7	2.30×10^7	2.51×10^7	2.66×10^7	9.50×10^7	7.50×10^7	5.50×10^7	8.10×10^7		2.00×10^7	2.00×10^7
L. Ronchi	1.20×10^6	1.47×10^6											
L. Bosman	6.02×10^6												
L. Simmons							5.00×10^6	5.50×10^6	5.50×10^6	5.50×10^6			
M.D. Lange							3.00×10^6	3.00×10^6	3.00×10^6				
M. Henriques				2.30×10^6									
M. Hussy							5.00×10^7						
M. Markande											2.00×10^6	2.00×10^6	
M. Mcclennaghan								3.00×10^6	3.00×10^6	3.00×10^6	1.00×10^7	1.00×10^7	1.00×10^7
M. Patel				3.22×10^7	3.22×10^7	3.22×10^7							
M. Pandey	6.00×10^5												
M. Johnson					1.51×10^7	1.51×10^7				2.00×10^7			
MD. Nidheesh											2.00×10^6		
M. Khan											2.00×10^6		
M. Rahman											2.20×10^7		
N. Pooran										3.00×10^6			

Name								
N.C. Nile						2.40×10^7		8.00×10^7
N. Rana			1.00×10^6	1.00×10^6	1.00×10^6			
P. Cummins		5.40×10^7					2.00×10^6	
P. Jaiswal								
P. Huges					5.33×10^6			
P. Ojha			2.30×10^7	3.25×10^7	2.30×10^7			
P. Suyal	1.00×10^6		1.00×10^6	5.00×10^6	1.00×10^6	1.00×10^6		
P. Patel			1.40×10^7	1.40×10^7	1.40×10^7			
P. Shah	1.20×10^6	1.20×10^6						
P. Kumar			5.00×10^6					
P. Sangwan		1.50×10^7				2.80×10^7		
Q. Decock					2.80×10^7	2.80×10^7		
R. Salam					2.00×10^6			
R. Chahar		1.90×10^7	1.90×10^7	1.90×10^7	1.90×10^7			
R. Pawar	1.20×10^6							
R. Utthappa	3.20×10^7							
R. Levi			2.51×10^6					
R. Mclaren	1.47×10^6	1.39×10^6						
R.P. Singh			2.76×10^7					
R. Peterson			5.03×10^6					
R. Raje	4.00×10^5	4.00×10^5						
R. Satish	1.20×10^6	3.00×10^6						
R. Shukla			8.00×10^5					
Ra shaikh	4.00×10^5	6.00×10^5						
R. Shukla								
R. Price		2.30×10^6						

(Continued)

TABLE 1.8 (Continued)

Player	2008	2009	2010	2011	2012	2013	2014	2015	2016	2017	2018	2019	2020
R. Ponting						2.13×10^7							
R. Dhawan						2.00×10^6							
R. Sharma				9.20×10^7	9.20×10^7	9.20×10^7	1.25×10^8	1.25×10^8	1.50×10^8	1.50×10^8	1.50×10^8	1.50×10^8	1.50×10^8
S. Chitnis	8.00×10^5												
S. Pollock	2.21×10^7												
S. Dhawan		1.20×10^6	1.20×10^6										
S. Kanwar				1.00×10^6									
S. Lad								1.00×10^6	1.00×10^6	1.00×10^6	2.00×10^6	2.00×10^6	
S. Marathe					8.00×10^5	8.00×10^5	1.00×10^6						
S. Nayak					8.00×10^5								
S. Rutherford													2.00×10^7
S. Tendulkar	4.49×10^7	4.49×10^7	4.49×10^7	8.28×10^7	8.28×10^7	8.28×10^7							
S. Jayasurya	3.92×10^7	4.79×10^7	4.51×10^7										
S. Gopal							1.00×10^6	1.00×10^6	1.00×10^6				
S. Lamba											2.00×10^6		
S. Tiwari	1.20×10^6	1.20×10^6	1.20×10^6						3.00×10^6		8.00×10^6		5.00×10^6
S. Yadav				1.00×10^6	1.00×10^6	1.00×10^6				3.20×10^7	3.20×10^7	3.20×10^7	3.20×10^7
S. Singh	4.00×10^5												
S. Shahabuddin			6.00×10^5										
T. Bolt													2.20×10^7
T. Dhillon											5.50×10^6		
T. Parera					3.27×10^7								
Southee										2.50×10^7			
T. Suman				3.00×10^6	3.00×10^6								
T. Sunnman													

Name			
U. Chand	6.50×10^6	6.50×10^6	
V. Yeligati	6.00×10^5		
V. Kumar	3.00×10^7	3.00×10^7	3.00×10^7
Y. Takawale	2.00×10^6		
Y. Chahal	1.00×10^6	1.00×10^6	1.00×10^6
Y. Singh	1.00×10^7		
Z. Khan	1.80×10^7	1.80×10^7	2.60×10^7

TABLE 1.9 Batting performance of Mumbai Indians players.

Player	Span	Mat	Inns	NO	Runs	HS	Ave	BF	SR	100	50	0	4s	6s
R.G. Sharma	2011–21	162	158	22	4310	109*	31.69	3309	130.25	1	32	11	380	173
K.A. Pollard	2010–21	171	154	50	3191	87*	30.68	2115	150.87	0	16	4	207	211
A.T. Rayudu	2010–17	114	107	18	2416	81*	27.14	1915	126.16	0	14	9	205	79
S.R. Tendulkar	2008–13	78	78	11	2334	100*	34.83	1948	119.81	1	13	4	295	29
S.A. Yadav	2012–21	54	52	5	1589	79*	33.80	1163	136.62	0	11	4	189	42
H.H. Pandya	2015–21	87	80	29	1401	91	27.47	891	157.23	0	4	5	91	95
Q. de Kock	2019–21	38	38	4	1187	81	34.91	888	133.67	0	9	2	106	50
K.H. Pandya	2016–21	78	67	21	1100	86	23.91	778	141.38	0	1	2	103	44
L.M.P. Simmons	2014–17	29	29	2	1079	100*	39.96	852	126.64	1	11	2	109	44
Ishan Kishan	2018–21	40	36	4	965	99	30.15	726	132.92	0	6	4	69	53
P.A. Patel	2015–17	40	40	1	911	81	23.35	691	131.83	0	5	5	119	17
Harbhajan Singh	2008–17	136	84	35	799	64	16.30	561	142.42	0	1	13	76	41
S.T. Jayasuriya	2008–10	30	30	2	768	114*	27.42	532	144.36	1	4	2	84	39
K.D. Karthik	2012–13	36	33	2	748	86	24.12	624	119.87	0	2	3	84	16
Dr Smith	2008–13	24	22	2	620	87*	31.00	479	129.43	0	5	2	63	27
S.S. Tiwary	2008–20	31	26	3	613	61	26.65	464	132.11	0	4	1	49	22
J.P. Duminy	2009–18	26	23	8	565	62	37.66	496	113.91	0	5	1	42	17
J.C. Buttler	2016–17	24	24	3	527	77	25.09	361	145.98	0	1	1	50	26
A.M. Nayar	2008–10	30	24	5	457	45*	24.05	341	134.01	0	0	0	34	18
D.J. Bravo	2008–10	30	25	4	457	70*	21.76	390	117.17	0	3	0	37	17
N. Rana	2016–17	17	15	1	437	70	31.21	339	128.90	0	4	0	31	25
E. Lewis	2018–19	16	16	0	430	65	26.87	328	131.09	0	2	2	36	26
C.J. Anderson	2014–15	16	15	3	379	95*	31.58	278	136.33	0	3	0	32	21
J.E.C. Franklin	2011–12	20	16	5	327	79	29.72	301	108.63	0	1	0	25	8
R.V. Uthappa	2008–08	14	14	5	320	48	35.55	279	114.69	0	0	0	34	9
A.P. Tare	2010–15	29	23	4	313	59	16.47	235	133.19	0	1	2	36	11
S. Dhawan	2009–10	15	14	0	231	56	16.50	215	107.44	0	2	1	26	3
M.E.K. Hussey	2014–14	9	9	0	209	56	23.22	182	114.83	0	2	0	17	7
A.M. Rahane	2008–09	10	9	1	148	62*	18.50	140	105.71	0	2	2	13	3
S.M. Pollock	2008–08	13	8	0	147	33	18.37	111	132.43	0	0	2	12	8
R. Sathish	2010–11	21	14	5	137	24	15.22	130	105.38	0	0	1	12	0
A. Symonds	2011–11	11	9	5	135	44*	33.75	138	97.82	0	0	0	9	3

(Continued)

TABLE 1.9 (Continued)

Player	Span	Mat	Inns	NO	Runs	HS	Ave	BF	SR	100	50	0	4s	6s
C.M. Gautam	2014–14	9	9	2	121	33	17.28	111	109.00	0	0	0	13	5
A.C. Blizzard	2011–12	7	7	0	120	51	17.14	90	133.33	0	1	1	21	2
B.C.J. Cutting	2018–19	12	9	3	114	37	19.00	75	152.00	0	0	0	6	9
U.B.T. Chand	2015–16	7	6	0	102	58	17.00	87	117.24	0	1	1	13	2
Yuvraj Singh	2019–19	4	4	0	98	53	24.50	75	130.66	0	1	0	7	6
D.J. Jacobs	2011–12	7	7	0	92	32	13.14	98	93.87	0	0	1	10	4
Y.V. Takawale	2008–09	11	5	2	88	27	29.33	87	101.14	0	0	0	9	2
S.L. Malinga	2009–19	122	25	9	88	17	5.50	99	88.88	0	0	6	6	5
P.R. Shah	2008–09	14	9	2	87	29	12.42	86	101.16	0	0	1	8	2
M.J. McClenaghan	2015–19	56	24	11	85	20	6.53	70	121.42	0	0	6	5	7
R.E. Levi	2012–12	6	6	0	83	50	13.83	73	113.69	0	1	2	10	4
H.H. Gibbs	2012–12	3	3	1	81	66*	40.50	88	92.04	0	1	0	8	2
T.L. Suman	2011–12	10	9	1	80	36	10.00	70	114.28	0	0	0	6	6
R. McLaren	2010–10	10	7	4	66	40	22.00	69	95.65	0	0	1	7	0
M.G. Johnson	2013–17	22	9	5	59	13*	14.75	53	111.32	0	0	0	3	3
M.J. Guptill	2016–16	3	3	0	57	48	19.00	55	103.63	0	0	0	3	3
R.T. Ponting	2013–13	6	5	0	52	28	10.40	75	69.33	0	0	1	3	1

*Not out.

TABLE 1.10 Bowling performance of Mumbai Indians players.

Player	Span	Mat	Inns	Overs	Mdns	Runs	Wkts	BBI	Ave	Econ	SR	4	5
S.L. Malinga	2009–19	122	122	471.1	8	3365	170	5/13	19.79	7.14	16.6	6	1
Harbhajan Singh	2008–17	136	134	486.3	5	3385	127	5/18	26.65	6.95	22.9	1	1
J.J. Bumrah	2013–21	99	99	375.4	6	2778	115	4/14	24.15	7.39	19.6	2	0
M.J. McClenaghan	2015–19	56	56	212.2	1	1803	71	4/21	25.39	8.49	17.9	1	0
K.A. Pollard	2010–21	171	97	228.0	0	2014	63	4/44	31.96	8.83	21.7	1	0
K.H. Pandya	2016–21	78	75	224.3	0	1636	49	3/14	33.38	7.28	27.4	0	0
H.H. Pandya	2015–21	87	60	144.5	0	1313	42	3/20	31.26	9.06	20.6	0	0
M.M. Patel	2011–13	31	31	116.0	3	862	40	5/21	21.55	7.43	17.4	2	1
R.D. Chahar	2019–21	35	35	128.0	0	943	39	4/27	24.17	7.36	19.6	1	0
D.S. Kulkarni	2008–21	35	35	113.1	1	916	36	3/18	25.44	8.09	18.8	0	0

(Continued)

TABLE 1.10 (Continued)

Player	Span	Mat	Inns	Overs	Mdns	Runs	Wkts	BBI	Ave	Econ	SR	4	5
T.A. Boult	2020–21	22	22	83.4	3	680	33	4/18	20.60	8.12	15.2	1	0
M.G. Johnson	2013–17	22	22	84.0	1	600	31	3/26	19.35	7.14	16.2	0	0
P.P. Ojha	2012–15	38	37	130.2	1	1004	29	3/11	34.62	7.70	26.9	0	0
Z. Khan	2009–14	26	26	91.4	1	664	26	3/21	25.53	7.24	21.1	0	0
D.J. Bravo	2008–10	30	30	87.4	1	719	26	3/24	27.65	8.20	20.2	0	0
C.R.D. Fernando	2008–10	10	10	39.0	0	294	17	4/18	17.29	7.53	13.7	1	0
M. Markande	2018–19	17	17	50.0	0	427	16	4/23	26.68	8.54	18.7	1	0
K.V. Sharma	2017–17	9	9	30.4	0	214	13	4/16	16.46	6.97	14.1	1	0
S.T. Jayasuriya	2008–10	30	21	49.0	1	390	13	3/14	30.00	7.95	22.6	0	0
A. Nehra	2008–08	14	14	44.5	0	348	12	3/13	29.00	7.76	22.4	0	0
T.G. Southee	2016–17	14	14	53.0	1	425	12	3/24	35.41	8.01	26.5	0	0
R. Vinay Kumar	2015–17	17	17	55.3	1	463	12	2/17	38.58	8.34	27.7	0	0
S.M. Pollock	2008–08	13	13	46.0	1	301	11	3/12	27.36	6.54	25.0	0	0
J.L. Pattinson	2020–20	10	10	35.3	0	320	11	2/19	29.09	9.01	19.3	0	0
R.P. Singh	2012–12	11	11	41.0	0	318	10	3/28	31.80	7.75	24.6	0	0
J. Suchith	2015–16	14	13	41.0	0	368	10	2/14	36.80	8.97	24.6	0	0
J.E.C. Franklin	2011–12	20	15	25.1	0	220	9	2/18	24.44	8.74	16.7	0	0
Dr Smith	2008–13	24	13	29.0	0	237	9	3/26	26.33	8.17	19.3	0	0
A.N. Ahmed	2010–13	10	10	31.0	1	257	8	2/13	32.12	8.29	23.2	0	0
S. Gopal	2014–16	6	6	19.1	0	154	7	2/25	22.00	8.03	16.4	0	0
Mustafizur Rahman	2018–18	7	7	27.3	0	230	7	3/24	32.85	8.36	23.5	0	0
A.S. Joseph	2019–19	3	3	8.4	1	87	6	6/12	14.50	10.03	8.6	0	1
A.G. Murtaza	2010–11	8	8	32.0	0	208	6	2/18	34.66	6.50	32.0	0	0
R.R. Raje	2008–09	10	10	23.1	0	209	6	2/16	34.83	9.02	23.1	0	0
N.M. Coulter-Nile	2013–21	9	9	34.0	0	270	6	2/29	45.00	7.94	34.0	0	0
A.M. Nayar	2008–10	30	9	19.0	0	152	5	3/13	30.40	8.00	22.8	0	0
J.P. Behrendorff	2019–19	5	5	19.0	0	165	5	2/22	33.00	8.68	22.8	0	0
J.P. Duminy	2009–18	26	10	26.0	0	166	5	2/15	33.20	6.38	31.2	0	0
C.J. Anderson	2014–15	16	11	22.0	0	217	5	2/18	43.40	9.86	26.4	0	0
R. McLaren	2010–10	10	10	34.0	0	270	4	2/28	67.50	7.94	51.0	0	0
D.J. Thornely	2008–08	6	4	7.0	0	40	3	2/7	13.33	5.71	14.0	0	0

(Continued)

TABLE 1.10 (Continued)

Player	Span	Mat	Inns	Overs	Mdns	Runs	Wkts	BBI	Ave	Econ	SR	4	5
R.J. Peterson	2012–12	5	4	8.0	0	70	3	3/37	23.33	8.75	16.0	0	0
P. Kumar	2014–14	3	3	12.0	0	78	3	2/31	26.00	6.50	24.0	0	0
K. Santokie	2014–14	2	2	8.0	0	90	3	2/50	30.00	11.25	16.0	0	0
J. Yadav	2019–21	7	7	25.0	0	175	3	1/25	58.33	7.00	50.0	0	0
B.C.J. Cutting	2018–19	12	8	19.0	0	195	3	1/12	65.00	10.26	38.0	0	0

TABLE 1.11 Run summary section of year-wise win% of Mumbai Indians.

Parameter	Value	Parameter	Value
Dependent variable	Mumbai Indians win	Rows processed	13
Independent variable	Years	Rows used in estimation	13
Frequency variable	None	Rows with X missing	0
Weight variable	None	Rows with Freq missing	0
Intercept	−18.7653	Rows prediction only	0
Slope	0.0096	Sum of frequencies	13
R-squared	0.1026	Sum of weights	13
Correlation	0.3202	Coefficient of variation	0.1992
Mean square error	0.01335879	Square root of MSE	0.1155802

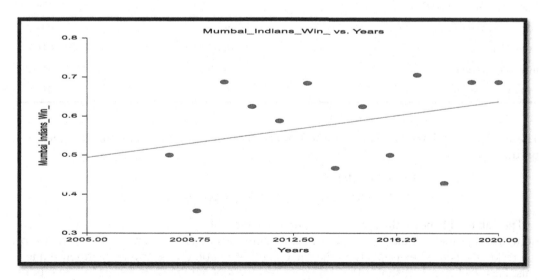

FIGURE 1.10 Year-wise percentage of Mumbai Indians wins.

TABLE 1.12 Descriptive statistics section.

Parameter	Dependent	Independent
Variable	Mumbai Indians Win	Years
Count	13	13
Mean	0.5802	2014.0000
Standard deviation	0.1168	3.8944
Minimum	0.3571	2008.0000
Maximum	0.7058	2020.0000

TABLE 1.13 Linear regression report.

Intercept Parameter	Slope	
	B(0)	B(1)
Regression coefficients	−18.7653	0.0096
Lower 95% confidence limit	−56.7426	−0.0093
Upper 95% confidence limit	19.2121	0.0285
Standard error	17.2547	0.0086
Standardized coefficient	0.0000	0.3202
t value	−1.0875	1.1212
Prob level (t test)	0.3001	0.2861
Reject H0 (Alpha = 0.0500)	No	No
Power (Alpha = 0.0500)	0.1688	0.1764
Regression of Y on X	−18.7653	0.0096
Inverse regression from X on Y	−188.0540	0.0937
Orthogonal regression of Y and X	−18.7809	0.0096

These results are based on several assumptions that should be validated before they are used.

Estimated model

$(-18.765250549448) + (0.00960549450549308) \times (\text{Years})$

The Table 1.14 shows the F-ratio for testing whether the slope is zero, the degrees of freedom, and the mean square error. The mean square error, which estimates the variance of the residuals, is used extensively in the calculation of hypothesis tests and confidence intervals. Figs. 1.11 and 1.12 shows the Year-wise residuals of MI win% and distributional plots of residuals of win%. Fig. 1.13 shows the normal probability plot of residuals of MI win%.

TABLE 1.14 Analysis of variance section.

Source	DF	Sum of squares	Mean square	F-ratio	Prob level	Power (5%)
Intercept	1	4.376449	4.376449			
Slope	1	0.01679233	0.01679233	1.2570	0.2861	0.1764
Error	11	0.1469467	0.01335879			
Adj. total	12	0.163739	0.01364492			
Total	13	4.540187				

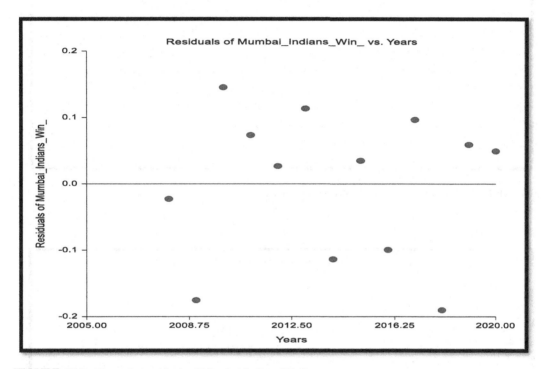

FIGURE 1.11 Year-wise residuals of Mumbai Indians Win%.

After the individual assessment of salaries of MI players and win% of MI, now the year-wise relationship between salaries of MI and win% of MI is given by

$$Years = 2002.90413352717 + 0.0186286938224725 \times salaries\ of\ MI$$

$$+ 1.51634173330256 \times Win\%\ of\ MI$$

Table 1.15 shows the regression coefficient confidence intervals of MI with the parameters of salaries and win% of MI. Fig. 1.14 shows the surface plot of year-wise salaries in Millions versus Win% of MI.

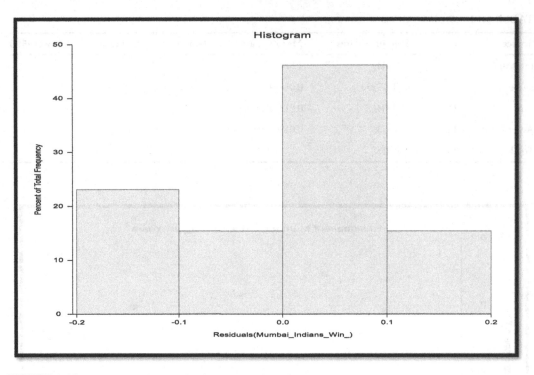

FIGURE 1.12   Histogram of residuals of Mumbai Indians Win%.

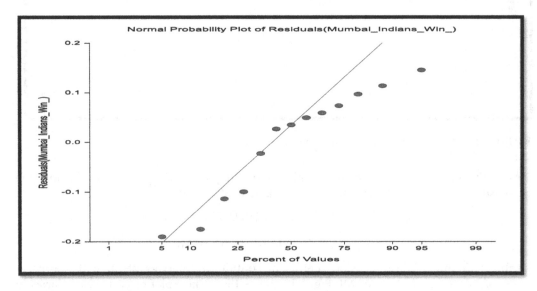

FIGURE 1.13   Normal probability plot of residuals of Mumbai Indians Win%.

TABLE 1.15 Regression coefficients confidence intervals of MI.

Independent variable	Regression coefficient b(i)	Standard error Sb(i)	Lower 95% conf. limit of β(i)	Upper 95% conf. limit of β(i)
Intercept	2002.904	1.572133	1999.401	2006.407
Salaries of MI	0.01862869	0.001566818	0.01513761	0.02211978
Win of MI	1.516342	2.680308	−4.455757	7.488441

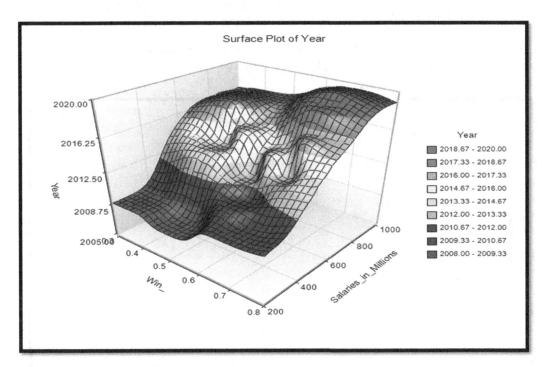

FIGURE 1.14 Surface plot of year-wise salaries in millions versus Win% of MI.

1.6.1.4 Michaelis–Menten curve of Mumbai Indians data

The Michaelis–Menten equation is a well-known model used in enzyme kinetics. It is a special arrangement of a two-parameter rectangular hyperbola. The mathematical model is given by

$$V = \frac{C(V_{\max})}{C + K_m}$$

where V is the dependent variable, C is the independent variable, and V_{max} and K_m are parameters to be estimated. In enzyme kinetics, V is the velocity (rate) of an enzyme reaction and C is the substrate concentration. V_{max} and K_m have simple physical interpretations. V_{max} is the maximum velocity and serves as a horizontal asymptote. K_m, the

Michaelis constant, is the value of C the results a velocity of $V_{max}/2$. Fig. 1.15 shows Michaelis–Menten curve of salaries in millions versus Win%.

In this case model is fit for Y = Salary in Millions, X = Win%

$$\text{Salaries in Millions of MI} = \frac{V_{max} \times \text{Win\% of MI}}{K_m + \text{Win\% of MI}}$$

According to the data set estimated nonlinear-regression model according to the Michaelis–Menten concept is given by

$$\text{Salaries in Millions of MI} = \frac{1045.9274405185 \times \text{Win\% of } MI}{0.514810315548479 + \text{Win\% of } MI}$$

Table 1.16 shows the value of V_{max} and K_m after the five iteration. When put the maximum likelihood value of V_{max} and K_m then decrease the value of salaries rather than salary

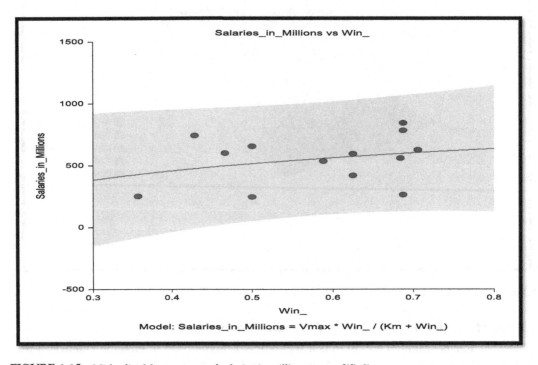

FIGURE 1.15 Michaelis–Menten curve of salaries in millions versus Win%.

TABLE 1.16 Michaelis–Menten parameter estimation.

Groups	Count	Iter's	R^2	Nonlinear regression V_{max}	Maximum likelihood V_{max}	Nonlinear regression K_m	Maximum likelihood K_m
All	13	5	0.08749	1045.92744	834.21277	0.51481	0.29662

TABLE 1.17 Michaelis–Menten based maximum-likelihood parameter estimation.

Parameter name	Parameter estimate	Asymptotic standard error	Lower 95% C.L.	Upper 95% C.L.
V_{max}	834.21277	549.44405	−375.10542	2043.53096
K_m	0.29662	0.56019	−0.93636	1.52960

TABLE 1.18 Michaelis–Menten based nonlinear regression parameter estimation.

Parameter name	Parameter estimate	Asymptotic standard error	Lower 95% C.L.	Upper 95% C.L.
V_{max}	1045.92744	1036.64041	−1235.70271	3327.55760
K_m	0.51481	1.09213	−1.88895	2.91857

estimation through the conventional formula. Tables 1.17 and 1.18 shows the maximum likelihood and non-linear regression based value of V_{max} and K_m at the different level.

1.6.1.5 Key findings of Mumbai Indians

Solid middle and lower order: The MI are the only team with two middle-order batsmen in the top ten run scorers in 2020 IPL. Ishan Kishan has been excellent for the MI this season, averaging 53 and striking out at a pace of 144. Suryakumar Yadav, however, has been the real standout, hitting fifties at critical times to get the team over the line. Suryakumar Yadav has a strike rate of close to 150 and an average of 48. MI′ middle-order is formidable thanks to the combination of Ishan Kishan and Suryakumar Yadav. In the event that both Suryakumar and Ishan Kishan falter, they have Kieron Pollard and the Pandya brothers to bat out the game in the death overs. MI slammed 62 in three overs against Kings XI Punjab, thanks to Kieron Pollard and Hardik Pandya's attack. Hardik Pandya and Suryakumar smashed 51 runs in the final three overs against Rajasthan Royals in another game. Hardik Pandya hit 37 off 14 balls in Qualifier 1, and MI scored 55 runs in the last three overs to beat Delhi Capitals.

Boult and Bumrah Duo: Trent Boult will get you if Jasprit Bumrah doesn't. MI′ opening and death bowling combinations are among the best in the game. In IPL 2020, Bumrah and Boult have combined for 49 wickets, with Bumrah's 27 wickets being the most by an Indian bowler in a single edition. With a 6.71 economy rate, Bumrah is in a different league. The MI are a formidable team because they play in pairs. The performance of MI can be attributed to Rohit Sharma's captaincy, which included brilliant use of Jasprit Bumrah at the outset, in the middle overs, and at the end. The fact that nine out of eleven members contribute and are not too dependent on one person is the primary reason for MI′ dominance in the IPL.

1.6.2 Analyzing Starbucks' value chain

The value chain notion can be better explained and understood by looking at Starbucks. In the year 1971, there was only one Starbucks location in Seattle. From that point on, it developed to become one of the most recognizable brands in the entire globe. The aim of Starbucks is to "inspire and nurture the human spirit-one person, one cup, and one neighborhood at a time," according to its website. Table 1.19 shows the value chain analysis of Starbucks'.

1.6.2.1 Starbucks' primary activities

Inbound logistics: Starbucks' inbound logistics refer to the process through which specially hired coffee buyers choose the best coffee beans from growers in Latin America, Africa, and Asia. In the case of Starbucks, the green or unroasted beans are purchased by the company's purchasers directly from the plantations. These are delivered to storage facilities, where the beans are then dried, roasted, and packaged. Starbucks' unique roasting and packaging processes add value to the beans, which helps to raise their retail price. The beans are subsequently sent to distribution facilities, some of which are owned by the corporation and others of which are run by other logistical firms.

Operations: Starbucks has direct company-owned outlets or businesses with a license in more than 80 markets. Globally, the corporation operates more than 32,000 outlets. In addition, it owns a number of brands, such as Teavana, Seattle's Best Coffee, and Evolution Fresh. According to its financial filings, during the first half of its fiscal year 2020, the company's company-operated stores contributed 81% of its total net sales, while licensed stores contributed 11%.

Outbound logistics: In the product sales process for Starbucks, there are either hardly any or none at all. Stores are where most of the things are sold. However, delivery to retail locations and storage are crucial.

Marketing and sales: Starbucks puts more money on providing top-notch customer service and high-quality goods than it does in aggressive marketing. However, the business engages in need-based marketing operations during the introduction of new products by providing samples in the vicinity of the stores.

Service: Through its in-store customer service, Starbucks tries to increase customer loyalty. Giving customers a distinctive Starbucks experience has always been one of Starbucks' defining retail goals. A crucial link in the value chain that contributes to the distinctiveness of its services is service training. The value that baristas add when they prepare drinks for consumers is considerable.

1.6.2.2 Starbucks' support activities

Infrastructure: This covers the divisions needed to maintain the company's retail locations, such as management, finance, legal, etc. Additionally, it has store managers on-site

TABLE 1.19 Value chain analysis of Starbucks'.

Case study domain	Value chain analytics
Data collection	Investopedia and website of Starbucks'
Attribute selection	Inbound logistics and outbound logistics
Data assessment	Qualitative assessment

who assist in managing attractive, well-designed stores that are complemented by excellent customer service offered by the committed team of employees wearing green aprons.

Human resource management: The loyal personnel are seen as a crucial factor in the business's success and growth over the years. Starbucks provides considerable incentives and bonuses to keep staff motivated. Because of the company's reputation for caring for its employees, there is a low employee turnover rate, which is a sign of excellent human resource management. Employees participate in a variety of training programs in a work environment that fosters employee motivation and productivity.

Technology development: Starbucks is well known for using technology not only to engage with its consumers but also for coffee-related procedures. Because Starbucks cafes offer free, unrestricted Wi-Fi, many consumers use them as temporary offices or gathering places. Starbucks has introduced a number of venues where users can share their experiences, make comments, and ask questions. Particularly in the area of its rewards program, technology aids in the implementation of this input.

1.6.3 Case study on the big data analysis

1.6.3.1 *Walmart*

For its clients, Walmart uses big data and data mining to generate customized product recommendations. Walmart can find useful patterns revealing the most often purchased products, most popular products, and even the most popular product bundles with the aid of these two cutting-edge technologies. Walmart develops appealing and unique recommendations for certain consumers based on these insights. The retail behemoth has significantly increased conversion rates and enhanced customer service by successfully applying Data Mining techniques. Additionally, Walmart leverages NoSQL and Hadoop technologies to make it possible for customers to access real-time data gathered from various sources.

1.6.3.2 *Uber*

Uber is one of the major cab service providers in the world. It leverages customer data to track and identify the most popular and most used services by the users. Once this data is collected, Uber uses data analytics to analyze the usage patterns of customers and determine which services should be given more emphasis and importance. Apart from this, Uber uses big data in another unique way. Uber closely studies the demand and supply of its services and changes the cab fares accordingly. It is the surge pricing mechanism that works something like this suppose when you are in a hurry, and you have to book a cab from a crowded location, Uber will charge you double the normal amount!

1.6.4 Conclusion

The field of analytics has become increasingly important in recent years, as businesses and organizations seek to leverage data to make more informed decisions. Analytics involves the use of statistical and mathematical methods to analyze data and uncover insights that can inform business strategy and decision-making. One of the key conclusions that can be drawn from the field of analytics is that data-driven decision-making can be highly effective. By analyzing data and uncovering insights, businesses and organizations can gain a better understanding of their customers, identify trends and patterns, and make more informed decisions about product development, marketing strategies, and other key areas.

Another conclusion from the field of analytics is that there is a significant need for skilled professionals in this area. As more businesses and organizations adopt analytics as a core part of their operations, there is a growing demand for professionals with expertise in data analysis, statistics, and other related areas.

Looking to the future, there are a number of exciting developments and opportunities in the field of analytics. One key area of growth is in the use of machine learning and AI to analyze data and uncover insights. As these technologies continue to advance, we can expect to see even more powerful and sophisticated analytics tools emerging. Another area of future growth is in the use of analytics to drive innovation and new product development. By analyzing data on customer behavior, market trends, and other factors, businesses can identify new opportunities for innovation and develop new products and services that meet evolving customer needs.

1.7 Exercise

1.7.1 Objective type question

1. _____ is the process which converts conventional information into the intelligent information.
   a. Regression
   b. Analytics
   c. Blockchain
   d. Internet of Things

2. To identify relationship between two or more than two parameters from one of best method is
   a. Cluster analysis
   b. Value chain analysis
   c. Regression analysis
   d. Cognitive analysis

3. _____ are the programming language which can be used for data analysis.
   a. C
   b. C + +
   c. Java
   d. Python

4. _____ is an interdisciplinary field that integrates knowledge from linguistics, psychology and neurology.
   a. Forensic Science
   b. General Science
   c. Cognitive Science
   d. Earth Science

5. To ask the question in the form of "What Happened" is the part of one of the following analytics approach
   a. Diagnostic
   b. Prescriptive
   c. Descriptive
   d. Predictive

6. To ask the question in the form of "What will Happen Next" is the part of one of the following analytics approach
   a. Diagnostic
   b. Prescriptive
   c. Predictive
   d. Descriptive

7. To ask the question in the form of "Why did it Happen" is the part of one of the following analytics approach
   a. Diagnostic
   b. Prescriptive
   c. Predictive
   d. Descriptive

8. To ask the question in the form of "What Action should be Taken" is the part of one of the following analytics approach
   a. Descriptive
   b. Predictive
   c. Diagnostic
   d. Prescriptive

9. Reports, Visualization and _____ is the use case of descriptive analytics.
   a. Mathematical equation
   b. Models
   c. Flow chart
   d. Dashboard

10. With _____, data pattern in the past and present are examined to see, if they are likely to occur.
    a. Descriptive analytics
    b. Predictive analytics
    c. Predictive analytics
    d. Prescriptive analytics

11. One of the following is the initial step of data analysis
    a. Data visualization
    b. Data cleaning
    c. Data requirement
    d. Data deployment

12. The conversion of quantitative data into the graphical view is called as
    a. Data cleaning
    b. Data requirement
    c. Data deployment
    d. Data visualization

13. One of the following is the initial step of Business analytics
    a. Data cleaning
    b. Data requirement
    c. Data aggregation
    d. Data deployment

14. For both qualitative and quantitative research, _____ examines unstructured text data sets like documents, emails, social media posts, blog comments, call center scripts, and other text-based sources.
    a. Text mining
    b. Web mining
    c. Data mining
    d. None of the above

15. _____ represent the total amount of times a page on your website has been visited.
    a. Sessions
    b. Events
    c. Page views
    d. Entity

16. A _____ is a collection of activities that happen on your website over a specific period of time, such as page views, CTA clicks, and events.
    a. Events
    b. Page views
    c. Sessions
    d. Entity

17. _____ is a method for visually examining a company's operations to determine how the company might gain a competitive edge.
    a. Descriptive analytics
    b. Predictive analytics
    c. Data analysis
    d. Value chain analysis

18. Businesses will need to devise a means to find, extract, organize, and store the data in order for it to be useful is called as_____
    a. Unusability
    b. Analysis
    c. Usability
    d. Assessment

19. _____ makes predictions about future events using historical data, while _____ calculates the possibility that these predictions will come true using cutting-edge methods.
    a. Predictive analytics, Regression analysis
    b. Regression analysis, Regression analysis
    c. Forecasting, Predictive analytics
    d. Predictive analytics, Forecasting

20. Case study of Starbucks' is related to the concept of
    a. Descriptive analytics
    b. Predictive analytics
    c. Value chain analysis
    d. Data Analysis

1.7.2 Assessment question

1. Apply the concept of analytics in health care industry and automobile industry and categorize the assessment into conventional and intelligent information.

2. How we can apply the concept of descriptive, diagnostic, predictive and prescriptive analytics in the following industry:
    a. Health care industry
    b. Automobile industry
    c. Software industry
    d. Consultancy services

3. Explain how prediction and forecasting are the key components of Business Analytics.

4. Analyze the key business components of Amazon and Flipcart based on the following parameters:
    a. Data aggregation
    b. Data mining
    c. Forecasting and prediction

5. Apply the concept of Big data analytics in the Tourism industry and find out the key parameters.

6. Apply the concept of value chain analysis in the following industry:
    a. Health care industry
    b. Automobile industry
    c. Software industry
    d. Consultancy services

7. Develop a case study on the performance of Brazil in the FIFA WORLD CUP from 1950 to 2022.

8. Develop Big data based case study on the Microsoft Azure system.

9. Develop case study on the performance comparison between Roger Federer and Rafael Nadal.

10. Find out different example of web scrapping from real world problems.

11. Find out role of Analytics in the following recent technology:
    a. Artificial intelligence
    b. Cloud computing
    c. Blockchain
    d. Augmented reality
    e. Virtual reality

Further reading

M.M. Botvinick, Realizing the promise of AI: a new calling for cognitive science, Trends Cogn. Sci. 26 (12) (2022) 1013–1014.

S.C. Emily, Mind meets machine: towards a cognitive science of human–machine interactions, Trends Cogn. Sci. 25 (3) (2021) 200–212.

V. Khare, Prediction, investigation, and assessment of novel tidal–solar hybrid renewable energy system in India by different techniques, Int. J. Sustain. Energy 38 (5) (2019) 447–468.

V. Khare, Status of tidal energy system in India, J. Mar. Eng. Technol. 20 (5) (2021) 289–298.

V. Khare, C. Khare, S. Nema, P. Baredar, Renewable energy system paradigm change from trending technology: a review, Int. J. Sustain. Energy 40 (7) (2021) 697–718.

V. Khare, S. Nema, P. Barear, Optimisation of the hybrid renewable energy system by HOMER, PSO and CPSO for the study area, Int. J. Sustain. Energy 36 (4) (2017) 326–343.

R.S. Marquez, Diagnosis of quality management systems using data analytics—a case study in the manufacturing sector, Comput. Indus. 115 (2020)103183.

J.A. Mazanec, Hidden theorizing in big data analytics: with a reference to tourism design research, Ann. Tour. Res. 83 (2020)102931. July.

S.J. Quin, Advances and opportunities in machine learning for process data analytics, Comput. Chem. Eng. 126 (2019) 465–473. 12 July.

W. Sun, Opportunities in tensorial data analytics for chemical and biological manufacturing processes, Comput. Chem. Eng. 143 (5) (2020) 107099.

P. Thagard, The cognitive science of COVID-19: acceptance, denial, and belief change, Methods 195 (2021) 92–102.

Foundation of cognitive science

Abbreviations

AI	artificial intelligence
NLP	natural language processing
MNIST	Modified National Institute of Standards and Technology
CNS	central nervous system
IPT	information processing theory
STM	short-term memory
CLIL	content and language integrated learning
GDN	geography disciplines network
ICP	inclusive curriculum project
STS	short-term storage

2.1 Introduction

Science is a systematic approach that generates and organizes knowledge by formulating explanations and predictions pertaining to the universe, which can be empirically tested. Archeological evidence dating back tens of thousands of years indicates the existence of scientific reasoning, suggesting that science may be as ancient as humanity itself. Science serves as a means of acquiring knowledge about the constituents of the universe and comprehending their functioning across different temporal realms: the present, the past, and the anticipated future. The exhilaration derived from observing or comprehending previously unexplored phenomena motivates scientists in their pursuit of knowledge.

Nowadays lots of study to be done in the field of human mind and the study of the human mind and brain is called cognitive science, which is shown in Fig. 2.1, and it focuses on how the mind represents and manipulates information as well as how mental representations and processes are realized in the brain. The study of the mind, including its composition and activities, is known as cognitive science. Several research sciences are included in it, which is shown in Fig. 2.2. Following are the description of each factor of the cognitive science:

2.2 Education

Cognitive science is the study of how the mind works, including processes such as attention, memory, problem-solving, and language. This field of study has important

Cognitive Science, Computational Intelligence, and Data Analytics
DOI: https://doi.org/10.1016/B978-0-443-16078-3.00005-8
© 2024 Elsevier Inc. All rights are reserved, including those for text and data mining, AI training, and similar technologies.

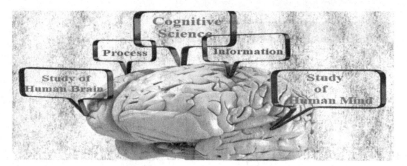

FIGURE 2.1 Cognitive science.

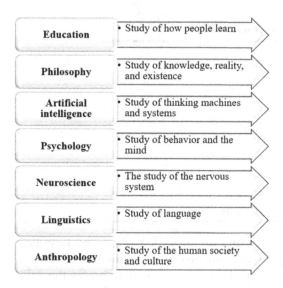

FIGURE 2.2 Different fields of cognitive science.

implications for education as it helps educators understand how students learn and how to improve teaching methods. Cognitive science is investigating how the structure and functioning of the brain affect our ability to learn. It is a field of study that takes into account pupils' brain architecture while determining how to instill knowledge in their brains. To this purpose, working memory (also known as short-term memory [STM]) and long-term memory can be used to broadly classify human cognition. Cognitive science research has identified several principles of effective learning that can be applied in the classroom. For example, studies have shown that students learn best when information is presented in a way that is easy to understand and remember. This can be achieved through the use of clear explanations, visual aids, and analogies.

Cognitive science also emphasizes the importance of active learning. Students learn more effectively when they are actively engaged in the learning process, rather than just passively receiving information. This can be achieved through activities such as group discussions, problem-solving tasks, and hands-on experiments. Additionally, cognitive science has shed light on the importance of feedback in the learning process. Providing students with feedback on their work helps them identify areas where they need to improve and reinforces what they have learned.

At the end, cognitive science provides valuable insights into how students learn and how educators can improve teaching methods to enhance student learning outcomes.

2.3 Philosophy

The systematic study of broad and fundamental issues, such as those pertaining to existence, reason, knowledge, values, the mind, and language, is known as philosophy. The most general definition of philosophy is the search for knowledge, wisdom, and truth. In fact, the world's Greek definition is "love of wisdom." Philosophy addresses fundamental issues. Here is a typical classification, about which particular questions is philosophy concerned with? Fig. 2.3 shows the classification of philosophy.

- *Logic*: Logicians research both sound and flawed justifications, as well as formal symbolic languages used to represent premises, phrases, and arguments.
- *Metaphysics*: The types of entities that exist, the nature of the universe and its elements, and the relationships between things or events are all topics of study for metaphysicians.
- *Epistemology*: Epistemologists research information, proof, and logically sound beliefs. An epistemologist might investigate the reliability of science and the veracity of our senses.
- *Values*: Philosophers examine a variety of subjects in value theory, including politics, art, and morality. For instance: What is a wrong action? How do we recognize moral individuals and decent lives? What causes a society to be fair or unfair?

FIGURE 2.3   Classification of philosophy.

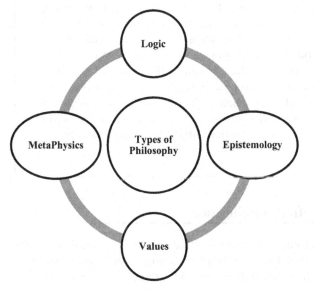

Python Program on the epistemology—knowledge acquisition through observation:

```python
class Observation:
    def __init__(self, description):
        self.description = description

    def analyze(self):
        print("Analyzing the observation...")
        # Perform analysis on the observation here
        # This can include logical reasoning, data processing, etc.
        print("Analysis complete.")

    def interpret(self):
        print("Interpreting the observation...")
        # Perform interpretation of the observation here
        # This can involve making inferences, drawing conclusions, etc.
        print("Interpretation complete.")

    def present(self):
        print("Presenting the observation:")
        print(self.description)

# Create an observation instance
observation = Observation("The sky is cloudy today.")

# Analyze, interpret, and present the observation
observation.analyze()
observation.interpret()
observation.present()
```

In this program, we have an Observation class that represents an observation. The Observation class has methods such as analyze(), interpret(), and present().

When you create an instance of the Observation class, you pass in a description of the observation. In this example, the observation is "The sky is cloudy today." The analyze() method represents the process of analyzing the observation, which can involve logical reasoning, data processing, or any other relevant analysis techniques. The interpret() method represents the process of interpreting the observation, such as making inferences or drawing conclusions based on the observation. The present() method simply displays the description of the observation.

This program illustrates a simplified concept of how observation, analysis, interpretation, and presentation are integral to the process of acquiring knowledge, which is a fundamental topic in epistemology.

2.4 Artificial intelligence

Artificial intelligence (AI) is a field of computer science that focuses on creating intelligent machines that can perform tasks that typically require human intelligence, such as visual perception, speech recognition, decision-making, and language translation. AI uses a combination of algorithms, statistical models, and data to mimic human cognitive abilities and solve complex problems. It can be divided into several subfields, including machine learning, natural language processing (NLP), robotics, and computer vision. AI has applications in various industries, including healthcare, finance, transportation, and manufacturing, and is expected to have a significant impact on society in the coming years. The study of AI and its effects on our knowledge and understanding of intelligence, ethics, consciousness and epistemology is the focus of the philosophy of AI, which is also a subfield of technology. Understanding common knowledge and skills is a major issue for both AI and philosophy. The idea of the common sense informatics scenario, or the situation a human or computer program finds themselves in while using ill-defined notions since the knowledge that is available is incomplete both in terms of observation and theory. Cognitive science and AI are closely related fields of study. Cognitive science focuses on understanding how the human mind works, while AI aims to create machines that can perform tasks that typically require human intelligence, such as reasoning, problem-solving, and language understanding. Cognitive science has provided insights into how the brain processes information and how people learn, which has informed the development of AI systems. For example, cognitive science research on visual perception has helped to inform the development of computer vision algorithms used in image recognition tasks.

In turn, AI research has also contributed to our understanding of cognition. For example, deep learning models have been used to model neural networks in the brain, providing insights into how the brain processes information. Cognitive science and AI are also connected through the field of cognitive computing, which combines the strengths of both fields to create intelligent systems that can reason and learn like humans. Cognitive computing systems can process vast amounts of data, understand natural language, and make decisions based on complex information. In that case, cognitive science and AI are mutually beneficial fields of study, with cognitive science providing insights into how the human mind works, which can inform the development of AI systems, and AI providing tools and models that can be used to study cognition.

One of the main ways that AI contributes to cognitive science is through the development of computational models of cognition. These models are designed to simulate the processes that underlie cognitive tasks and provide a framework for understanding how the brain works. For example, researchers can use AI to develop models of visual perception that simulate the way that the brain processes visual information. By comparing the output of these models to the behavior of human subjects, researchers can test theories about how the brain processes visual information and gain insights into the underlying neural mechanisms. AI can also be used to develop new methods for analyzing and interpreting data from cognitive experiments. For example, machine learning algorithms can be used to identify patterns in large datasets, allowing researchers to uncover new relationships between cognitive processes and behavior. NLP algorithms can be used to analyze language data, providing insights into the cognitive processes involved in language comprehension and production.

Finally, AI can be used to develop new technologies that can help people with cognitive impairments. For example, researchers are exploring the use of AI-based virtual assistants to help people with dementia or other cognitive impairments maintain their independence and improve their quality of life. At the end, AI is a valuable tool for cognitive scientists, providing new insights into the workings of the mind and helping to develop new technologies to improve cognitive functioning.

2.5 Psychology

The scientific study of the mind and behavior is called psychology. The study of conscious and unconscious events, such as emotions and thoughts, is included in psychology. It is a field of study that bridges the natural and social sciences and has a huge scope. The science of mind, brain, and social behavior can be roughly divided into two parts: a large profession of practitioners and a smaller but developing science. Although the two have different objectives, curricula, and methods, some psychologists combine the two.

Cognitive science and psychology are closely related fields of study that both focus on understanding the human mind and behavior. Cognitive science is an interdisciplinary field that draws on research from psychology, neuroscience, linguistics, philosophy, and computer science to understand how the mind works. Cognitive scientists study mental processes such as perception, attention, memory, language, and reasoning, and use this knowledge to develop theories and models of cognition.

Psychology is a broader field that encompasses the study of behavior and mental processes. Psychologists use a variety of methods to study human behavior, including observation, experimentation, and statistical analysis. Psychology includes a range of subfields, such as social psychology, developmental psychology, clinical psychology, and cognitive psychology. Cognitive psychology is a subfield of psychology that focuses specifically on the study of mental processes such as perception, attention, memory, language, and reasoning, and is closely related to cognitive science. Fig. 2.4 shows the subfield of the psychology.

FIGURE 2.4   Subfields of psychology.

Cognitive science and psychology share many research methods and approaches, and both fields contribute to our understanding of the human mind and behavior. Research in cognitive science has informed the development of theories and models of cognition, while research in psychology has provided insights into the social and emotional factors that influence behavior. Overall, cognitive science and psychology are complementary fields that together provide a rich understanding of the human mind and behavior.

2.6 Neuroscience

The scientific study of the nervous system's functioning and diseases includes the study of the brain, spinal cord, and peripheral nervous system. The study of the anatomy and operation of the nervous system and the brain is known as neuroscience. To map the brain mechanistically, neuroscientists draw on cellular and molecular biology, anatomy and physiology, human behavior and cognition, and other fields. Cognitive science and neuroscience are closely related fields of study that both focus on understanding the brain and its functions. Cognitive science is an interdisciplinary field that draws on research from psychology, linguistics, philosophy, computer science, and neuroscience to understand how the mind works. Cognitive scientists study mental processes such as perception, attention, memory, language, and reasoning, and use this knowledge to develop theories and models of cognition.

2.7 Theoretical neuroscience

Theoretical neuroscience is a field of study that focuses on developing mathematical and computational models to explain the functions of the brain and nervous system. Theoretical neuroscientists use mathematical and computational tools to simulate the behavior of neurons and neural circuits, and to test hypotheses about the underlying mechanisms of neural processing. They develop models to explain phenomena such as neural coding, synaptic plasticity, learning, memory, attention, and perception. Theoretical neuroscience offers a quantitative foundation for defining what neurological systems accomplish, figuring out how they work, and figuring out the fundamental laws that govern them. Applications in a number of fields, including vision, sensory-motor integration, development, learning, and memory are presented in this text, along with an introduction to the fundamental mathematical and computational techniques of theoretical neuroscience. The knowledge gained from examining a successful, complicated, and behaviorally sophisticated system should be revolutionary for creating the next wave of intelligent robots in the context of information technology. We do not have the right tools for creating massive, complicated systems, as has been amply demonstrated (for instance, just 30% of large software projects are successful). Nature has, however, found solutions to these issues in ways that humans do not yet fully comprehend. The study of theoretical neurology offers fresh perspectives on how nature solves problems. The most advanced algorithms in various fields are those inspired by neural networks. Reverse engineering the brain, however, can teach us a lot more about dynamical systems, complicated control, pattern recognition, and learning. Theoretical neuroscience is an interdisciplinary field that draws on research from neuroscience, physics, mathematics, computer science, and engineering. Theoretical neuroscientists collaborate with experimental neuroscientists to develop and test their models using data from experiments.

Theoretical neuroscience has led to many important insights into the workings of the brain and nervous system. For example, theoretical models have helped to explain how neural circuits process information and how the brain learns and adapts to new information. Theoretical models have also helped to identify the neural mechanisms that underlie diseases such as epilepsy and Parkinson's disease. So that, theoretical neuroscience is a vital field of study that provides important insights into the workings of the brain and nervous system, and has the potential to lead to new treatments for neurological and psychiatric disorders. Theoretical neuroscience is an interdisciplinary field that combines neuroscience, mathematics, physics, and computer science to develop mathematical models and theoretical frameworks for understanding how the brain processes information and generates behavior. There are several types of theoretical neuroscience, including:

Computational neuroscience: Computational neuroscience focuses on developing mathematical models of the brain's information processing and functional organization. These models use computational techniques to simulate neural activity and investigate how neurons interact with each other to process information and generate behavior.

Systems neuroscience: Systems neuroscience focuses on understanding how the brain's networks of neurons and circuits are organized and how they generate behavior. This field combines experimental techniques with mathematical modeling to investigate the functional organization of the brain at the level of networks of neurons and circuits.

Cognitive neuroscience: Cognitive neuroscience focuses on understanding how the brain processes information and generates behavior in humans and other animals. This field combines experimental techniques from psychology and neuroscience with computational modeling to investigate the neural mechanisms underlying cognitive processes such as perception, attention, memory, language, and decision-making.

Theoretical neurobiology: Theoretical neurobiology focuses on developing mathematical models of the structure and function of individual neurons and neural circuits. These models can be used to investigate how neural circuits generate behavior and to understand the mechanisms underlying neural plasticity and learning.

Mathematical neuroscience: Mathematical neuroscience focuses on developing mathematical models of neural systems at various levels of organization, from individual neurons to large-scale networks. These models are used to investigate the principles underlying neural computation and to develop new insights into brain function and dysfunction.

In summary, theoretical neuroscience is a diverse field that encompasses many different subfields and approaches, all aimed at developing mathematical models and theoretical frameworks for understanding how the brain processes information and generates behavior.

Python program that demonstrates a basic concept related to computational neuroscience—the Hodgkin-Huxley model for simulating action potentials:

```
import numpy as np
import matplotlib.pyplot as plt

# Constants for the Hodgkin-Huxley model
Cm = 1.0  # Membrane capacitance (uF/cm^2)
g_Na = 120.0  # Sodium conductance (mS/cm^2)
g_K = 36.0  # Potassium conductance (mS/cm^2)
g_L = 0.3  # Leak conductance (mS/cm^2)
E_Na = 50.0  # Sodium reversal potential (mV)
E_K = -77.0  # Potassium reversal potential (mV)
E_L = -54.4  # Leak reversal potential (mV)

# Simulation parameters
dt = 0.01  # Time step (ms)
t_start = 0.0  # Start time (ms)
t_end = 50.0  # End time (ms)

# Function for simulating action potentials using the Hodgkin-Huxley model
def simulate_action_potential():
    # Create arrays to store time and voltage values
    t = np.arange(t_start, t_end, dt)
    V = np.zeros(len(t))

    # Set initial conditions
    V[0] = -65.0  # Membrane potential (mV)
    m = alpha_m(V[0]) / (alpha_m(V[0]) + beta_m(V[0]))  # Sodium activation variable
    h = alpha_h(V[0]) / (alpha_h(V[0]) + beta_h(V[0]))  # Sodium inactivation variable
    n = alpha_n(V[0]) / (alpha_n(V[0]) + beta_n(V[0]))  # Potassium activation variable

    # Simulate action potentials using the Euler method
    for i in range(1, len(t)):
        # Calculate membrane currents
        I_Na = g_Na * m**3 * h * (V[i-1] - E_Na)
        I_K = g_K * n**4 * (V[i-1] - E_K)
        I_L = g_L * (V[i-1] - E_L)

        # Update membrane potential
        V[i] = V[i-1] + (1 / Cm) * (I_Na + I_K + I_L) * dt

        # Update gating variables
        m += (alpha_m(V[i-1]) * (1 - m) - beta_m(V[i-1]) * m) * dt
        h += (alpha_h(V[i-1]) * (1 - h) - beta_h(V[i-1]) * h) * dt
        n += (alpha_n(V[i-1]) * (1 - n) - beta_n(V[i-1]) * n) * dt

    # Plot the membrane potential over time
    plt.plot(t, V)
    plt.xlabel('Time (ms)')
    plt.ylabel('Membrane Potential (mV)')
    plt.title('Action Potential Simulation')
    plt.show()

# Functions for calculating rate constants (alpha and beta) for gating variables
def alpha_m(V):
    return 0.1 * (V + 40) / (1 - np.exp(-(V + 40) / 10))

def beta_m(V):
    return 4.0 * np.exp(-(V + 65) / 18)

def alpha_h(V):
    return 0.07 * np
```

2.8 Linguistics

The systematic examination of the features of both specific languages and of language in general is the main goal of linguistics, which is the scientific study of language. The scientific study of human language is called linguistics. Because it involves a thorough, methodical, objective, and accurate analysis of all facets of language, including its nature and structure, it is referred to as a scientific study. The social and cognitive facets of language are both of interest to linguists. Linguistics and cognitive science are closely interconnected fields of study that both focus on understanding language and how it relates to the mind and cognition. Linguistics is the study of language and its structure, including phonetics, syntax, semantics, and pragmatics. Linguists study the rules that govern language and how it is used in communication. In turn, linguistics provides insights into the structure and use of language, which can inform cognitive science research. For example, the study of syntax and semantics in linguistics can provide insights into the mental processes involved in language comprehension. Fig. 2.5 shows the different form of the study of the language.

So that, linguistics and cognitive science are interconnected fields that together provide a rich understanding of language and its relationship to the mind and cognition.

2.8.1 Role of linguistics in the cognitive science

Linguistics plays a crucial role in cognitive science, which is the interdisciplinary study of the mind and how it processes information. Linguistics is the scientific study of language, including its structure, function, and use, and it provides an important framework for understanding how language is processed and represented in the brain. One of the main contributions of linguistics to cognitive science is the development of theories and models of language processing. Linguists have developed models of language acquisition, language production, and language comprehension, which have been used to inform research in cognitive psychology and neuroscience. These models help researchers understand how the brain processes language and how language interacts with other cognitive processes such as attention, memory, and decision-making.

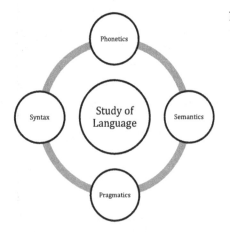

FIGURE 2.5   Study of language.

Linguistics also provides a foundation for investigating the relationship between language and thought. Researchers in cognitive science use linguistic analysis to explore how language reflects and shapes the way we think and perceive the world. For example, researchers have studied how different languages encode spatial relationships, and how this encoding affects spatial cognition.

Linguistics also plays an important role in the study of language disorders such as aphasia, dyslexia, and specific language impairment. By studying the linguistic patterns of these disorders, researchers can gain insights into the underlying cognitive mechanisms and develop new treatments. Finally, linguistics is critical for developing NLP technology, which allows computers to understand, generate, and translate human language. NLP has many applications, including chatbots, speech recognition, and machine translation, and linguistics provides the theoretical and computational tools necessary for developing these technologies. In summary, linguistics is a vital component of cognitive science, providing a framework for understanding language processing and representation in the brain, exploring the relationship between language and thought, and developing NLP technology.

Python program that demonstrates a basic concept related to linguistics—counting the frequency of words in a text:

```python
import string

def count_word_frequency(text):
    # Remove punctuation and convert text to lowercase
    text = text.translate(str.maketrans('', '', string.punctuation))
    text = text.lower()

    # Split the text into individual words
    words = text.split()

    # Create a dictionary to store word frequencies
    word_freq = {}

    # Count the frequency of each word
    for word in words:
        if word in word_freq:
            word_freq[word] += 1
        else:
            word_freq[word] = 1

    return word_freq

# Example text
text = "The quick brown fox jumps over the lazy dog. The dog barks, and the fox runs away."

# Count word frequency in the text
word_frequency = count_word_frequency(text)

# Print the word frequency
for word, freq in word_frequency.items():
    print(f"{word}: {freq}")
```

(cont'd)

In this program, we define the count word frequency function that takes a text as input and returns a dictionary containing the frequency of each word in the text. The function first removes punctuation from the text and converts it to lowercase to ensure consistent word counting. Then, it splits the text into individual words using the split method.

A dictionary named word freq is initialized to store the word frequencies. The function iterates over each word in the text and updates the corresponding frequency in the dictionary. If a word already exists in the dictionary, its frequency is incremented by 1; otherwise, a new entry is created with an initial frequency of 1.

Finally, the program demonstrates the usage of the count word frequency function by providing an example text. The resulting word frequencies are printed, displaying each word and its corresponding frequency.

2.9 Anthropology

The genesis and development of human civilizations and cultures are the subject of anthropology. People's learned behaviors, including their languages, belief systems, social structures, organizations, and material possessions, are referred to as culture. The systematic study of humans is known as anthropology, and its objectives include gaining an understanding of human evolution, our uniqueness as a species, and the wide variety of human social structures that exist today and throughout human history. Understanding our shared humanity and diversity, as well as interacting with various worldviews, are the main goals of anthropology. Anthropology is a social science that focuses on the study of human societies and cultures, both past and present. It encompasses a wide range of topics, including human evolution, cultural diversity, social organization, language, religion, and economic systems. Anthropologists use a variety of research methods, including participant observation, interviews, surveys, and ethnographic research, to collect data and analyze human behavior and social patterns.

One of the main goals of anthropology is to understand the diversity of human cultures and the ways in which societies have adapted to different environments and historical contexts. Anthropologists also study the ways in which societies change over time, including the impacts of globalization, colonialism, and other social and political forces. Anthropology is a broad and interdisciplinary field, and it is divided into several subfields, including:

- *Cultural anthropology*: Cultural anthropology focuses on the study of human cultures and societies, including their beliefs, values, customs, and practices.
- *Biological anthropology*: Biological anthropology focuses on the study of human evolution and variation, including genetics, anatomy, and primatology.
- *Archeology*: Archeology focuses on the study of human societies and cultures through the analysis of material remains, including artifacts, architecture, and other physical traces.
- *Linguistic anthropology*: Linguistic anthropology focuses on the study of language and its role in human communication, social organization, and culture.

Python program that demonstrates a basic concept related to anthropology—calculating the average height of a population:

```python
def calculate_average_height(heights):
    total_height = sum(heights)
    num_people = len(heights)
    average_height = total_height / num_people
    return average_height

# Example heights of individuals in centimeters
heights = [165, 170, 158, 173, 180, 155, 168]

# Calculate the average height
average_height = calculate_average_height(heights)

# Print the average height
print(f"The average height is: {average_height} cm")
```

In this program, we define the calculate average height function that takes a list of heights as input and returns the average height of the population. The function calculates the total height by summing all the heights in the list using the sum function. It then determines the number of people by finding the length of the list using the len function. Finally, the average height is calculated by dividing the total height by the number of people.

To demonstrate the usage of the calculate average height function, an example list of heights in centimeters is provided. The program calculates the average height using the function and prints the result.

This program showcases a basic application of anthropology by analyzing the average height of a population, which is a common anthropological study related to physical characteristics and human variation.

2.9.1 Role of anthropology in the cognitive science

Anthropology plays a significant role in cognitive science, the interdisciplinary study of the mind and how it processes information. Anthropologists provide important insights into the cultural and historical contexts in which cognitive processes develop, and the role that culture and language play in shaping cognitive processes. One of the main contributions of anthropology to cognitive science is the study of cultural variation in cognitive processes. Anthropologists have documented how cultural practices, beliefs, and values shape the development and expression of cognitive processes such as perception, memory, and reasoning. For example, anthropologists have shown how cultural practices such as storytelling, ritual, and art can shape the development of memory and imagination.

Anthropology also provides important insights into the relationship between language and cognition. Linguistic anthropologists have shown how language reflects and shapes the way people think and perceive the world, and how different languages encode and structure concepts in different ways. This research has helped cognitive scientists to better understand the relationship between language and thought, and the ways in which language influences cognitive processes such as categorization, attention, and memory.

In addition, anthropology contributes to cognitive science through the study of cultural evolution and cultural transmission. Anthropologists have documented how cultural practices, beliefs, and values change over time, and how they are transmitted across generations. This research has helped cognitive scientists to better understand the mechanisms of cultural transmission and how cultural practices and beliefs influence cognitive processes.

Finally, anthropology contributes to the development of cognitive science by providing a broad perspective on the diversity of human cultures and the ways in which cultural practices and beliefs shape cognitive processes. This perspective is important for developing a more comprehensive understanding of the human mind and its evolution.

2.10 Cognitive science theories

There are many cognitive science theories that represent how the mind works and also these theories create interaction between cognitive science and data analysis. These include:

Formal logic: The study of logical truths or deductively sound inferences is known as formal logic. It is a formal science that examines how conclusions inherently flow from premises. The word "a logic" designates a logical formal system that articulates a proof system when employed as a countable noun. The formal study of assertions, statements, or declarative sentences as well as deductive reasoning the discipline separates the structures or logical shapes that these items embody from their substance. To express such structures in an understandable and unambiguous manner and to make manipulations and validity checks easier to apply, the logician typically uses a symbolic notation.

Rules: The three basic principles of rules:

- The law of contradiction,
- The law of the excluded middle (or third),
- The principle of identity has traditionally been referred to as the laws of thought.

Concepts: Concepts are mental images, or entities "in the head," with a structure that reflects the outside world. A logical conclusion is that concepts are just rules for categorizing objects based on their features since our focus is with concepts that are used to distinguish between objects.

Analogies: The essence of human cognition, referred to as analogical cognition, has been thoroughly studied over the past 35 years by Dedre Gentner and her colleagues, and it is what gives us the ability to employ so many different words. Despite the fact that this research offers important new information about the nature of word meaning, linguists and philosophers of language have chosen to ignore it. Human mind is notable for its capacity to manage higher-order relations. First, think about the following task, which is to perceptually match one of the target letters with the base sample (the letter X) shown in Tables 2.1 and 2.2:

It has been said that the sine qua non of biological cognition is the capacity to assess the perceptual similarity between two stimuli, such as the capacity to match the base "X" to the target "X" (Penn et al., 2008). Comparing the features of the various tokens is the basis for the matching.

TABLE 2.1 Base and target values.

Base		Target
X	X	Y

TABLE 2.2 Comparison of the various tokens.

Base		Target
XX	YY	CD
ABA	AAD	UVU

It is not possible to solve this relational-match-to-sample test by comparing the letters in the base and the target's perceptual similarity. The matching is instead dependent on the persistence of a relation that exists between the tokens. Because the same relation (specifically, sameness) applies between X and X as it does between Y and Y, XX matches to YY but not to CD. Similar to how ABA matches UVU but not AAD due to their shared symmetry.

Python program that demonstrates a basic concept related to formal logic in cognitive science—evaluating logical propositions using truth tables:

```python
import itertools
def generate_truth_table(variables, expression):
    num_variables = len(variables)
    truth_table = []

    for assignment in itertools.product([False, True], repeat=num_variables):
        row = list(assignment)
        row.append(eval(expression, dict(zip(variables, assignment))))
        truth_table.append(row)

    return truth_table

# Example variables and expression
variables = ['P', 'Q']
expression = 'P and Q'

# Generate the truth table
truth_table = generate_truth_table(variables, expression)

# Print the truth table
header = variables + [expression]
print('\t'.join(header))
for row in truth_table:
    print('\t'.join(str(value) for value in row))
```

Connectionism: An approach to studying human cognition known as connectionism makes use of mathematical models called connectionist networks or artificial neural networks. These frequently take the shape of intricately linked processing units that resemble neurons. Although there is no clear boundary separating connectionism from computational neuroscience, connectionists frequently abstract from the specifics of neural activity in order to concentrate on high-level cognitive processes. In its ideological heyday in the late 20th century, connectionism sought to displace formal rules of inference and cognitive representations that take the form of sentences with simultaneous processing of diffuse patterns of brain activity. The goal of the connectionism movement in cognitive science is to use artificial neural networks, commonly referred to as "neural networks" or "neural nets," to explain intellectual skills. Neural networks are streamlined representations of the brain that are made up of numerous units (analogs of neurons) and weights that reflect the strength of the connections between the units. The effects of the synapses, which connect one neuron to another, are modeled by these weights. Studies using these models have shown that they can pick up abilities including face recognition, reading comprehension, and rudimentary grammatical structure identification. Connectionism has attracted the attention of philosophers because it aims to offer an alternative to the conventional theory of the mind, which holds that the mind is rather like a digital computer processing a symbolic language.

By the 1960s, connectionism, which was developed in the 1940s, had garnered a lot of interest. However, significant problems in the connectionist modeling methods were soon discovered, which decreased interest in and funding for connectionist research. However, connectionism experienced a strong, long-lasting resurgence in the 1980s. In the latter half of the 20th century, connectionism would be promoted by many as the brain-inspired alternative to the "classical" approach to the study of cognition that was influenced by computational artifacts. Similar to classicism, connectionism drew and inspired a sizable group of naturalistic philosophers. The two major systems disagreed on whether connectionism had the capacity to address fundamental problems with regard to minds, language, rationality, and knowledge.

Bayesian: Based on Bayes' theorem, Bayesian statistics is a method of data analysis where the parameters of a statistical model are updated with the help of observed data. The concept of Bayesian with cognitive science is always related to Bayesian inference. A statistical inference method known as Bayesian inference uses the Bayes' theorem to update a hypothesis' probability when new data or information becomes available. In statistics, particularly in mathematical statistics, Bayesian inference is a crucial method. When analyzing a sequence of data in a dynamic manner, Bayesian updating is very crucial. Numerous fields, including science, engineering, philosophy, medicine, sport, and law have used Bayesian inference. Subjective probability, sometimes known as "Bayesian probability," is closely related to Bayesian inference in the philosophy of decision theory.

The field of cognitive research known as Bayesian cognitive science, commonly referred to as computational cognitive science, focuses on the rational examination of cognition using Bayesian inference and cognitive modeling. The cognitive sciences have recently paid a great deal of attention to Bayesian theories. These theories claim that the mind assigns probability to hypotheses and changes them in accordance with accepted probabilistic inference rules. The study of vision, learning, memory, reasoning, language, decision-making, and many other areas have all benefited from the application of Bayesian theories. The term "computational" refers to David Marr's concept of the computational level of analysis. Testing the idea that certain sorts of cognitive tasks cause cognitive systems to behave like rational Bayesian agents is a common element of this research. This concept has been used in the past to study categories, language, motor control, reinforcement learning, theory of mind, and sequence learning.

Bayesian theories raise many foundational questions, the answers to which have been controversial: does the brain actually use Bayesian rules? Or are they merely approximate descriptions of behavior? How well can Bayesian theories accommodate irrationality in cognition? Do they require an implausibly uniform view of the mind? Are Bayesian theories near-trivial due to their many degrees of freedom? What are their implications for the relationship between perception, cognition, rationality, and consciousness?

Indeed, current research in the fields of perception, action, and cognition points to the ubiquitous use of Bayesian behavior across a wide range of modalities and species. As a result, numerous models have proposed that the brain is constructed using straightforward Bayesian ideas.

Python program that demonstrates a basic concept related to Bayesian statistics—calculating posterior probabilities using Bayes' theorem:

```python
def calculate_posterior_probability(prior, likelihood, evidence):
    # Calculate the denominator using the law of total probability
    denominator = sum(prior[i] * likelihood[i][evidence] for i in range(len(prior)))

    # Calculate the posterior probabilities using Bayes' theorem
    posterior = [prior[i] * likelihood[i][evidence] / denominator for i in range(len(prior))]

    return posterior

# Example prior probabilities
prior = [0.4, 0.6]  # Prior probabilities for two hypotheses H1 and H2

# Example likelihoods
likelihood = [
    [0.2, 0.8],  # Likelihood of evidence E given H1 and H2
    [0.6, 0.4]
]

# Example observed evidence
evidence = 1  # Observed evidence E

# Calculate the posterior probabilities
posterior = calculate_posterior_probability(prior, likelihood, evidence)

# Print the posterior probabilities
for i in range(len(posterior)):
    print(f"P(H{i+1}|E) = {posterior[i]}")
```

Deep learning: Deep learning, which is simply a neural network with three or more layers, is a subset of Machine learning. These neural networks make an effort to mimic the function of the human brain, however they fall well short of matching its capacity for "learning" from vast amounts of data. AI has undergone a revolution in recent years thanks to the family of algorithms collectively referred to as "deep learning," which has allowed robots to perform many challenging cognitive tasks at levels comparable to those of humans. Although deep learning models have their roots in the connectionist paradigm, their most recent developments were mostly driven by engineering objectives. Deep learning models finally appear fruitful for cognitive objectives, notwithstanding their applied concentration. This can be viewed as a form of biological exaptation, when a physiological structure is used for a purpose other than the one for which it was originally chosen. Deep learning is a subfield of AI that uses artificial neural networks to model and solve complex problems. It has many applications in cognitive science, where it is used to model and understand cognitive processes such as perception, memory, and decision-making. One of the main applications of deep learning in cognitive science is in the development of computer vision systems. Deep learning algorithms can be trained to recognize and classify visual patterns, such as faces, objects, and scenes. This research has helped cognitive scientists to better understand how the brain processes visual information, and how visual perception is influenced by factors such as attention and memory.

Deep learning is also used to model and simulate neural networks in the brain. These models can be used to test hypotheses about how neural networks process information and how different neural circuits interact to produce cognitive behaviors. Another application of deep learning in cognitive science is in NLP. Deep learning algorithms can be used to model the complex patterns of language use, including grammar, syntax, and semantics. This research has helped cognitive scientists to better understand how the brain processes language and how language is used to communicate and convey meaning.

Finally, deep learning is used in cognitive science to develop predictive models of human behavior. These models can be used to predict how people will respond to different stimuli, and how their behavior will change over time. This research has important applications in fields such as marketing, psychology, and economics.

Python program that demonstrates a basic concept related to deep learning—training a simple neural network for image classification using the Tensor Flow library:

```
import tensorflow as tf
from tensorflow import keras
from tensorflow.keras import layers

# Load and prepare the dataset (MNIST)
(x_train, y_train), (x_test, y_test) = keras.datasets.mnist.load_data()

# Preprocess the data
x_train = x_train.reshape(-1, 28 * 28).astype("float32") / 255.0
x_test = x_test.reshape(-1, 28 * 28).astype("float32") / 255.0
```

(cont'd)

```
# Define the model architecture
model = keras.Sequential([
    layers.Dense(64, activation="relu"),
    layers.Dense(10),
])

# Compile the model
model.compile(optimizer="adam",
loss=tf.keras.losses.SparseCategoricalCrossentropy(from_logits=True), metrics=["accuracy"])

# Train the model
model.fit(x_train, y_train, batch_size=32, epochs=5, verbose=2)

# Evaluate the model
loss, accuracy = model.evaluate(x_test, y_test, verbose=2)
print(f"Test loss: {loss}")
print(f"Test accuracy: {accuracy}")
```

In this program, we use the TensorFlow library to train a simple neural network for image classification on the MNIST dataset, which consists of handwritten digits. The program starts by loading and preparing the dataset using the keras.datasets.mnist.load_data() function. The data is then preprocessed by reshaping the input images and scaling the pixel values between 0 and 1. Next, we define the model architecture using the sequential class from Keras. In this example, we have a simple feedforward neural network with one hidden layer consisting of 64 neurons and a ReLU activation function. The output layer has 10 neurons corresponding to the 10 classes (digits 0–9).

After defining the model, we compile it using the Adam optimizer, sparse categorical cross-entropy loss function, and accuracy as the evaluation metric. We then train the model using the fit function, specifying the training data, batch size, and number of epochs.

Finally, we evaluate the trained model on the test data using the evaluate function and print the test loss and accuracy. This program demonstrates a basic application of deep learning by training a neural network for image classification. However, keep in mind that deep learning models can be much more complex with additional layers, different architectures, and more advanced techniques based on the specific problem and dataset.

2.11 Evaluation of cognitive science

Language, perception, memory, attention, reasoning, and emotion are among the mental processes that cognitive scientists study. To do so, they draw on linguistics, psychology, AI, philosophy, neuroscience, and anthropology. In the 1800s, as psychology as a science, and particularly experimental psychology, started to grow, scientists started looking for distinctive traits that the human mind shared in common. The scientific community accepted behaviorism, a viewpoint that considered the human mind as little more than a collection of programmed behaviors that entirely occurred as biological reactions to stimuli, in its quest for consistency and explanation. In other words, you weren't much different from a dog or a single-celled organism in the behaviorists' eyes. They perceived people as just more developed examples of "cause and effect," stimuli, and response.

Scientists started to propose the theory that there is much more to the human mind than only preprogrammed answers in more recent periods, at the beginning of the 1900s. Scientists gained a better understanding of the reasoning process as computer simulations of human thought processes were developed, and they became aware of the intricacy of the operations that take place inside the mind. Additionally, scientists started to wrestle with the dichotomy between the wide range of potential human cognition and the constrained set of options imposed by a strictly genetic approach to human construction.

Cognitive science is a multidisciplinary field of study that emerged in the 1950s and 1960s, with the goal of understanding the nature of the mind and cognition. The origins of cognitive science can be traced back to the work of researchers such as George Miller, Noam Chomsky, and Herbert Simon, who were interested in the study of language and the mind. Miller's classic paper "The Magical Number Seven, Plus or Minus Two" (1956) argued that the limits of human memory could be explained by the capacity of STM, while Chomsky's influential book "Syntactic Structures" (1957) proposed that the rules of language are innate and universal.

In the 1960s, the development of the computer provided a new model for understanding the mind as an information processing system. Researchers such as Allen Newell and Herbert Simon developed computer programs that simulated human problem-solving and decision-making processes. In the 1970s, cognitive science became an established field of study, with the founding of the Cognitive Science Society in 1979. The field continued to grow and expand, incorporating insights from neuroscience, psychology, linguistics, philosophy, and AI.

Today, cognitive science is a thriving field of study with a wide range of applications, from the development of AI and robotics to the treatment of neurological and psychiatric disorders. The field continues to evolve, incorporating new technologies and approaches to understand the nature of the mind and cognition.

2.11.1 Significance of cognitive science in the field of data analysis

Cognitive science is a multidisciplinary field that studies the cognitive processes of the human mind, including perception, attention, memory, reasoning, decision-making, and language. It has significant implications for data analysis, as it provides insights into the ways in which people process and interpret information.

One of the main contributions of cognitive science to data analysis is the development of theories and models of human cognition. These models provide a framework for understanding how people process information and make decisions, which can be applied to the analysis of data. For example, cognitive models can be used to understand how people search for and process information on websites, or how they make decisions based on financial data. Cognitive science also provides insights into how people perceive and interpret visual information. This is particularly relevant in the field of data visualization, where the goal is to present data in a way that is meaningful and easy to understand. Cognitive research has shown that people are more likely to understand and remember information that is presented in a clear and visually appealing manner, and that certain visual cues (such as color, shape, and size) can be used to highlight important data points.

Another contribution of cognitive science to data analysis is the development of theories and models of human learning and memory. These models can be used to design more effective methods for presenting and organizing data, such as through the use of mnemonic devices, repetition, and chunking. At the end, cognitive science provides insights into how people make decisions based on incomplete or ambiguous information. This is particularly relevant in fields such as data analysis and decision-making, where uncertainty and ambiguity are common. Cognitive models of decision-making can be used to develop more effective methods for analyzing data and making decisions in uncertain environments. Cognitive science has significant implications for data analysis, as it provides insights into how people process and interpret information, how they perceive and interpret visual information, how they learn and remember information, and how they make decisions based on incomplete or ambiguous information. By applying these insights to data analysis, researchers and practitioners can develop more effective methods for presenting, organizing, and analyzing data, and for making informed decisions in uncertain environments.

2.12 Understanding brain and sensory motor information

The brain, a highly advanced organ, oversees numerous bodily functions such as cognition, memory, emotions, sensory perception, motor abilities, vision, respiration, temperature regulation, and hunger. The central nervous system (CNS) consists of the spinal cord, which extends from the brain. In an average adult, the brain weighs approximately 3 pounds and comprises about 60% fat, while the remaining 40% is composed of a combination of water, protein, carbohydrates, and salts. Although the brain is not a muscle in its own right, it consists of nerves, blood vessels, neurons, and glial cells.

The brain communicates with the rest of the body via electrical and chemical impulses. Your brain interprets each signal, which controls a distinct process. For instance, some make you feel worn out while others make you uncomfortable. Some messages are stored in the brain, while others are transmitted to distant extremities by way of the spine and the extensive network of nerves in the body. The CNS uses billions of neurons to accomplish these nerve cells. The brain and sensory motor information systems are closely connected and work together to allow us to perceive, process, and respond to the world around us.

The sensory motor information systems consist of the sensory organs (such as the eyes, ears, and skin) and the motor system (including muscles and nerves). These systems work together to allow us to perceive and respond to stimuli in the environment. For example, the eyes capture visual information, which is then processed by the brain to create a representation of the world around us. The motor system then responds by directing movement, such as reaching for an object or walking towards a destination. The brain plays a critical role in processing and interpreting sensory motor information. Different regions of the brain are specialized to process different types of sensory information, such as visual, auditory, or tactile information. These regions work together to create a coherent representation of the environment.

In addition to sensory processing, the brain also plays a key role in motor control. The motor cortex is responsible for planning and executing movement, while the cerebellum helps to coordinate movement and maintain balance. Recent research has also shown that sensory and motor systems are interconnected in more complex ways. For example, motor imagery (the mental simulation of movement) has been shown to activate similar brain regions as actual movement. This suggests that the brain may use similar processes to plan and execute both actual and imagined movements.

At the end, the brain and sensory motor information systems work together to allow us to perceive and interact with the world around us. By understanding the mechanisms behind sensory processing and motor control, researchers can develop new insights and treatments for conditions that affect these systems, such as Parkinson's disease or sensory processing disorders.

2.12.1 Main parts of the brain and their functions

At a high level, the brain can be divided into the cerebrum, brainstem and cerebellum.

Cerebrum: Cerebrum is the largest part of the brain and is responsible for conscious thought, learning, memory, and voluntary movement. It is divided into two hemispheres, left and right, which are connected by a bundle of fibers called the corpus callosum. The surface of the cerebrum is highly convoluted with ridges called gyri and grooves called sulci, which increase the surface area and allow for more complex processing. The cerebrum is composed of different regions, each with specialized functions. The frontal lobe is involved in decision-making, planning, and voluntary movement; the parietal lobe processes sensory information such as touch, taste, and temperature; the temporal lobe is responsible for hearing, language comprehension, and memory; and the occipital lobe processes visual information. Overall, the cerebrum plays a vital role in human behavior, perception, and cognition. Speech, judgment, thinking and reasoning, problem-solving, emotions, and learning are all made possible by different regions of the cerebrum. Other functions deal with the senses of sight, sound, touch, and others.

Cerebral cortex: There are two hemispheres, or halves, of the cerebral cortex. It has folds and ridges (gyri) all over it (sulci). The interhemispheric fissure, also known as the medial longitudinal fissure, connects the two hemispheres of the brain and extends from the front to the rear of the skull. The left half of the brain controls the right side of the body, and the right half the left. The corpus callosum, a sizable, C-shaped mass of white matter and nerve connections, serves as the communication link between the two hemispheres. The cerebrum's corpus callosum is located in the middle.

Brainstem: The cerebrum and spinal cord are linked by the brainstem, which is in the center of the brain. The midbrain, pons, and medulla are all parts of the brainstem.

- *Midbrain*: With a variety of distinct neuron clusters, neuronal pathways, and other structures, the midbrain (or mesencephalon) is a tremendously complicated structure. These traits make it easier to do a variety of tasks, including listening, moving, responding to environmental changes, and calculating responses. The substantia nigra, a region of the basal ganglia that facilitates movement and coordination and is damaged by Parkinson's disease, is also located in the midbrain.

- *Pons*: Four of the 12 cranial nerves, which enable a variety of functions like tear generation, chewing, blinking, concentrating eyesight, balance, hearing, and facial expression, originate in the pons. The pons, which means "bridge" in Latin, serves as the link between the midbrain and the medulla.
- *Medulla*: At the bottom of the brainstem, the medulla is where the brain meets the spinal cord. The medulla is essential to survival. Functions of the medulla regulate many bodily activities, including heart rhythm, breathing, blood flow, and oxygen and carbon dioxide levels. The medulla produces reflexive activities such as sneezing, vomiting, coughing and swallowing.

Cerebellum: The cerebellum, sometimes known as the "little brain," is a fist-sized section of the brain situated in the rear of the head, above the brainstem and below the temporal and occipital lobes. The cerebellum is a part of the brain located at the back of the head, beneath the cerebrum. It is responsible for coordinating and regulating motor movements, balance, and posture. It works in conjunction with other parts of the brain, including the cerebral cortex and the brainstem, to control movements and maintain equilibrium. The cerebellum contains numerous small, tightly packed cells called Purkinje cells, which are responsible for integrating and processing information from other parts of the brain and the body. It also receives input from sensory systems, such as the inner ear, to help maintain balance and coordinate movement.

Damage to the cerebellum can result in a range of motor coordination and balance problems, such as ataxia, dysmetria, and tremors. It can also lead to speech and language problems, as the cerebellum is involved in the planning and execution of speech movements. Overall, the cerebellum plays a crucial role in motor coordination and balance, and its proper functioning is essential for normal movement and posture.

2.12.2 Lobes of the brain and what they control

The frontal, parietal, temporal, and occipital lobes are the four portions that make up each cerebral hemisphere (part of the cerebrum). Specific functions are controlled by each lobe.

Frontal lobe: The frontal lobe, the largest part of the brain, controls personality traits, judgment, and movement. It is situated in the front of the head. A portion of the frontal lobe is typically involved in smell recognition. The Broca's region, which is connected to speech capacity, is located in the frontal lobe.

Parietal lobe: The parietal lobe, located in the middle of the brain, aids in object identification and the comprehension of spatial relationships, which include comparing one's body to the surroundings. The interpretation of touch and pain experienced by the body also involves the parietal lobe. Wernicke's region, which aids the brain in comprehending spoken language, is located in the parietal lobe.

Occipital lobe: The back portion of the brain that controls vision is called the occipital lobe.

Temporal lobe: The temporal lobes on the sides of the brain have a role in STM, speech, musical rhythm, and to some extent, smell perception.

2.12.3 Cranial system

The cranial system, also known as the skull, is the bony structure that encloses and protects the brain. There are several types of cranial systems found in different organisms, including:

Chondrichthyes cranial system: This type of cranial system is found in cartilaginous fishes such as sharks and rays. It is composed of cartilage and is relatively flexible compared to other cranial systems.

Osteichthyes cranial system: This type of cranial system is found in bony fishes such as salmon and trout. It is composed of bone and is more rigid than the Chondrichthyes cranial system.

Amphibian cranial system: This type of cranial system is found in amphibians such as frogs and salamanders. It is composed of bone and cartilage and is more complex than the cranial systems of fish.

Reptilian cranial system: This type of cranial system is found in reptiles such as snakes and lizards. It is also composed of bone and cartilage but is more heavily armored and protective than the amphibian cranial system.

Avian cranial system: This type of cranial system is found in birds. It is composed of bone and is highly specialized for flight.

Mammalian cranial system: This type of cranial system is found in mammals, including humans. It is composed of bone and is the most complex and highly developed of all the cranial systems. It includes the bones of the face and skull and is specialized for chewing, swallowing, and speaking.

2.12.4 Sensory motor information

Sensory motor information refers to the flow of information between the sensory and motor systems in the brain. This information is responsible for the coordination and control of movement and behavior. Sensory information is processed in various sensory organs such as the eyes, ears, nose, tongue, and skin, and is transmitted to the brain via the sensory nerves. The sensory information is then integrated and processed in the sensory cortex, which is located in the parietal lobe of the cerebrum. The sensory cortex interprets and analyzes the sensory information and sends the processed information to other areas of the brain for further processing and decision-making.

Motor information, on the other hand, originates in the motor cortex, which is located in the frontal lobe of the cerebrum. The motor cortex plans and executes movement commands and sends them to the muscles via the motor neurons. The motor neurons activate the muscles and produce the desired movement. The sensory and motor systems work together to produce coordinated movements. During movement, sensory feedback is continuously sent to the brain, providing information about the position and movement of the body. This feedback is used to adjust and modify the movement, ensuring that it is precise and accurate. Sensory processing deals with how the brain processes sensory input from multiple sensory modalities. These include the five classic senses of vision (sight), audition (hearing), tactile stimulation (touch), olfaction (smell), and gustation (taste). Studies have made it possible for us to map the regions of the brain where the processing of sensory data takes place. Initially, this research was laborious and rather haphazard because it included observing people who had sensory deficits and then examining their brains after they had passed away to determine if there had been any obvious pathological alterations. The motor and sensory systems are closely connected. The brain receives crucial information from sensory stimulation and feedback via senses like smell, touch, vision, hearing, and balance. Your body and brain respond to sensory stimulation through motor function.

Python program that demonstrates a basic concept related to sensory motor information—simulating a simple sensory-motor loop:

```python
import time

def simulate_sensory_motor_loop(duration):
    start_time = time.time()

    while True:
        # Read sensory input
        sensory_input = read_sensory_input()

        # Process sensory input
        processed_input = process_input(sensory_input)

        # Generate motor command
        motor_command = generate_motor_command(processed_input)

        # Execute motor command
        execute_motor_command(motor_command)

        # Check if the specified duration has elapsed
        elapsed_time = time.time() - start_time
        if elapsed_time >= duration:
            break

def read_sensory_input():
    # Simulate reading sensory input from sensors
    sensory_input = "Sensory input"
    return sensory_input

def process_input(sensory_input):
    # Simulate processing the sensory input
    processed_input = f"Processed {sensory_input}"
    return processed_input
```

(cont'd)

```
def generate_motor_command(processed_input):
    # Simulate generating a motor command based on processed input
    motor_command = f"Motor command for {processed_input}"
    return motor_command

def execute_motor_command(motor_command):
    # Simulate executing the motor command
    print(f"Executing motor command: {motor_command}")

# Specify the duration of the simulation in seconds
duration = 5

# Simulate the sensory-motor loop for the specified duration
simulate_sensory_motor_loop(duration)
```

In this program, we simulate a simple sensory-motor loop that processes sensory input and generates motor commands. The program consists of several functions:

Simulate sensory motor loop: This function simulates the sensory-motor loop for a specified duration. It runs in a continuous loop, reading sensory input, processing it, generating motor commands, and executing them. The loop continues until the specified duration has elapsed.

Read sensory input: This function simulates reading sensory input from sensors. In this example, it returns a placeholder string "Sensory input."

Process input: This function simulates processing the sensory input. It takes the sensory input as input and returns a processed version of it. In this example, it adds the prefix "Processed" to the sensory input.

Generate motor command: This function simulates generating a motor command based on the processed input. It takes the processed input as input and returns a motor command. In this example, it adds the prefix "Motor command for" to the processed input.

Execute motor command: This function simulates executing the motor command. It takes the motor command as input and prints it to the console.

The program specifies the duration of the simulation in seconds and calls the simulate Sensory motor loop function with the specified duration to start the simulation.

This program demonstrates a basic simulation of a sensory-motor loop, where sensory input is processed, motor commands are generated, and actions are executed based on the generated commands.

2.13 Language and linguistic knowledge

A structured system of communication is language. A language's grammar is its structure, while its vocabulary is its free-form elements. Humans primarily communicate using languages, which can be expressed orally, visually, or in writing. Language is portrayed as a system of rules, or grammar, which defines all of the language's potential sentences. Linguistic competence, as used in linguistics, refers to the unconscious knowledge one possesses when speaking a language. It differs from linguistic performance, which refers to any other elements that enable one to utilize their language in practice.

The study of how language interacts with the psychological and neural processes that underpin it is called cognitive science of language, commonly referred to as psycholinguistics. Students who study in cognitive science and language learn how to apply scientific reasoning and research techniques to develop hypotheses and verify predictions regarding communication and language use, spanning from social behaviors to individual differences in communication and language impairments. Students who major in cognitive science and language learn to use scientific reasoning and research techniques to develop hypotheses and test predictions about communication and language use, ranging from social behaviors to individual differences in communication and language impairments.

Although it is frequently written with all lowercase letters, one of the approaches to cognitive linguistics is known as cognitive linguistics, with capital initials. When Ronald Langacker's Cognitive Grammar and George Lakoff's metaphor theory were combined in the early 1980s, the Construction Grammar movement was born. Subsequent models of Construction Grammar were developed by various writers. The merger involves two different theories of how language and culture have evolved: conceptual metaphor theory and construction theory. In contrast to generative grammar, cognitive linguistics positions language processing in the brain to follow general cognitive principles. The theories of Lakoff and Langacker are applicable to all the fields. Cognitive linguistics has an impact on linguistics and translation theory as well as literary studies, education, sociology, musicology, computer technology, and theology.

Creative linguistics: Creative linguistics is a subscience of linguistics that studies creative aspects of language/speech and language aspects of creativity. The realm of meaning transformations is where linguistic creativity is represented and displays itself at various levels of language expression. In terms of the correlation between linguistic and conceptual meaning, which has to do with comprehension and interpretation as well as the process of forming world views, linguistic meaning may also be seen as a cultural information container and a bearer of world knowledge. Linguistic creativity can be viewed as the process of generating new meaning in order to attain a certain stylistic or rhetorical effect in order to accomplish a communicative pragmatic goal throughout the information transfer process. Creative language use can take various forms, such as puns, metaphors, wordplay, and poetry. It involves manipulating language to create new associations and connections between words, and to express ideas and emotions in innovative ways. It can also involve breaking the rules of grammar and syntax to create new forms of expression. Creative language use has been studied in various fields, including linguistics, psychology, and literature. It is often seen as a form of artistic expression, and has been used in literature, music, comedy, and advertising.

At the end, creative language use involves using language in creative and unexpected ways to produce new meanings and interpretations, and to express ideas and emotions in innovative ways.

2.14 Theory of information processing

An approach to cognitive development studies called information processing theory (IPT) seeks to explain how information is stored in memory. It is predicated on the notion that people don't just react to environmental cues, instead information is processed by people. These include the manner in which the brain interprets data. The idea of information processing describes not only how information is captured but also how it is stored and retrieved. Receiving input, also known as stimuli, from the environment through different senses is the first step in the process. After that, the input is described and stored in the memory, where it can later be accessed. The brain or mind is compared to a computer that can process data from the outside world. As a result, information processing has an impact on the behavior. According to the expectation theory of motivation, a person processes knowledge about the connections between conduct and results. They might then decide based on expectations they have formed based on the facts.

2.14.1 Origins of information processing theory

The IPT is a cognitive psychology theory that explains how humans acquire, store, and use information. The IPT emerged in the 1950s and 1960s as an alternative to behaviorism, which dominated psychology at the time. The IPT was heavily influenced by the work of computer scientists who were developing early models of information processing. These models involved the flow of information through a system of inputs, processing, and outputs. Psychologists at the time saw a parallel between this process and the way that humans process information.

One of the earliest and most influential IPT researchers was George Miller, who published a seminal paper in 1956 called "The Magical Number Seven, Plus or Minus Two: Some Limits on Our Capacity for Processing Information." Miller proposed that humans have a limited capacity for processing information, and that this capacity could be increased by chunking information into meaningful units. Other important figures in the development of the IPT include Ulric Neisser, Allen Newell, and Herbert Simon. Neisser, in particular, helped to define the IPT as a distinct field of study with his 1967 book "Cognitive Psychology."

Since its emergence in the mid-20th century, the IPT has had a significant impact on the study of cognition and has contributed to our understanding of a wide range of mental processes, including perception, attention, memory, and problem-solving.

2.14.2 Elements of information processing theory

Information stores: Information storage areas across the brain, including sensory memory, STM, long-term memory, semantic memory, episodic memory, and others.

Cognitive processes: The numerous methods used to move data between different memory storage. Perception, coding, recording, chunking, and retrieval are a few of the processes.

Executive cognition: The person's awareness of how information is processed inside of them. It also has to do with being aware of their advantages and disadvantages. This and metacognition are quite similar.

2.14.3 Models of information processing theory

Various initiatives have been made to create models of information processing. The working memory model by Baddeley and Hitch and the multistore model by Atkinson and Shiffrin are the two most widely used.

2.14.3.1 Atkinson and Shiffrin model

The multistore model was proposed by John William Atkinson and Richard Shiffrin in 1968 to show their theory on human memory. The three divisions of human memory are depicted in the model, along with how they interact. Fig. 2.6 shows the Atkinson and Shiffrin model of the IPT.

Sensory memory: It stores the knowledge that the mind gathers through several senses, such as sight, smell, or hearing. These senses frequently experience a constant flood of stimuli. The mind, however, ignores and forgets the majority of them in order to avoid becoming overloaded. STM is used to store sensory information that captures the mind's interest.

STM: STM can only store information for about 30 seconds. The way that people process information in working memory depends on their cognitive ability. Additionally, paying attention to and concentrating on the most crucial information is essential for helping it get stored in long-term memory. Furthermore, repetition considerably improves one's capacity for long-term memory.

Long-term memory: As long-term memory may store memories from the past to be recalled at a later time, it is believed to have an infinite amount of space. Information is stored in the long-term memory via a variety of techniques, including repetition, linking concepts, connecting concepts to relevant experiences or other information, and breaking the information up into smaller chunks.

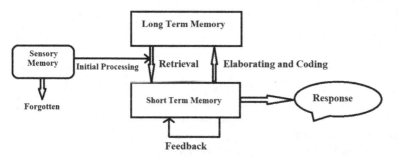

FIGURE 2.6 Model of information process theory.

Python program for the Atkinson and Shiffrin model for the information processing theory:

```python
import time

def sensory_memory(input_data):
    # Simulate sensory memory by briefly holding the input data
    print("Sensory Memory")
    print(f"Input: {input_data}")
    time.sleep(1)

    # Pass the data to short-term memory
    short_term_memory(input_data)

def short_term_memory(input_data):
    # Simulate short-term memory by holding a limited amount of information
    print("\nShort-Term Memory")
    print(f"Received: {input_data}")
    time.sleep(1)

    # Process the information and transfer it to long-term memory
    processed_data = process_data(input_data)
    long_term_memory(processed_data)

def long_term_memory(input_data):
    # Simulate long-term memory by storing and retaining information
    print("\nLong-Term Memory")
    print(f"Stored: {input_data}")
    time.sleep(1)

    # Retrieve information from long-term memory
    retrieved_data = retrieve_data()
    print(f"Retrieved: {retrieved_data}")
    time.sleep(1)

def process_data(input_data):
    # Simulate processing the input data
    processed_data = f"Processed {input_data}"
    return processed_data

def retrieve_data():
    # Simulate retrieving information from long-term memory
    retrieved_data = "Retrieved information"
    return retrieved_data

# Simulate the Atkinson and Shiffrin Model
input_data = "Input data"
sensory_memory(input_data)
```

In this program, each stage of the Atkinson and Shiffrin model is represented by a function:

Sensory memory: Simulates the sensory memory stage by briefly holding the input data (e.g., visual or auditory stimuli) and then passing it to STM.

STM: Simulates the STM stage by holding a limited amount of information and processing it. In this example, the input data is processed and then transferred to long-term memory.

Long-term memory: Simulates the long-term memory stage by storing and retaining

<hr>

(cont'd)

<hr>

information. In this example, the processed data is stored in long-term memory. It also simulates retrieving information from long-term memory.

Process data: Simulates the processing of input data. In this example, it adds the prefix "Processed" to the input data.

Retrieve data: Simulates retrieving information from long-term memory. In this example, it returns a placeholder string "Retrieved information."

The program starts by defining the input data. It then calls the sensory_memory function to simulate the flow of information through the Atkinson and Shiffrin model. Each stage of the model is sequentially executed, with a brief delay between stages for visualization purposes.

This program provides a simplified demonstration of the Atkinson and Shiffrin model for the IPT, showcasing the flow of information from sensory memory to STM and then to long-term memory.

Python program for memory recall:

```python
import random

# List of phone numbers for memory recall exercise
phone_numbers = ["555-1234", "987-6543", "123-4567", "999-8888", "111-2222"]

def memory_recall():
    # Randomly select a phone number
    selected_number = random.choice(phone_numbers)

    # Display the phone number to the user
    print("Try to remember this phone number:")
    print(selected_number)

    # Prompt the user to recall the phone number
    user_input = input("Enter the recalled phone number: ")

    # Check if the user's input matches the selected number
    if user_input == selected_number:
        print("Congratulations! You remembered the phone number correctly.")
    else:
        print("Oops! Your recalled phone number does not match.")

# Run the memory recall exercise
memory_recall()
```

(cont'd)

In this program, we have a list of phone numbers stored in the phone_numbers variable. The memory_recall() function randomly selects a phone number from the list and displays it to the user. The user is then prompted to enter the recalled phone number. The program checks if the user's input matches the selected number and provides appropriate feedback.

This simple program illustrates the concept of memory recall, which is a crucial aspect of cognitive science. It demonstrates how our brain processes and retrieves information from memory.

2.14.3.2 *Baddeley and Hitch model of working memory*

In 1974, Graham Hitch and Alan Baddeley proposed the working memory concept. They gave a thorough grasp of the mind and information processing. To further explain the IPT, four more elements are included (Goldstein & Mackewn, 2005), namely:

Central executive: It is regarded as the brain's "control center," where information flow between different memory stores is managed. It directs and carries out the cognitive operations that encode and decode information. The episodic buffer, phonological loop, and visuospatial sketchpad also provide information to the central executive. Since all active decisions are processed in the frontal lobe of the brain, this area is believed to be the location of the central executive.

Phonological loop: The fourth component of the model, which likewise contains information, was later added by Baddeley. It improves the mind's capacity to store knowledge. He thought that information is passed between STM, perception, and long-term memory via the episodic buffer.

Visuospatial sketchpad: It is regarded as an additional component of the central executive that stores spatial and visual data. It aids in the mind's ability to visualize things and navigate spaces.

Episodic buffer: The fourth component of the model, which likewise contains information, was later added by Baddeley. It improves the mind's capacity to store knowledge. He thought that information is passed between STM, perception, and long-term memory via the episodic buffer.

Key takeaways: information processing models:

- Cognitive psychology's IPT, which employs computers as a metaphor for how the human mind functions, is a cornerstone of the field.
- American psychologists like George Miller first put forth the theory in the middle of the 1950s to explain how people translate information into memory.
- The Atkinson and Shiffrin stage theory, which describes the three phases information passes through before being stored into long-term memory, is considered to be the most significant theory in the field of information processing.

Python program on the Baddeley and Hitch model of working memory:

```python
import time

class WorkingMemory:
    def __init__(self):
        self.central_executive = CentralExecutive()
        self.phonological_loop = PhonologicalLoop()
        self.visuospatial_sketchpad = VisuospatialSketchpad()

    def process_task(self, task):
        print(f"Task: {task}")

        # Delegate task processing to the respective components
        self.central_executive.execute_task(task)
        self.phonological_loop.process_task(task)
        self.visuospatial_sketchpad.process_task(task)

        time.sleep(1)

class CentralExecutive:
    def __init__(self):
        self.processed_tasks = []

    def execute_task(self, task):
        # Simulate the role of the central executive in coordinating and controlling cognitive
processes
        self.processed_tasks.append(task)
        print(f"Central Executive: Executing task - {task}")

class PhonologicalLoop:
    def __init__(self):
        self.phonological_store = PhonologicalStore()
        self.articulatory_loop = ArticulatoryLoop()

    def process_task(self, task):
        # Simulate processing of the task in the phonological loop
        self.phonological_store.store(task)
        self.articulatory_loop.rehearse(task)
        print("Phonological Loop: Processing task")

class PhonologicalStore:
    def __init__(self):
        self.stored_items = []
    def store(self, item):
        # Simulate storing items in the phonological store
        self.stored_items.append(item)

class ArticulatoryLoop:
    def __init__(self):
        self.rehearsed_items = []

    def rehearse(self, item):
        # Simulate rehearsing items in the articulatory loop
        self.rehearsed_items.append(item)
```

(cont'd)

```
class VisuospatialSketchpad:
    def __init__(self):
        self.visual_cache = VisualCache()
        self.inner_scribe = InnerScribe()

    def process_task(self, task):
        # Simulate processing of the task in the visuospatial sketchpad
        self.visual_cache.store(task)
        self.inner_scribe.update(task)
        print("Visuospatial Sketchpad: Processing task")

class VisualCache:
    def __init__(self):
        self.stored_items = []

    def store(self, item):
        # Simulate storing items in the visual cache
        self.stored_items.append(item)

class InnerScribe:
    def __init__(self):
        self.updated_items = []

    def update(self, item):
        # Simulate updating items in the inner scribe
        self.updated_items.append(item)

# Simulate the Baddeley and Hitch Model of Working Memory
working_memory = WorkingMemory()
working_memory.process_task("Task 1")
working_memory.process_task("Task 2")
```

In this program, the Baddeley and Hitch model of working memory is represented by a set of classes:

Working memory: Represents the working memory system and consists of three components: central executive, phonological loop, and visuospatial sketchpad. It coordinates the processing of tasks within each component.

Central executive: Simulates the role of the central executive component, which coordinates and controls cognitive processes. In this example, it keeps track of the processed tasks.

Phonological loop: Represents the phonological loop component, which deals with verbal and auditory information. It consists of the PhonologicalStore and ArticulatoryLoop subclasses.

2.15 Concept of short-term memory

The ability to temporarily store a small amount of knowledge in the mind and keep it accessible is known as STM. It is often referred to as active or primary memory. The majority of the data held in STM will be retained for only 20–30 seconds. STM can hold onto some knowledge for up to a minute, but unless you use rehearsal techniques like stating the information out loud or mentally repeating it, the majority of information spontaneously decays rather fast. STM has a range of storage capacities for data. George Miller, a psychologist, proposed that people may hold between five and nine items in STM in his seminal 1956 study, "The Magical Number Seven, Plus or Minus Two." According to more recent studies, the average person can hold four informational "chunks" or "pieces" in STM.

Think about trying to recall a phone number, for instance. When the other person mentions their 10-digit phone number, you quickly make a mental note of it. You remember the number only to learn later that you already forgot it. The information is quickly erased from STM if it is not practiced or repeatedly repeated until it is committed to memory. STM creates a kind of "visuospatial" sketch of information the brain has recently absorbed and will process into memories later on. By some estimates, STM can hold around seven items of information at one time. Information can move from STM into long-term memory, where the brain permanently stores the information for future recall when necessary. Long-term memory does not seem to have a specific limit or maximum capacity. Information held in long-term memory is usually related to how a person performs a skill, or to rules, events, facts, and concepts.

Working memory and STM are both temporary storage systems that handle incoming sensory memory. Between information ingested by sensory memory and the longer-term preservation of information in long-term memory, there lies the STM. If information is not transferred from STM to long-term memory, it will be lost. Because this is the system where memory "work" takes place, STM is also known as working memory. When it bring up knowledge from long-term memory, are transferring it to working memory, where it may consider it.

The cognitive processes for storing, maintaining, and manipulating information that is no longer present in the sensory world are collectively referred to as STM. Selective attention, on the other hand, has to do with mechanisms that control how sensory stimuli are processed during encoding. STM is the ability to store information in a system after it has been organized and processed by the brain. In fact, the information that a person is consciously aware of is sometimes compared to the information in STM. Short-term storage (STS) allows for continuous processing of information.

1. STM has three main characteristics:
   a. Brief duration that can only last up to 20 seconds.
   b. Its capacity is limited to 7 ± 2 chunks of independent information (Miller's law) and is vulnerable to interference and interruption.
   c. Its weakening (due to many reasons, such as medication, sleep deprivation, a stroke, or a head injury, for example) is the first step to memory loss.
2. STM is responsible for three operations:
   a. Iconic, which is the ability to store images. The primary function of our inborn, intrinsic STM is image storage.
   b. Acoustic, which is the ability to store sounds. We have a type of STM that explains how we can retain the noises that are constantly being presented to us.
   c. Working memory is the ability to hold knowledge until it is needed. Some scientists equate working memory with STM, but in reality, working memory is also employed for information manipulation in addition to information storage. Its flexibility and dynamic nature, which makes all the difference in learning achievement, are crucial.

Examples of STM:

- In order to comprehend a lengthy sentence in a conversation, you must first recall the first portion of the sentence. The system that enables you to briefly recall the start of a sentence called STM. Once you have grasped something, you don't need to recall it, and your brain will eventually forget the words.
- Your STM behaves similarly to the preceding case when you read. To comprehend a written statement or notion in its whole, you must retain its first few words. A long, complicated sentence will be harder to recall than a short, straightforward one. Naturally, this has a significant impact in academic environments. The key to academic achievement is reading comprehension, which is tied to STM.

2.16 Conclusion

In conclusion, cognitive science is a multidisciplinary field that has made significant contributions to our understanding of the human mind and behavior. By drawing on insights from psychology, neuroscience, linguistics, philosophy, anthropology, and computer science, cognitive scientists have developed theories and models of cognition that have been applied to a wide range of domains, from education to AI.

The future scope of cognitive science is promising, as researchers continue to make new discoveries about the human mind and brain. Advances in neuroimaging technology have allowed scientists to study brain function in more detail than ever before, and new techniques for analyzing big data have opened up new avenues for research. In addition, developments in AI and robotics have led to new opportunities for applying cognitive science research to real-world problems. One promising area of future research is the study of the social and emotional aspects of cognition. This includes research on empathy, social cognition, and emotional regulation, which have important implications for fields such as education, healthcare, and social robotics.

Another important area of future research is the development of more sophisticated models of cognition that can account for the complexity and variability of human behavior. This includes the development of computational models that can simulate the cognitive processes underlying decision-making, language processing, and other cognitive tasks. At the end, cognitive science research has important implications for society, as it can inform policy decisions and improve our understanding of how to address social and environmental problems. For example, research on decision-making can inform policy decisions related to healthcare or financial regulation, while research on cognitive development can inform educational policy and practice.

2.17 Case study

2.17.1 Case study: the cognitive science of learning

Introduction: Cognitive science is the interdisciplinary study of the mind and intelligence, including the study of perception, attention, memory, reasoning, and language. The field of cognitive science has made significant contributions to our understanding of how people learn and remember information. This case study will explore the cognitive science of learning by examining the case of a student named James, who is struggling in his studies.

Background: James is a college student who is struggling in his classes. He finds it difficult to focus on his studies, and he has trouble remembering information. James is frustrated because he wants to do well in his classes, but he feels like he is not making any progress.

Analysis: The cognitive science of learning can help us understand why James is struggling in his studies. There are several factors that may be contributing to his difficulties:

- *Attention*: James may be having trouble paying attention in class. Attention is a key component of learning, and if James is not able to focus on what the teacher is saying, he may not be able to remember the information.
- *Memory*: James may be having trouble remembering the information he is learning. Memory is another key component of learning, and if James is not able to remember what he has learned, he may struggle to apply it later.
- *Organization*: James may be having trouble organizing the information he is learning. When we learn new information, it is important to organize it in a meaningful way. If James is not able to do this, he may have difficulty recalling the information later.
- *Motivation*: James may be lacking motivation to learn. Motivation is an important factor in learning, and if James is not motivated to learn, he may not be putting in the effort needed to succeed.
- *Learning style*: James may have a learning style that is different from the way information is being presented in class. Everyone has a unique learning style, and if James is not able to learn in the way that works best for him, he may struggle to understand the material.

Recommendations: Based on the analysis above, there are several recommendations that may help James improve his academic performance:

Improve attention: James can try to improve his attention by minimizing distractions during class. He can turn off his phone and close any unnecessary tabs on his computer.

Memory strategies: James can try using memory strategies such as repetition or visualization to improve his memory of information.

Organizational strategies: James can try using organizational strategies such as note-taking or creating study guides to help him organize information.

Find motivation: James can try to find motivation to learn by setting goals for himself and finding ways to make the material more interesting or relevant to his life.

Learning style: James can try to identify his learning style and find ways to learn in the way that works best for him. For example, he may benefit from visual aids or hands-on activities.

Conclusion: The cognitive science of learning provides valuable insights into how people learn and remember information. By understanding the factors that can affect learning, we can make recommendations to help students like James improve their academic performance. By improving attention, memory, organization, motivation, and learning style, James can overcome his struggles and achieve his academic goals.

2.17.2 Case study: brain and sensory motor information

Introduction: The brain is responsible for processing sensory motor information, which includes the information we receive from our senses and the movements we make in response to that information. This case study will explore the role of the brain in processing sensory motor information by examining the case of a patient named Sarah, who has experienced a stroke.

Background: Sarah is a 55-year-old woman who recently suffered a stroke. As a result of the stroke, Sarah has difficulty with movement and sensation on the right side of her body. She is currently undergoing physical therapy to help her regain movement and function.

Analysis: The brain plays a crucial role in processing sensory motor information, and a stroke can disrupt this process. In Sarah's case, the stroke has affected the areas of the brain responsible for movement and sensation on the right side of her body. This has resulted in a loss of movement and sensation on that side.

The brain processes sensory motor information through a complex network of neurons and pathways. When we receive sensory information, such as touch or sound, it is processed by specific areas of the brain. These areas send signals to other parts of the brain, which integrate the information and generate a response. When we make a movement, such as reaching for an object, the brain sends signals to the muscles that control that movement. In Sarah's case, the stroke has disrupted this process. The areas of the brain that are responsible for processing sensory motor information on the right side of her body have been damaged. This means that signals from her right side are not being processed properly, resulting in a loss of movement and sensation on that side.

Recommendations: Based on the analysis above, there are several recommendations that may help Sarah regain movement and function:

- Physical therapy: Sarah should continue with her physical therapy, which will help her regain movement and function on the affected side of her body. The therapy will focus on exercises that promote the activation of the areas of the brain that control movement and sensation.
- Occupational therapy: Sarah can also benefit from occupational therapy, which will help her relearn daily activities such as dressing, grooming, and feeding. This therapy will focus on adapting to her physical limitations and learning new techniques to perform daily tasks.
- Brain training: Sarah can benefit from brain training exercises that target the areas of the brain that have been affected by the stroke. These exercises can help to rewire the brain and promote recovery.
- Supportive devices: Sarah can benefit from using supportive devices, such as braces or assistive devices, to help her with movement and function on the affected side of her body.

Conclusion: The brain plays a crucial role in processing sensory motor information, and a stroke can disrupt this process. In Sarah's case, the stroke has affected the areas of the brain responsible for movement and sensation on the right side of her body, resulting in a loss of movement and sensation on that side. Through physical therapy, occupational therapy, brain training exercises, and the use of supportive devices, Sarah can regain movement and function on the affected side of her body. The brain has the ability to rewire and adapt, and with the right interventions, Sarah can make significant progress in her recovery.

2.17.3 Case study: language and linguistic knowledge

Introduction: Language and linguistic knowledge are essential aspects of human communication. This case study will explore the role of language and linguistic knowledge by examining the case of a bilingual individual named Maria.

Background: Maria is a 35-year-old woman who was born and raised in Spain. She is fluent in both Spanish and English and has been living in the United States for the past 5 years. Maria works as a translator and interpreter, helping individuals and businesses communicate across languages.

Analysis: Language and linguistic knowledge play a significant role in Maria's life and career. As a bilingual individual, Maria has the ability to communicate effectively in two different languages. This skill is valuable in her work as a translator and interpreter, as she is able to help individuals and businesses bridge the communication gap between different languages and cultures. Maria's linguistic knowledge allows her to understand and use the grammatical and syntactic rules of both Spanish and English. This knowledge is essential for effective communication in both languages, as it allows her to use the appropriate vocabulary, grammar, and syntax for each language.

Furthermore, Maria's knowledge of the cultural nuances of both languages allows her to accurately interpret and translate language in a way that is culturally appropriate. This is particularly important in business settings, where cultural differences can impact communication and relationships.

Recommendations: Based on the analysis above, there are several recommendations that can help individuals develop their language and linguistic knowledge:

- *Language learning*: Learning a second language can help individuals develop their language and linguistic knowledge. This can be done through formal language classes or through immersion programs.
- *Linguistic study*: Studying linguistics can help individuals develop a deeper understanding of language structure and use. This can be particularly helpful for individuals working in fields such as translation, interpretation, or language teaching.
- *Cultural immersion*: Immersing oneself in different cultures can help individuals develop their cultural awareness and sensitivity. This can be done through travel, cultural exchange programs, or working in multicultural environments.

Conclusion: Language and linguistic knowledge are essential aspects of human communication, and the ability to communicate effectively in different languages is a valuable skill. Bilingual individuals, like Maria, have the ability to bridge the communication gap between different languages and cultures, making them valuable in a range of settings. Developing language and linguistic knowledge can be achieved through language learning, linguistic study, and cultural immersion, among other methods. By developing these skills, individuals can enhance their communication abilities and advance their careers in a globalized world.

TABLE 2.3 Participants' background.

InforMant A (age: 23)	InforMant B (age: 21)
Catalan Spanish at home (mother tongues)	Catalan/Spanish/Portuguese at home (mother tongues)
Catalan: language of school tuition	Semiimmersion in French in an International school (35 hours a week)
Advanced (C1) level in English	Advanced (C1) level in French
Upper intermediate level in German	Upper intermediate level in English
Beginner intermediate level in French	Upper intermediate level in Italian

2.17.4 A case study on the linguistic profile and self perception of multilingual university students by Johnston S.M., Garau M.J

The investigation of multilingual abilities and their application to the professional world is still developing. This case study aims to provide helping to better understand how people perceive themselves and how cognitive science is related to data analysis. It also refers to the topics directly related to the pupils' individual linguistic history, like the influence of varied learning settings on language gains, and the culture and language are related. The case study's data have been information gathered from two bilingual university students who have formal instruction, content and language integrated learning, and study abroad are three different venues for learning English. Table 2.3 shows the information of the participant's background.

According to Informant A, speaking more than one language is a success, and English is the language of choice for intercultural contact. One of the numerous benefits of being bilingual, according to the informant B, is that learning another language is easier once you are fluent in one. Young people are becoming more and more conscious of the value of learning a foreign language to advance their professional chances in times of crises. This is the situation with our case study participants, who place a high value on their bilingual profiles in a job market that is becoming more and more competitive.

2.17.5 Case study: the theory of information processing

Introduction: The theory of information processing is a cognitive psychology approach that explains how humans process, store, and retrieve information. This case study will explore the role of the theory of information processing by examining the case of a student named Tom, who struggles with reading comprehension.

Background: Tom is a 10-year-old student who is struggling with reading comprehension in school. Despite being a good reader, Tom has difficulty understanding what he reads and often needs to reread passages multiple times. Tom's teacher is concerned about his reading comprehension and has recommended that he receive additional support.

Analysis: The theory of information processing can provide insights into Tom's reading comprehension difficulties. According to this theory, information is processed in a series of stages, including sensory input, attention, perception, memory, and output. These stages are interdependent, and the processing of information can be influenced by factors such as attention, memory capacity, and cognitive load. Tom's reading comprehension difficulties may be related to his ability to process information in these stages. For example, Tom may have difficulty attending to and perceiving the information he is reading, which can impact his ability to store it in memory and retrieve it later. Additionally, Tom's working memory capacity may be limited, making it difficult for him to hold and manipulate information as he reads.

Recommendations: Based on the analysis above, there are several recommendations that can help individuals with reading comprehension difficulties:

- *Instructional support*: Tom may benefit from additional instructional support in reading comprehension, such as guided reading or comprehension strategies instruction. These interventions can help Tom develop his attention, perception, and memory skills and improve his comprehension.
- *Technology support*: Technology can provide additional support for individuals with reading comprehension difficulties. Text-to-speech software, for example, can read text aloud to help individuals better comprehend the material.
- Cognitive load reduction: Reducing cognitive load can help individuals better process and comprehend information. Strategies such as chunking information, breaking down complex tasks, and providing visual aids can help reduce cognitive load and improve comprehension.
- *Memory strategies*: Memory strategies such as mnemonics, repetition, and association can help individuals better encode and retrieve information. Teaching Tom these strategies can help him better retain and recall information as he reads.

Conclusion: The theory of information processing can provide insights into how individuals process, store, and retrieve information, which can help address reading comprehension difficulties. Interventions such as instructional support, technology support, cognitive load reduction, and memory strategies can help individuals improve their reading comprehension skills. By understanding the stages of information processing and the factors that influence it, educators and clinicians can provide targeted interventions to support individuals with reading comprehension difficulties.

2.17.6 The following case study is taken from: the Geography Disciplines Network (GDN) Inclusive Curriculum Project (ICP) Case Studies, HEFCE Project, University of Gloucestershire, http://www2.glos.ac.uk/gdn/icp/caseintro.htm (information extracted and accessed September 2006)

Chris is just coming to the end of the first year of his degree. His major subject is psychology but about one third of his time in the first year has been given to geography courses, and he hopes to continue to include geography as a minor subject in his second and third years. He was diagnosed as having dyslexia in the early years of secondary school.

Chris had some contact with the Disability Adviser before he arrived and has since used this central service to arrange an update to his statement of needs, to support his claim for Disabled Students Allowances to buy a laptop, and to arrange extra time for his exams. Although staff have been mostly very helpful, his experiences with the service have been mixed. The exam arrangements were straightforward to organize, but Chris had sent psychologists' reports to the office which subsequently went missing; and he found the process for obtaining the laptop very long winded.

At first tutors did not seem to be aware of Chris's dyslexia, but the Disability Adviser wrote to departments about half way through the first term and things got easier after that. His chief problem has been with lecturers who deliver their content very quickly and run through crowded power point slides too fast to allow him to keep up with notes. The educational psychologist recommended that Chris be given lecture notes in advance, to help remedy this situation, but this has not happened. Chris is determined to follow up this issue in his second year and is confident of approaching his departments first, and the Disability Adviser afterwards for extra support if necessary, to ensure that the psychologist's recommendations are implemented.

Chris finds the library a very daunting place. "I often find myself disorientated, frustrated and confused." It is very large, and he says he has difficulty focusing on the specific task he is there to do because of feeling bombarded by information from all the written sources around him. The fact that books are not always in just the right place on the shelf compounds his difficulty. A successful solution has been for him to have a helper with him in the library to locate the texts he needs. At the moment he is using a friend from his course for this support; their time is being paid for from Disabled Students Allowances. He finds route finding around the library moderately difficult the color coding of different sections helps a bit but is not a complete solution as colors are repeated on different floors. Chris wasn't aware at the start of the course that individual introductions to the library were offered to disabled students by a library assistant with particular responsibility for disability services. He reckons he would have made use of this service if he had known about it as well as doing the regular tour with other students.

He was offered additional learning support but hasn't taken this up. He is happy and confident with strategies developed during school and college from supportive parents who are teachers, from a private tutor—and his own trial and error. So far, he has not used the system of attaching yellow stickers to his essays, reminding tutors about his dyslexia. He may use these in his second year but is determined not to fall back on them as an excuse for poor work. He does, though, find invaluable the extra time allocated in exams. He uses it to plan out his answers more than would have been possible; and to avoid the problem of overload when lots of ideas crowd in at once and risk getting lost.

Chris advises other students with dyslexia to make sure staff know about their difficulties, to be clear about how it affects their studies, and to use the help available in the department and around the university.

2.17.7 Case study: short-term memory

Introduction: STM is a critical component of cognitive function, enabling individuals to temporarily store and manipulate information. This case study will explore the role of

STM by examining the case of a college student named Jane, who struggles with remembering information presented in class.

Background: Jane is a 20-year-old college student who is struggling with retaining information presented in her classes. Despite taking diligent notes, Jane finds that she is unable to recall much of the information when it comes time for exams. Jane's academic advisor is concerned about her ability to succeed in her courses and has recommended that she seek additional support.

Analysis: STM plays a critical role in an individual's ability to retain and manipulate information. STM is a limited capacity system, with the capacity to store only a limited amount of information for a brief period of time. Jane's difficulty in retaining information presented in class may be related to the limitations of her STM. As Jane takes notes during class, she may be able to hold only a limited amount of information in her STM, which can impact her ability to process and retain additional information. Furthermore, if Jane does not have effective strategies for transferring information from her STM to her long-term memory, she may struggle to recall the information at a later time.

Recommendations: Based on the analysis above, there are several recommendations that can help individuals improve their STM and ability to retain information: -

Active listening: Active listening can help individuals retain information presented in class. Encouraging Jane to actively engage with the material by asking questions, summarizing key points, and making connections to prior knowledge can help her better process and retain the information.

Chunking: Chunking is the process of breaking information down into smaller, more manageable chunks. Encouraging Jane to chunk information into smaller, more meaningful units can help her better store and recall the information.

Repetition: Repetition is a memory strategy that involves rehearsing information multiple times. Encouraging Jane to repeat information to herself or to others can help her better retain the information in her STM.

Mnemonics: Mnemonics are memory strategies that involve creating associations between new information and existing knowledge. Encouraging Jane to use mnemonic devices, such as acronyms or rhymes, can help her better remember information.

Conclusion: STM is a critical component of cognitive function, enabling individuals to temporarily store and manipulate information. Strategies such as active listening, chunking, repetition, and mnemonics can help individuals better retain information in their STM. By understanding the limitations of STM and providing targeted interventions to improve retention, individuals such as Jane can improve their ability to process and retain information presented in their classes.

2.17.8 Case study: Butterworth B., Campbell R., Howard D., "The Uses of Short-Term Memory: A Case Study," The Quarterly Journal of Experimental Psychology (1986) 38A, 705—737

It has been generally asserted that the systems utilized in immediate memory tasks serve a purpose in speech comprehension; it has been postulated that these systems are used to hold a representation of the speech until a syntactic analysis and interpretation have been finished.

Such a holding function is intended to be particularly significant in situations where the spoken sentences are lengthy or complex. Thus, it has been expected that individuals with poor STM will have trouble understanding such sentences. In this case study, one participant underwent testing on a variety of tasks involving syntactic analysis, memory, and comprehension of lengthy and complex material. This participant also had drastically limited digit span and poor phonological processing. On tests of syntactic analysis and comprehension but not of sentence repetition, she was judged to be unimpaired. Discussion is had regarding the implications for STM models. In this case study, we re-examine the function of phonemic processing in executing STM tasks as well as the function of STM in the memory and comprehension of prose in a subject, RE, who has demonstrable impairments on tasks involving both phonemic processing and STM.

- Following working hypotheses have been evaluated in this study

A loss in phonological processing is sufficient to cause an impairment in STM activities that use this store since normal phonemic processing is required for the phonological short-term store to function properly. Because the proper operation of syntactic analysis in comprehension depends on the phonological STS, which is involved in STM tasks, a deficiency in STS is enough to cause a problem with its functioning. In the theories outlined below, comprehension and syntactic analysis rely on keeping a verbatim record of the input sentence in STS while syntactic and interpretive processes are ongoing.

2.18 Exercise

1.   The study of the mind, including its composition and activities, is known as _____

     A Philosophy

     B Psychology

     C Neuroscience

     D Cognitive science

2.   The systematic study of broad and fundamental issues, such as those pertaining to existence, reason, knowledge, values, the mind, and language, is known as _____

     A Cognitive science

     B Philosophy

     C Psychology

     D Neuroscience

3.   The study of conscious and unconscious events, such as emotions and thoughts, is included in

     _____.

     A Psychology

     B Philosophy

     C Neuroscience

     D Cognitive science

4. The study of the anatomy and operation of the nervous system and the brain is known as
_____.

    A Cognitive science

    B Neuroscience

    C Philosophy

    D Psychology

5. The scientific study of human language is called _____

    A Knowledge

    B Information

    C Concepts

    D Linguistics

6. An approach to studying human cognition known as _____ makes use of mathematical models
called connectionist networks or artificial neural networks

    A Linguistics

    B Information

    C Concepts

    D Connectionism

7. _____ offers a quantitative foundation for defining what neurological systems accomplish,
figuring out how they work, and figuring out the fundamental laws that govern them.

    A Philosophy

    B Neuroscience

    C Cognitive science

    D Theoretical neuroscience

8. Based on _____, Bayesian statistics is a method of data analysis where the parameters of a statistical
model are updated with the help of observed data.

    A Random Forest

    B Bayes' theorem

    C Gaussian function

    D Probability

9. At a high level, the brain can be divided into the cerebrum, _____ and cerebellum.

    A Parietal lobe

    B Little brain

    C Occipital lobe

    D Brainstem

10. The cerebellum, sometimes known as the "_____," is a fist-sized section of the brain situated in the rear of the head, above the brainstem and below the temporal and occipital lobes. It features two hemispheres, just like the cerebral cortex.

    A Parietal lobe

    B Little brain

    C Occipital lobe

    D Brainstem

11. The _____, located in the middle of the brain, aids in object identification and the comprehension of spatial relationships, which include comparing one's body to the surroundings.

    A Parietal lobe

    B Little brain

    C Occipital lobe

    D Brainstem

12. _____ is a subscience of linguistics that studies creative aspects of language/speech and language aspects of creativity.

    A Creative linguistics

    B Philosophy

    C Neuroscience

    D Cognitive science

13. An approach to cognitive development studies called _____ seeks to explain how information is stored in memory.

    A Knowledge representation

    B Constraint satisfaction

    C Information processing theory

    D Short-term memory

14. The multistore model was proposed by _____ and Richard Shiffrin in 1968 to show their theory on human memory.

    A John Cooper

    B John William Atkinson

    C Allen Turing

    D William Starling

15. Short-term memory can only store information for about _____ seconds.

    A 60

    B 5

    C 45

    D 30

2.19 Assessment question

1. What is cognitive science and how does it relate to other fields of study such as psychology, neuroscience, linguistics, philosophy, and computer science?
2. What are some of the key theoretical frameworks and research methods used in cognitive science, and how have they contributed to our understanding of human cognition and behavior?
3. What are some of the practical applications of cognitive science, both in terms of improving our understanding of the human mind and in terms of developing new technologies and applications based on that understanding?
4. How does the brain process sensory motor information, and what are some of the key mechanisms involved in this process?
5. What are some of the key brain regions and neural networks that are involved in sensory motor processing, and how do they work together to produce coordinated movement and sensory perception?
6. How do factors such as attention, learning, and experience influence sensory motor processing, and how can this knowledge be used to develop new therapies and technologies for individuals with sensory motor impairments or disorders?
7. What are some of the ethical and societal implications of research on sensory motor processing, and how can we ensure that this research is conducted in a responsible and ethical manner?
8. What is the theory of information processing, and how does it relate to our understanding of human cognition and behavior?
9. What are some of the key theoretical frameworks and research methods used in IPT, and how have they contributed to our understanding of topics such as attention, memory, perception, and problem-solving?
10. How has the theory of information processing evolved over time, and what are some of the key debates and controversies within the field?
11. What are some of the practical applications of IPT, both in terms of developing new technologies and therapies and in terms of understanding and addressing issues such as cognitive impairment and learning disabilities?
12. What is STM, and how does it differ from other forms of memory such as long-term memory and working memory?
13. What are some of the key theoretical models and frameworks that have been developed to explain the mechanisms of STM, and how have these models been tested and refined over time?
14. How do factors such as attention, rehearsal, and chunking affect the capacity and duration of STM, and how can this knowledge be applied in practical settings such as education and cognitive rehabilitation?
15. What are some of the challenges and limitations associated with research on STM, and how can we address these challenges to further advance our understanding of this important cognitive process?

Further reading

S. Ariel, An information processing theory of family dysfunction, Psychother.: Theory Res. Pract. Train. 24 (3S) (1987) 477−495. Available from: https://doi.org/10.1037/h0085745.

R. Atkinson, R. Shiffrin, Human memory: a proposed system and its control processes, Human Memory (1977) 7−113. Available from: https://doi.org/10.1016/b978-0-12-121050-2.50006-5.

A. Baddeley, Working memory, in: S. Pickering (Ed.), Working Memory and Education, Scientific Research: An Academic Publisher, 2006, pp. 1−31. Available from: https://doi.org/10.1016/b978-012554465-8/50003-x.

A.D. Baddeley, G.J. Hitch, The phonological loop as a buffer store: an update, Cortex 112 (2019) 91−106. Available from: https://doi.org/10.1016/j.cortex.2018.05.015.

N. Çeliköz, Y. Erişen, M. Şahin, Cognitive learning theories with emphasis on latent learning, Gestalt and information processing theories, J. Educ. Instr. Stud. World 9 (3) (2019).

S. Chen, N. Lin, Global dispersion of offshore service providers: an information processing perspective, J. Knowl. Manag. 20 (5) (2016) 1065−1082. Available from: https://doi.org/10.1108/jkm-11-2015-0449.

J.R. Galbraith, Organization design: an information processing view, Interfaces 4 (3) (1974) 28−36. Available from: https://doi.org/10.1287/inte.4.3.28.

E.B. Goldstein, A. Mackewn, Cognitive Psychology Connecting Mind, Research, and Everyday Experience, Thomson Wadsworth. Google Books, Belmont, CA, 2005.

I. Hann, K. Hui, S.T. Lee, I.P. Png, Overcoming online information privacy concerns: an information-processing theory approach, J. Manag. Inf. Syst. 24 (2) (2007) 13−42. Available from: https://doi.org/10.2753/mis0742-1222240202.

J.L. Kmetz, Information Processing Theory of Organization: Managing Technology Accession in Complex Systems, Routledge. Google Books, Abingdon-on-Thames, England, 2020.

D. Laberge, S. Samuels, Toward a theory of automatic information processing in reading, Cogn. Psychol. 6 (2) (1974) 293−323. Available from: https://doi.org/10.1016/0010-0285(74)90015-2.

P. Langley, The central role of cognition in learning, Adv. Cogn. Syst. 4 (2016). Semantic Scholar.

P.R. Rogers, A. Miller, W.Q. Judge, Using information-processing theory to understand planning/performance relationships in the context of strategy, Strateg. Manag. J. 20 (6) (1999) 567−577.

S.D. Sala, Tall Tales About the Mind and Brain: Separating Fact from Fiction, Oxford University Press, Oxford, 2007.

Y. Wang, D. Liu, Y. Wang, Discovering the capacity of human memory, Brain and Mind 4 (2003) 89−198. Available from: https://doi.org/10.1023/A:1025405628479.

Data theory and taxonomy of data

Abbreviations

SQL	structured query language
XML	extensible markup language
JSON	JavaScript Object Notation
API	application programming interfaces
IOT	Internet of Things
NPS	net promoter score
IQ	interquartile
TURF	totally unduplicated reach and frequency
SPSS	statistical package for social sciences
EDA	exploratory data analysis
CAD	computer aided design
3D	three dimension

3.1 Introduction

Data theory and taxonomy of data play a fundamental role in understanding the nature, structure, and characteristics of data in various fields such as statistics, computer science, and data analysis. In this context, the concept of data as a whole, different views of data, measurement and scaling concepts, and various types of scales are essential components to comprehend the complexity and diversity of data. Data, in its broadest sense, refers to any collection of information or facts. It encompasses both qualitative and quantitative observations, measurements, or records that are collected, stored, and analyzed for various purposes. In today's data-driven world, the abundance and variety of data have become a valuable resource for decision-making, insights generation, and knowledge discovery. To gain a deeper understanding of data, it is essential to explore different views of data. Data can be viewed as raw, unprocessed observations or as structured and organized information with a specific context. The different views of data include the conceptual view, representing the meaning and relationships within the data; the logical view, defining the organization and structure of the data; and the physical view, focusing on the storage and retrieval of the data. Measurement and scaling concepts are fundamental in data theory, providing a framework for assigning numerical values to observations and categorizing them into meaningful categories. Measurement refers to the process of assigning numbers to variables or

Cognitive Science, Computational Intelligence, and Data Analytics
DOI: https://doi.org/10.1016/B978-0-443-16078-3.00003-4
© 2024 Elsevier Inc. All rights are reserved, including those for text and data mining, AI training, and similar technologies.

attributes, enabling quantitative analysis. Scaling, on the other hand, involves creating a continuum of values to represent the intensity or magnitude of a variable.

Various types of scales are used in data analysis to measure different types of variables. Nominal scales categorize data into distinct categories without any inherent order or numerical value. Ordinal scales order data categories but do not provide a fixed measurement unit or equal intervals. Interval scales provide a fixed measurement unit and equal intervals between values but lack a true zero point. Ratio scales possess all the properties of interval scales with the additional feature of a true zero point, allowing for meaningful ratio comparisons. Understanding the taxonomy of data and the different types of scales is crucial in selecting appropriate analytical techniques, designing data collection instruments, and interpreting the results accurately. It provides a foundation for organizing and classifying data based on their nature, allowing researchers and analysts to choose the most suitable methods for data analysis and interpretation. The field of data theory and taxonomy of data encompasses the study of data as a whole, different views of data, measurement and scaling concepts, and various types of scales. These concepts form the basis for comprehending the complexity and diversity of data and play a vital role in data analysis, interpretation, and decision-making. By applying these principles, researchers and analysts can effectively handle and extract meaningful insights from the vast amount of data available today.

3.2 Data as a whole

Data as a whole refers to all of the information that has been collected, stored, and analyzed in a particular context. This can include structured data (such as numbers and dates stored in spreadsheets or databases) and unstructured data (such as text, images, and videos). The term "data as a whole" emphasizes the importance of considering all available data when making decisions or drawing conclusions, rather than focusing on a narrow subset of information. It is often used in the context of big data, which refers to extremely large and complex datasets that require specialized tools and techniques to analyze the data effectively. Data analysis is the process of modifying, processing, and cleaning raw data in order to obtain useful, pertinent information that supports for the commercial decision-making. The process offers helpful insights and statistics, frequently presented in charts, graphics, tables, and graphs, which lessen the risks associated with decision-making. Whenever we make a choice in our day-to-day existence, we are essentially engaging in a fundamental form of data analysis by evaluating past events or anticipating future outcomes. This process is straightforward, involving an examination of previous occurrences or future possibilities, followed by a decision based on the analysis. Data is categorized in the different forms such as structured, unstructured, qualitative, and quantitative.

3.2.1 Structured data

Structured data is data that follows a pre-established data model and is easy to analyze. Structured data refers to data that is organized and stored in a specific format, usually within a database or a spreadsheet. This data is highly organized and easily searchable because it is stored in a predefined structure with fixed fields and values. Structured data can be processed and analyzed using software tools such as SQL (structured query language), which allows for complex queries and data manipulation.

Examples of structured data include:

- Customer information such as name, address, and phone number
- Sales transactions with details such as date, amount, and product
- Inventory data with details such as SKU, stock levels, and location
- Financial data such as income statements and balance sheets
- Time-series data such as stock prices or temperature readings

A tabular format with relationships between the various rows and columns is that structured data follows. Excel spreadsheets and SQL databases are typical instances of structured data. Each of them has structured, sortable rows and columns. Fig. 3.1 shows the sources of the structure of the data.

A data model, which is a representation of how data can be stored, processed, and accessed, is necessary for the existence of structured data. Each field is discrete and can be accessed independently or in conjunction with data from other fields to convert the effective structured data. Because it is feasible to swiftly aggregate data from many areas in the database, where structured data is incredibly powerful. Since the early versions of database management systems could store, analyze, and access structured data, structured data is regarded as the most "conventional" type of the data storage. Following are the characteristics of the structured data:

- Characteristics of structured data:
  - Data is structured clearly and complies with a data model.
  - In the form of rows and columns, data is saved.

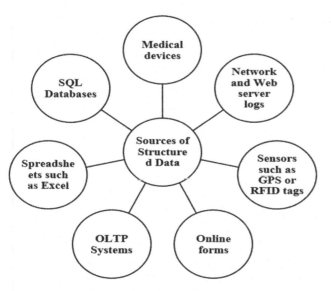

FIGURE 3.1 Sources of the structured data.

- Data is organized so that its definition, format, and meaning are all well understood.
- Within a record or file, data is stored in fixed fields.
- Classes or relations are formed by grouping together similar things.
- The properties of entities in the same group are the same.
- Data is easily accessed and queried, making it accessible to other programs.
- Addressable data pieces allow for quick analysis and processing.

- Advantages of structured data
  - Data can be indexed based on text strings as well as attributes since structured data has a well-defined structure that makes it easy to store and access data. This makes conducting searches simple.
  - Data mining is simple, making it simple to extract knowledge from data.
  - Operations like updating and deleting are simple since the data is well-structured.
  - Operations involving business intelligence, such as data warehousing, are simple to carry out.
  - Data security is simple to ensure.

Python program of the structured data:

```python
# Define a list of dictionaries representing students' information
students = [
    {"name": "John", "age": 18, "grade": "A"},
    {"name": "Emily", "age": 17, "grade": "B"},
    {"name": "Michael", "age": 18, "grade": "A+"},
    {"name": "Sophia", "age": 17, "grade": "A"}
]
# Function to display student information
def display_student_info(student):
    print(f"Name: {student['name']}")
    print(f"Age: {student['age']}")
    print(f"Grade: {student['grade']}")
    print()

# Display information for each student
for student in students:
    display_student_info(student)


Outcome:
Name: John
Age: 18
Grade: A

Name: Emily
Age: 17
Grade: B

Name: Michael
Age: 18
Grade: A+

Name: Sophia
Age: 17
Grade: A
```

(cont'd)

In this program, we have a list called students, which contains dictionaries representing student information. Each dictionary represents a single student and contains keys such as "name," "age," and "grade," with corresponding values.

We also define a function called display student info() that takes a student dictionary

as a parameter and prints out the student's name, age, and grade.

Finally, we iterate over the list of students using a for loop and call the display student info() function for each student to display their information.

3.2.2 Semistructured data

Data that has some structure but does not adhere to a data model is referred to as semistructured data. It doesn't have a set or rigid structure. The data that does not belong in a logical database but has some organizational characteristics is what makes analysis easier. We can store some processes in the relational database. Semistructured data is a type of data that has some structure but does not conform to the rigid structure of traditional relational databases. It is sometimes also referred to as "semistructured" or "partially structured" data. Semistructured data typically consists of data that is organized in a flexible and dynamic way, allowing for changes and variations in the structure over time. It may also contain both structured and unstructured data elements, such as metadata, tags, or annotations.

One of the most common types of semistructured data is XML (extensible markup language), which allows for flexible representation of data using tags and attributes. Another example is JSON (JavaScript Object Notation), which is often used in web applications and application programming interfaces to exchange data between systems. Fig. 3.2 shows the sources of the semistructure dataset.

- Examples of semistructured data include:
  - Web pages with HTML markup
  - Emails with headers and metadata
  - Social media posts with hashtags and mentions
  - Documents with metadata and annotations
  - Sensor data with varying data structures and formats
- Characteristics of semistructured data:
  - Although data does not follow a data model, it does have some structure.
  - Rows and columns, as used in databases, cannot be used to store data.
  - Semistructured data includes tags and components (metadata) that are used to categorize and define the storage of the data.
  - Similar objects are gathered and arranged in a hierarchy.

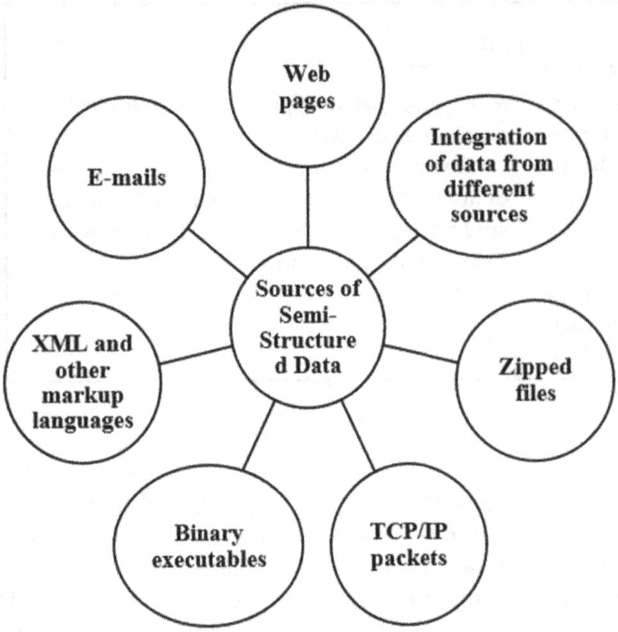

FIGURE 3.2 Sources of the semistructure data.

- Group members may or may not have the same characteristics or qualities.
- Similar features in a group may vary in size and type.
- It lacks a clear structure, making it difficult for computer programmes to utilize it.
- Advantages of semistructured data:
  - There is no fixed schema that restricts the data.
  - Flexible, i.e., schema changes are simple.
  - Transportable data.
  - It aids users whose needs cannot be expressed in SQL.
  - It can manage the diversity of sources with ease.
- Disadvantages of semistructured data:
  - Lack of fixed, rigid schema makes it difficult in storage of the data.
  - Interpreting the relationship between data is difficult as there is no separation of the schema and the data.
  - Queries are less efficient as compared to structured data.

Python program on semistructured data:

```python
import json

# Sample JSON data representing books
books_json = '''
{
  "books": [
    {
      "title": "The Great Gatsby",
      "author": "F. Scott Fitzgerald",
      "year": 1925
    },
    {
      "title": "To Kill a Mockingbird",
      "author": "Harper Lee",
      "year": 1960
    },
    {
      "title": "1984",
      "author": "George Orwell",
      "year": 1949
    }
  ]
}
'''

# Load JSON data into Python object
books_data = json.loads(books_json)

# Extract and display book information
for book in books_data["books"]:
    title = book["title"]
    author = book["author"]
    year = book["year"]
    print(f"Title: {title}")
    print(f"Author: {author}")
    print(f"Year: {year}")
    print()
```

Outcome:
Title: The Great Gatsby
Author: F. Scott Fitzgerald
Year: 1925

Title: To Kill a Mockingbird
Author: Harper Lee
Year: 1960

Title: 1984
Author: George Orwell
Year: 1949

(cont'd)

In this program, we have a sample JSON data string representing information about books. We use the json.loads() function to parse the JSON data and load it into a Python object called books_data.

We then iterate over the list of books within the books key of the books_data object. For each book, we extract the title, author, and year using dictionary indexing (book["title"], book["author"], book["year"]). We then print out this information.

You can modify the books_json string to include your own semistructured data in JSON format, or you can load data from a file using json.load() function instead of json.loads().

3.2.3 Unstructured data

Unstructured data is any data that deviates from a data model and lacks a clearly defined structure, making it difficult for computer programmes to use. Unstructured data is not organized in a predetermined way or does not have a predetermined data model, hence it does not work well with relational databases in general. Unstructured data refers to any type of data that does not have a specific structure or format, making it difficult to organize and process using traditional database tools. This type of data often comes in the form of text, images, audio, or video files, and may contain information that is difficult to categorize or classify.

- Examples of unstructured data include:
  - Text documents such as email messages, reports, and articles
  - Social media content such as tweets, posts, and comments
  - Images and videos, including photos, videos, and surveillance footage
  - Audio recordings, such as podcasts and voicemails
  - Sensor data, such as data collected by Internet of Things (IOT) devices, which can include a variety of data types

Unstructured data can be analyzed using specialized techniques such as natural language processing, image recognition, and sentiment analysis, which allow for the extraction of insights and trends from large volumes of unstructured data. These techniques are often used in data mining, machine learning, and big data analytics applications. Unstructured data is often contrasted with structured data, which has a predefined format and is easily organized and processed using traditional database tools. There is also a middle ground between structured and unstructured data, known as semistructured data, which has some structure but is not fully structured. Fig. 3.3 shows the sources of the unstructured data.

- Characteristics of unstructured data:
  - Data is unstructured and does not follow a data model.
  - Rows and columns, as used in databases, cannot be used to store data.

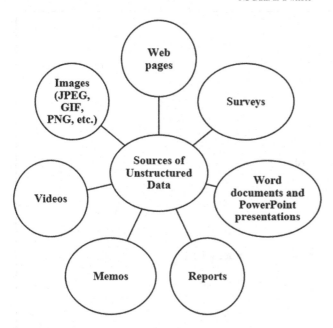

FIGURE 3.3 Sources of unstructured data.

- Data does not adhere to any rules or semantics.
- Data does not follow a specific format or order.
- Data lacks a well-defined structure.
- The lack of a recognizable structure makes it difficult for computer programmes to use.
- Advantages of unstructured data:
  - It supports information that is not properly formatted or ordered.
  - There is no fixed schema that restricts the data.
  - Due to the lack of a schema, it is very flexible.
  - Data is scalable and portable.
  - It can manage the diversity of sources with ease.
  - There are several business intelligence and analytics applications for this type of data.
- Disadvantages of unstructured data:
  - Due to a lack of schema and organization, it is challenging to store and handle unstructured data.
  - Due to the data's ambiguous structure and lack of predefined properties, indexing is challenging and error-prone. Search results are therefore not particularly accurate.
  - Data security is a challenging issue.

Python program on unstructured data:

```python
# Sample unstructured text
text = '''
The quick brown fox jumps over the lazy dog.
The dog is barking loudly.
I love eating pizza.
'''

# Convert the text to lowercase
text = text.lower()

# Count the number of occurrences of a word
word = "dog"
word_count = text.count(word)
print(f"The word '{word}' appears {word_count} times.")

# Split the text into sentences
sentences = text.split('.')
sentences = [sentence.strip() for sentence in sentences if sentence.strip()]
print("Sentences:")
for sentence in sentences:
    print(sentence)

# Extract words from the text
words = text.split()
print("Words:")
for word in words:
    print(word)
```

Outcome:
The word 'dog' appears 2 times.

Sentences:
the quick brown fox jumps over the lazy dog
the dog is barking loudly
i love eating pizza
Words:
the
quick
brown
fox
jumps
over
the
lazy
dog.
the
dog
is
barking
loudly.
i
love
eating
pizza.

(cont'd)

In this program, we start with a sample unstructured text. We convert the text to lowercase using the lower() method to make it case-insensitive.

Next, we count the number of occurrences of a specific word ("dog" in this case) using the count() method.

We then split the text into sentences by splitting it at every period (.) using the split() method. We remove any leading or trailing whitespace using the strip() method. The resulting sentences are stored in a list and printed.

Finally, we split the text into individual words using the split() method without any arguments. The resulting words are stored in a list and printed.

You can modify the text variable to work with your own unstructured data or load the data from a file. Depending on your specific requirements, you may need to apply more advanced text processing techniques like tokenization, stemming, or named entity recognition.

3.2.4 Quantitative and qualitative data analysis

3.2.4.1 *Qualitative data*

Qualitative data is the term used to describe information that cannot be expressed in numerical or quantitative terms. The objective of analyzing qualitative data is to provide insights into the actions people undertake and the underlying factors that influence those actions. Gathering and processing this type of data can be time-consuming as it requires the analyst to reflect on the information. A qualitative researcher or analyst is someone who specializes in working with qualitative data, which is descriptive in nature rather than numerical. It is often collected through observations, interviews, focus groups, surveys, and other methods that involve gathering data from people's subjective experiences, opinions, and perceptions. Qualitative data can include written or spoken responses, images, video recordings, and other non-numerical sources.

Qualitative data is commonly used in social sciences, market research, and other fields where understanding people's experiences and perspectives is important. It is often analyzed using qualitative methods such as content analysis, thematic analysis, and grounded theory, which involve identifying patterns and themes within the data.

- Examples of qualitative data include:
  - *Interview transcripts*: written or recorded transcripts of interviews with participants, which can be analyzed to understand their experiences, opinions, and beliefs.
  - *Focus group recordings*: audio or video recordings of group discussions, which can be analyzed to understand shared perspectives and experiences.
  - *Observation notes*: written notes or field notes taken by researchers during observations of participants, which can provide insights into their behaviors and interactions.
  - *Survey open-ended responses*: written responses to open-ended survey questions, which can provide more detailed and nuanced insights into participants' opinions and experiences.

3.2.4.1.1 Types of qualitative data

Binary data: Binary data is expressed numerically as a mix of zeros and ones. The only type of data that a computer can directly comprehend, and process is binary data. The frequency with which the study subject is likely to be positive or negative, up or down, right or wrong based on a zero scale is predicted using binary data by data analysts using statistical models. Binary data refers to data that can only take on one of two possible values. These values are often represented as 0 or 1, true or false, yes or no, or on or off. Binary data can be stored electronically using binary code, which is a system of representing data using only two digits, 0 and 1. Binary data is commonly used in computer science and digital technology, where it is used to represent information in a way that can be easily processed by machines. For example, in computer programming, binary data is used to represent computer instructions and data in a form that can be understood and executed by the computer's processor.

- Examples of binary data include:
  - *Binary code*: a system of representing data using only two digits, 0 and 1.
  - *Boolean values*: a data type that can only take on one of two values, true or false.
  - *Bitmapped images*: images that are represented as a grid of pixels, where each pixel is either on or off.
  - *Binary files*: files that are stored in binary format, such as executable files, image files, and sound files.

Binary data can be analyzed using techniques such as binary classification, which is a machine learning technique used to classify data into one of two categories based on binary features.

Nominal data: Nominal data is any sort of data that is used to label something without assigning it a number value. It is sometimes referred to as "named, labeled data" or "nominal scaled data." Nominal data are used by data scientists to identify statistically significant variations between sets of qualitative data. Nominal data is a type of categorical data that is used to classify observations into discrete categories or groups. Nominal data is often used to describe characteristics or attributes of people, objects, or events, such as gender, ethnicity, religion, political affiliation, or product type. Unlike ordinal data, which has a natural ordering or ranking, nominal data has no inherent order or hierarchy among the categories. The categories are simply labels that are used to group the observations into distinct categories. Nominal data is commonly used in social sciences, marketing, and other fields where categorical data is useful in understanding patterns and trends. It can be analyzed using descriptive statistics, such as frequency counts and percentages, or inferential statistics, such as chi-square tests and logistic regression.

- Examples of nominal data include:
  - Gender: male or female
  - Ethnicity: Hispanic, Caucasian, African American, Asian, etc.
  - Religion: Christianity, Islam, Hinduism, Buddhism, etc.
  - Political affiliation: Democrat, Republican, Independent, etc.
  - Product type: food, clothing, electronics, etc.

Nominal data can also be represented using nominal scales, which assign a numerical value or code to each category for ease of data management and analysis. However, these numerical values do not imply any inherent order or ranking among the categories.

Python program on nominal data:

```python
# Sample nominal data
categories = ['Red', 'Blue', 'Green', 'Red', 'Yellow', 'Green']

# Count the frequency of each category
category_counts = {}
for category in categories:
    if category in category_counts:
        category_counts[category] += 1
    else:
        category_counts[category] = 1

# Display the frequency of each category
print("Category Counts:")
for category, count in category_counts.items():
    print(f"{category}: {count}")

# Find unique categories
unique_categories = set(categories)

# Display unique categories
print("\nUnique Categories:")
for category in unique_categories:
    print(category)
# Check if a category is present
category_to_check = 'Blue'
if category_to_check in categories:
    print(f"\n{category_to_check} is present in the data.")
else:
    print(f"\n{category_to_check} is not present in the data.")
```

Outcome:
Category Counts:
Red: 2
Blue: 1
Green: 2
Yellow: 1

Unique Categories:
Blue
Green
Yellow
Red

Blue is present in the data.

(cont'd)

In this program, we start with a sample nominal data represented by a list called categories. The categories can be any strings without any particular order or numerical value.

To count the frequency of each category, we iterate over the list and update the category_counts dictionary accordingly. If a category is already in the dictionary, we increment its count; otherwise, we initialize it to 1.

We then display the frequency of each category by iterating over the category_counts dictionary.

To find the unique categories in the data, we convert the list to a set using the set() function. Sets only contain unique elements, so duplicates are automatically removed.

We display the unique categories by iterating over the set.

Lastly, we demonstrate how to check if a specific category is present in the data using the in operator.

You can customize the categories list with your own nominal data or load the data from an external source. Depending on your requirements, you can extend the program to perform additional operations or analyses on the nominal data.

Ordinal data: Ordinal data is qualitative data that has been ranked or scaled in a certain way. The order of the qualitative data counts more than the distinctions between each category when researchers employ ordinal data. Researchers may use ordinal data to categorize groups such as age, gender, or class, while data analysts may use it to create visualizations. For instance, the results of a net promoter score survey are expressed as satisfaction levels ranging from 0 to 10. Ordinal data is a type of categorical data that has an inherent order or ranking among the categories. It is used to measure the magnitude or intensity of a characteristic or attribute, such as satisfaction, agreement, or frequency of use. Ordinal data is often collected through surveys, rating scales, or Likert scales, where respondents are asked to rate their level of agreement or satisfaction on a scale that ranges from low to high, or from disagree to agree. Ordinal data can be analyzed using descriptive statistics, such as median and mode, or inferential statistics, such as ordinal regression and Spearman's rank correlation coefficient.

- Examples of ordinal data include:
  - Educational level: elementary school, high school, some college, associate's degree, bachelor's degree, master's degree, or doctoral degree.
  - Income level: less than $25,000, $25,000–$50,000, $50,000–$75,000, $75,000–$100,000, or more than $100,000.
  - Satisfaction level: very dissatisfied, somewhat dissatisfied, neutral, somewhat satisfied, or very satisfied.
  - Pain intensity level: no pain, mild pain, moderate pain, severe pain, or extreme pain.
  - Likelihood of recommendation: not likely, somewhat likely, or very likely.

Ordinal data can be graphically represented using bar charts or histograms, which show the frequency or proportion of each category, or using box plots, which show the median, quartiles, and range of the data.

Python program on ordinal data:

```python
# Sample ordinal data
ranks = ['First', 'Second', 'Third', 'Second', 'Fourth', 'Third']

# Count the frequency of each rank
rank_counts = {}
for rank in ranks:
    if rank in rank_counts:
        rank_counts[rank] += 1
    else:
        rank_counts[rank] = 1

# Display the frequency of each rank
print("Rank Counts:")
for rank, count in rank_counts.items():
    print(f"{rank}: {count}")

# Find unique ranks
unique_ranks = sorted(set(ranks))

# Display unique ranks
print("\nUnique Ranks:")
for rank in unique_ranks:
    print(rank)

# Sort the ranks
sorted_ranks = sorted(ranks)

# Display the sorted ranks
print("\nSorted Ranks:")
for rank in sorted_ranks:
    print(rank)

# Convert ranks to numerical values
rank_values = {'First': 1, 'Second': 2, 'Third': 3, 'Fourth': 4}
numerical_ranks = [rank_values[rank] for rank in ranks]

# Display numerical ranks
print("\nNumerical Ranks:")
for rank in numerical_ranks:
    print(rank)
```

Outcome:
Rank Counts:
First: 1
Second: 2
Third: 2
Fourth: 1

Unique Ranks:
First
Fourth
Second
Third

Sorted Ranks:
First
Fourth
Second
Second
Third
Third

Numerical Ranks:
1
2
3
2
4
3

In this program, we start with a sample ordinal data represented by a list called ranks. The ranks represent categories with a meaningful order or hierarchy.

To count the frequency of each rank, we iterate over the list and update the rank_counts dictionary accordingly. If a rank is already in the dictionary, we increment its count; otherwise, we initialize it to 1.

We then display the frequency of each rank by iterating over the rank_counts dictionary.

To find the unique ranks in the data, we convert the list to a set using the set () function to remove duplicates. We then sort the set using the sorted () function to obtain a sorted list of unique ranks.

We display the unique ranks by iterating over the sorted list.

To sort the ranks in ascending order, we use the sorted () function directly on the ranks list.

If you have a specific order mapping for the ordinal data, like a mapping from ranks to numerical values, you can convert the ranks to numerical values. In this example, we use a rank values dictionary to define the mapping. We create a new list called numerical ranks by mapping each rank to its corresponding numerical value using a list comprehension.

We display the numerical ranks by iterating over the numerical ranks list.

You can customize the ranks list with your own ordinal data or load the data from an external source. Depending on your requirements, you can extend the program to perform additional operations or analyses on the ordinal data.

3.2.4.1.2 Importance of qualitative data

In order to ascertain the specific frequency of traits or features, qualitative data is crucial. It enables statisticians or researchers to create parameters by which they can study larger data sets. Observers can quantify their environment with the help of qualitative data. A market researcher can answer questions like who their clients are, what problems or troubles they are having, and where they should concentrate their efforts to find solutions by gathering qualitative data. Qualitative data focuses on people's feelings, perceptions, and emotions. These sensations and feelings are recorded in quantifiable data. It enables the market researchers to address the issue effectively and efficiently by enabling them to comprehend the language spoken by their customers.

3.2.4.1.3 Role of qualitative data in the industry 4.0

Qualitative data plays an important role in industry 4.0, which is characterized by the integration of various technologies such as IOT, AI (artificial intelligence), and big data. Qualitative data refers to non-numerical data that provides insights into the attitudes, opinions, and experiences of individuals.

- In industry 4.0, qualitative data is used in various ways, such as:
  - *Understanding customer needs*: Qualitative data is used to understand customer preferences, opinions, and experiences with products and services. This helps businesses to design products that meet customer needs and preferences.
  - *Product design*: Qualitative data is used to understand user behavior, preferences, and expectations, which helps in designing products that are more user-friendly and efficient.
  - *Human resource management*: Qualitative data is used to understand the needs, expectations, and experiences of employees, which helps in creating a positive work environment and improving employee satisfaction.
  - *Risk management*: Qualitative data is used to identify potential risks and opportunities in the market, which helps in developing strategies to mitigate risks and capitalize on opportunities.
  - *Market research*: Qualitative data is used to gather insights about the market, competitors, and customer behavior, which helps businesses to make informed decisions about product development, pricing, and marketing.
  - Finally, qualitative data plays an important role in industry 4.0 by providing insights into the human aspects of technology integration, such as customer preferences, employee satisfaction, and market behavior.

3.2.4.1.4 Main approaches to qualitative data analysis

Deductive approach: The deductive method entails examining qualitative data in accordance with a specified structure. The questions might serve as a roadmap for a researcher as they analyze the data. When a researcher has a good sense of the expected replies he or she will obtain from the sample population, they can use this quick and simple method. The deductive approach of qualitative analysis involves starting with a pre-existing theory or framework and then using data to test and support or refute that theory. This approach is also known as top-down or theory-driven approach. In deductive qualitative analysis, the researcher begins by developing a hypothesis or research question based on a pre-existing theory or model. The researcher then collects data through interviews, surveys, observations, or other methods, and analyzes the data to test the hypothesis or answer the research questions.

The deductive approach typically involves a structured data collection and analysis process, where the data is categorized according to predetermined themes or codes. The researcher uses these themes or codes to identify patterns and connections in the data that either support the pre-existing theory. The deductive approach is useful when the researcher has a pre-existing theory or hypothesis that needs to be tested, or when the researcher wants to build on existing research in a particular field. This approach allows for a systematic and rigorous analysis of data, and can provide strong support for the pre-existing theory or framework.

However, the deductive approach may also have limitations, such as potential bias in the interpretation of data or an overreliance on pre-existing theories or frameworks that may not be fully applicable to the research context. It is important for the researcher to be aware of these limitations and to balance the deductive approach with other qualitative research methods.

Inductive approach: Contrarily, the inductive approach does not rely on preconceived guidelines or a predefined framework. It is a more extensive and time-consuming method of qualitative data analysis. When a researcher has very little or no knowledge of the investigated phenomenon, they frequently employ an inductive approach. The inductive approach of qualitative data analysis involves starting with the data itself and then developing theories or models based on patterns and themes that emerge from the data. This approach is also known as bottom-up or data-driven approach.

In inductive qualitative analysis, the researcher begins by collecting data through interviews, surveys, observations, or other methods, without any preconceived theories or hypotheses. The researcher then systematically analyzes the data, looking for patterns, themes, and connections. The researcher organizes the data into categories and codes based on the emerging themes and patterns, and then uses these codes to develop theories or models that explain the data. This approach allows for the creation of new theories or models that are grounded in the data, rather than being limited by pre-existing theories. The inductive approach is useful when the researcher wants to explore a new area of research, or when the researcher wants to gain a deeper understanding of a phenomenon without being limited by pre-existing theories. This approach allows for a more flexible and open-ended analysis of data, and can lead to the discovery of new and unexpected insights.

However, the inductive approach may also have limitations, such as potential subjectivity in the interpretation of data, or the risk of missing important insights that may be outside of the researcher's initial focus. It is important for the researcher to be aware of these limitations and to balance the inductive approach with other qualitative research methods.

3.2.4.1.5 Steps to qualitative data analysis

- Step 1: Arrange your data:
    When you have gathered the data, it is generally unstructured and somewhat confusing at first glance. As a result, it is crucial that you as a researcher first transcribe the information gathered. The methodical organization of your data is the initial stage in the analysis process. Data organization entails text conversion of all the data. The data can be manually entered, exported into a spreadsheet, or analyzed using any of the computer-assisted qualitative data analysis methods.
- Step 2: Organize all your data:
    The next thing to do is organize your data after it has been transformed and arranged. There is a good probability that you have a lot of information that needs to be organized, so do so now. Going back to your study goals and then structuring the data based on the questions you posed are two of the greatest ways to organize the data. Create a table with your study objective set up so that it is easily readable. Stay away from the temptation to deal with disorganized data at all costs. Time will be wasted, and no definitive outcomes will be attained.
- Step 3: Set a code to the data collected:
    One of the best ways to compress the vast amount of information gathered is through coding. Coding qualitative data is the process of classifying and appointing characteristics and patterns to the gathered information. Coding is a crucial phase in the study of qualitative data since it allows you to draw theories from the results of pertinent research. After giving your data codes, you may start to build on the patterns to get a deeper understanding of the data and make wiser judgements.
- Step 4: Validate your data:
    One of the essential phases of qualitative data analysis for productive research is data validation. Since data is fundamental to study, it is crucial to make sure that the data are accurate. Please be aware that data validation is a continuous process that must be carried out throughout the research process and is not simply one phase in the study of qualitative data.
    There are two aspects to data validation one of that precision of your research strategy or techniques and reliability, or the consistency with which the processes consistently provide accurate data.
- Step 5: Concluding the analysis process:
    It is important to finally conclude the data, which means systematically presenting the data, a report that can be readily used. The report should state the method that, as a researcher, used to conduct the research studies, the positives, and negatives and study limitations. In the report, you should also state the suggestions/inferences of your findings and any related areas for future research.

3.2.4.1.6 Qualitative data collection methods

Qualitative data collection methods are used to gather non-numerical data or information that cannot be quantified. Following are the common qualitative data collection methods:

1. Interviews

Because of its individualized approach, it is one of the most often utilized data gathering tools for qualitative research. One-on-one data collection takes place between the interviewer or researcher and the interviewee. The interview may be conversational, casual, and unstructured. Most of the time, open-ended questions are asked impulsively by the interviewer, who lets the interview's natural flow determine what to ask. Interviews are a common method for collecting qualitative data. Qualitative interviews involve asking open-ended questions and allowing participants to provide detailed responses in their own words. Interviews can be conducted in-person, over the phone, or via video conferencing.

There are several advantages to using interviews as a qualitative data collection method:
- *In-depth data*: Interviews can provide detailed, in-depth data that allows researchers to gain a rich understanding of participants' experiences, perspectives, and opinions.
- *Flexibility*: Interviews can be flexible and allow participants to expand on their responses, providing researchers with a more comprehensive view of the topic being studied.
- *Participant perspective*: Interviews allow researchers to gain insight into the participants' perspective and experiences, which can help to identify important issues and concerns.
- *Probing questions*: Researchers can use probing questions to clarify responses into a particular topic, allowing for a more nuanced analysis of the data.

However, there are also some limitations to using interviews as a qualitative data collection method:
- *Potential bias*: The interviewer's own biases and beliefs can influence the data collected, potentially skewing the results.
- *Time-consuming*: Interviews can be time-consuming to conduct and transcribe, making it difficult to collect data from a large sample size.
- *Limited generalizability*: Because qualitative interviews focus on a small sample size, the results may not be generalizable to a larger population.
- *Response bias*: Participants may provide responses that they believe the researcher wants to hear, rather than providing their honest opinions and experiences.

At the end interviews can be a valuable qualitative data collection method, particularly when the research question involves exploring participants' experiences, attitudes, and perspectives. It is important for researchers to be aware of the limitations and to take steps to mitigate potential biases in the data collection process.

2. Focus group

This is done in a setting of a group discussion. The group is limited to 6–10 participants, and a moderator is chosen to oversee the conversation as it progresses. A focus group is a qualitative data collection method that involves a small group of people, typically between 6 and 12 individuals, who participate in a structured discussion or interview about a particular topic or issue of interest. The focus group is led by a moderator who guides the discussion and asks open-ended questions to elicit participants' thoughts, opinions, and attitudes about the topic.

The goal of a focus group is to gain insights and perspectives from a diverse group of individuals who share similar characteristics related to the research topic. The data collected through focus groups is qualitative in nature, meaning it provides rich and detailed information about participants' experiences, beliefs, and attitudes. Focus groups are commonly used in market research to gather information about consumers' preferences, opinions, and behaviors related to a particular product or service. They can also be used in social science research to explore topics such as attitudes towards public policies, experiences with healthcare services, or perceptions of social issues.

One of the main advantages of focus groups is that they allow researchers to gather data from a diverse group of individuals in a relatively short period of time. Additionally, the group discussion can facilitate the generation of new ideas and insights, as participants build on each other's comments and feedback. However, focus groups also have some limitations. For example, the data collected may be influenced by group dynamics, such as social pressure to conform to others' opinions or the dominance of a few participants. Additionally, the sample size is typically small, and the findings may not be generalizable to the larger population. Therefore, it is important to use other methods, such as surveys or interviews, to corroborate the findings from the focus groups.

3. Record keeping

As a data source, this strategy uses already-existing, trustworthy documents and other sources of information. The new study can make use of this data. It is comparable to visiting a library. There, one can look through books and other reference materials to gather pertinent information for the study. Record keeping is a qualitative data collection method that involves the systematic and detailed documentation of observations, experiences, and interactions related to a particular research topic or question. Record keeping can involve a variety of sources, including field notes, photographs, audio or video recordings, memos, and other forms of documentation.

The goal of record keeping is to collect and preserve detailed, accurate, and comprehensive information about a particular phenomenon or situation. This data can then be analyzed and used to generate insights and understanding about the topic under study. Record keeping is commonly used in qualitative research methods such as ethnography, where the researcher immerses themselves in the community or setting being studied and records their observations and interactions with the people and environment. In this context, record keeping serves as a way to capture the complexity and richness of the setting and the experiences of the people involved.

One of the main advantages of record keeping is that it allows for detailed and comprehensive documentation of the research context and the experiences and perspectives of the participants. This can help to generate a rich and nuanced understanding of the topic under study. However, record keeping also has some limitations. For example, it can be time-consuming and labor-intensive to document and organize large amounts of data. Additionally, there may be ethical considerations related to privacy and confidentiality when recording people's interactions or experiences.

Record keeping can be a valuable qualitative data collection method for generating detailed and comprehensive information about a research topic or phenomenon. However, it should be used in conjunction with other qualitative methods and data sources to provide a more complete understanding of the topic under study.

4. Process of observation

In this strategy of gathering qualitative data, the researcher becomes fully immersed in the environment where his respondents are present, maintains a close eye on them, and makes notes about what they say. This is referred to as the observation process. Other kinds of documentation, such as video and audio recording, photography, and similar techniques, can be utilized in addition to taking notes. Observation is a qualitative data collection method that involves systematically watching and recording behavior, interactions, and events in a natural setting or environment. The process of observation involves several steps, including:

- *Defining the research question*: The researcher must first determine the specific research question or objective that will guide the observation. This involves identifying the phenomenon or behavior that will be observed and the context in which it occurs.
- *Selecting the observation site*: The researcher must select the site or setting where the observation will take place. This may involve identifying a specific location or group of people to observe.
- *Planning the observation*: The researcher must plan the observation, including selecting the appropriate observational techniques and tools, such as checklists, field notes, or audio or video recording.
- *Conducting the observation*: The researcher observes and records the behavior, interactions, and events in the selected setting or environment. This may involve taking field notes, recording audio or video, or using other observational tools.
- *Analyzing the data*: The researcher analyzes the observational data to identify patterns, themes, and insights related to the research question or objective. This may involve organizing and categorizing the data, looking for relationships and connections between different behaviors and events, and identifying key themes and trends.

Observation can be conducted in a variety of settings and contexts, including natural environments, public spaces, and social situations. It is commonly used in fields such as anthropology, sociology, and psychology to gain a deeper understanding of human behavior, social interaction, and cultural practices. One of the main advantages of observation as a qualitative data collection method is that it allows researchers to gain a first-hand and detailed understanding of the phenomenon or behavior being studied. However, there are also limitations to observation, such as the potential for observer bias, the need for specialized training and skills, and the difficulty of generalizing findings beyond the specific context of the observation.

5. Longitudinal studies

The same data source is used frequently over a lengthy period of time in this data collection approach. It is a form of observational research that lasts for a number of years, and in some circumstances, even for decades. Through an empirical investigation of participants with similar qualities, this data collection technique seeks to identify correlations. Longitudinal studies are often considered a quantitative research method, as they typically involve the collection and analysis of numerical data over time. However, longitudinal studies can also incorporate qualitative data collection methods, such as interviews or observations, to provide richer and more nuanced insights into participants' experiences and perspectives.

Qualitative data collection in longitudinal studies can be particularly valuable for understanding the context and meaning behind participants' quantitative data. For example, qualitative interviews conducted at multiple points in time can provide deeper insights into how participants' attitudes and beliefs are changing over time, and how these changes might be related to other factors in their lives.

Qualitative data collection in longitudinal studies can also help to identify unexpected or unanticipated changes or outcomes. By collecting detailed qualitative data, researchers can more easily identify patterns and trends that might not be apparent in quantitative data alone, and can use this information to generate new hypotheses or research questions. Longitudinal studies are typically considered a quantitative research method, the inclusion of qualitative data collection methods can enhance the depth and richness of the data collected, and provide valuable insights into participants' experiences and perspectives over time.

6. Case studies

With this approach, data is acquired by carefully examining case studies. This method's ability to be applied to both simple and difficult subjects exemplifies how adaptable it is. The advantage of this approach is how carefully it combines one or more qualitative data collection techniques to make judgements. Case studies are a qualitative research method that involves the in-depth exploration of a particular case or set of cases. Case studies can be particularly useful for exploring complex or sensitive issues, and can provide detailed insights into the perspectives and experiences of individuals or groups.

One of the key advantages of case studies as a qualitative data collection method is that they allow researchers to explore a particular phenomenon in-depth, and to generate detailed and nuanced data about the experiences and perspectives of participants. Case studies can also be particularly useful for generating new hypotheses or theories, as they allow researchers to explore complex relationships and interactions in real-world contexts.

Case studies can be conducted using a range of qualitative data collection methods, including interviews, observations, and document analysis. Interviews can be particularly useful for gathering detailed information about participants' experiences and perspectives, while observations can provide insights into the context and environment in which the case study is taking place. However, it is important to note that case studies have some limitations as a qualitative data collection method. Because they focus on a particular case or set of cases, the findings may not be generalizable to other contexts or populations. Additionally, the subjective interpretation of the researcher can influence the results of the study. Overall, case studies are a useful qualitative data collection method for exploring complex phenomena and generating detailed insights into the perspectives and experiences of participants. However, researchers should be mindful of the limitations of case studies and the potential for researcher bias when interpreting the data.

3.2.4.2 *Quantitative data*

Quantitative data is information that is expressed as counts or numbers, each of which has a specific numerical value. Data is any quantifiable information that may be used by academics for statistical analysis and mathematical computations so that they can derive practical conclusions. It makes measuring various parameters controllable due to the ease of mathematical derivations they come with. It is usually collected for statistical analysis using surveys, polls, or questionnaires sent across to a specific section of a population. Quantitative data refers to numerical data that can be measured and analyzed using mathematical or statistical methods. This type of data is expressed in terms of quantities or numbers, such as age, height, weight, income, and so on. Quantitative data can be either discrete or continuous. Discrete data takes on specific, distinct values, while continuous data can take on any value within a range. Examples of discrete data include the number of siblings someone has, while examples of continuous data include height or weight. Quantitative data is often used in scientific research, market research, and other fields to analyze and make predictions based on numerical information.

3.2.4.2.1 Types of Quantitative Data

Discrete data Discrete data is a kind of quantitative information that contains countable statistics and non-divisible numbers. Discrete data points are often expressed as integers that correspond to precise values. The phrase "the number of" is frequently used to indicate discrete data, such as the number of customers in a business. Single events that have already happened are typically represented as discrete data. When evaluating discrete data, can examine precise numbers like the quantity sold on a certain day or the number of hours a worker put in over a specific week. Discrete data is a type of quantitative data that represents specific, distinct values. These values are often counted or enumerated, and cannot be divided into smaller units. Discrete data can take only specific numerical values, and there are no intermediate values between these points.

Examples of discrete data include:

Number of children in a family: This is discrete data as it can only take integer values such as 0, 1, 2, 3, etc.
Number of red cars in a parking lot: This is also discrete data as it can only take integer values such as 0, 1, 2, 3, etc.
Number of days a person exercises in a week: This is also discrete data as it can only take integer values such as 0, 1, 2, 3, etc.

Discrete data is often analyzed using statistical methods such as frequency distributions, histograms, and bar charts.

Python program on discrete data:

```python
# Sample discrete data
numbers = [5, 2, 3, 5, 4, 2, 1, 3, 4]

# Count the frequency of each number
number_counts = {}
for number in numbers:
    if number in number_counts:
        number_counts[number] += 1
    else:
        number_counts[number] = 1

# Display the frequency of each number
print("Number Counts:")
for number, count in number_counts.items():
    print(f"{number}: {count}")

# Find unique numbers
unique_numbers = sorted(set(numbers))

# Display unique numbers
print("\nUnique Numbers:")
for number in unique_numbers:
    print(number)

# Sort the numbers
sorted_numbers = sorted(numbers)

# Display the sorted numbers
print("\nSorted Numbers:")
for number in sorted_numbers:
    print(number)

# Calculate the sum of the numbers
sum_of_numbers = sum(numbers)
print(f"\nSum of the numbers: {sum_of_numbers}")
    # Calculate the average of the numbers
    average = sum_of_numbers / len(numbers)
    print(f"Average of the numbers: {average}")
```

Outcome:
Number Counts:
5: 2
2: 2
3: 2
4: 2
1: 1

Unique Numbers:
1
2
3
4
5

(cont'd)

Sorted Numbers:
1
2
2
3
3
4
4
5
5

Sum of the numbers: 29
Average of the numbers: 3.2222222222222223

In this program, we start with a sample discrete data represented by a list called numbers. The numbers represent discrete values within a defined range.

To count the frequency of each number, we iterate over the list and update the number_counts dictionary accordingly. If a number is already in the dictionary, we increment its count; otherwise, we initialize it to 1.

Display the frequency of each number by iterating over the number_counts dictionary.

To find the unique numbers in the data, we convert the list to a set using the set() function to remove duplicates. We then sort the set using the sorted() function to obtain a sorted list of unique numbers.

Display the unique numbers by iterating over the sorted list.

To sort the numbers in ascending order, we use the sorted() function directly on the numbers list.

Calculate the sum of the numbers using the sum() function and display it.

Calculate the average of the numbers by dividing the sum of the numbers by the length of the list and display it.

Can customize the numbers list with your own discrete data or load the data from an external source. Depending on your requirements, you can extend the program to perform additional operations or analyses on the discrete data.

Continuous data Measurable data is referred to as continuous data. The values in this data are not constant and can take on an endless number of different forms. You can also divide these measures up into smaller, independent components. Continuous data is a type of quantitative data that can take any value within a certain range or interval. Unlike discrete data, which consists of specific values that cannot be divided into smaller units, continuous data can be measured to any degree of accuracy. Examples of continuous data include:

- *Height and weight*: These are continuous data as they can take any value within a certain range. For example, a person's height can be measured to any degree of accuracy in inches or centimeters.
- *Temperature*: This is also continuous data as it can be measured to any degree of accuracy in Celsius or Fahrenheit.
- *Time*: Time is also an example of continuous data, as it can be measured to any degree of accuracy in hours, minutes, and seconds.

Continuous data is often analyzed using statistical methods such as histograms, frequency polygons, and scatter plots. These methods help to summarize and visualize the distribution of the data and can be used to make inferences about the population from which the data was collected.

Python program on continuous data:

```
# Sample continuous data
data = [3.2, 2.5, 4.7, 6.1, 5.3, 4.2, 3.9, 5.8]

# Find the minimum and maximum values
minimum = min(data)
maximum = max(data)

print(f"Minimum value: {minimum}")
print(f"Maximum value: {maximum}")

# Calculate the range
range_val = maximum - minimum
print(f"Range: {range_val}")

# Calculate the mean (average)
mean = sum(data) / len(data)
print(f"Mean: {mean}")

# Calculate the median
sorted_data = sorted(data)
n = len(sorted_data)
if n % 2 == 0:
    median = (sorted_data[n // 2 - 1] + sorted_data[n // 2]) / 2
else:
    median = sorted_data[n // 2]
print(f"Median: {median}")

# Calculate the standard deviation
sum_squares = sum((x - mean) ** 2 for x in data)
standard_deviation = (sum_squares / len(data)) ** 0.5
print(f"Standard Deviation: {standard_deviation}")
```

(cont'd)

Outcome:
Minimum value: 2.5
Maximum value: 6.1
Range: 3.5999999999999996
Mean: 4.4624999999999995
Median: 4.45
Standard Deviation: 1.175731155494316

In this program, we start with a sample continuous data represented by a list called data. The data consists of numerical values without any specific gaps or intervals.

Find the minimum and maximum values in the data using the min() and max() functions, respectively.

Calculate the range by subtracting the minimum value from the maximum value.

To calculate the mean (average) of the data, we sum all the values and divide by the number of data points.

The median is the middle value of the sorted data. We first sort the data using the sorted() function. Then, we check if the number of data points is even or odd to determine how to calculate the median accordingly.

The standard deviation is a measure of the spread of the data. We calculate it by first summing the squares of the differences between each data point and the mean. Then, we divide this sum by the number of data points and take the square root.

Interval data Interval data, also called an integer, is defined as a data type which is measured along a scale, in which each point is placed at equal distance from one another. Interval data always appears in the form of numbers or numerical values where the distance between the two points is standardized and equal. Interval data is crucial in market research as well as other types of social, economic, and commercial research. The fact that interval data enables virtually all statistical tests and transformations in order to generate quantitative data is what makes interval data so well-liked and in-demand. Comparing interval data to nominal data, ordinal data, or even ratio data, one can see that interval data has several very unique characteristics. In contrast to ratio data, interval data lacks a clear absolute zero point. Interval data is a type of quantitative data where the distance or interval between two values is meaningful and consistent. The values of interval data are numeric, and the differences between the values are equal or uniform throughout the scale, but there is no true zero point. In other words, there is no inherent meaning to a value of zero in interval data. Examples of interval data include:

Temperature measured in Celsius or Fahrenheit: The difference between 20 °C and 30 °C is the same as the difference between 30 °C and 40 °C, but there is no true zero point on the temperature scale.

IQ scores: IQ scores are interval data because the difference between a score of 100 and 110 is the same as the difference between a score of 110 and 120, but there is no true zero point on the IQ scale.

Dates and times: Dates and times are also interval data because the difference between January 1st and February 1st is the same as the difference between February 1st and March 1st, but there is no true zero point on the calendar.

Interval data is often analyzed using statistical methods such as mean, standard deviation, and correlation coefficient. It is important to note that while interval data can be manipulated using mathematical operations such as addition and subtraction, it cannot be multiplied or divided.

Python program on interval data:

```python
# Sample interval data
temperatures = [24.5, 25.1, 23.8, 26.6, 25.9, 24.2, 23.7, 25.4]

# Find the minimum and maximum values
minimum = min(temperatures)
maximum = max(temperatures)

print(f"Minimum temperature: {minimum}")
print(f"Maximum temperature: {maximum}")

# Calculate the range
range_val = maximum - minimum
print(f"Range: {range_val}")

# Calculate the mean (average)
mean = sum(temperatures) / len(temperatures)
print(f"Mean: {mean}")

# Calculate the median
sorted_temperatures = sorted(temperatures)
n = len(sorted_temperatures)
if n % 2 == 0:
    median = (sorted_temperatures[n // 2 - 1] + sorted_temperatures[n // 2]) / 2
else:
    median = sorted_temperatures[n // 2]

print(f"Median: {median}")

# Calculate the standard deviation
sum_squares = sum((x - mean) ** 2 for x in temperatures)
standard_deviation = (sum_squares / len(temperatures)) ** 0.5
print(f"Standard Deviation: {standard_deviation}")
```

Outcome:
Minimum temperature: 23.7
Maximum temperature: 26.6
Range: 2.900000000000002
Mean: 24.9
Median: 24.8
Standard Deviation: 0.9669539802906859

(cont'd)

In this program, we have a sample interval data represented by a list called temperatures. The data consists of numerical values where the difference between two values is meaningful, but there is no absolute zero point.

Find the minimum and maximum temperatures in the data using the min() and max() functions, respectively.

Calculate the range by subtracting the minimum temperature from the maximum temperature.

To calculate the mean (average) of the temperatures, we sum all the values and divide by the number of data points.

The median is the middle value of the sorted data. We first sort the temperatures using the sorted() function. Then, we check if the number of data points is even or odd to determine how to calculate the median accordingly.

The standard deviation is a measure of the spread of the data. We calculate it by first summing the squares of the differences between each temperature and the mean. Then, we divide this sum by the number of data points and take the square root.

Trend analysis   A common method for analyzing interval data is trend analysis, which is used to identify patterns and insights in survey data across time. In other words, an interval scale survey is used to collect data for a trend analysis on interval data by asking the same question repeatedly. Trend analysis is a statistical technique used to identify and evaluate patterns or trends in quantitative data over time. The aim of trend analysis is to identify changes or shifts in the data that occur over time, as well as to predict future changes based on past trends. This technique can be applied to various fields such as finance, economics, social sciences, and marketing.

- The process of trend analysis involves the following steps:
  - *Collecting data*: Data is collected over a specific period, which could be daily, weekly, monthly, or annually, depending on the nature of the data being analyzed.
  - *Preparing the data*: The collected data is then organized and arranged into a time series dataset.
  - *Graphical representation*: The data is then plotted on a graph to show the trend over time. The graph can be a line graph, scatter plot, or any other appropriate visual representation.
  - *Statistical analysis*: Statistical techniques such as regression analysis, moving averages, and exponential smoothing are used to identify and evaluate trends in the data.
  - *Interpretation*: The trends in the data are then interpreted to identify patterns, relationships, and underlying factors that may have caused the trend.
  - *Prediction*: Finally, based on the identified trends, predictions are made for future trends and changes in the data.

Trend analysis is a valuable tool for decision-making, as it can help individuals and organizations to identify and respond to changes in their environment, plan for the future, and make informed decisions based on data.

Python program on trend analysis:

```
# Trend Analysis with Linear Regression:
Import numpy as np
from sklearn.linear_model import LinearRegression
import matplotlib.pyplot as plt

# Sample data
x = np.array([1, 2, 3, 4, 5, 6, 7])
y = np.array([2, 4, 6, 8, 10, 12, 14])

# Reshape the data to match the expected input shape of the linear regression
model
x = x.reshape(-1, 1)
y = y.reshape(-1, 1)

# Create a linear regression model and fit the data
model = LinearRegression()
model.fit(x, y)

# Predict the y values for the given x values
y_pred = model.predict(x)

# Plot the original data and the predicted trend line
plt.scatter(x, y, color='blue', label='Original data')
plt.plot(x, y_pred, color='red', label='Trend line')
plt.xlabel('x')
plt.ylabel('y')
plt.title('Trend Analysis')
plt.legend()
plt.show()

Outcome:
```

(cont'd)

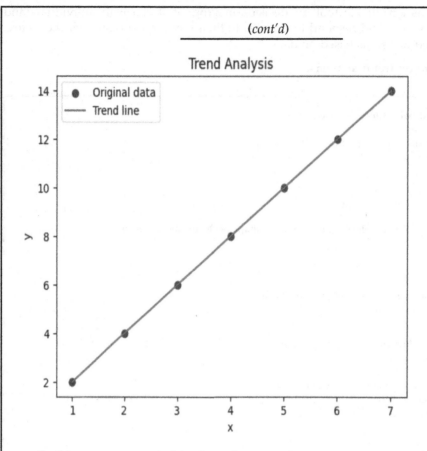

In this program, we start by importing the necessary libraries: numpy for numerical operations, sklearn.linear_model for the linear regression model, and matplotlib. pyplot for data visualization.

Next, define the sample data for the x and y variables. You can modify these arrays with your own data.

Then, reshape the data using reshape (−1, 1) to match the expected input shape of the linear regression model.

Create an instance of the Linear Regression class and fit the data using the fit method.

After fitting the model, we use it to predict the y values for the given x values using the predict method.

Finally, we plot the original data points as blue dots and the predicted trend line as a red line using plt.scatter and plt.plot. We also add labels and a title to the plot and display it using plt.show().

Conjoint analysis Conjoint analysis is a sophisticated method of market research that is frequently used to examine how people choose between options. Which elements are crucial for customers when they have a wide range of options before making a decision. Conjoint analysis is a statistical technique used in market research to determine how consumers value different attributes of a product or service. It helps to understand the relative importance of different features and how they influence consumer choices. Conjoint analysis assumes that consumers make trade-offs between different attributes of a product or service and aims to identify the most important factors that influence their purchasing decisions.

- Conjoint analysis involves the following steps:
  - *Define the attributes*: The first step is to identify the attributes that are important to consumers, such as price, quality, design, and brand.
  - *Create product profiles*: A set of product profiles is then created by combining different levels of the identified attributes.
  - *Develop a questionnaire*: A survey questionnaire is developed, where respondents are asked to choose their preferred product from a set of product profiles.
  - *Analyze the data*: The data collected from the survey is then analyzed using statistical techniques to determine the relative importance of each attribute and the optimal combination of attributes that consumers prefer.
  - *Interpret the results*: Finally, the results are interpreted to identify the key drivers of consumer preference and to make recommendations for product development and marketing strategies.

Conjoint analysis is a powerful tool for businesses to understand consumer preferences and to design products that meet their needs. It can be used in a variety of industries, such as automotive, technology, and consumer goods. It provides insights into consumer behavior that can inform pricing, product design, and marketing strategies.

Python program on conjoint analysis:

```python
# Conjoint Analysis
import pandas as pd
import pyconjoint

# Sample data
data = {
    'Product': ['Product A', 'Product B', 'Product C'],
    'Price': [10, 20, 30],
    'Color': ['Red', 'Blue', 'Red'],
    'Size': ['Small', 'Large', 'Small'],
    'Preference': [5, 7, 3]
}
```

(cont'd)

```
# Create a pandas DataFrame from the data
df = pd.DataFrame(data)

# Define the attribute levels for each attribute
attribute_levels = {
    'Price': [10, 20, 30],
    'Color': ['Red', 'Blue'],

    'Size': ['Small', 'Large']
}

# Create the conjoint experiment
experiment = pyconjoint.Experiment(df, attribute_levels)

# Run the conjoint analysis
results = experiment.run()

# Print the utility scores for each attribute level
print(results['utilities'])

# Print the importance scores for each attribute
print(results['importances'])
```

In this program, we start by importing the necessary libraries: pandas for data manipulation and pyconjoint for performing the conjoint analysis. Next, define the sample data as a dictionary, where each key represents an attribute, and the corresponding values represent the attribute levels and customer preferences.

Create a pandas DataFrame from the data using pd.DataFrame(). Define the attribute levels for each attribute in a dictionary called attribute_levels. This dictionary maps each attribute to its respective levels. Create the conjoint experiment using pyconjoint. Experiment(), passing in the DataFrame and the attribute levels. Run the conjoint analysis using experiment.run () and store the results in the results variable. Print the utility scores for each attribute level using results ['utilities']. Print the importance scores for each attribute using results['importances'].

TURF analysis A marketer might use the TURF analysis method, which stands for Totally Unduplicated Reach and Frequency analysis, to assess the potential of market research for a variety of goods and services. It assesses the frequency and interval data of the clients reached by a specific communication source. Researchers utilize this study technique to determine whether a new good or service will be favorably received in the target market. The main application of this analysis technique was for creating media campaigns, but it has since been extended to product distribution and line analysis. TURF analysis is a marketing research technique that helps businesses determine the potential reach of a product or service in a given market. It is used to identify the optimal combination of products or services to offer to maximize the total reach of a target audience.

The process of TURF analysis involves the following steps:

- *Define the target audience*: The first step is to define the target audience for the product or service.
- *Identify the product or service attributes*: The next step is to identify the different attributes or features of the product or service that may be of interest to the target audience.
- *Create product/service combinations*: A set of different product or service combinations is then created by varying the attributes of the product or service.
- *Conduct a survey*: A survey is then conducted to determine the level of interest in each product or service combination among the target audience.
- *Analyze the data*: The data collected from the survey is then analyzed using statistical techniques to determine the total reach of each product or service combination and to identify the optimal combination that maximizes the total reach of the target audience.
- *Interpret the results*: Finally, the results are interpreted to identify the most effective product or service combination to offer to the target audience.

TURF analysis is a valuable tool for businesses to understand the potential reach of their products or services and to develop effective marketing strategies. It can be used in a variety of industries, such as entertainment, consumer goods, and healthcare. TURF analysis provides insights into the preferences of the target audience, which can inform product development, pricing, and promotion strategies.

Python program on TURF analysis:

```
# TURF Analysis:
import pandas as pd
import pyturfcut

# Sample data
data = {
    'Respondent': [1, 2, 3, 4, 5, 6, 7, 8, 9, 10],
    'Attribute1': [1, 1, 0, 1, 0, 0, 1, 1, 0, 0],
    'Attribute2': [0, 1, 0, 1, 1, 0, 1, 0, 0, 1],
    'Attribute3': [1, 0, 1, 0, 0, 1, 1, 0, 1, 1]
}

# Create a pandas DataFrame from the data
df = pd.DataFrame(data)

# Define the attributes to be included in the TURF analysis
attributes = ['Attribute1', 'Attribute2', 'Attribute3']

# Perform the TURF analysis
results = pyturfcut.calculate_turf(df, attributes)

# Print the TURF analysis results
print(results)
```

(cont'd)

In this program, we start by importing the necessary libraries: pandas for data manipulation and pyturfcut for performing the TURF analysis.

Next, define the sample data as a dictionary, where the keys represent the attributes and the values represent the presence or absence of those attributes for each respondent.

Create a pandas DataFrame from the data using pd.DataFrame().

Define the attributes to be included in the TURF analysis by listing their column names in the attributes list.

Perform the TURF analysis using pyturfcut.calculate_turf(), passing in the DataFrame and the attributes.

The TURF analysis results, which include the optimal combinations of attributes, reach, and frequency, are stored in the results variable.

Print the TURF analysis results using print(results).

3.2.4.2.2 Quantitative data collection methods

Probability sampling   Probability sampling is a sampling technique that involves random selection to gather data from the target audience, allowing researchers to obtain a probability statement. This approach offers researchers a chance to collect information from specific population members they wish to investigate, making it one of its most advantageous features. Additionally, the fact that the data was drawn at random from the chosen sample eliminates the risk of sampling bias.

There are three significant types of probability sampling:

- *Simple random sampling*: More often, the targeted demographic is chosen for inclusion in the sample.
- *Systematic random sampling*: Any of the targeted demographic would be included in the sample, but only the first unit for inclusion in the sample is selected randomly, rest are selected in the ordered fashion as if 1 out of every 10 people on the list.
- *Stratified random sampling*: It allows selecting each unit from a particular group of the targeted audience while creating a sample. It is useful when the researchers are selective about including a specific set of people in the sample, i.e., only males or females, managers or executives, people working within a particular industry.

Surveys/questionnaires   Online questionnaires and surveys made with survey software are essential for gathering data online for both quantitative and qualitative research. The surveys are created in a way that validates the actions and confidence of the responders. The majority of quantitative surveys frequently use checklists and rating scale items because they make measuring respondents' attitudes and their behaviors. There are two significant types of survey questionnaires used to collect online data for quantitative market research.

Web-based questionnaire   This is one of the most popular and reliable ways to conduct online or internet-based research. In a web-based survey, respondents receive an email containing a link to the survey, which when clicked, directs them to a secure online survey platform where they can complete the survey or take it. Researchers favor web-based surveys more because they are more time and money efficient, have a wider audience, and are more cost effective. A web-based survey offers the most flexibility because respondents can complete it whenever it is convenient for them on a desktop, laptop, tablet, or mobile device.

A web-based questionnaire is a survey that is administered online through a web-based platform. The questionnaire can be accessed through a link and completed using a web browser on a computer or mobile device. Web-based questionnaires are increasingly popular due to their convenience and cost-effectiveness compared to traditional paper-based questionnaires.

- The process of creating a web-based questionnaire involves the following steps:
  - *Define the research question*: The first step is to define the research question and the objectives of the survey.
  - *Identify the target audience*: The next step is to identify the target audience for the survey and the best way to reach them online.
  - *Choose a web-based platform*: There are many web-based platforms available for creating and administering surveys, such as Survey Monkey, Google Forms, and Qualtrics. Choose the one that best fits your needs and budget.
  - *Design the questionnaire*: Design the questionnaire with clear and concise questions that are easy to understand and answer. Make sure to use skip logic and branching to ensure that respondents only answer questions relevant to them.
  - *Test the questionnaire*: Test the questionnaire on a small group of people to ensure that it works correctly and is easy to use.
  - *Distribute the questionnaire*: Distribute the questionnaire to the target audience using email, social media, or other online channels. Make sure to provide clear instructions on how to access and complete the questionnaire.
  - *Analyze the data*: Once the survey is completed, the data can be analyzed using statistical software such as SPSS or Excel.

Web-based questionnaires offer several advantages over traditional paper-based surveys. They are cost-effective, easy to administer, and can reach a wider audience. They also allow for real-time data analysis and can provide instant feedback to respondents. However, web-based questionnaires may suffer from low response rates, and respondents may not be representative of the general population. Careful planning and execution are needed to ensure that the survey is effective and yields valid and reliable results.

Mail questionnaire   A mail questionnaire enables the researcher to reach a variety of audiences by mailing the survey to a large portion of the sample population. The mail questionnaire usually comes in a packet with a cover sheet that informs the audience about the type of study being done and why, as well as a pre-paid return to gather data online. Even though the postal survey has a larger churn rate than other quantitative data gathering techniques, including incentives and reminders to finish the survey helps to significantly lower the churn rate. A mail questionnaire is a survey that is administered by sending a paper questionnaire by mail to potential respondents. Mail questionnaires have been widely used in the past, but with the advent of web-based questionnaires, they have become less popular.

The process of creating a mail questionnaire involves the following steps:

- *Define the research question*: The first step is to define the research question and the objectives of the survey.
- *Identify the target audience*: The next step is to identify the target audience for the survey and obtain their mailing addresses.
- *Design the questionnaire*: Design the questionnaire with clear and concise questions that are easy to understand and answer. Make sure to use skip logic and branching to ensure that respondents only answer questions relevant to them.
- *Test the questionnaire*: Test the questionnaire on a small group of people to ensure that it works correctly and is easy to use.
- *Print and mail the questionnaire*: Print and mail the questionnaire to the target audience along with a cover letter explaining the purpose of the survey and instructions on how to complete and return the questionnaire.
- *Follow-up*: Follow-up with non-respondents by sending reminders or contacting them by phone to encourage them to complete the questionnaire.
- *Collect and analyze the data*: Once the survey is completed and returned, the data can be analyzed using statistical software such as SPSS or Excel.

Mail questionnaires have several advantages, such as allowing respondents to complete the survey at their own pace, providing a written record of responses, and reaching a wider audience than web-based questionnaires. However, mail questionnaires may suffer from low response rates, and respondents may not always provide accurate or complete information. They are also more time-consuming and expensive to administer than web-based questionnaires. Careful planning and execution are needed to ensure that the survey is effective and yields valid and reliable results.

Observations It is a rather easy and uncomplicated means of gathering quantitative data, as the name would imply. By using approaches like counting the number of individuals present at a certain event at a specific time and a specific venue, or the number of people attending the event in a defined spot, researchers can get quantitative data through systematic observations in this manner. More often than not, researchers use a naturalistic observation strategy to get quantitative data, which calls for good observational abilities and senses in order to gather data about the "what" rather than the "why" and "how." Naturalistic observation is used to collect both types of data; qualitative and quantitative. However, structured observation is more used to collect quantitative rather than qualitative data.

Structured observation: In contrast to naturalistic or participant observation, this form of observation method requires the researcher to make thorough observations of one or more specified behaviors in a more extensive or structured context. In a structured observation, the researchers narrow their attention to only a few key behaviors of interest rather than watching everything. It enables them to put the behaviors they are seeing into numbers. It is frequently referred to as "coding" when the observations call for the observers to make a judgment. To do this, a set of target behaviors must be precisely defined.

Document review in quantitative data collection   Document review is a process used to collect data after reviewing the existing documents. It is an efficient and effective way of gathering data as documents are manageable and are the practical resource to get qualified data from the past. Apart from strengthening and supporting the research by providing supplementary research data, document review has emerged as one of the beneficial methods to gather quantitative research data. Three primary document types are being analyzed for collecting supporting quantitative research data:

- *Public records*: The official, continuing records of an organization are examined for further investigation as part of this document review. For instance, annual reports, policy guides, student events, university game activities, etc.
- *Personal documents*: This kind of document analysis examines private reports of people's behaviors, conduct, health, physique, etc. as opposed to public records. For instance, the size and weight of the students, the travel time students take to go to school, etc.
- *Physical evidence*: Physical evidence or physical documents deal with previous achievements of an individual or of an organization in terms of monetary and scalable growth.

Table 3.1 shows the difference between quantitative and qualitative data.

TABLE 3.1   Difference between quantitative and qualitative data.

Basis for comparison	Qualitative data	Quantitative data
Meaning	Qualitative data is the data in which the classification of objects is based on attributes and properties	Quantitative data is the type of data which can be measured and expressed numerically
Data type	Nominal and ordinal	Ratio and interval
Research methodology	Exploratory	Conclusive
Approach	Subjective	Objective
Analysis	Non-statistical	Statistical
Collection of data	Unstructured	Structured
Determines	Depth of understanding	Level of occurrences
Asks	Why	How many or how much
Samples	Small number of non-representative samples	Large number of representatives samples

3.3 Views of data

One of the most promising and in-demand job options for competent professionals is data science, a multidisciplinary discipline that is constantly evolving. In order to extract knowledge and insights from noisy, structured, and unstructured data and apply knowledge and actionable insights from data across a wide range of application domains, it is considered to be a strong application that encompasses and uses scientific methods, processes, algorithms, and systems. Applying the idea of in-depth analysis of a vast amount of data, data science involves taking the raw, structured, and unstructured data and extracting something useful from it. The use of statistical approaches and algorithms, scientific procedures, various other technologies, etc., are required to extract the useful information from massive volumes of data. Data science therefore has an impact on and influences the types of applications in the majority of fields, including search engines, transportation, finance, e-commerce, health care, image recognition, targeting recommendation, airline routing planning, gaming, medicine and drug development, delivery logistics, etc. Statistical analysis is the process of collecting and analyzing data in order to discern patterns and trends. It is a method for removing bias from evaluating data by employing numerical analysis. This technique is useful for collecting the interpretations of research, developing statistical models, and planning surveys and studies. With the aid of statistical analysis, which is a scientific instrument, enormous amounts of data may be gathered, analyzed, and turned into useful information by spotting common patterns and trends. Simply said, statistical analysis is a method for data analysis that assists in deriving meaningful conclusions from unstructured and raw data.

3.3.1 Types of statistical analysis

3.3.1.1 Descriptive analysis

In descriptive analysis, data must be gathered, understood, summarized, and statistically analyzed in order to be presented as tables, charts, and graphs. It just makes the complicated data easier to read and understand, rather than offering any conclusions. Descriptive analysis is a statistical analysis that involves describing and summarizing data using measures such as central tendency, variability, and frequency distribution. It is often used to explore and understand data in a meaningful way, without making any conclusions or predictions about the data.

The main steps involved in descriptive analysis include:

- *Collecting data*: The first step in descriptive analysis is collecting the data that needs to be analyzed. This can be done through surveys, experiments, or observational studies.
- *Organizing and summarizing the data*: Once the data is collected, it needs to be organized and summarized. This involves calculating measures such as mean, median, mode, variance, and standard deviation to describe the central tendency and variability of the data.
- *Creating frequency distributions*: Frequency distributions are used to summarize the data in terms of the frequency of occurrence of each value or range of values. This can be done using histograms, bar charts, or pie charts.

- *Interpreting the data*: After organizing and summarizing the data, it is important to interpret the results. This involves analyzing the measures of central tendency and variability, looking for patterns in the frequency distributions, and drawing conclusions based on the findings.

Descriptive analysis is useful in a wide range of fields, such as market research, public health, and social sciences. It can be used to describe the characteristics of a population, to identify trends and patterns in the data, and to summarize the data in a meaningful way that can be easily understood by others. Descriptive analysis is an important tool for understanding data and providing insights that can be used to inform decision-making.

3.3.1.2 Inferential analysis

The inferential statistical analysis focuses on drawing meaningful conclusions on the basis of the data analyzed. It studies the relationship between different variables or makes predictions for the whole population. Inferential analysis is a statistical analysis that involves drawing conclusions or making predictions about a population based on a sample of data. It involves using sample data to infer or make inferences about the population as a whole.

- The main steps involved in inferential analysis include:
  - Formulating *a research question or hypothesis*: The first step in inferential analysis is to formulate a research question or hypothesis that can be tested using statistical analysis.
  - *Selecting a sample*: The next step is to select an illustrative sample from the population of interest. It is important to use random sampling techniques to ensure that the sample is illustrative of the population.
  - *Conducting statistical tests*: Once the sample data is collected, statistical tests are conducted to draw conclusions or make predictions about the population. These tests can include hypothesis testing, confidence intervals, and regression analysis.
  - Interpreting *the results*: After conducting statistical tests, it is important to interpret the results in the context of the research question or hypothesis. This involves assessing the strength of the evidence and drawing conclusions about the population.

Inferential analysis is useful in a wide range of fields, such as medicine, social sciences, and engineering. It can be used to test hypotheses, make predictions, and estimate population parameters. However, it is important to ensure that the sample is representative of the population and that the statistical tests are appropriate for the data being analyzed. Incorrect or inappropriate statistical analysis can lead to incorrect conclusions and predictions.

3.3.1.3 Predictive analysis

A sort of statistical analysis known as predictive statistical analysis examines data to identify historical trends and make predictions about the future based on those trends. The statistical analysis of data is carried out using AI, data mining, and machine learning techniques. Predictive analysis is a statistical analysis that involves using data, statistical algorithms, and machine learning techniques to make predictions about future events or behaviors. It involves analyzing historical data to identify patterns and relationships, and then using this information to make predictions about future outcomes.

- The main steps involved in predictive analysis include:
  - *Collecting and preparing data*: The first step in predictive analysis is to collect and prepare the data that will be used for analysis. This can involve cleaning, transforming, and integrating data from multiple sources.
  - *Exploratory data analysis (EDA)*: Once the data is prepared, it is important to conduct EDA to identify patterns and relationships in the data. This can involve using techniques such as correlation analysis, regression analysis, and data visualization.
  - *Building predictive models*: Once the patterns and relationships in the data are identified, predictive models can be built using statistical algorithms and machine learning techniques. These models can be used to make predictions about future events or behaviors.
  - *Evaluating and refining models*: Once the predictive models are built, they need to be evaluated to ensure that they are accurate and effective. This involves testing the models on new data to see how well they predict outcomes. If the models are not accurate, they may need to be refined or adjusted.
  - *Deploying and monitoring models*: Once the models are refined and effective, they can be deployed in a production environment and monitored over time to ensure that they continue to be accurate and effective.

Predictive analysis is useful in a wide range of fields, such as finance, marketing, and healthcare. It can be used to identify patterns and trends in data, make predictions about future events or behaviors, and inform decision-making. However, it is important to ensure that the data is accurate and representative, and that the predictive models are evaluated and refined to ensure their effectiveness over time.

3.3.1.4 Prescriptive analysis

The prescriptive analysis conducts the analysis of data and prescribes the best course of action based on the results. It is a type of statistical analysis that helps you make an informed decision. Prescriptive analysis is a statistical analysis that involves identifying the best course of action to take in a given situation based on data, business rules, and constraints. It involves using optimization and simulation techniques to determine the best decision or action to take.

- The main steps involved in prescriptive analysis include:
  - *Collecting and preparing data*: The first step in prescriptive analysis is to collect and prepare the data that will be used for analysis. This can involve cleaning, transforming, and integrating data from multiple sources.
  - *Analyzing and modeling data*: Once the data is prepared, it is important to analyze and model the data to identify patterns, relationships, and constraints. This can involve using techniques such as regression analysis, decision trees, and clustering.
  - *Identifying constraints and objectives*: Based on the data analysis, constraints and objectives are identified that need to be taken into account when making decisions.

For example, there may be constraints on resources or time, or objectives related to profitability or customer satisfaction.

- *Developing optimization and simulation models*: Based on the constraints and objectives, optimization and simulation models are developed to identify the best course of action to take. These models can help identify the optimal allocation of resources or the best decision given the constraints and objectives.
- *Implementing and monitoring the decision*: Once the optimal decision is identified, it is important to implement and monitor the decision over time to ensure that it continues to be effective.

Prescriptive analysis is useful in a wide range of fields, such as logistics, supply chain management, and finance. It can be used to identify the best course of action to take in a given situation based on data and business rules. However, it is important to ensure that the data is accurate and representative, and that the models are designed and evaluated to ensure their effectiveness over time.

3.3.1.5 *Exploratory data analysis*

Inferential analysis and exploratory analysis are similar, but exploratory analysis entails looking into unidentified data relationships. It examines any potential connections in the data. EDA is a process of examining and understanding the structure and characteristics of a dataset. It involves using statistical and visualization techniques to summarize and analyze the main features of the data, such as its distribution, relationships between variables, and outliers.

- The main steps involved in EDA include:
  - *Data collection and preparation*: The first step in EDA is to collect and prepare the data that will be used for analysis. This can involve cleaning, transforming, and integrating data from multiple sources.
  - *Data visualization*: Once the data is prepared, it is important to visualize the data using techniques such as histograms, box plots, and scatter plots. These visualizations can help identify patterns and relationships in the data.
  - *Summary statistics*: In addition to data visualization, summary statistics such as mean, median, and standard deviation can be used to summarize the data and identify its main features.
  - *Data cleaning and transformation*: EDA also involves cleaning and transforming the data to address issues such as missing data, outliers, and skewness.
  - *Hypothesis testing*: Finally, hypothesis testing can be used to test assumptions about the data and identify relationships between variables.

EDA is useful for identifying patterns and relationships in the data, detecting outliers and missing values, and identifying potential issues with the data. It can help inform the development of predictive and prescriptive models by providing insights into the main features of the data. However, it is important to ensure that the data is representative and accurate before conducting EDA, as this can impact the results of the analysis.

Python program on EDA:

```python
import pandas as pd
import matplotlib.pyplot as plt

# Read the data from a CSV file
data = pd.read_csv('your_data.csv')

# Display the first few rows of the dataset
print("First few rows of the dataset:")
print(data.head())

# Display the summary statistics of the dataset
print("Summary statistics:")
print(data.describe())

# Check the data types of each column
print("Data types:")
print(data.dtypes)

# Check the missing values in the dataset
print("Missing values:")
print(data.isnull().sum())

# Visualize the distribution of a numerical variable
plt.hist(data['numerical_column'], bins=10)
plt.xlabel('Value')
plt.ylabel('Frequency')
plt.title('Histogram of Numerical Column')
plt.show()

# Visualize the relationship between two numerical variables
plt.scatter(data['numerical_column1'], data['numerical_column2'])
plt.xlabel('Numerical Column 1')
plt.ylabel('Numerical Column 2')
plt.title('Scatter Plot of Numerical Columns')
plt.show()

# Visualize the distribution of a categorical variable
plt.bar(data['categorical_column'].value_counts().index,
data['categorical_column'].value_counts().values)
plt.xlabel('Category')
plt.ylabel('Count')
plt.title('Bar Chart of Categorical Column')
plt.show()

# Generate a correlation matrix for numerical variables

correlation_matrix        =        data[['numerical_column1',        'numerical_column2',
'numerical_column3']].corr()
print("Correlation Matrix:")
print(correlation_matrix)
```

(cont'd)

In this program, we assume you have a dataset stored in a CSV file named your_data. csv. Modify this file name to match the name of your dataset.

Start by importing the necessary libraries: pandas for data manipulation and analysis, and matplotlib.pyplot for data visualization.

Read the data from the CSV file using pd. read_csv() and store it in the data variable.

Display the first few rows of the dataset using data.head().

Display the summary statistics of the dataset using data.describe().

Check the data types of each column using data.dtypes.

Check the missing values in the dataset using data.isnull().sum().

Visualize the distribution of a numerical variable using plt.hist().

Visualize the relationship between two numerical variables using plt.scatter().

Visualize the distribution of a categorical variable using plt.bar().

Generate a correlation matrix for numerical variables using data.corr().

3.3.1.6 Causal analysis

The causal statistical analysis focuses on determining the cause and effect relationship between different variables within the raw data. In simple words, it determines why something happens and its effect on other variables. This methodology can be used by businesses to determine the reason for failure. Causal analysis is a statistical method used to investigate the relationship between a dependent variable and one or more independent variables to determine whether there is a cause-and-effect relationship between them. In other words, it involves identifying whether changes in one variable cause changes in another variable, while holding all other variables constant.

- The main steps involved in causal analysis include:
  - *Identify the variables*: The first step in causal analysis is to identify the dependent variable and the independent variable(s) that may have a causal effect on the dependent variable.
  - *Formulate a hypothesis*: Based on the relationship between the variables, formulate a hypothesis that explains the causal relationship.
  - *Collect data*: Collect data on the dependent and independent variables for the relevant time period.
  - *Analyze the data*: Use statistical techniques such as regression analysis or structural equation modeling to analyze the data and test the hypothesis.
  - *Draw conclusions*: Based on the results of the analysis, draw conclusions about the causal relationship between the variables.

Causal analysis is used in various fields such as economics, social sciences, and healthcare to identify the factors that influence outcomes. It can help organizations and policymakers make informed decisions about strategies and interventions that may lead to positive outcomes. However, it is important to use caution when interpreting the results of causal analysis, as there may be other factors that influence the dependent variable that were not measured in the study.

3.3.1.7 Different statistical method

3.3.1.7.1 Central tendency

A single number that seeks to characterize a set of data by pinpointing the center position within that set of data is referred to as a measure of central tendency. As a result, measures of central location are occasionally used to refer to measures of central tendency. They also fit within the category of summary statistics. If anyone are probably most familiar with the mean (sometimes known as the average), but there are additional central tendency measures, including the median and the mode. The mean, median and mode are all valid measures of central tendency, but under different conditions, some measures of central tendency become more appropriate to use than others. In the following sections, will look at the mean, mode and median, and learn how to calculate them and under what conditions they are most appropriate to be used.

Mean The mean (or average) is the most popular and well known measure of central tendency. It can be used with both discrete and continuous data, although its use is most often with continuous data. The mean is equal to the sum of all the values in the dataset divided by the number of values in the dataset. So, if we have $x_1, x_2, x_3.........x_n,$

$$\text{Then ean} = (x_1 + x_2 + x_3 + x_4 + x_5)/n$$

Why do not use the mean The mean has one main disadvantage: It is particularly susceptible to the influence of outliers. These are values that are unusual compared to the rest of the dataset by being especially small or large in numerical value. For example, consider the wages of staff at a factory shown in Table 3.2.

The mean salary for these 10 staff is $30.7k. However, inspecting the raw data suggests that this mean value might not be the best way to accurately reflect the typical salary of a worker, as most workers have salaries in the $12k to 18k range. The mean is being skewed by the two large salaries. Therefore, in this situation, would like to have a better measure of central tendency. Another time when usually prefer the median over the mean (or mode) is when our data is skewed. If we consider the normal distribution as this is the most frequently assessed in statistics when the data is perfectly normal, the mean, median, and mode are identical. Moreover, they all represent the most typical value in the dataset. However, as the data becomes skewed the mean loses its ability to provide the best central location for the data because the skewed data is dragging it away from the typical value. However, the median best retains this position and is not as strongly influenced by the skewed values.

TABLE 3.2 Wages of staff at a factory.

Staff	1	2	3	4	5	6	7	8	9	10
Salary	15	18	16	14	15	15	12	17	90	95

Median The median is the middle score for a set of data that has been arranged in order of magnitude. The median is less affected by outliers and skewed data. In order to calculate the median, suppose we have the data below:

Mode The mode is the most frequent score in our dataset. On a histogram it represents the highest bar in a bar chart or histogram. Therefore, sometimes consider the mode as being the most popular option. Table 3.3 shows that variable and their central tendency.

There can often be a "best" measure of central tendency with regards to the data are analyzing, but there is no one "best" measure of central tendency. This is because whether use the median, mean or mode will depend on the type of data they have, such as nominal or continuous data; whether your data has outliers and/or is skewed; and what are trying to show from the data. It is usually inappropriate to use the mean in such situations where data is skewed. All continuous data has a median, mode, and mean. However, strictly speaking, ordinal data has a median and mode only, and nominal data has only a mode. However, a consensus has not been reached among statisticians about whether the mean can be used with ordinal data, and can often see a mean reported for Likert data in research. The mean is usually the best measure of central tendency to use when the data distribution is continuous and symmetrical, such as when data is normally distributed. However, it all depends on what are trying to show from the data. The mode is the least used of the measures of central tendency and can only be used when dealing with nominal data. For this reason, the mode will be the best measure of central tendency (as it is the only one appropriate to use) when dealing with nominal data. The mean and/or median are usually preferred when dealing with all other types of data, but this does not mean it is never used with these data types. The median is usually preferred to other measures of central tendency when the dataset is skewed or are dealing with ordinal data. However, the mode can also be appropriate in these situations, but is not as commonly used as the median. The median is usually preferred in these situations because the value of the mean can be distorted by the outliers. However, it will depend on how influential the outliers are. If they do not significantly distort the mean, using the mean as the measure of central tendency will usually be preferred.

Variance and standard deviation In statistics, the standard deviation is a measure of the amount of variation or dispersion of a set of values. A low standard deviation indicates that the values tend to be close to the mean of the set, while a high standard deviation indicates that the values are spread out over a wider range. In statistics, variance and

TABLE 3.3 Variable and their central tendency.

Type of variable	Best measures of central tendency
Nominal	Mode
Ordinal	Median
Interval/ratio (not skewed)	Mean
Interval/ratio (skewed)	Median

standard deviation are related with each other since the square root of variance is considered the standard deviation for the given dataset. Below are the definitions of variance and standard deviation.

Variance is the measure of how notably a collection of data is spread out. If all the data values are identical, then it indicates the variance is zero. All non-zero variances are considered to be positive. A little variance represents that the data points are close to the mean, and to each other, whereas if the data points are highly spread out from the mean and from one another indicates the high variance. In short, the variance is defined as the average of the squared distance from each point to the mean.

Standard Deviation is a measure which shows how much variation (such as spread, dispersion, spread) from the mean exists. The standard deviation indicates a "typical" deviation from the mean. It is a popular measure of variability because it returns to the original units of measure of the dataset. Like the variance, if the data points are close to the mean, there is a small variation whereas the data points are highly spread out from the mean, then it has a high variance. Standard deviation calculates the extent to which the values differ from the average. Standard deviation, the most widely used measure of dispersion, is based on all values. Therefore, a change in even one value affects the value of standard deviation. It is independent of origin but not of scale. It is also useful in certain advanced statistical problems.

Python program on variance and standard deviation:

```
# Variance and Standard Deviation
import numpy as np

# Sample dataset
data = [4, 5, 6, 7, 8, 9]

# Calculate variance
variance = np.var(data)

# Calculate standard deviation
std_dev = np.std(data)

# Print the results
print("Variance:", variance)
print("Standard Deviation:", std_dev)

Outcome:
Variance: 2.9166666666666665
Standard Deviation: 1.707825127659933
```

In this program, we start by importing the numpy library, which provides functions for mathematical operations and statistical calculations. Define a sample dataset in the data list. Modify this list to include your own dataset. Calculate the variance using np.var(data), which computes the sample variance of the dataset. Calculate the standard deviation using np.std (data), which calculates the sample standard deviation of the dataset. Print the results using print() statements.

Z-score Z-score is a statistical measurement that describes a value's relationship to the mean of a group of values. Z-score is measured in terms of standard deviations from the mean. If a Z-score is 0, it indicates that the data point's score is identical to the mean score. A Z-score of 1.0 would indicate a value that is one standard deviation from the mean. Z-scores may be positive or negative, with a positive value indicating the score is above the mean and a negative score indicating it is below the mean.

In investing and trading, Z-scores are measures of an instrument's variability and can be used by traders to help determine volatility. The Z-score is sometimes confused with the Altman Z-score, which is calculated using factors taken from a company's financial reports. The Altman Z-score is used to calculate the likelihood that a business will go bankrupt in the next two years, while the Z-score can be used to determine how far a stock's return differs from it's average return and much more.

The statistical formula for a value's Z-score is calculated using the following formula:

$$z = (x - \mu)/\sigma$$

where z is a Z-score, x is the value being evaluated, μ is the mean, and σ is the standard deviation.

In its most basic form, the Z-score allows you to determine how far (measured in standard deviations) the returns for the stock you're evaluating are from the mean of a sample of stocks. The average score you have could be the mean of a stock's annual return, the average return of the index it is listed on, or the average return of a selection of stocks you've picked. Some traders use the Z-scores in more advanced evaluation methods, such as weighting each stock's return to use factor investing, where stocks are evaluated based on specific attributes using Z-scores and standard deviation. In the forex markets, traders use Z-scores and confidence limits to test the capability of a trading system to generate winning and losing streaks.

Quartiles Quartiles are values that separate the data into four equal parts.
The quartiles (Q0, Q1, Q2, Q3, Q4) are the values that separate each quarter.
Between Q0 and Q1 are the 25% lowest values in the data. Between Q1 and Q2 are the next 25%. And so on.

- Q0 is the smallest value in the data.
- Q1 is the value separating the first quarter from the second quarter of the data.
- Q2 is the middle value (median), separating the bottom from the top half.
- Q3 is the value separating the third quarter from the fourth quarter
- Q4 is the largest value in the data.

Percentile Percentiles arc values that separate the data into 100 equal parts.
For example, the 95th percentile separates the lowest 95% of the values from the top 5%
The 25th percentile ($P25\%$) is the same as the first quartile ($Q1$).
The 50th percentile ($P50\%$) is the same as the second quartile ($Q2$) and the median.
The 75th percentile ($P75\%$) is the same as the third quartile ($Q3$).

Python program on percentile and quartile:

```python
# Percentile and Quartile
import numpy as np

# Sample dataset
data = [12, 34, 56, 23, 45, 67, 89, 90, 32, 67]

# Calculate quartiles
q1 = np.percentile(data, 25)
q2 = np.percentile(data, 50)
q3 = np.percentile(data, 75)

# Calculate percentiles
p10 = np.percentile(data, 10)
p90 = np.percentile(data, 90)

# Print the results
print("Quartiles:")
print("Q1:", q1)
print("Q2:", q2)
print("Q3:", q3)

print("Percentiles:")
print("P10:", p10)
print("P90:", p90)
```

Outcome:
Quartiles:
Q1: 32.5
Q2: 50.5
Q3: 67.0
Percentiles:
P10: 21.9
P90: 89.1

In this program, we start by importing the numpy library, which provides functions for mathematical operations and statistical calculations. Define a sample dataset in the data list. Modify this list to include your own dataset. Calculate the quartiles using np.percentile(data, q), where data is the dataset and q is the desired percentile (25 for $Q1$, 50 for $Q2$, and 75 for $Q3$).

Calculate percentiles using np.percentile (data, p), where data is the dataset and p is the desired percentile (e.g., 10 for $P10$ and 90 for $P90$). Finally, we print the results using print() statements.

3.4 Measurement and scaling concepts

Measurement is the actual assignment of a number from 1 to 100 to each respondent. Scaling is the process of placing the respondents on a continuum with respect to their attitude toward department stores. There are two main types of measurement scales, namely; comparative scales and non-comparative scales.

3.4.1 Comparative scales

In comparative scaling, respondents are asked to make a comparison between one object and the other. When used in market research, customers are asked to evaluate one product in direct comparison to the others. Comparative scales can be further divided into pair comparison, rank order, constant sum, and q-sort scales.

3.4.1.1 Paired comparison scale

Paired comparison scale is a scaling technique that presents the respondents with two objects at a time and asks them to choose one according to a predefined criterion. Product researchers use it in comparative product research by asking customers to choose the most preferred to them in between two closely related products. For example, there are three new features in the last release of a software product. But the company is planning to remove 1 of these features in the new release. Therefore, the product researchers are performing a comparative analysis of the most and least preferred feature. Which feature is most preferred to you between the following pairs?

Filter—Voice recorder
Filter—Video recorder
Voice recorder—Video recorder

3.4.1.2 Rank order scale

In rank order scaling technique, respondents are simultaneously provided with multiple options and asked to rank them in order of priority based on a predefined criterion. It is mostly used in marketing to measure preference for a brand, product, or feature. When used in competitive analysis, the respondent may be asked to rank a group of brands in terms of personal preference, product quality, customer service, etc. The results of this data collection are usually obtained in the conjoint analysis, as it forces customers to discriminate among options. The rank order scale is a type of ordinal scale because it orders the attributes from the most preferred to the least preferred but does not have a specific distance between the attributes. For example: Rank the following brands from the most preferred to the least preferred.

Coca-Cola
Pepsi-Cola
Dr-pepper
Mountain Dew

3.4.1.3 Constant sum scale

Constant sum scale is a type of measurement scale where the respondents are asked to allocate a constant sum of units such as points, dollars, chips, or chits among the stimulus objects according to some specified criterion. The constant sum scale assigns a fixed number of units to each attribute, reflecting the importance a respondent attach to it. This type of measurement scale can be used to determine what influences a customer's decision when choosing which product to buy. For example, you may wish to determine how important price, size, fragrance, and packaging is to a customer when choosing which brand of perfume to buy. Some of the major setbacks of this technique are that respondents may be confused and end up allocating more or fewer points than those specified. The researchers are left to deal with a group of data that is not uniform and may be difficult to analyze.

3.4.1.4 Q-sort scale

Q-sort scale is a type of measurement scale that uses a rank order scaling technique to sort similar objects with respect to some criterion. The respondents sort the number of statements or attitudes into piles, usually of 11. The Q-sort scaling helps in assigning ranks to different objects within the same group, and the differences among the groups (piles) are clearly visible. It is a fast way of facilitating discrimination among a relatively large set of attributes. For example, a new restaurant that is just preparing its menu may want to collect some information about what potential customers like: The document provided contains a list of 50 meals. Please choose 10 meals you like, 30 meals you are neutral about (neither like nor dislike) and 10 meals you dislike.

3.4.2 Non-comparative scales

In non-comparative scaling, customers are asked to only evaluate a single object. This evaluation is totally independent of the other objects under investigation. Sometimes called monadic or metric scale, non-comparative scale can be further divided into continuous and the itemized rating scales.

3.4.2.1 Continuous rating scale

In continuous rating scale, respondents are asked to rate the objects by placing a mark appropriately on a line running from one extreme of the criterion to the other variable criterion. Also called the graphic rating scale, it gives the respondent the freedom to place the mark anywhere based on personal preference. Once the ratings are obtained, the researcher splits up the line into several categories and then assigns the scores depending on the category in which the ratings fall. This rating can be visualized in both horizontal and vertical form.

Although easy to construct, the continuous rating scale has some major setbacks, giving it limited usage in market research.

3.4.2.2 *Itemized rating scale*

The itemized rating scale is a type of ordinal scale that assigns numbers to each attribute. Respondents are usually asked to select an attribute that best describes their feelings regarding a predefined criterion. Itemized rating scale is further divided into 2, namely; Likert scale, Stapel scale, and semantic scale.

3.4.2.2.1 Likert scale

A Likert scale is an ordinal scale with five response categories, which is used to order a list of attributes from the best to the least. This scale uses adverbs of degree like very strongly, highly, etc. to indicate the different levels.

3.4.2.2.2 Stapel scale

This a scale with 10 categories, usually ranging from −5 to 5 with no zero point. It is a vertical scale with three columns, where the attributes are placed in the middle and the least (−5) and highest (5) is in the first and third columns, respectively.

3.4.2.2.3 Semantic differential scale

This is a seven-point rating scale with endpoints associated with bipolar labels (e.g., good or bad, happy, etc.). It can be used for marketing, advertising and in different stages of product development.

3.5 Various types of scale

There are four different scales of measurement. The data can be defined as being one of the four scales. The four types of scales which are shown in Fig. 3.4:

FIGURE 3.4   Types of measuring scale.

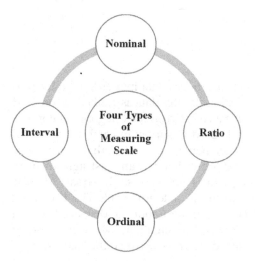

3.5.1 Nominal

The first level of measuring scales are called nominal scales, and they use numbers as "tags" or "labels" to categorize or identify various items. Usually, non-numeric variables or numbers without any meaning are dealt with by a nominal scale. In the example below, the measurement of the popularity of a political party is measured on a nominal scale. In statistics, a nominal scale is a type of categorical variable measurement scale in which data is measured in categories or labels that have no intrinsic order or numerical value. Nominal scales are used to represent characteristics such as race, gender, political affiliation, or types of car models. These categories are mutually exclusive and collectively exhaustive, which means that each observation falls into one and only one category, and all possible categories are included. For example, the "color of cars" variable can be measured on a nominal scale with categories such as "red," "blue," "green," "black," and "white." Each category is considered equal in value, and there is no inherent order or numerical relationship between them.

Which political party are you affiliated with?

Labeling Independent as "1," Republican as "2" and Democrat as "3" does not in any way mean any of the attributes are better than the other. They are just used as an identity for easy data analysis.

3.5.2 Ordinal

The second level of measurement, the ordinal scale, reports data's ordering and ranking without determining the degree of variance among them. Ordinal is a symbol for "order." Ordinal data is also referred to as categorical or qualitative data. It can be named, ranked, and categorized.

For example: A software company may need to ask its users:
How would you rate our app?

- Excellent
- Very good
- Good
- Bad
- Poor

An ordinal scale is a type of measurement scale that categorizes data into ordered categories based on some kind of ranking or order. In an ordinal scale, the data is ranked or ordered according to some characteristic or attribute, but the distance between the categories is not necessarily equal or measurable. For example, a Likert scale used in survey research is an ordinal scale where respondents rate their agreement with a statement using a scale that ranges from "strongly disagree" to "strongly agree." The categories are ordered from least agreement to most agreement, but the distance between the categories is not necessarily equal. Another example of an ordinal scale is a ranking of sports teams in a tournament. The teams are ordered from the first to the last place based on their performance, but the distance between the places is not necessarily equal. Ordinal scales are useful in situations where we need to order or rank data, but do not need to measure the exact differences between the categories.

3.5.3 Interval

The third level of measurement scale is the interval scale. It is described as a quantitative measuring scale where a noticeable difference may be found between the two variables. In other words, the measurements are precise rather than relative, where the occurrence of zero is arbitrary. An interval scale is a type of measurement scale where the distance between the values or intervals is equal and can be measured. In an interval scale, the values or intervals are ordered and the numerical difference between them is meaningful. One example of an interval scale is the Fahrenheit temperature scale, where each degree represents a consistent and measurable difference in temperature. Another example is the IQ test score, where the difference between scores of 100 and 110 is the same as the difference between scores of 110 and 120.

It is important to note that an interval scale does not have a true zero point. A zero point in an interval scale does not represent the absence of the measured quantity but rather a point on the scale. For example, 0 degrees Fahrenheit does not represent the complete absence of temperature. Interval scales are widely used in many fields such as physics, engineering, economics, and psychology. They allow for precise measurement of quantities and are useful in statistical analyses.

3.5.4 Ratio

The fourth level of measuring scale, which is quantitative, is the ratio scale. A changeable measurement scale of this kind is used. It enables researchers to contrast intervals or differences. The ratio scale has a distinguishing quality. It has zero points' or the origin's character. A ratio scale is the highest level of measurement in which data is not only categorized, ordered, and measured, but also has a true zero point that represents the absence of the attribute being measured. In a ratio scale, not only is the distance between values or intervals equal and measurable, but also ratios between values are meaningful and can be calculated. Examples of ratio scales include height, weight, and length measurements, where a zero value represents the complete absence of the measured quantity. For instance, a person with a weight of 0 kg represents a complete absence of weight or mass.

The ratio scale enables researchers to perform all mathematical operations, including addition, subtraction, multiplication, and division, making it the most versatile of all the measurement scales. This scale is used in many fields, including science, engineering, medicine, and finance, where precise measurements are essential. In summary, the ratio scale is a measurement scale that provides a true zero point and allows for meaningful ratios between values. It enables researchers to perform mathematical operations and is used in various fields to make accurate and reliable measurements. Table 3.4 shows the properties of scales of measurement.

3.6 Primary data analysis with Python

Python is one of the most popular programming languages for data analysis due to its simplicity, versatility, and a wide range of libraries and tools available for data

TABLE 3.4 Properties of Scales of measurement.

Data	Nominal	Ordinal	Interval	Ratio
Labeled	Yes	Yes	Yes	Yes
Meaningful order	No	Yes	Yes	Yes
Measurable difference	No	No	Yes	Yes
True zero starting point	No	No	No	Yes

manipulation, exploration, and visualization. Here are some of the reasons why Python is important in data analysis:

Easy to learn and use: Python is a simple and easy-to-learn programming language. It has a simple syntax and a large number of libraries and tools for data analysis.

Large community and ecosystem: Python has a vast community of users and developers. The large number of users has led to the development of a vast ecosystem of libraries and tools for data analysis.

Versatility: Python can be used for various purposes, such as web development, scientific computing, and data analysis. This makes it a versatile language for data analysis.

Libraries and tools: Python has many libraries and tools for data analysis, including NumPy, Pandas, Matplotlib, Scikit-learn, and TensorFlow. These libraries provide efficient and easy-to-use functions for data manipulation, exploration, visualization, and machine learning.

Data visualization: Python provides excellent data visualization capabilities through libraries such as Matplotlib, Seaborn, and Plotly. These libraries help to create interactive and informative visualizations to better understand and communicate data insights.

Machine learning: Python has become the de facto language for machine learning and AI. The powerful libraries and tools such as Scikit-learn, TensorFlow, and Keras provide efficient and easy-to-use functions for machine learning tasks such as classification, regression, clustering, and deep learning.

In conclusion, Python is an essential tool for data analysis due to its simplicity, versatility, and the vast array of libraries and tools available for data manipulation, exploration, and visualization.

Python is a powerful programming language that is widely used in data analysis. Here are some steps you can follow for primary data analysis with Python:

Importing data: You can import your data into Python using various libraries like Pandas, Numpy, etc. Pandas is a commonly used library for data analysis.

Data cleaning: Before starting the analysis, it is important to clean the data by removing duplicates, dealing with missing values, and correcting any inconsistencies.

Descriptive analysis: Once the data is cleaned, you can perform some basic descriptive analysis to understand the data. You can use various Python libraries like Pandas,

Matplotlib, Seaborn, etc. to create graphical representations of the data, such as histograms, box plots, scatter plots, etc.

Statistical analysis: After the initial analysis, you can perform statistical analysis to understand the relationship between different variables. Python has several libraries like Scipy, Statsmodels, etc. that can be used for statistical analysis.

Machine learning: You can also use Python to perform machine learning algorithms like regression, clustering, classification, etc. These algorithms can help you make predictions or identify patterns in your data.

Visualization: Finally, you can use Python libraries like Matplotlib, Seaborn, Plotly, etc. to create interactive and informative visualizations of your data, which can be used to communicate your findings to others.

These are some basic steps that you can follow for primary data analysis with Python. However, the exact process will depend on the specific data and research question you are trying to answer.

3.7 Conclusion

In conclusion, the study of data theory and taxonomy of data provides valuable insights into the nature, structure, and characteristics of data. By examining data as a whole and considering different views of data, such as the conceptual, logical, and physical views, researchers and analysts can gain a comprehensive understanding of its meaning, organization, and storage. In a data-driven world, where the volume and complexity of data continue to increase, understanding data theory and taxonomy of data is essential. It allows researchers and analysts to navigate through the vast amount of data available, ensuring that data analysis is accurate, meaningful, and aligned with the research objectives.

In summary, data theory and taxonomy of data provide a comprehensive framework for understanding the complexity and diversity of data. By exploring data as a whole, considering different views of data, understanding measurement and scaling concepts, and classifying data based on their characteristics, researchers and analysts can effectively analyze and interpret data, leading to valuable insights and informed decision-making.

3.8 Case study

3.8.1 Case study: taxonomy of data in a healthcare organization

Background: A healthcare organization is collecting vast amounts of data from various sources such as patient records, medical devices, research studies, and clinical trials. This data includes patient demographics, medical histories, lab results, imaging studies, and other clinical data. The organization needs to organize and classify this data to ensure easy accessibility, accuracy, and interoperability across different systems.

Objective: The objective of this case study is to create a taxonomy of data for the healthcare organization that will enable efficient data management, enhance data analysis, and improve patient care.

Approach: To develop a taxonomy of data, the healthcare organization needs to follow a systematic approach that includes the following steps:

Step 1: Identify the data elements

The first step is to identify all the data elements that are being collected, stored, and processed by the healthcare organization. This includes data from different sources such as patient records, lab results, imaging studies, research studies, and clinical trials. The data elements can be classified into different categories based on their attributes such as type, format, source, and usage.

Step 2: Define the data categories

Once all the data elements have been identified, the next step is to define the data categories. The categories can be defined based on different criteria such as clinical specialty, patient demographics, medical conditions, and treatments. For example, data categories can include patient demographics, medical history, lab results, imaging studies, and clinical notes.

Step 3: Create a hierarchical structure

The next step is to create a hierarchical structure for the data categories. This will enable the healthcare organization to organize and classify the data elements based on their relationships and dependencies. The hierarchical structure can include parent categories and subcategories, with each subcategory containing specific data elements. For example, patient demographics can be a parent category, and subcategories can include age, gender, ethnicity, and address.

Step 4: Develop a data dictionary

The final step is to develop a data dictionary that defines each data element in the taxonomy. The data dictionary should include the data element's name, description, format, source, usage, and relationships with other data elements in the taxonomy. The data dictionary can also include rules and standards for data collection, storage, and processing to ensure data quality and integrity.

Results: Using the above approach, the healthcare organization developed a taxonomy of data that included the following categories:

Patient demographics
Medical history
Medications
Lab results
Imaging studies
Clinical notes
Research studies
Clinical trials

Each category had multiple subcategories, and each subcategory had specific data elements. For example, the patient demographics category had subcategories such as age, gender, ethnicity, and address. The data dictionary defined each data element in detail and provided rules and standards for data collection, storage, and processing.

Conclusion: Developing a taxonomy of data is a critical step in managing and analyzing data effectively. The healthcare organization was able to organize and classify the vast amounts of data it collected into a hierarchical structure, making it easy to access and analyze the data. The data dictionary provided a standardized approach for collecting, storing, and processing data, ensuring data quality and integrity. This taxonomy of data will enable the healthcare organization to improve patient care, conduct research studies, and enhance clinical decision-making.

3.8.2 Case study: taxonomy of data in the automobile industry

The automobile industry generates vast amounts of data throughout the entire vehicle lifecycle, from design and production to sales and post-sale services. This data can be classified into different categories based on their source, format, and purpose. In this case study, we will discuss the taxonomy of data in the automobile industry.

Vehicle design data: Vehicle design data includes information about the vehicle's exterior and interior design, including CAD drawings, 3D models, and simulations. This data is used by design teams to create and modify vehicle designs, optimize performance, and test different scenarios.

Production data: Production data includes information about the manufacturing process, including production schedules, assembly line operations, quality control checks, and supply chain management. This data is used to optimize the production process, reduce defects, and improve efficiency.

Vehicle performance data: Vehicle performance data includes information about the vehicle's performance, including engine speed, acceleration, fuel consumption, and emissions. This data is collected from sensors and other monitoring systems in the vehicle and is used by engineers to optimize the vehicle's performance and meet regulatory requirements.

Customer data: Customer data includes information about the customers who purchase and use the vehicles, including demographic data, purchase history, and customer feedback. This data is used by marketing teams to target customers, improve product offerings, and enhance the customer experience.

Sales data: Sales data includes information about the sales process, including pricing, promotions, and sales performance. This data is used by sales teams to track sales performance, identify trends, and adjust sales strategies.

Service data: Service data includes information about the vehicle's maintenance and repair history, including service records, warranty claims, and customer complaints. This data is used by service teams to diagnose and repair vehicle issues, improve service offerings, and enhance the customer experience.

Telematics data: Telematics data includes information about the vehicle's location, speed, and driving behavior, collected through onboard sensors and connected devices. This data is used by insurance companies to assess risk, by fleet managers to optimize operations, and by car manufacturers to improve vehicle design and performance.

Overall, the taxonomy of data in the automobile industry can be quite complex and diverse, spanning various categories and applications. However, by understanding the different types of data and their respective uses, companies in the industry can leverage data to improve performance, enhance customer experience, and drive innovation.

3.8.3 Case study on the data theory

Data theory, also known as information theory, is a branch of mathematics and computer science that deals with the quantification, storage, and communication of information. It provides a framework for understanding the fundamental limits of information processing and communication, as well as methods for optimizing the performance of information systems. One notable case study in data theory is the development of error-correcting codes. In the early days of digital communication, errors were a major problem due to noise and other sources of interference. Information theory provided a solution to this problem by introducing the concept of redundancy. By adding extra bits to a message, it is possible to detect and correct errors that occur during transmission.

The most famous example of an error-correcting code is the Hamming code, developed by Richard Hamming in the 1950s. Hamming codes are simple yet powerful, and they are still used today in a variety of applications, including data storage and transmission. They work by encoding a message with parity bits that allow the receiver to detect and correct errors. Another important application of data theory is in data compression. In this case, the goal is to represent a message using as few bits as possible. Information theory provides a way to measure the entropy of a message, which is a measure of its randomness. By exploiting the patterns and structure in the message, it is possible to compress it without losing any information.

One of the most widely used compression algorithms is the Lempel-Ziv algorithm, which was first proposed in 1977. The Lempel-Ziv algorithm works by identifying repeated patterns in the message and encoding them using a dictionary. This allows the message to be compressed without losing any information.

In summary, data theory has played a fundamental role in the development of modern communication and information systems. By providing a rigorous mathematical framework for understanding information, it has enabled the development of error-correcting codes, data compression algorithms, and other tools that are essential for modern computing.

3.9 Exercise

3.9.1 Objective type question

1. Which of the following best describes data taxonomy?
    a. The study of data structures and algorithms.
    b. The process of organizing and classifying data based on their characteristics.
    c. The analysis of data patterns and trends.
    d. The interpretation of data visualizations.

2. True or False: Data taxonomy refers to the measurement and scaling of data variables.
    a. True
    b. False.

3. What is the purpose of data taxonomy?
   a. To assign numerical values to categorical data.
   b. To organize and classify data based on their nature and characteristics.
   c. To determine the statistical significance of data variables.
   d. To measure the variability of data in a dataset.

4. Which of the following is NOT a component of data taxonomy?
   a. Measurement and scaling
   b. Data visualization
   c. Categorization and classification
   a. Data patterns and trends.

5. Which type of scale is used in data taxonomy to categorize data into distinct categories without any inherent order?
   a. Nominal scale
   b. Ordinal scale
   c. Interval scale
   d. Ratio scale

6. What is the main difference between nominal and ordinal scales?
   a. Nominal scales provide equal intervals between values, while ordinal scales do not.
   b. Nominal scales have a true zero point, while ordinal scales do not.
   c. Nominal scales order data categories, while ordinal scales do not provide a fixed measurement unit.
   d. Nominal scales are used for continuous variables, while ordinal scales are used for discrete variables.

7. Which of the following is an example of using data taxonomy in practice?
   a. Creating a scatter plot to analyze the relationship between two variables.
   b. Categorizing survey responses into different age groups.
   c. Calculating the mean and standard deviation of a dataset.
   d. Applying regression analysis to predict future trends.

8. True or False: Data taxonomy is a static process and does not evolve over time.
   a. True
   b. False

9. Which of the following is a benefit of using data taxonomy?
   a. It provides insights into data patterns and trends.
   b. It allows for precise measurements of data variables.
   c. It automates the data analysis process.
   d. It eliminates the need for data visualization techniques.

10. Which step of the data analysis process does data taxonomy typically occur in?
    a. Data collection
    b. Data preprocessing
    c. Data visualization
    d. Data interpretation

11. Which programming language is commonly used for primary data analysis?
    a. Python
    b. Java
    c. C++
    d. Ruby

12. True or False: Python is an open-source programming language.
    a. True
    b. False

13. Which Python library is commonly used for data analysis?
    a. Matplotlib
    b. TensorFlow
    c. Django
    d. NumPy

14. What is the purpose of primary data analysis?
    a. To gather data from secondary sources
    b. To analyze and interpret data collected directly from the source
    c. To perform statistical hypothesis testing
    d. To create data visualizations

15. Which Python library provides tools for data manipulation and analysis, such as data cleaning and transformation?
    a. Pandas
    b. SciPy
    c. Scikit-learn
    d. PyTorch

16. True or False: Python is not suitable for handling large datasets.
    a. True
    b. False

17. Which Python library is commonly used for data visualization?
    a. Seaborn
    b. BeautifulSoup
    c. Requests
    d. SQLAlchemy

18. What is the purpose of using Jupyter Notebook in primary data analysis with Python?
    a. To write and execute Python code
    b. To create interactive data visualizations
    c. To document and share data analysis workflows
    d. All of the above

19. Which Python library is commonly used for statistical analysis and hypothesis testing?
    a. Statsmodels
    b. Keras
    c. Pygame
    d. Flask

20. What is the advantage of using Python for primary data analysis?
    a. It has a large and active community for support and resources.
    b. It is a highlys specialized language for data analysis.
    c. It provides faster execution time compared to other programming languages.
    d. It is only compatible with specific operating systems.

3.9.2 Descriptive type question

1. Explain the concept of data as a whole and its significance in various fields.
2. Discuss the different views of data, including the conceptual, logical, and physical views, and provide examples of each.
3. What is the role of measurement in data analysis? Explain the process of assigning numerical values to variables and its importance in quantitative analysis.
4. Describe the concept of scaling in data analysis. How does scaling create a continuum of values for variables? Provide examples of scaling techniques.
5. Explore the various types of scales used in data analysis, such as nominal, ordinal, interval, and ratio scales. Explain the characteristics and applications of each scale type.
6. How does the taxonomy of data contribute to the organization and classification of data? Discuss the importance of classifying data based on their nature and characteristics.
7. Provide examples of how different types of scales, such as nominal and interval scales, are used in real-world scenarios or research studies.
8. Explain the implications and considerations when choosing an appropriate scale for a specific data analysis task. How does the choice of scale impact data interpretation?
9. Discuss the challenges and limitations associated with measurement and scaling in data analysis. How can researchers address these challenges to ensure accurate and meaningful results?
10. Explore the interplay between measurement, scaling, and data analysis techniques such as regression analysis or factor analysis. How do these concepts relate to each other in the context of data analysis?

Further reading

E. Gurarie, R.D. Andrews, K.L. Laidre, A novel method for identifying behavioral changes in animal movement data, Ecol. Lett. 12 (5) (2009) 395–408.

T. Hagerstrand, Time geography: focus on the corporeality of man, society and environment, in: S. Aida (Ed.), The Science and Praxis of Complexity, The United Nations University, Tokyo, 1985, pp. 193–216.

K.C. Heesch, M. Langdon, The usefulness of GPS bicycle tracking data for evaluating the impact of infrastructure change on bicycling behaviour, Health Promot. J. Austr. 27 (3) (2017) 222–229.

E. Heinen, K. Maat, B. Van Wee, Day-to-day choice to commute or not by bicycle, Transp. Res. Rec. 2230 (1) (2011) 9–18.

B. Jestico, T. Nelson, M. Winters, Mapping ridership using crowdsourced cycling data, J. Transp. Geogr. 52 (2016) 90–97.

J.-Y. Kang, J. Aldstadt, Using multiple scale spatio-temporal patterns for validating spatially explicit agent-based models, Int. J. Geogr. Inf. Sci. 33 (1) (2019) 193–213.

T. Knudsen, B.P. Olsen, Automated change detection for updates of digital map databases, Photogramm. Eng. Remote. Sens. 69 (11) (2003) 1289–1296.

M.-P. Kwan, Time, information technologies, and the geographies of everyday life, Urban. Geogr. 23 (5) (2002) 471−482. Available from: https://doi.org/10.2747/0272-3638.23.5.471.

M.-P. Kwan, T. Neutens, Space-time research in GIScience, Int. J. Geogr. Inf. Sci. 28 (5) (2014) 851−854. Available from: https://doi.org/10.1080/13658816.2014.889300.

S. Lee, S. Jung, Combined analysis of amplitude and phase variations in functional data, arXiv Prepr. arXiv 1603 (2016) 01775.

D.-J. Lee, Z. Zhu, P. Toscas, Spatio-temporal functional data analysis for wireless sensor networks data, Environmetrics 26 (5) (2015) 354−362.

X. Liu, Q. Huang, S. Gao, Exploring the uncertainty of activity zone detection using digital footprints with multi-scaled DBSCAN, Int. J. Geogr. Inf. Sci. 33 (6) (2019) 1196−1223.

S. Lohit, Q. Wang, P. Turaga. Temporal transformer networks: Joint learning of invariant and discriminative time warping. In: Proceedings - 2019 IEEE/CVF Conference on Computer Vision and Pattern Recognition, CVPR, 2019, pp. 12418−12427.

M. Loidl, G. Wallentin, R. Wendel, B. Zagel, Mapping bicycle crash risk patterns on the local scale, Safety 2 (3) (2016) 17.

Multivariate data analytics and cognitive analytics

Abbreviations

PCA   principal component analysis
EFA   exploratory factor analysis
ANOVA   analysis of variance

4.1 Introduction

In today's data-driven world, organizations across various domains are faced with the challenge of extracting valuable insights from complex datasets. The field of data analytics provides powerful tools and techniques to make sense of such multivariate data, enabling informed decision-making and strategic planning. This chapter explores the fascinating realm of multivariate data analytics and cognitive analytics, focusing on key methodologies such as factor analysis, principal component analysis (PCA), regression analysis, logistic analysis, and multivariate analysis. Multivariate data analytics involves the examination and interpretation of datasets with multiple variables simultaneously. It recognizes that real-world phenomena are often influenced by multiple factors, and understanding the relationships and patterns between these variables is crucial for uncovering meaningful insights. By analyzing multivariate data, organizations can gain a comprehensive understanding of complex systems, leading to enhanced predictions, improved performance, and optimized decision-making.

Factor analysis is a statistical method utilized to uncover latent variables or underlying factors that explain the correlations observed among a set of observed variables. It helps in reducing the dimensionality of data and identifying the essential components driving the observed patterns. By extracting these underlying factors, researchers can simplify complex datasets and gain a deeper understanding of the underlying constructs influencing the data.

PCA is another powerful technique in multivariate data analytics. It transforms a set of correlated variables into a smaller set of uncorrelated variables known as principal components. These components capture the maximum variance in the original data, allowing for

Cognitive Science, Computational Intelligence, and Data Analytics
DOI: https://doi.org/10.1016/B978-0-443-16078-3.00002-2
© 2024 Elsevier Inc. All rights reserved, including those for text and data mining, AI training, and similar technologies.

dimensionality reduction while retaining as much information as possible. PCA is particularly useful in visualizing data, identifying outliers, and highlighting the most influential variables in a dataset.

Regression analysis is a widely used statistical method that examines the relationship between a dependent variable and one or more independent variables. It helps to understand how changes in independent variables affect the dependent variable, enabling predictions and forecasting. Regression analysis provides valuable insights into causality and helps researchers identify the key drivers behind observed phenomena. Logistic analysis, on the other hand, focuses on modeling and predicting binary outcomes or categorical variables. It is particularly useful when analyzing data that involves predicting the probability of an event occurring or classifying observations into distinct categories. By employing logistic regression, researchers can assess the impact of multiple variables on the likelihood of a specific outcome, enabling effective decision-making and risk management.

Finally, multivariate analysis encompasses a range of techniques that allow for the simultaneous examination of multiple variables and their relationships. These techniques include multivariate regression, discriminant analysis, cluster analysis, and factor analysis, among others. Multivariate analysis provides a holistic perspective on complex datasets, revealing intricate patterns and uncovering valuable insights that would be difficult to discern using univariate or bivariate approaches alone.

At the end, multivariate data analytics and cognitive analytics offer powerful methodologies to extract meaningful insights from complex datasets. Through techniques such as factor analysis, PCA, regression analysis, logistic analysis, and multivariate analysis, organizations can gain a comprehensive understanding of multivariate data, leading to more accurate predictions, informed decision-making, and improved business outcomes. The following sections will delve into these methodologies in more detail, exploring their underlying principles, applications, and benefits in the realm of data analytics.

4.2 Factor analytics

Factor analysis is a statistical technique used to identify underlying factors or dimensions that explain the pattern of correlations among a set of observed variables. These underlying factors are latent variables that cannot be directly observed, but can be inferred from the patterns of correlations among the observed variables.

For example, consider a survey that measures attitudes towards different political issues. The survey may include questions about taxes, healthcare, immigration, and other topics. These questions are the observed variables, and the underlying factors or dimensions may be things like "economic conservatism," "social liberalism," "foreign policy interventionism," and so on. Factor analysis can help identify these underlying factors and determine which observed variables are most strongly associated with each factor.

Another example of factor analysis is in finance, where it is used to identify the underlying factors that drive the returns of different assets. For example, the returns of a portfolio of stocks may be influenced by factors such as the overall performance of the stock market, the performance of specific industries, or macroeconomic variables like interest rates and inflation. Factor analysis can help identify these underlying factors and determine how much of the variation in the returns of different stocks can be attributed to each factor.

For the example, factor rating is a simple methodology to assess the attractiveness of each potential location for the software company. This method involves four steps in which the relevant parameters are identified, their relative importance established, the performance of each location in each factor assessed and finally, all this information is combined to rank the locations.

Example: One of the software company is actively considering five alternative locations to open the new branch of the company. Based on the survey related to software industry, company has six factors to be considered for final site selection. The ratings of each factor on a scale of 1–100 provide this information of location of software company in Table 4.1.

The first step in the solution is to develop the relative importance of each parameters using a normalization factor. The sum of all the parameters related to software company is 415. Therefore, by dividing each parameter rating by 415 one can obtain the relative weight of the parameters, which is shown in Tables 4.2 and 4.3.

TABLE 4.1 Factor rating.

Factors	Rating (1–100)
Market access	80
Cost of living and business	75
Industry hub	70
Availability of talent pool	60
Government incentives and support	65
Risk and stability	65

TABLE 4.2 Factor rating.

Factors	Rating (1–100)	Relative weight
Market access	80	0.192771084
Cost of living and business	75	0.180722892
Industry hub	70	0.168674699
Availability of talent pool	60	0.144578313
Government incentives and support	65	0.156626506
Risk and stability	65	0.156626506
Sum of all factor rating	415	1

TABLE 4.3   Rating of each location of solar energy system against each factor.

Factors	Relative weight	Location 1	Location 2	Location 3	Location 4	Location 5
Market access	0.192771084	45	60	75	62	42
Cost of living and business	0.180722892	30	58	70	56	55
Industry hub	0.168674699	35	41	63	45	47
Availability of talent pool	0.144578313	30	45	55	25	51
Government incentives and support	0.156626506	40	40	60	42	50
Risk and stability	0.156626506	35	30	55	35	45
Sum of all factor rating		36.084	46.433	63.698	45.337	48.216
Ranking of the locations		5	3	1	4	2

Since the normalized weight of each parameter, one can compute how each location fares by weighing the rating of the location against each factor with the weight for the factor. The computation for location 1 is as follows:

$$(45 \times 0.192771084) + (30 \times 0.180722892) + (35 \times 0.168674699) + (30 \times 0.144578313)$$
$$+ (40 \times 0.156626506) + (35 \times 0.156626506)$$
$$= 36.084$$

Similarly, factor rating of location 2, 3, 4, and 5 is 46.433, 63.698, 45.337, and 48.216, respectively. So according to the above assessment location 3 is more feasible location for software company. Factor-rating systems are the most widely used location techniques as they combine diverse factors in an easy-to-understand format. Lot of factors are taken into consideration which other processes don't take into consideration.

Python program for the above dataset:

```python
import numpy as np
# Define the factors and ratings
factors = [
    'Market Access',
    'Cost of living and business',
    'Industry Hub',
    'Availability of talent pool',
    'Government incentives and support',
    'Risk and stability'
]
ratings = [80, 75, 70, 60, 65, 65]

# Normalize the ratings
normalized_ratings = np.array(ratings) / 100
```

(cont'd)

```
# Calculate the eigenvalues and eigenvectors
covariance_matrix = np.outer(normalized_ratings, normalized_ratings)
eigenvalues, eigenvectors = np.linalg.eig(covariance_matrix)

# Sort eigenvalues and eigenvectors in descending order
sorted_indices = np.argsort(eigenvalues)[::-1]
sorted_eigenvalues = eigenvalues[sorted_indices]
sorted_eigenvectors = eigenvectors[:, sorted_indices]

# Calculate the explained variance ratio
explained_variance_ratio = sorted_eigenvalues / np.sum(sorted_eigenvalues)

# Print the factor analysis results
print("Factor Analysis Results:")
for i, factor in enumerate(factors):
    print(f"Factor: {factor}")
    print(f"Eigenvalue: {sorted_eigenvalues[i]}")
    print(f"Explained Variance Ratio: {explained_variance_ratio[i]*100:.2f}%")
    print()

# Print the cumulative explained variance ratio
cumulative_variance_ratio = np.cumsum(explained_variance_ratio)
print("Cumulative Explained Variance Ratio:")
for i, factor in enumerate(factors):
    print(f"Factor: {factor}")
    print(f"Cumulative          Explained          Variance          Ratio:
{cumulative_variance_ratio[i]*100:.2f}%")
    print()
```

This program uses the numpy library to perform the factor analysis calculations. It normalizes the ratings, calculates the covariance matrix, eigenvalues, and eigenvectors. It then sorts them in descending order to determine the importance of each factor. The program prints the eigenvalues, explained variance ratio, and cumulative explained variance ratio for each factor.

4.3 Principal component analytics

PCA is a statistical technique used to reduce the dimensionality of a dataset by identifying the most important underlying patterns of variation. In PCA, a set of correlated variables is transformed into a set of uncorrelated variables called principal components. Each principal component is a linear combination of the original variables and captures a unique pattern of variation in the data.

Following are the steps how PCA can be applied to a numerical problem:

Suppose we have a dataset of 100 observations on four variables $(X_1 - X_4)$ and we want to identify the underlying patterns of variation in the data. We can perform PCA using the following steps:

- Standardize the data to ensure that each variable has a mean of 0 and a standard deviation of 1.
- Calculate the correlation matrix for the four variables.
- Compute the eigenvalues and eigenvectors of the correlation matrix.
- Sort the eigenvalues in descending order and select the top k eigenvectors corresponding to the k largest eigenvalues. These k eigenvectors are the principal components.
- Transform the original data into the space defined by the principal components.

Problems based on PCA:
Consider the two-dimensional pattern: [(3, 4), (4, 5), (4, 3), (5, 7), (6, 8), (8, 9)]

Step 1: Get data
The given feature vector is:

$$X_1 = (3, 4)$$
$$X_2 = (4, 5)$$
$$X_3 = (4, 3)$$
$$X_4 = (5, 7)$$
$$X_5 = (6, 8)$$
$$X_6 = (8, 9)$$

$$\begin{bmatrix} 3 \\ 4 \end{bmatrix} \quad \begin{bmatrix} 4 \\ 5 \end{bmatrix} \quad \begin{bmatrix} 4 \\ 3 \end{bmatrix} \quad \begin{bmatrix} 5 \\ 7 \end{bmatrix} \quad \begin{bmatrix} 6 \\ 8 \end{bmatrix} \quad \begin{bmatrix} 8 \\ 9 \end{bmatrix}$$

Step 2: Calculate the mean vector (μ)

$$\text{Mean vector} = ((3 + 4 + 4 + 5 + 6 + 8)/6, (4 + 5 + 3 + 7 + 8 + 9)/6)$$
$$= (5, 6)$$

Thus mean vector $(\mu) = \begin{bmatrix} 5 \\ 6 \end{bmatrix}$

Step 3: Subtract mean vector (μ) from the given features vectors

$$X_1 - \mu = (3 - 5, 4 - 6) = (-1, -2)$$
$$X_2 - \mu = (4 - 5, 5 - 6) = (-1, -1)$$
$$X_3 - \mu = (4 - 5, 3 - 6) = (-1, -3)$$
$$X_4 - \mu = (5 - 5, 7 - 6) = (0, 1)$$
$$X_5 - \mu = (6 - 5, 8 - 6) = (1, 2)$$
$$X_6 - \mu = (8 - 5, 9 - 6) = (3, 3)$$

Features vectors (X_i) after subtracting mean vector (μ) are:

$$\begin{bmatrix} -1 \\ -2 \end{bmatrix}, \begin{bmatrix} -1 \\ -1 \end{bmatrix}, \begin{bmatrix} -1 \\ -3 \end{bmatrix}, \begin{bmatrix} 0 \\ 1 \end{bmatrix}, \begin{bmatrix} 1 \\ 2 \end{bmatrix}, \begin{bmatrix} 3 \\ 3 \end{bmatrix}$$

Step 4: Covariance matrix is given by

$$\text{Covariance matrix} = \frac{\sum (X_i - \mu)(X_i - \mu)^t}{n}$$

$$M_1 = (X_1 - \mu)(X_1 - \mu)^t = \begin{bmatrix} -1 \\ -2 \end{bmatrix} \begin{bmatrix} -1 & -2 \end{bmatrix} = \begin{bmatrix} 1 & 2 \\ 2 & 4 \end{bmatrix}$$

$$M_2 = (X_2 - \mu)(X_2 - \mu)^t = \begin{bmatrix} -1 \\ -1 \end{bmatrix} \begin{bmatrix} -1 & -1 \end{bmatrix} = \begin{bmatrix} 1 & 1 \\ 1 & 1 \end{bmatrix}$$

$$M_3 = (X_3 - \mu)(X_3 - \mu)^t = \begin{bmatrix} -1 \\ -3 \end{bmatrix} \begin{bmatrix} -1 & -3 \end{bmatrix} = \begin{bmatrix} 1 & 3 \\ 3 & 9 \end{bmatrix}$$

$$M_4 = (X_4 - \mu)(X_4 - \mu)^t = \begin{bmatrix} 0 \\ 1 \end{bmatrix} \begin{bmatrix} 0 & 1 \end{bmatrix} = \begin{bmatrix} 0 & 0 \\ 0 & 1 \end{bmatrix}$$

$$M_5 = (X_5 - \mu)(X_5 - \mu)^t = \begin{bmatrix} 1 \\ 2 \end{bmatrix} \begin{bmatrix} 1 & 2 \end{bmatrix} = \begin{bmatrix} 1 & 2 \\ 2 & 4 \end{bmatrix}$$

$$M_6 = (X_6 - \mu)(X_6 - \mu)^t = \begin{bmatrix} 3 \\ 3 \end{bmatrix} \begin{bmatrix} 3 & 3 \end{bmatrix} = \begin{bmatrix} 9 & 9 \\ 9 & 9 \end{bmatrix}$$

Now covariance matrix $= (M_1 + M_2 + M_3 + M_4 + M_5 + M_6)/6$

On adding the above matrices and dividing by 6, we get

$$\text{Covariance matrix} = \frac{1}{6} \begin{bmatrix} 13 & 17 \\ 17 & 28 \end{bmatrix} = \begin{bmatrix} 2.16 & 2.83 \\ 2.83 & 4.67 \end{bmatrix}$$

Step 7: Calculate the Eigen values and Eigen vectors of the covariance matrix
λ is an eigen value for a matrix M if it is a solution of the characteristic equation $|M - \lambda I| = 0$.
So, we have

$$\begin{vmatrix} 2.16 & 2.83 \\ 2.83 & 4.67 \end{vmatrix} - \begin{bmatrix} \lambda & 0 \\ 0 & \lambda \end{bmatrix} = 0$$

$$\begin{vmatrix} 2.16 - \lambda & 2.83 \\ 2.83 & 4.67 - \lambda \end{vmatrix} = 0$$

From here,

$$(2.16 - \lambda)(4.67 - \lambda) - (2.83 \times 2.83) = 0$$

$$10.08 - 2.16\lambda - 4.67\lambda + \lambda^2 - 8 = 0$$

$$\lambda^2 - 6.83\lambda + 2.08 = 0$$

To find the values of the quadratic equation $\lambda^2 - 6.83\lambda + 2.08 = 0$, we can use the quadratic formula:

$$\lambda = \left(-b \pm \sqrt{(b^2 - 4ac)}\right)/(2a)$$

For this equation, $a = 1$, $b = -6.83$, and $c = 2.08$. Plugging these values into the quadratic formula, we get:

$$\lambda = \left(-(-6.83) \pm \sqrt{((-6.83)^2 - 4(1)(2.08))}\right)/(2(1))$$

Simplifying further:

$$\lambda = \left(6.83 \pm \sqrt{(46.6689 - 8.32)}\right)/2$$
$$\lambda = \left(6.83 \pm \sqrt{38.3489}\right)/2$$

Now, let's calculate the square root:

$$\lambda = (6.83 \pm 6.190729583)/2$$

Splitting it into two separate equations:

$$\lambda_1 = (6.83 + 6.190729583)/2 \approx 6.51$$
$$\lambda_2 = (6.83 - 6.190729583)/2 \approx 0.32$$

Therefore, the values of the quadratic equation $\lambda^2 - 6.83\lambda + 2.08 = 0$ are approximately $\lambda_1 \approx 6.51$ and $\lambda_2 \approx 0.32$.

Clearly second eigen value is very small compared to the first eigen value, so the second eigen value is left out.

Now we use the following equation to find the eigen vector
$MX = \lambda x$
where M is a covariance matrix, X is an Eigen vector, and λ is an Eigen value.

Substituting the values in the above equation, we get

$$\begin{bmatrix} 2.16 & 2.83 \\ 2.83 & 4.67 \end{bmatrix} \begin{bmatrix} X_1 \\ X_2 \end{bmatrix} = 6.51 \begin{bmatrix} X_1 \\ X_2 \end{bmatrix}$$

To perform PCA on the given two-dimensional dataset [(3, 7), (4, 9), (4, 3), (8, 6), (6, 8), (8, 9)], we can follow these steps:

Step 1: Compute the mean of the dataset.
To find the mean, sum up the x-coordinates and y-coordinates separately and divide by the number of data points (which is 6 in this case):

$$\text{Mean\_}x = (3 + 4 + 4 + 8 + 6 + 8)/6 = 33/6 = 5.5$$
$$\text{Mean\_}y = (7 + 9 + 3 + 6 + 8 + 9)/6 = 42/6 = 7$$

So, the mean of the dataset is (Mean_x, Mean_y) = (5.5, 7).
Step 2: Center the dataset by subtracting the mean from each data point.
Subtract the mean from each coordinate of the data points:

$$(3, 7) - (5.5, 7) = (-2.5, 0)$$
$$(4, 9) - (5.5, 7) = (-1.5, 2)$$

$$(4,3) - (5.5,7) = (-1.5, -4)$$
$$(8,6) - (5.5,7) = (2.5, -1)$$
$$(6,8) - (5.5,7) = (0.5,1)$$
$$(8,9) - (5.5,7) = (2.5,2)$$

The centered dataset becomes: $[(-2.5, 0), (-1.5, 2), (-1.5, -4), (2.5, -1), (0.5, 1), (2.5, 2)]$.
Step 3: Compute the covariance matrix of the centered dataset.
The covariance matrix can be computed using the formula:

$$\text{Covariance matrix} = (1/n) \times X^T \times X,$$

where n is the number of data points and X is the centered dataset matrix.

$$X = [(-2.5,0),(-1.5,2),(-1.5,-4),(2.5,-1),(0.5,1),(2.5,2)]$$
$$X^T = [(-2.5,-1.5,-1.5,2.5,0.5,2.5),(0,2,-4,-1,1,2)]$$

Now, we can calculate the covariance matrix:

$$\text{Covariance matrix} = (1/6) \times X^T \times X$$

Multiplying X^T and X gives:

$$X^T \times X = [(30.5, -7),(-7,24)]$$
$$\text{Covariance matrix} = (1/6) \times [(30.5, -7),(-7,24)]$$
$$\text{Covariance matrix} = [(5.083, -1.167),(-1.167,4)]$$

So, the covariance matrix of the centered dataset is $[(5.083, -1.167), (-1.167, 4)]$.

Python program of PCA:

```python
import numpy as np
from sklearn.decomposition import PCA

# Sample data
data = np.array([[1, 2, 3], [4, 5, 6], [7, 8, 9]])

# Create PCA object
pca = PCA(n_components=2)

# Perform PCA
pca.fit(data)

# Transform the data
transformed_data = pca.transform(data)

# Print the transformed data
print("Transformed data:")
print(transformed_data)
```

(cont'd)

Outcome:
Transformed data:
[[-5.19615242e+00 -1.33226763e-15]
 [0.00000000e+00 0.00000000e+00]
 [5.19615242e+00 1.33226763e-15]]

In this example, use the numpy library to create a sample dataset data with three observations and three features. We then import the PCA class from the sklearn. decomposition module, which provides a simple and efficient implementation of PCA.

Create an instance of the PCA class, specifying the number of components we want to keep (n_components = 2). In this case, we want to reduce the dimensionality of the data to two components.

Call the fit method of the PCA object to compute the principal components using the input data. The fit method analyzes the data and calculates the eigenvectors and eigenvalues. Afterward, we use the transform method to project the original data onto the principal components. The transformed data is stored in the transformed_data variable.

4.4 Cluster analytics

Cluster analysis is a statistical technique used to group similar observations into clusters or segments. It is often used in market research, customer segmentation, and data mining to identify patterns and structures in large datasets. There are many different methods for clustering data, including hierarchical clustering and k-means clustering. Table 4.4 shows the data of organization with the parameters of number of product and sales in thousand. Table 4.5 shows the month wise overall performance index of the employee. Fig. 4.1 shows the cluster of the dataset of Table 4.4. Fig. 4.2 shows the cluster of the dataset of Table 4.5.

Following are the example of how cluster analysis can be applied to a dataset:

Suppose we have a dataset of 200 customers that includes information on their age, income, and spending habits. We want to segment the customers into distinct groups based on their behavior and can perform cluster analysis using the following steps:

- Choose a clustering algorithm and set the number of clusters.
- Select the variables to be used in the analysis and standardize them if necessary.
- Run the clustering algorithm and assign each observation to a cluster.
- Evaluate the quality of the clustering using a clustering validation index.
- Interpret the results and assign a label to each cluster.

4.4.1 K-means

K-means clustering intends to partition n objects into k clusters in which each object belongs to the cluster with the nearest mean. This method produces exactly k different clusters of greatest possible distinction. The best number of clusters k leading to the greatest separation (distance) is not known as a priori and must be computed from the data.

TABLE 4.4 Data of organization.

Organization	Number of product	Sales in thousand
A	4	8
B	16	4
C	18	6
D	2	10
E	17	2

TABLE 4.5 Month-wise overall performance index.

Month	Overall performance index-1	Overall performance index-2
Jan.	1.4	6
Feb.	4.5	7.4
March	5	7.8
April	1.3	6.1
May	5.5	7.5
June	1.2	6.3
July	6	7.6
August	2.2	8.1
Sep.	4	7.3
Oct.	2.3	8.3
Nov.	2.4	8.2
Dec.	2.5	8.4

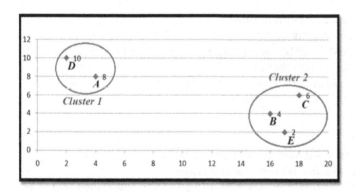

FIGURE 4.1 Cluster analysis of the dataset of table.

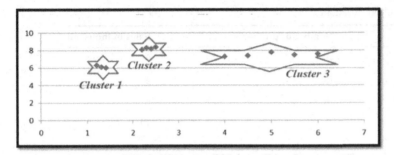

FIGURE 4.2 Cluster analysis of the dataset.

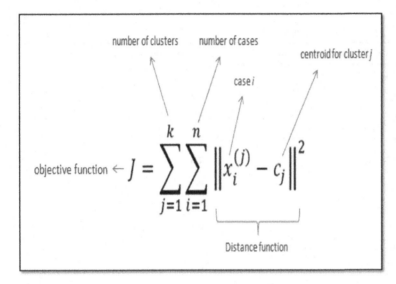

FIGURE 4.3 Formulation of K-means algorithm.

The objective of K-means clustering is to minimize total intra-cluster variance, or, the squared error function. Fig. 4.3 shows the formation of the K-means algorithm.

4.4.1.1 Algorithms

1. Cluster the data into k groups where k is predefined.
2. Select k points at random as cluster centres.
3. Assign objects to their closest cluster centre, according to the *Euclidean distance* function.
4. Calculate the centroid or mean of all objects in each cluster.
5. Repeat steps 2, 3, and 4 until the same points are assigned to each cluster in consecutive rounds.

4.4.1.2 K-means clustering

- K-Means clustering is an unsupervised iterative clustering technique.
- It partitions the given dataset into k predefined distinct clusters.
- A cluster is defined as a collection of data points exhibiting certain similarities (Fig. 4.4).

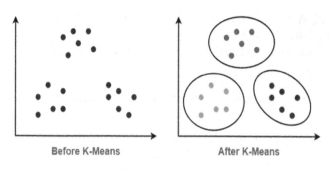

FIGURE 4.4 Collection of data points exhibiting certain similarities.

It partitions the dataset such that

- Each data point belongs to a cluster with the nearest mean.
- Data points belonging to one cluster have high degree of similarity.
- Data points belonging to different clusters have high degree of dissimilarity.

4.1.2.1 Steps of the K-means clustering algorithm

K-means clustering algorithm involves the following steps.

Step-01:

- Choose the number of clusters K.

Step-02:

- Randomly select any K data points as cluster centers.
- Select cluster centers in such a way that they are as farther as possible from each other.

Step-03:

- Calculate the distance between each data point and each cluster center.
- The distance may be calculated either by using given distance function or by using Euclidean distance formula.

Step-04:

- Assign each data point to some cluster.
- A data point is assigned to that cluster whose center is nearest to that data point.

Step-05:

- Re-compute the center of newly formed clusters.
- The center of a cluster is computed by taking mean of all the data points contained in that cluster.

Step-06:
Keep repeating the procedure from Step-03 to Step-05 until any of the following stopping criteria is met.

- Center of newly formed clusters do not change.
- Data points remain present in the same cluster.
- Maximum number of iterations are reached.

4.1.2.2 Practice problems based on K-means clustering algorithm

Cluster the following eight points (with (x, y) representing locations) into three clusters:

A1(2, 10), A2(2, 5), A3(8, 4), A4(5, 8), A5(7, 5), A6(6, 4), A7(1, 2), A8(4, 9)
Initial cluster centers are: A1(2, 10), A4(5, 8), and A7(1, 2).
The distance function between two points $a = (x1, y1)$ and $b = (x2, y2)$ is defined as

$$P(a, b) = |x2 - x1| + |y2 - y1|$$

Use K-means algorithm to find the three cluster centers after the second iteration.

Solution:
We follow the above discussed K-means clustering algorithm.
Iteration-01:

- We calculate the distance of each point from each of the center of the three clusters.
- The distance is calculated by using the given distance function.

The following illustration shows the calculation of distance between point A1(2, 10) and each of the center of the three clusters:
Calculating distance between A1(2, 10) and C1(2, 10):

$$P(A1, C1)$$
$$= |x2 - x1| + |y2 - y1|$$
$$= |2 - 2| + |10 - 10|$$
$$= 0$$

Calculating distance between A1(2, 10) and C2(5, 8):

$$P(A1, C2)$$
$$= |x2 - x1| + |y2 - y1|$$
$$= |5 - 2| + |8 - 10|$$
$$= 3 + 2$$
$$= 5$$

Calculating distance between A1(2, 10) and C3(1, 2):

$$P(A1, C3)$$
$$= |x2 - x1| + |y2 - y1|$$
$$= |1 - 2| + |2 - 10|$$
$$= 1 + 8$$
$$= 9$$

In the similar manner, we calculate the distance of other points from each of the center of the three clusters. Table 4.6 shows the assessment of the new cluster at the given points. Next,

- We draw a table showing all the results.
- Using the table, we decide which point belongs to which cluster.
- The given point belongs to that cluster whose center is nearest to it.

From here, new clusters are-

Cluster-01:
First cluster contains points

- A1(2, 10)

TABLE 4.6 Assessment of new cluster.

Given points	Distance from center (2, 10) of Cluster-01	Distance from center (5, 8) of Cluster-02	Distance from center (1, 2) of Cluster-03	Point belongs to cluster
A1(2, 10)	0	5	9	C1
A2(2, 5)	5	6	4	C3
A3(8, 4)	12	7	9	C2
A4(5, 8)	5	0	10	C2
A5(7, 5)	10	5	9	C2
A6(6, 4)	10	5	7	C2
A7(1, 2)	9	10	0	C3
A8(4, 9)	3	2	10	C2

Cluster-02:
Second cluster contains points

- A3(8, 4)
- A4(5, 8)
- A5(7, 5)
- A6(6, 4)
- A8(4, 9)

Cluster-03:
Third cluster contains points

- A2(2, 5)
- A7(1, 2)

Now,

- We re-compute the new cluster clusters.
- The new cluster center is computed by taking mean of all the points contained in that cluster.

For Cluster-01:

- We have only one point A1(2, 10) in Cluster-01.
- So, cluster center remains the same.

For Cluster-02:

$$\text{Center of Cluster-02}$$
$$= ((8 + 5 + 7 + 6 + 4)/5, (4 + 8 + 5 + 4 + 9)/5)$$
$$= (6, 6)$$

For Cluster-03:

$$\text{Center of Cluster-03}$$
$$= ((2 + 1)/2, (5 + 2)/2)$$
$$= (1.5, 3.5)$$

This is completion of Iteration-01.
Iteration-02:

- We calculate the distance of each point from each of the center of the three clusters.
- The distance is calculated by using the given distance function.

The following illustration shows the calculation of distance between point A1(2, 10) and each of the center of the three clusters-
Calculating distance between A1(2, 10) and C1(2, 10)

$$P(A1, C1)$$
$$= |x2 - x1| + |y2 - y1|$$
$$= |2 - 2| + |10 - 10|$$
$$= 0$$

Calculating distance between A1(2, 10) and C2(6, 6)

$$P(A1, C2)$$
$$= |x2 - x1| + |y2 - y1|$$
$$= |6 - 2| + |6 - 10|$$
$$= 4 + 4$$
$$= 8$$

Calculating distance between A1(2, 10) and C3(1.5, 3.5)

$$P(A1, C3)$$
$$= |x2 - x1| + |y2 - y1|$$
$$= |1.5 - 2| + |3.5 - 10|$$
$$= 0.5 + 6.5$$
$$= 7$$

In the similar manner, we calculate the distance of other points from each of the center of the three clusters.
Next,

- We draw a table showing all the results.
- Using the table, we decide which point belongs to which cluster.
- The given point belongs to that cluster whose center is nearest to it. Table 4.7 shows the cluster analysis of the given points.

From here, new clusters are
Cluster-01:
First cluster contains points

- A1(2, 10)
- A8(4, 9)

Cluster-02:
Second cluster contains points

- A3(8, 4)
- A4(5, 8)

TABLE 4.7 Cluster analysis of the given dataset.

Given points	Distance from center (2, 10) of Cluster-01	Distance from center (6, 6) of Cluster-02	Distance from center (1.5, 3.5) of Cluster-03	Point belongs to cluster
A1(2, 10)	0	8	7	C1
A2(2, 5)	5	5	2	C3
A3(8, 4)	12	4	7	C2
A4(5, 8)	5	3	8	C2
A5(7, 5)	10	2	7	C2
A6(6, 4)	10	2	5	C2
A7(1, 2)	9	9	2	C3
A8(4, 9)	3	5	8	C1

- A5(7, 5)
- A6(6, 4)

  Cluster-03:
  Third cluster contains points

- A2(2, 5)
- A7(1, 2)

  Now,

- We re-compute the new cluster clusters.
- The new cluster center is computed by taking mean of all the points contained in that cluster.

  For Cluster-01:

$$\text{Center of Cluster-01}$$
$$= ((2+4)/2, (10+9)/2)$$
$$= (3, 9.5)$$

  For Cluster-02:

$$\text{Center of Cluster-02}$$
$$= ((8+5+7+6)/4, (4+8+5+4)/4)$$
$$= (6.5, 5.25)$$

  For Cluster-03:

$$\text{Center of Cluster-03}$$
$$= ((2+1)/2, (5+2)/2)$$
$$= (1.5, 3.5)$$

This is completion of Iteration-02.

After second iteration, the center of the three clusters are

- C1(3, 9.5)
- C2(6.5, 5.25)
- C3(1.5, 3.5)

Python program for K-means cluster:

```python
import numpy as np
from sklearn.cluster import KMeans
import matplotlib.pyplot as plt
# Input data
data = np.array([[2, 10], [2, 5], [8, 4], [5, 8], [7, 5], [6, 4], [1, 2], [4, 9]])
# Number of clusters
k = 3
# Create a K-means clustering model
model = KMeans(n_clusters=k, random_state=0)
# Fit the model to the data
model.fit(data)
# Get the cluster labels and cluster centers
labels = model.labels_
centers = model.cluster_centers_
# Plot the data points and cluster centers
plt.scatter(data[:, 0], data[:, 1], c=labels, cmap='viridis')
plt.scatter(centers[:, 0], centers[:, 1], c='red', marker='X')
plt.xlabel('X')
plt.ylabel('Y')
plt.title('K-means Clustering')
plt.show()
```

This program uses the scikit-learn library (sklearn) to perform K-means clustering. It creates a K-Means model with the desired number of clusters (k) and fits it to the input data. Then, it retrieves the cluster labels and cluster centers. Finally, it plots the data points with different colors representing different clusters, and marks the cluster centers with red crosses.

4.4.2 Cluster analysis of driverless car dataset

4.4.2.1 *Problem*

Suppose have a dataset for a driverless car. The dataset consists of two features: average speed and distance from the obstacle. We want to perform cluster analysis to group the driving scenarios into different clusters based on these features. Table 4.8 shows the dataset of the driver less car.

TABLE 4.8 The dataset of driverless car.

Average speed (km/h)	Distance (m)
60	20
40	30
70	25
50	40
45	35
55	15

Python program for the dataset of driverless car of Table 4.8:

```
import pandas as pd
from sklearn.cluster import KMeans
import matplotlib.pyplot as plt
# Create a DataFrame from the dataset
data = pd.DataFrame({
    'Average Speed': [60, 40, 70, 50, 45, 55],
    'Distance': [20, 30, 25, 40, 35, 15]
})
# Perform cluster analysis
num_clusters = 2  # Number of clusters to identify
kmeans = KMeans(n_clusters=num_clusters)
kmeans.fit(data)
# Get the cluster labels and centroids
cluster_labels = kmeans.labels_
centroids = kmeans.cluster_centers_
# Add the cluster labels to the dataset
data['Cluster'] = cluster_labels
# Visualize the clusters
plt.scatter(data['Average Speed'], data['Distance'], c=data['Cluster'])
plt.scatter(centroids[:, 0], centroids[:, 1], marker='X', color='red', label='Centroids')
plt.xlabel('Average Speed (km/h)')
plt.ylabel('Distance (m)')
plt.legend()
plt.show()
# Print the cluster labels
print("Cluster Labels:")
print(cluster_labels)
```

In this example, we create a DataFrame containing the "Average Speed" and "Distance" columns from the given dataset. Then apply the k-means algorithm with num_clusters = 2, indicating that want to identify two clusters. The cluster labels assigned by the algorithm are added to the DataFrame.

4.5 Linear regression analysis

Linear regression analysis is a statistical technique used to study the relationship between two continuous variables. It is commonly used in many fields such as economics, social sciences, engineering, and business to explore the association between two variables and to make predictions. In simple linear regression, one variable is considered as the independent variable, which is used to predict the dependent variable. The dependent variable is also known as the response variable and the independent variable is known as the predictor variable.

Following are the steps involved in linear regression analysis:

- Identify the research question and the variables of interest.
- Collect the data for the variables of interest.
- Identify dependent and independent variable.
- Plot the data to visualize the relationship between the variables.
- Calculate the correlation coefficient to measure the strength and direction of the relationship.
- Fit a linear regression model to the data using a suitable software tool.
- Interpret the results of the model by examining the coefficients and the goodness of fit statistics.
- Use the model to make predictions and test hypotheses.

Suppose want to study the relationship between the years of experience and salary of employees in a company. Collect data on 50 employees and record their years of experience and their corresponding salaries. Following are the steps we might take to perform linear regression analysis on this data:

- *Research question and variables of interest*: What is the relationship between years of experience and salary?
- *Independent variable*: Years of experience
- *Dependent variable*: Salary
- *Data collection*: Collect the data for years of experience and salary for 50 employees.
- *Data visualization*: Plot the data on a scatter plot to visualize the relationship between the variables.
- *Correlation coefficient*: Calculate the correlation coefficient to measure the strength and direction of the relationship between the variables. A value close to 1 indicates a strong positive relationship, while a value close to −1 indicates a strong negative relationship. A value close to 0 indicates a weak or no relationship.

- *Linear regression model*: Fit a linear regression model to the data using a suitable software tool such as R or Python. The model will estimate the slope and intercept of the line of best fit for the data.
- *Interpretation of results*: Examine the coefficients of the model to determine the strength and direction of the relationship between the variables. Also, look at the goodness of fit statistics such as R-squared, adjusted R-squared, and root mean square error to determine how well the model fits the data.
- *Prediction and hypothesis testing*: Use the model to make predictions about the salary of an employee with a given number of years of experience. Also, test hypotheses about the relationship between the variables using appropriate statistical tests such as t-tests or ANOVA.

4.5.1 Mathematical expression for regression analysis

$$y = AB^x$$

where A and B are constant
Taking the log on both sides of the equation, we get

$$\log y = \log A + x \log B$$

Putting $\log y = Y$, $\log A = a$, $\log B = b$ in equation

$$Y = a + bx$$

From equation, we get

$$\sum Y = \sum a + \sum bx$$

or

$$\sum Y = na + b \sum x$$
$$\sum xY = \sum ax + \sum bx^2$$

or

$$\sum xY = a \sum x + b \sum x^2$$

Taking an x = clearness index = C and by y = radiation = R, we get required data for x, y, Y, x^2, and Yx from the Table 4.9.
Substituting the values from table in equation we get

$$8.724207 = 12a + 7.19b$$

Substituting the values from table in equation we get

$$5.254343 = 7.19a + 4.414616b$$

TABLE 4.9 Regression analysis calculation.

Performance index (x)	Increment in % = (y)	Y = log10y	x²	Yx
0.659	4.55	0.658011	0.434281	0.43363
0.678	5.42	0.733999	0.459684	0.497652
0.658	6.14	0.788168	0.432964	0.518615
0.654	6.83	0.834421	0.427716	0.545711
0.632	6.96	0.842609	0.399424	0.532529
0.532	5.95	0.774517	0.283024	0.412043
0.438	4.85	0.685742	0.191844	0.300355
0.401	4.25	0.628389	0.160801	0.251984
0.531	5.14	0.710963	0.281961	0.377521
0.678	5.67	0.753583	0.459684	0.510929
0.672	4.79	0.680336	0.451584	0.457185
0.657	4.3	0.633468	0.431649	0.416189
Σ7.19	Σ64.85	Σ8.724207	Σ4.414616	Σ5.254343

From the above equations, respectively, we get

$$a = 0.5747692, b = 0.2540996$$

$$A = 10^a = 10^{0.5747692} = 3.756377236$$

$$B = 10^b = 10^{0.2540996} = 1.795145274$$

$$Y = AB^x \quad = 3.756377236(1.795145274)^x$$

$$Y = 3.75e^{0.58508x}$$

Substituting $x = C$ and $y = R$, $R = 3.75e^{0.58508x}$

$$\text{Salary increament} = 3.75e^{0.58508 \times \text{Performance Index}}$$

Python program of linear regression analysis for dataset mentioned in the table:

```
import numpy as np
from sklearn.linear_model import LinearRegression

# Input data
x = np.array([0.659, 0.678, 0.658, 0.654, 0.632, 0.532, 0.438,  0.401, 0.531, 0.678, 0.672,
0.657])
y = np.array([4.55, 5 42, 6.14, 6.83, 6.96, 5.95, 4.85, 4.25, 5.14, 5.67, 4.79, 4.3])
```

(cont'd)

```
# Reshape the input arrays
x = x.reshape(-1, 1)
y = y.reshape(-1, 1)

# Create a linear regression model
model = LinearRegression()

# Fit the model to the data
model.fit(x, y)

# Get the slope (coefficient) and intercept of the linear regression line
slope = model.coef_[0][0]
intercept = model.intercept_[0]

# Print the equation of the regression line
print(f"Regression line equation: y = {slope:.3f} * x + {intercept:.3f}")

# Predict the y-values for the given x-values
y_pred = model.predict(x)

# Print the predicted values
print("Predicted values:")
for i in range(len(x)):
    print(f"x = {x[i][0]:.3f}, y_pred = {y_pred[i][0]:.3f}")
```

This program uses the scikit-learn library (sklearn) to perform linear regression. It creates a linear regression model, fits it to the input data, and then predicts the values for the given *x*-values. The program also prints the equation of the regression line and the predicted values. Make sure you have scikit-learn installed (pip install scikit-learn) before running this program.

Python program for the regression analysis, where salary is the dependent parameter and years of experience is the independent parameter:

```
import pandas as pd
data1 = pd.read_csv('data.csv')
data1.head()
```

	YearsExperience	Salary
0	1.1	39343
1	1.3	46205
2	1.5	37731
3	2.0	43525
4	2.2	39891

Outcome

(cont'd)

data1.describe()   # statistical assessment

	YearsExperience	Salary
count	30.000000	30.000000
mean	5.313333	76003.000000
std	2.837888	27414.429785
min	1.100000	37731.000000
25%	3.200000	56720.750000
50%	4.700000	65237.000000
75%	7.700000	100544.750000
max	10.500000	122391.000000

Outcome

 # 2. Extract data from Years' Experience column is a variable named X
x = data1["YearsExperience"]
x

```
0     1.1
1     1.3
2     1.5
3     2.0
4     2.2
5     2.9
6     3.0
7     3.2
8     3.2
9     3.7
10    3.9
11    4.0
12    4.0
13    4.1
14    4.5
15    4.9
16    5.1
17    5.3
18    5.9
19    6.0
20    6.8
21    7.1
22    7.9
23    8.2
24    8.7
25    9.0
26    9.5
27    9.6
```

 # 3. Extract data from salary column is a variable named y
y = data1["Salary"]
y

0	39343
1	46205
2	37731
3	43525
4	39891
5	56642
6	60150
7	54445
8	64445
9	57189
10	63218
11	55794
12	56957
13	57081
14	61111
15	67938
16	66029
17	83088
18	81363
19	93940
20	91738
21	98273
22	101302

```
# 4. divide the dataset into two parts for training and testing  in 67% and 33% proportion
from sklearn.model_selection import train_test_split
x_train,x_test,y_train,y_test = train_test_split(x,y,test_size= 0.33, random_state =42)
x_train_reshaped= x_train.values.reshape(-1,1)
y_train_reshaped= y_train.values.reshape(-1,1)
x_test_reshaped= x_test.values.reshape(-1,1)
y_test_reshaped= y_test.values.reshape(-1,1)

x_train_reshaped

array([[ 2.2],
       [ 5.1],
       [ 2.9],
       [ 4.1],
       [ 4. ],
       [ 7.9],
       [ 1.3],
       [ 1.5],
       [ 9. ],
       [ 2. ],
       [ 7.1],
       [ 9.5],
       [ 5.9],
       [10.5],
       [ 6.8],
       [ 3.2],
       [ 3.9],
       [ 4.5],
       [ 6. ],
       [ 3. ]])
```

(cont'd)

```
# 5create and train linearregression model on training set
from sklearn.linear_model import LinearRegression
lin_reg = LinearRegression().fit(x_train_reshaped,y_train_reshaped)

# 6. Make prediction based on the testing set using the trained model
y_pred = lin_reg.predict(x_test_reshaped)
y_pred
   array([[115814.30756236],
          [ 71511.92534771],
          [102617.85328566],
          [ 75282.34085534],
          [ 55487.65944028],
          [ 60200.67882482],
          [122412.53470072],
          [107330.8726702 ],
          [ 63028.49045554],
          [ 35692.97802523]])

y_pred1= lin_reg.predict(y_test_reshaped)
y_pred1
   array([[1.06172720e+09],
          [6.40411546e+08],
          [1.07282165e+09],
          [7.83216034e+08],
          [6.07486393e+08],
          [5.39091055e+08],
          [1.15368764e+09],
          [1.03152617e+09],
          [5.36904215e+08],
          [3.70873968e+08]])

y_train_pred = lin_reg.predict(x_train_reshaped)
y_train_pred
```

<hr>

(*cont'd*)

```
array([[  46061.62067121],
       [  73397.13310153],
       [  52659.84780956],
       [  63971.09433245],
       [  63028.49045554],
       [  99790.04165494],
       [  37578.18577904],
       [  39463.39353286],
       [110158.68430092],
       [  44176.41291739],
       [  92249.21063968],
       [114871.70368546],
       [  80937.96411679],
       [124297.74245453],
       [  89421.39900895],
       [  55487.65944028],
       [  62085.88657864],
       [  67741.50984008],
       [  81880.56799369],
       [  53602.45168647]])
print(lin_reg.coef_)
print(lin_reg.intercept_)
# 7. r2 score
from sklearn.metrics import r2_score
print(r2_score(y_train_reshaped,y_train_pred))
  0.9549236946181227
```

<hr>

4.5.2 Solved example of linear regression analysis of driverless car

4.5.2.1 Problem

Suppose we have a dataset of driving data for a driverless car. The dataset consists of two features: distance traveled and time taken. We want to build a linear regression model to predict the time taken by the driverless car to travel a given distance. Table 4.10 shows the dataset of driverless car with distance and time.

TABLE 4.10   The dataset of driverless car with distance and time.

Distance (km)	Time (minutes)
10	15
20	30
30	40
40	50
50	60
60	70

4.5.2.2 *Solution*

Use Python and the scikit-learn library to solve this problem

```
import numpy as np
from sklearn.linear_model import LinearRegression
# Input data
X = np.array([[10], [20], [30], [40], [50], [60]])
y = np.array([15, 30, 40, 50, 60, 70])
# Create a linear regression model
model = LinearRegression()
# Fit the model to the data
model.fit(X, y)
# Test the model on new data
test_distance = np.array([[25], [35]])
# Predict the time taken
predictions = model.predict(test_distance)
# Print the predictions
for i in range(len(test_distance)):
    print(f"Distance: {test_distance[i][0]} km, Predicted Time: {predictions[i]:.2f} minutes")
```

4.6 Logistic regression analysis

Logistic regression is a statistical technique used to model the relationship between a binary dependent variable and one or more independent variables. The dependent variable can take one of two values, usually denoted as 0 and 1. The independent variables can be continuous or categorical, and the goal is to determine how they influence the probability of the dependent variable being 1 or 0.

Following are the steps involved in logistic regression analysis:

- Identify the research question and the variables of interest.
- Collect the data for the variables of interest.
- Explore the data to understand the distribution of the variables and check for outliers and missing values.
- Transform the dependent variable if necessary to ensure that it follows a binomial distribution.
- Fit a logistic regression model to the data using a suitable software tool.
- Interpret the results of the model by examining the coefficients and the goodness of fit statistics.
- Use the model to make predictions and test hypotheses.

Suppose we want to study the factors that influence whether or not a customer will purchase a product from an online store. We collect data on 500 customers and record whether they made a purchase (1) or not (0), as well as their age, gender, income, and website traffic.

Following are the steps we might take to perform logistic regression analysis on this data:

- *Research question and variables of interest*: What factors influence whether or not a customer will purchase a product?
- *Dependent variable*: Purchase (0/1)
- *Independent variables*: Age, gender, income, website traffic
- *Data collection*: Collect the data for the variables of interest for 500 customers.
- *Data exploration*: Explore the data to understand the distribution of the variables and check for outliers and missing values.
- *Dependent variable transformation*: Transform the dependent variable to ensure that it follows a binomial distribution. For example, we might use a logit or probit transformation.
- *Logistic regression model*: Fit a logistic regression model to the data using a suitable software tool such as R or Python. The model will estimate the coefficients of the independent variables and their effect on the probability of making a purchase.
- *Interpretation of results*: Examine the coefficients of the model to determine the influence of each independent variable on the probability of making a purchase. Also, look at the goodness of fit statistics such as the likelihood ratio test, Hosmer–Lemeshow test, and area under the receiver operating characteristic curve to determine how well the model fits the data.
- *Prediction and hypothesis testing*: Use the model to make predictions about the probability of a customer making a purchase based on their age, gender, income, and website traffic. Also, test hypotheses about the relationship between the variables using appropriate statistical tests such as Wald tests or likelihood ratio tests.

Python program of logistic regression analysis for diabetes dataset:

```
import pandas as pd
data2 = pd.read_csv("diabetes.csv")
data2.head(20)
```

	Glucose	BloodPressure	SkinThickness	Insulin	BMI	DiabetesPedigreeFunction	Age	Outcome
0	148	72	35	0	33.6	0.627	50	1
1	85	66	29	0	26.6	0.351	31	0
2	183	64	0	0	23.3	0.672	32	1
3	89	66	23	94	28.1	0.167	21	0
4	137	40	35	168	43.1	2.288	33	1
5	116	74	0	0	25.6	0.201	30	0
6	78	50	32	88	31.0	0.248	26	1
7	115	0	0	0	35.3	0.134	29	0
8	197	70	45	543	30.5	0.158	53	1
9	125	96	0	0	0.0	0.232	54	1
10	110	92	0	0	37.6	0.191	30	0
11	168	74	0	0	38.0	0.537	34	1

```
#2. Extract data from outcome as Y variable
y = data2["Outcome"]
y
```

(cont'd)

```
0      1
1      0
2      1
3      0
4      1
      ..
763    0
764    0
765    0
766    1
767    0
Name: Outcome, Length: 768, dtype: int64
```

# 3. extract data from every column except Outcome column in a variable named X
x = data2.iloc[:,:-1] # all row and only left last column
x

	Glucose	BloodPressure	SkinThickness	Insulin	BMI	DiabetesPedigreeFunction	Age
0	148	72	35	0	33.6	0.627	50
1	85	66	29	0	26.6	0.351	31
2	183	64	0	0	23.3	0.672	32
3	89	66	23	94	28.1	0.167	21
4	137	40	35	168	43.1	2.288	33
...	...	...	...	...	...	...	...
763	101	76	48	180	32.9	0.171	63
764	122	70	27	0	36.8	0.340	27
765	121	72	23	112	26.2	0.245	30
766	126	60	0	0	30.1	0.349	47
767	93	70	31	0	30.4	0.315	23

768 rows × 7 columns

# 4. divide the dataset into train and test 70 and 30 percent
from sklearn.model_selection import train_test_split
x_train,x_test,y_train,y_test = train_test_split(x,y,train_size= 0.7, random_state =10)
# 5. Create and Train Logistic Regression model on training set
from sklearn.linear_model import LogisticRegression
log_model = LogisticRegression().fit(x_train,y_train)

```
/usr/local/lib/python3.7/dist-packages/sklearn/linear_model/_logistic.py:818: ConvergenceWarning: lbfgs failed to converge (status=1):
STOP: TOTAL NO. of ITERATIONS REACHED LIMIT.

Increase the number of iterations (max_iter) or scale the data as shown in:
    https://scikit-learn.org/stable/modules/preprocessing.html
Please also refer to the documentation for alternative solver options:
    https://scikit-learn.org/stable/modules/linear_model.html#logistic-regression
extra_warning_msg=_LOGISTIC_SOLVER_CONVERGENCE_MSG,
```

# 6. make prediction based on the testing set using the trained model
y_pred = log_model.predict(x_test)
y_pred

(cont'd)

```
array([1, 0, 1, 0, 0, 0, 0, 0, 0, 1, 0, 0, 1, 0, 0, 1, 1, 0, 0, 1, 0, 0,
       0, 0, 0, 1, 0, 0, 1, 1, 0, 0, 0, 0, 0, 0, 0, 1, 0, 0, 0, 0, 0,
       0, 0, 0, 1, 0, 0, 1, 0, 0, 0, 0, 0, 0, 0, 0, 0, 0, 0, 0, 0, 0,
       1, 0, 0, 1, 1, 0, 0, 1, 0, 0, 1, 1, 0, 0, 0, 1, 0, 0, 0, 1, 0, 0,
       1, 0, 0, 0, 0, 0, 0, 0, 1, 0, 0, 0, 1, 0, 0, 0, 0, 1, 1, 1, 0, 1,
       0, 1, 0, 0, 0, 0, 0, 1, 0, 1, 0, 0, 0, 1, 0, 0, 0, 0, 0, 0, 1, 0,
       1, 0, 0, 0, 0, 1, 1, 1, 0, 0, 0, 1, 0, 0, 1, 1, 0, 0, 0, 1, 0,
       1, 0, 0, 0, 0, 0, 0, 1, 0, 0, 0, 0, 0, 1, 0, 0, 1, 0, 0, 0, 1, 0,
       0, 1, 0, 0, 0, 0, 0, 0, 0, 0, 0, 0, 0, 0, 1, 1, 0, 1, 0, 0, 0,
       0, 1, 1, 0, 0, 0, 1, 0, 0, 0, 1, 1, 0, 0, 0, 1, 0, 1, 0, 0, 0, 1,
       0, 0, 0, 1, 0, 0, 1, 1, 0, 0, 0])
```

y_test
```
  568    0
  620    0
  456    0
  197    1
  714    0
        ..
  345    0
  408    1
  304    0
  686    0
  202    0
Name: Outcome, Length: 231, dtype: int64
```

# 7. Check the performance by calculating the confusion matrix and accuracy score of the model
from sklearn.metrics import accuracy_score, confusion_matrix
accuracy_score(y_test,y_pred)

confusion_matrix(y_test,y_pred)

```
0.7445887445887446

array([[128,  16],
       [ 43,  44]])
```

TABLE 4.11   The dataset of exam score.

Exam 1 score	Exam 2 score	Pass/fail
84	78	1
90	87	1
69	56	0
70	65	0
91	89	1
76	75	1

Following are the example of solving a numerical problem using logistic regression analysis:

Problem:

Suppose we have a dataset of students' exam scores and their corresponding pass/fail outcomes. The dataset consists of two features: Exam 1 score and Exam 2 score. Now want to build a logistic regression model to predict whether a student will pass (1) or fail (0) based on their exam scores. Table 4.11 shows the dataset of exam score.

Use Python and the scikit-learn library to solve this problem:

```python
import numpy as np
from sklearn.linear_model import LogisticRegression

# Input data
X = np.array([[84, 78], [90, 87], [69, 56], [70, 65], [91, 89],  [76, 75]])
y = np.array([1, 1, 0, 0, 1, 1])

# Create a logistic regression model
model = LogisticRegression()

# Fit the model to the data
model.fit(X, y)

# Test the model on new data
test_scores = np.array([[80, 70], [95, 80], [60, 50]])

# Predict the pass/fail outcomes
predictions = model.predict(test_scores)

# Print the predictions
for i in range(len(test_scores)):
    print(f"Exam 1 score: {test_scores[i][0]}, Exam 2 score: {test_scores[i][1]}, Prediction:
{'Pass' if predictions[i] == 1 else 'Fail'}")
```

TABLE 4.12 Dataset of speed and distance.

Speed (km/h)	Distance (m)	Visibility (1–5)	Action (Stop = 0, Continue = 1)
60	20	3	1
40	30	2	0
70	25	5	1
50	40	4	0
45	35	3	0
55	15	2	1

Solution:

In this example, we first define the input data X as a NumPy array containing the exam scores, and the output data y as a NumPy array containing the pass/fail outcomes. Then, we create a logistic regression model and fit it to the data using the fit method. Next, we define some new test scores in the test_scores array and use the trained model to predict the pass/fail outcomes for these scores using the predict method. Finally, we print the predictions for each test score.

Problem:

Suppose we have a dataset of driving data for a driverless car. The dataset consists of three features: speed, distance from the obstacle, and visibility conditions. The target variable is whether the car should stop (0) or continue (1). We want to build a logistic regression model to predict the action of the driverless car based on the given features. Table 4.12 shows the dataset of speed and distance.

Solution:

Use Python and the scikit-learn library to solve this problem.

```
import numpy as np
from sklearn.linear_model import LogisticRegression
# Input data
X = np.array([[60, 20, 3], [40, 30, 2], [70, 25, 5], [50, 40, 4], [45, 35, 3], [55, 15, 2]])
y = np.array([1, 0, 1, 0, 0, 1])
# Create a logistic regression model
model = LogisticRegression()
# Fit the model to the data
model.fit(X, y)
# Test the model on new data
test_data = np.array([[65, 22, 4], [42, 32, 3]])
# Predict the actions (stop/continue)
predictions = model.predict(test_data)
# Print the predictions
for i in range(len(test_data)):
    print(f"Speed: {test_data[i][0]} km/h, Distance: {test_data[i][1]} m, Visibility: {test_data[i][2]}, Action: {'Continue' if predictions[i] == 1 else 'Stop'}")
```

In this example, first define the input data X as a NumPy array containing the speed, distance, and visibility features, and the output data y as a NumPy array containing the corresponding actions (stop/continue). Then, create a logistic regression model and fit it to the data using the fit method. Next, we define some new test data in the test_data array and use the trained model to predict the actions (stop/continue) based on these features using the predict method. Finally, we print the predictions for each test data point.

4.7 Application of analytics across value chain

Value chain analytics is the process of analyzing the various activities that create value for a business and identifying opportunities for optimization and improvement. The value chain is a concept developed by Michael Porter that describes the activities involved in creating a product or service, from the raw materials to the finished product or service.

There are two types of value chain analytics:

- *Internal value chain analysis*: This involves analyzing the activities within a company that contribute to its overall value creation. This includes functions such as production, marketing, logistics, and customer service. The goal of internal value chain analysis is to identify areas where a company can improve its efficiency and effectiveness, such as reducing costs or improving product quality.
- *External value chain analysis*: This involves analyzing the activities of the suppliers, customers, and other partners that contribute to a company's value creation. This includes functions such as research and development, distribution, and sales. The goal of external value chain analysis is to identify opportunities for collaboration and partnership that can improve a company's overall performance.

Following are the steps involved in conducting value chain analytics:

- *Identify the activities involved in the value chain*: This involves breaking down the value chain into its constituent parts and identifying the specific activities involved in each part.
- *Collect data on the activities*: This involves gathering data on the inputs, outputs, and processes involved in each activity, as well as any costs and performance metrics.
- *Analyze the data*: This involves using statistical and analytical tools to identify patterns and trends in the data, as well as to identify areas of inefficiency or opportunity for improvement.
- *Identify areas for improvement*: This involves using the insights from the analysis to identify specific areas where improvements can be made, such as reducing costs, improving quality, or enhancing customer service.
- *Implement improvements*: This involves putting into action the improvements identified through the analysis and monitoring their impact on the business.

    Value chain analytics can provide valuable insights into a company's operations and help identify areas for improvement. By understanding the activities involved in creating value for customers, companies can optimize their performance, reduce costs, and improve their competitive advantage.

Let's walk through an example of conducting a value chain analysis for a fictional company operating in the electronics industry.

Example:

Suppose have a company called "TechElectro" that manufactures and sells consumer electronics. It will perform a value chain analysis to identify the primary and support activities within the company's value chain and assess their strengths and weaknesses.

Step 1: Identify primary activities

The primary activities in the value chain are directly involved in creating and delivering the product or service. For TechElectro, the primary activities can include:

1. *Inbound logistics*: Procuring raw materials, components, and parts from suppliers.
2. *Operations*: Assembling and manufacturing electronic products.
3. *Outbound logistics*: Warehousing finished goods and distributing them to retailers or customers.
4. *Marketing and sales*: Promoting and selling the electronic products.
5. *Customer service*: Providing after-sales support and addressing customer inquiries.

Step 2: Identify support activities

Support activities provide the necessary infrastructure and resources to enable the primary activities. Some support activities for TechElectro can include:

1. *Procurement*: Negotiating contracts and managing relationships with suppliers.
2. *Technology and R&D*: Conducting research and development to innovate and improve product offerings.
3. *Human resources*: Recruiting, training, and managing a skilled workforce.
4. *Infrastructure*: Maintaining facilities, equipment, and IT systems required for operations.
5. *Firm infrastructure*: Overseeing strategic planning, finance, and legal functions.

Step 3: Assess strengths and weaknesses

For each primary and support activity, we assess its strengths and weaknesses to identify areas of competitive advantage and potential improvement. Following are the example:

Primary activities:

1. *Inbound logistics*:
   • *Strengths*: Established relationships with reliable suppliers, efficient inventory management.
   • *Weaknesses*: High transportation costs due to global sourcing, occasional supply chain disruptions.
2. *Operations*:
   • *Strengths*: Advanced manufacturing processes, stringent quality control measures.
   • *Weaknesses*: Relatively higher production costs compared to competitors.
3. *Outbound logistics*:
   • *Strengths*: Efficient warehousing and distribution network, timely delivery.
   • *Weaknesses*: Limited visibility into the supply chain beyond the distributors.
4. *Marketing and sales*:
   • *Strengths*: Strong brand recognition, effective digital marketing campaigns.
   • *Weaknesses*: Limited presence in emerging markets, heavy reliance on retail partners.

5. *Customer service*:
   - *Strengths*: Dedicated customer support team, prompt resolution of issues.
   - *Weaknesses*: Lack of self-service options, occasional delays in response time.

   Support activities:

1. *Procurement*:
   - *Strengths*: Favorable supplier contracts, regular evaluation of supplier performance.
   - *Weaknesses*: Limited supplier diversification, occasional quality control issues.
2. *Technology and R&D*:
   - *Strengths*: Ongoing investment in research and development, strong intellectual property portfolio.
   - *Weaknesses*: Longer time-to-market for new product releases, limited collaboration with external partners.
3. *Human resources*:
   - *Strengths*: Skilled and motivated workforce, robust training, and development programs.
   - *Weaknesses*: High employee turnover, limited diversity in the workforce.
4. *Infrastructure*:
   - *Strengths*: Modern manufacturing facilities, reliable IT systems.
   - *Weaknesses*: High energy consumption, occasional equipment maintenance challenges.
5. *Firm infrastructure*:
   - *Strengths*: Effective strategic planning, strong financial management.
   - *Weaknesses*: Limited agility in decision-making, bureaucratic processes.

By conducting this analysis, TechElectro can identify areas where they have a competitive advantage and areas that require improvement. This information can be used to develop strategies to enhance their value chain and gain a competitive edge in the market.

4.8 Multivariate data analytics with Python

Multivariate data analysis refers to the statistical analysis and exploration of datasets that contain multiple variables. It involves examining the relationships, patterns, and structures within the data to gain insights and make informed decisions. In multivariate data analysis, the variables are often interrelated, and analyzing them collectively provides a more comprehensive understanding of the underlying phenomena. Some common techniques used in multivariate data analysis include:

PCA: PCA is used to reduce the dimensionality of a dataset by identifying and retaining the most important features or variables that explain the maximum variance in the data.

Factor analysis: Factor analysis is used to identify underlying latent factors that explain the correlations among observed variables. It helps in understanding the common underlying dimensions or constructs in a dataset.

Cluster analysis: Cluster analysis is used to group similar data points or individuals into clusters based on their characteristics or variables. It helps in identifying homogeneous subgroups within a dataset.

Multivariate regression analysis: Multivariate regression analysis extends the concept of simple linear regression to multiple predictor variables. It helps in modeling and predicting the relationship between multiple independent variables and a dependent variable.

Discriminant analysis: Discriminant analysis is used to classify observations into predefined groups based on their measured characteristics. It helps in identifying the variables that contribute most to the separation of different groups.

Canonical correlation analysis: Canonical correlation analysis explores the relationship between two sets of variables and identifies linear combinations that are maximally correlated between the two sets. These are just a few examples of techniques used in multivariate data analysis. The choice of technique depends on the specific objectives, nature of the dataset, and the research questions being addressed.

Python program for multivariate analysis:

Problem:

Suppose we have a dataset of housing prices with multiple features such as the area (in square feet), number of bedrooms, and number of bathrooms. Want to build a multivariate regression model to predict the price of a house based on these features. Table 4.13 shows the dataset of multivariate analytics.

Solution:

Use Python and the scikit-learn library to solve this problem:

```
import numpy as np
from sklearn.linear_model import LinearRegression

# Input data
X = np.array([[1500, 3, 2], [2000, 4, 2.5], [1800, 3, 2], [2200, 3, 2.5], [2500, 4, 3], [1900, 3,
2]])
y = np.array([250000, 350000, 300000, 400000, 500000, 320000])

# Create a multivariate linear regression model
model = LinearRegression()

# Fit the model to the data
model.fit(X, y)

# Test the model on new data
test_data = np.array([[2100, 3, 2.5], [1800, 2, 1.5]])

# Predict the prices
predictions = model.predict(test_data)

# Print the predictions
for i in range(len(test_data)):
    print(f"Test Data: Area = {test_data[i][0]} sq. ft., Bedroo        ms = {test_data[i][1]},
Bathrooms ={test_data[i][2]}, Predicted Price = ${predictions[i]:,.2f}")
```

TABLE 4.13   Dataset of multivariate analytics.

Area (sq. ft.)	Bedrooms	Bathrooms	Price ($)
1500	3	2	250,000
2000	4	2.5	350,000
1800	3	2	300,000
2200	3	2.5	400,000
2500	4	3	500,000
1900	3	2	320,000

TABLE 4.14   Dataset of multiregression analysis.

Average speed (km/h)	Distance (m)	Visibility (1−5)	Time taken (minutes)
60	20	3	15
40	30	2	25
70	25	5	12
50	40	4	20
45	35	3	22
55	15	2	18

In this example, we first define the input data X as a NumPy array containing the area, number of bedrooms, and number of bathrooms, and the output data y as a NumPy array containing the corresponding house prices. Then, we create a linear regression model and fit it to the data using the fit method. Next, we define some new test data in the test_data array and use the trained model to predict the house prices based on these features using the predict method. Finally, we print the predictions for each test data point.

1. Solved example of the multiregression analysis of driver less car:

Problem:

Suppose have a dataset of driving data for a driverless car. The dataset consists of three features: average speed, distance from the obstacle, and visibility conditions. Want to build a multivariate regression model to predict the time taken by the driverless car to reach a destination based on these features. Table 4.14 shows the dataset of multiregression analysis.

Solution:

We will use Python and the scikit-learn library to solve this problem:

```python
import numpy as np
from sklearn.linear_model import LinearRegression

# Input data
X = np.array([[60, 20, 3], [40, 30, 2], [70, 25, 5], [50, 40, 4], [45, 35, 3], [55, 15, 2]])
y = np.array([15, 25, 12, 20, 22, 18])

# Create a multivariate linear regression model
model = LinearRegression()

# Fit the model to the data
model.fit(X, y)

# Test the model on new data
test_data = np.array([[65, 22, 4], [42, 32, 3]])

# Predict the time taken
predictions = model.predict(test_data)

# Print the predictions
for i in range(len(test_data)):
print(f"Test Data: Average Speed = {test_data[i][0]} km/h, Dist ance = {test_data[i][1]} m,
Visibility = {test_data[i][2]}, Predicted Time Taken = {predictions[i]:.2f} minutes")
```

4.9 Conclusion

In conclusion, multivariate data analytics and cognitive analytics play crucial roles in extracting meaningful insights and patterns from complex datasets. The techniques discussed, including factor analysis, PCA, regression analysis, logistic analysis, and multivariate analysis, offer powerful tools for analyzing and interpreting multivariate data. However, it is important to consider the limitations and assumptions associated with these techniques. Researchers should be mindful of potential biases, data quality issues, and the need for appropriate model validation and interpretation.

In summary, the integration of multivariate data analytics and cognitive analytics empowers organizations to unlock valuable insights from complex datasets, enabling them to make informed decisions, gain a competitive edge, and drive progress in their respective fields. With continuous advancements in technology and data analysis techniques, the potential for these analytical approaches to revolutionize decision-making and innovation is ever-expanding.

4.10 Case study

4.10.1 Case study: factor analysis for customer satisfaction in a hotel chain

4.10.1.1 Introduction

A hotel chain operates multiple hotels across different locations. The management wants to understand the key factors influencing customer satisfaction to improve service quality and enhance the overall guest experience. To achieve this, they decide to conduct factor analysis on a dataset containing customer feedback.

4.10.1.2 Data collection

The hotel chain collects data from customer feedback surveys. The survey includes questions related to various aspects of the hotel experience, such as room cleanliness, staff friendliness, amenities, food quality, and overall satisfaction. Each question is rated on a scale of 1–5, with 1 being "strongly dissatisfied" and 5 being "strongly satisfied."

4.10.1.3 Data analysis

1. *Data preparation*:

   The collected survey data is organized into a dataset with each row representing a customer and each column representing a survey question. Numeric ratings from 1 to 5 are assigned to the responses.

2. *Exploratory factor analysis (EFA)*:

   EFA is performed to identify the underlying factors that contribute to customer satisfaction. The analysis seeks to uncover latent variables that explain the observed patterns in the data. Commonly used factor extraction methods include PCA and maximum likelihood estimation.

3. *Factor extraction*:

   The factor extraction process identifies the number of factors to retain based on eigenvalues, scree plots, and variance explained. The extraction method chosen determines the interpretation of the factors. Rotation methods such as Varimax or Oblimin are used to enhance the interpretability of the factors.

4. *Factor interpretation*:

   After extraction and rotation, each factor is interpreted based on the survey questions that load most strongly on it. For example, if a factor has high loadings on questions related to room cleanliness and amenities, it may be labeled as "Facilities Quality." Factors with loadings below a certain threshold may be excluded from further analysis.

5. *Factor scores*:

   Once the factors are identified and interpreted, factor scores can be computed for each customer. These scores represent the extent to which a customer's responses align with each factor. Higher factor scores indicate a higher level of satisfaction with the corresponding factor.

6. *Analysis of variance (ANOVA)*:

   ANOVA can be performed to assess whether there are significant differences in the mean factor scores across different customer segments, such as age groups or loyalty program membership. This analysis helps identify specific customer segments that exhibit varying satisfaction levels.

By conducting factor analysis, the hotel chain gains insights into the key factors driving customer satisfaction. They discover factors like "Facilities Quality," "Staff Service," and "Food and Beverage" that significantly influence guest satisfaction. Armed with this knowledge, the hotel chain can prioritize areas for improvement, allocate resources effectively, and tailor their service offerings to meet customer expectations. This case study provides an overview of the factor analysis process in the context of customer satisfaction. The actual implementation may vary depending on the specific dataset, software used, and analysis techniques employed.

4.10.2 Case study: regression analysis in real estate market

4.10.2.1 Introduction

Regression analysis is a powerful statistical tool widely used in various fields, including finance, economics, and market research. In this case study, we will explore the application of regression analysis in the real estate market. Specifically, we will examine the relationship between housing prices and several key factors, such as square footage, number of bedrooms, location, and proximity to amenities.

4.10.2.2 Background

A real estate agency wants to understand the factors that influence housing prices in a particular city. They have collected data on recent home sales, including information about the property characteristics and sale prices. The agency aims to build a regression model that can predict housing prices based on the available variables.

4.10.2.3 Data collection

The real estate agency gathered data from 200 recently sold properties in the city. The variables collected for each property include:

- *Sale price*: The final sale price of the property in dollars.
- *Square footage*: The total area of the property in square feet.
- *Number of bedrooms*: The number of bedrooms in the property.
- *Location*: A categorical variable indicating the neighborhood or district of the property.
- *Proximity to amenities*: A measure of the property's distance to amenities like schools, parks, and shopping centers.

4.10.2.4 Regression analysis

Data preprocessing: The dataset is cleaned and checked for missing values or outliers. Categorical variables, such as location, are converted into numerical dummy variables.

Model building: A multiple linear regression model is constructed to predict housing prices based on the available variables. The sale price is considered the dependent variable, while square footage, number of bedrooms, location, and proximity to amenities are treated as independent variables.

Assumptions checking: The assumptions of linear regression, including linearity, independence, homoscedasticity, and normality of residuals, are tested to ensure the validity of the regression model.

Variable selection: Variable selection techniques, such as stepwise regression or backward elimination, may be employed to identify the most significant predictors of housing prices.

Model evaluation: The regression model is evaluated using statistical metrics such as R-squared, adjusted R-squared, and P-values of the regression coefficients. These metrics help assess the overall fit of the model and the significance of individual predictors.

Prediction and interpretation: Once the model is deemed satisfactory, it can be used to predict housing prices for new properties based on their characteristics. The coefficients of the regression equation provide insights into the impact of each predictor on housing prices. For example, the coefficient of square footage indicates the average change in price per unit increase in square footage.

Regression analysis proves to be a valuable tool in understanding the relationship between housing prices and various factors in the real estate market. By building a regression model, the real estate agency can predict housing prices accurately and gain insights into the importance of factors such as square footage, number of bedrooms, location, and proximity to amenities. This information enables the agency to make informed decisions, provide accurate property valuations, and offer valuable advice to their clients.

4.11 Exercise

4.11.1 Objective type question

1. Factor analysis is a statistical method used for:
   a. Hypothesis testing
   b. Dimensionality reduction
   c. Causal inference
   d. Data visualization

2. The main goal of factor analysis is to:
   a. Identify hidden factors underlying observed variables
   b. Determine causality between variables
   c. Calculate the correlation coefficients between variables
   d. Predict future outcomes based on past data

3. In factor analysis, the factors are:
   a. Observed variables
   b. Categorical variables
   c. Latent variables
   d. Independent variables

4. The number of factors extracted in factor analysis is determined by:
   a. The researcher's choice
   b. The number of variables in the dataset
   c. The statistical software used
   d. The eigenvalues of the correlation matrix

5. Factor loading represents:
   a. The strength of the relationship between a variable and a factor
   b. The significance level of a variable in the analysis
   c. The number of factors extracted in the analysis
   d. The standard deviation of the variable

6. Principal Component Analysis (PCA) is a technique used for:
   a. Hypothesis testing
   b. Dimensionality reduction
   c. Causal inference
   d. Data clustering

7. The main goal of PCA is to:
   a. Identify hidden factors underlying observed variables
   b. Determine causality between variables
   c. Calculate the correlation coefficients between variables
   d. Transform the data into uncorrelated components

8. The components in PCA are:
   a. Observed variables
   b. Categorical variables
   c. Latent variables
   d. Independent variables

9. The number of components retained in PCA is determined by:
   a. The researcher's choice
   b. The number of variables in the dataset
   c. The statistical software used
   d. The amount of variance explained by each component

10. Eigenvalue in PCA refers to:
    a. The proportion of total variance explained by a component
    b. The correlation coefficient between two variables
    c. The sum of squared residuals in the analysis
    d. The p-value of a statistical test

11. Regression analysis is a statistical technique used to:
    a. Test the difference between two means
    b. Determine causality between variables
    c. Predict the value of a dependent variable based on independent variables
    d. Identify hidden factors underlying observed variables

12. The dependent variable in regression analysis is also known as the:
    a. Predictor variable
    b. Independent variable
    c. Response variable
    d. Explanatory variable

13. The purpose of a regression equation is to:
    a. Calculate the correlation coefficient between variables
    b. Identify the direction of the relationship between variables
    c. Estimate the values of the dependent variable based on the independent variables
    d. Test the significance of the relationship between variables

14. In multiple regression analysis, the number of independent variables is:
    a. One
    b. Two
    c. Three or more
    d. It can vary depending on the analysis

15. The coefficient of determination (R-squared) in regression analysis represents:
    a. The strength of the relationship between the variables
    b. The percentage of variation in the dependent variable explained by the independent variable(s)
    c. The standard deviation of the residuals
    d. The p-value of the regression model

4.11.2 Descriptive type question

1. Explain the concept of factor analysis and its role in multivariate data analytics. How does factor analysis help in reducing the dimensionality of a dataset and uncovering underlying factors?
2. Describe the process of PCA in multivariate data analytics. How does PCA transform correlated variables into uncorrelated principal components? What are the benefits of PCA in data visualization and dimensionality reduction?
3. Discuss the application of regression analysis in multivariate data analytics. How does regression analysis examine the relationship between a dependent variable and multiple independent variables? Provide an example of how regression analysis can be used to make predictions or understand causal relationships.
4. Explain the concept of logistic analysis and its significance in multivariate data analytics. How does logistic analysis differ from regression analysis? Provide an example of how logistic analysis can be used to predict binary outcomes or classify observations into distinct categories.
5. Discuss the importance of multivariate analysis in understanding complex datasets. What are some common techniques used in multivariate analysis, apart from factor analysis, PCA, regression analysis, and logistic analysis? Provide examples of situations where multivariate analysis is beneficial and how it contributes to enhanced insights and decision-making.

6. Explain how cognitive analytics complements multivariate data analytics. How does cognitive analytics leverage advanced technologies like artificial intelligence and machine learning to process and interpret complex datasets? Discuss the potential benefits and challenges of incorporating cognitive analytics in multivariate data analysis.
7. Compare and contrast factor analysis and PCA. What are the similarities and differences between these two techniques in multivariate data analytics? When would you choose one over the other?
8. Describe the steps involved in conducting a multivariate analysis. How would you approach analyzing a dataset with multiple variables using techniques such as factor analysis, PCA, regression analysis, logistic analysis, and other relevant methods? Discuss the considerations and challenges in implementing a comprehensive multivariate analysis.
9. Discuss the limitations or assumptions associated with the techniques mentioned in the title. What are some factors that researchers need to be mindful of when applying factor analysis, PCA, regression analysis, logistic analysis, and multivariate analysis? How can these limitations be addressed or mitigated?
10. Provide real-world examples of how multivariate data analytics and cognitive analytics have been applied in different industries or domains. Highlight the specific techniques used and the insights gained from these analyses. Discuss the potential impact of these analytics approaches on improving decision-making and driving innovation in various fields.

Further reading

J.O. Ramsay, B.W. Silverman, Functional Data Analysis, Springer, 2000.
J.O. Ramsay, B.W. Silverman, Functional Data Analysis, Springer, New York, NY, 2005.
G. Romanillos, M.Z. Austwick, D. Ettema, J. De Kruijf, Big data and cycling, Transp. Rev. 36 (1) (2016) 114–133.
A. Roy, T.A. Nelson, A. Stewart Fotheringham, M. Winters, Correcting bias in crowdsourced data to map bicycle ridership of all bicyclists, Urban. Sci. 3 (2) (2019) 62.
A. Roy, P. Turaga, T. Nelson, Data and code for FDA analysis functional data analysis for spatial-temporal change detection. figshare Software (2020). https://doi.org/10.6084/m9.figshare.13171862.
D. Saha, P. Alluri, A. Gan, W.U. Wanyang, Spatial analysis of macro-level bicycle crashes using the class of conditional autoregressive models, Accid. Anal. Prev. 118 (2018) 166–177.
A. Srivastava, S.H. Joshi, W. Mio, X. Liu, Statistical shape analysis: clustering, learning, and testing, IEEE Trans. pattern Anal. Mach. Intell. 27 (4) (2005) 590–602.
A. Srivastava, E. Klassen, S.H. Joshi, I.H. Jermyn, Shape analysis of elastic curves in euclidean spaces, IEEE Trans. pattern Anal. Mach. Intell. 33 (7) (2010) 1415–1428.
A. Srivastava, W. Wu, S. Kurtek, E. Klassen, J.S. Marron, Registration of functional data using Fisher-Rao metric. arXiv preprint arXiv:1103.3817 (2011).
D.A. Stow, Reducing the effects of misregistration on pixel-level change detection, Int. J. Remote. Sens. 20 (12) (1999) 2477–2483.
R. Tibshirani, G. Walther, T. Hastie, Estimating the number of clusters in a data set via the gap statistic, J. R. Stat. Soc. Ser. B (Stat Methodol. 63 (2) (2001) 411–423.
J.M. Torres, P.G. Nieto, L. Alejano, A.N. Reyes, Detection of outliers in gas emissions from urban areas using functional data analysis, J. Hazard. Mater. 186 (1) (2011) 144–149.

Artificial intelligence and machine learning application in data analysis

Abbreviations

ML	machine learning
AI	artificial intelligence
RL	reinforcement learning
NLP	natural language processing
UI	user interface
GUI	graphical user interfaces
ATM	automated teller machines
IOT	internet of technology
TOM	theory of mind
OWL	web ontology language
RDF	resource description framework
SLAM	simultaneous localization and mapping
ECU	electronic control units
IMU	inertial measurement units
CSP	constraint satisfaction problems
LDA	latent Dirichlet allocation
NER	Named entity recognition

5.1 Introduction

Artificial intelligence (AI) is a branch of computer science and engineering that aims to create intelligent machines that can perform tasks that normally require human intelligence, such as understanding natural language, recognizing objects, making decisions, and learning from experience. AI systems use algorithms and statistical models to analyze and interpret large amounts of data, and they can improve their performance over time through machine learning (ML) techniques such as supervised, unsupervised, and reinforcement learning (RL). AI is used in various applications, including image and speech recognition, natural language processing (NLP), autonomous vehicles, predictive analytics, robotics, and gaming. AI is playing an increasingly important role in today's technology. AI can automate routine tasks and processes, freeing up humans to focus on more creative and strategic work. It can analyze large amounts of data to create personalized experiences

Cognitive Science, Computational Intelligence, and Data Analytics
DOI: https://doi.org/10.1016/B978-0-443-16078-3.00001-0
© 2024 Elsevier Inc. All rights are reserved, including those for text and data mining, AI training, and similar technologies.

for users, such as personalized recommendations on websites or personalized healthcare plans. AI can analyze historical data and make predictions about future events, such as predicting equipment failures in a manufacturing plant or predicting customer behavior in marketing. AI is helping to make technology more intelligent, efficient, and effective, and is enabling new applications and services that were not possible before.

On the other hand, ML is a subset of AI that involves developing algorithms and statistical models that enable computer systems to learn from data, identify patterns, and make predictions or decisions without being explicitly programmed. In other words, ML systems can learn from experience, improve their performance over time, and adapt to new situations.

There are several types of ML, including:

1. Supervised learning:

Supervised learning is a subfield of ML where an algorithm learns from labeled training data to make predictions or take actions. In supervised learning, the algorithm is provided with input data, also known as features, and the corresponding correct outputs, known as labels or targets. The goal is for the algorithm to learn the mapping between the input features and their corresponding labels so that it can accurately predict the correct label for new, unseen inputs. The system undergoes training using labeled data, where correct answers are provided, enabling it to make predictions based on this acquired knowledge. Supervised learning, a form of ML, involves teaching computers to identify patterns in data through training on labeled examples. In essence, it entails educating a ML model by supplying it with labeled data and allowing it to discern the underlying patterns within that data. For instance, an illustration of supervised learning could involve the task of classifying images. Suppose we possess a dataset comprising images of fruits like apples, oranges, and bananas. Each image is accompanied by a label indicating the fruit it depicts. The objective of our supervised learning algorithm would involve training it to recognize the distinct fruits within the images. Fig. 5.1 shows the path of the supervised learning.

To achieve this, our initial step would involve partitioning the dataset into two segments: a training set and a testing set. The training set would encompass a considerable number of labeled images, serving as the data used to train our ML model. The testing set, on the other hand, would consist of a smaller number of labeled images utilized to assess the model's performance. Subsequently, we would employ a supervised learning algorithm like a convolutional neural network and input the training data into it. Through analyzing the labeled images, the algorithm would grasp

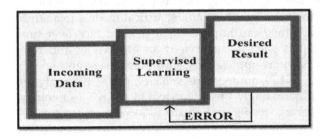

FIGURE 5.1   Path of supervised learning.

the distinctive features characterizing various fruits. Once the model has completed its training, would gauge its effectiveness on the testing set, assessing its ability to accurately classify the fruits. If the model exhibits strong performance on the testing set, it can then be employed to classify novel fruit images that it has never encountered before. This exemplifies the potency of supervised learning, as it empowers us to instruct machines in recognizing data patterns and employing that knowledge to generate predictions on new data.

2. Unsupervised learning:

Unsupervised learning is a subfield of ML where the algorithm learns patterns and structures in unlabeled data without any specific target or output variable to guide the learning process. Unlike supervised learning, there are no predefined labels or correct answers provided to the algorithm during training. Instead, the algorithm explores the data and identifies inherent patterns, relationships, or clusters within it. The system is trained on unlabeled data and must identify patterns and relationships on its own. Unsupervised learning is a type of ML algorithm in which the computer learns to identify patterns in data without being given any explicit guidance or labeled examples. Instead, the algorithm must identify the structure in the data on its own. An example of unsupervised learning can be clustering, which involves grouping data points that are similar to each other based on some similarity metric. For instance, a dataset of customer shopping behavior in a supermarket. The dataset contains information such as customer ID, age, gender, items purchased, and the amount spent. Fig. 5.2 shows the path of unsupervised learning.

To perform clustering, we would use an unsupervised learning algorithm such as K-means clustering. The algorithm would group the customers based on similarities in their purchasing behavior. It would do this by first randomly selecting k centroids (representative points) in the data space and assigning each data point to the centroid closest to it. Then, the algorithm would calculate the mean of each cluster and update the centroids to be the mean of the points in that cluster. This process is repeated until the centroids no longer move, and the algorithm converges to a stable set of clusters. The resulting clusters could reveal patterns such as groups of customers who purchase similar items or customers who tend to spend more than others. This information could be used by the supermarket to tailor their marketing strategies to each cluster's preferences and maximize sales. Unsupervised learning is a powerful technique for discovering hidden patterns in data that may not be easily recognizable using traditional methods. It can be used in a variety of applications, such as image and speech recognition, anomaly detection, and NLP.

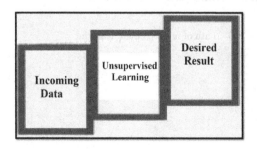

FIGURE 5.2   Path of unsupervised learning.

3. Reinforcement learning:

RL is a subfield of ML concerned with how an agent can learn to make sequential decisions in an environment to maximize a notion of cumulative reward. It is a type of learning where an agent interacts with an environment, learns from the consequences of its actions, and adapts its behavior over time to achieve specific goals. The system learns through trial and error, receiving feedback in the form of rewards or penalties for its actions. RL is a type of ML algorithm in which an agent learns to make decisions in an environment by receiving rewards or punishments for its actions. The goal of the agent is to learn to maximize its cumulative reward over time. An example of RL can be teaching a computer to play a game of chess. In this case, the environment would be the chessboard, and the agent would be the computer player. At the beginning of the game, the agent would receive an initial state of the chessboard as input. It would then choose a move based on its current policy, which could be a set of rules or a ML algorithm. The move would be executed on the chessboard, and the state of the game would be updated. Fig. 5.3 shows the path of RL.

The agent would then receive a reward signal based on the outcome of the move. If the move led to a favorable outcome, such as capturing an opponent's piece, the agent would receive a positive reward. If the move led to an unfavorable outcome, such as losing its own piece, the agent would receive a negative reward. The agent would continue to play the game, receiving rewards or punishments for each move, and updating its policy accordingly to maximize its cumulative reward over time. Eventually, the agent would learn to make better decisions and become more skilled at playing chess. RL is a powerful technique that has been used in a variety of applications, such as robotics, game playing, and autonomous driving. It allows machines to learn to make decisions and take actions in complex environments without human intervention, making it a key component of AI. ML is used in a wide variety of applications, including image and speech recognition, NLP, fraud detection, recommendation systems, and autonomous vehicles, among others. By providing insights and predictions based on large amounts of data, ML is helping businesses to make better decisions and improve their operations.

AI and ML are related concepts, but they are not the same thing. AI is a broad field of computer science that aims to create intelligent machines that can perform tasks that normally require human intelligence, such as understanding natural language, recognizing objects, making decisions, and learning from experience. On the other hand, ML is a subset of AI that involves developing algorithms and statistical models that enable computer systems to learn from data, identify patterns, and make

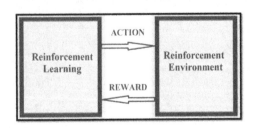

FIGURE 5.3   Path of reinforcement learning.

predictions or decisions without being explicitly programmed. In other words, ML is a specific technique used in AI to teach machines how to learn from data. AI is a broader field that includes various techniques and approaches to creating intelligent machines, of which ML is just one example. While both AI and ML are related and often used together, they are not interchangeable terms. To summarize, AI is the broader field of creating intelligent machines, while ML is a specific technique within AI that involves training machines to learn from data.

AI and ML are related concepts, and they share also some similarities. Few of the similarities in between them are:

- Both AI and ML involve computer systems that can perform tasks that normally require human intelligence, such as recognizing patterns, making predictions, and learning from experience.
- Both AI and ML require large amounts of data to train the computer systems.
- Both AI and ML involve algorithms and statistical models to analyze and interpret the data.
- Both AI and ML are used in a wide variety of applications, including image and speech recognition, NLP, fraud detection, recommendation systems, and autonomous vehicles, among others.
- Both AI and ML are rapidly advancing fields that are transforming many industries and sectors.

While there are some differences between AI and ML, they share many similarities and are often used together to create intelligent systems that can learn and improve over time.

5.2 Fundamentals of artificial intelligence

The fundamental of AI is the creation of intelligent machines that can perform tasks that normally require human intelligence, such as learning, reasoning, perception, and decision-making. Fig. 5.4 shows the fundamental of AI. Following are some key concepts that form the basis of AI:

5.2.1 Natural language processing

NLP involves developing algorithms that enable computers to understand, interpret, and generate human language. NLP is a field of AI that focuses on enabling computers to understand, interpret, and generate human language. NLP techniques are used to analyze and manipulate large amounts of natural language data, such as text, speech, and human conversation.

- Some of the common applications of NLP include:
  - Sentiment analysis: This involves using NLP techniques to analyze and classify text into positive, negative, or neutral sentiments. It can be used to monitor social media sentiment about a product or service.

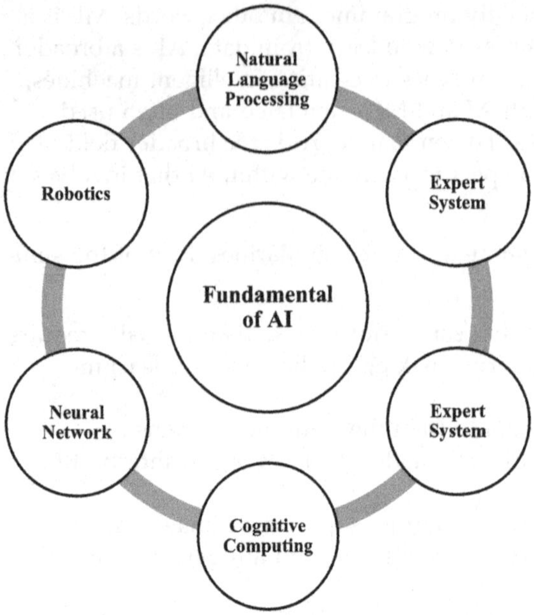

FIGURE 5.4 Fundamental of artificial intelligence.

- Machine translation: This involves using NLP techniques to automatically translate text from one language to another. For example, Google Translate uses NLP to translate text between different languages.
- Named entity recognition: This involves using NLP techniques to identify and classify named entities in text, such as people, organizations, and locations. This can be used in applications such as information retrieval and question answering.
- Chatbots: This involves using NLP techniques to create conversational agents that can understand and respond to human language. Chatbots are used in customer service and support applications.
- Text summarization: This involves using NLP techniques to automatically generate a summary of a longer text, such as a news article or research paper.

NLP algorithms use a variety of techniques such as ML, deep learning, and rule-based methods to understand and process human language. As the field of NLP continues to advance, it is expected to play an increasingly important role in many areas of our lives, including healthcare, education, and business.

5.2.2 Robotics

Robotics involves developing machines that can perform physical tasks and interact with the environment, often using sensors and machine vision. Robotics is a field of engineering and computer science that deals with the design, construction, and operation of robots. Robotics is closely related to AI as robots often use AI techniques to make decisions and perform tasks. One of the key applications of AI in robotics is in the area of autonomous robots. Autonomous robots are designed to operate without human intervention and to make their own decisions based on the environment and tasks at hand. These robots use a variety of AI techniques, such as ML, computer vision, and NLP, to perceive the environment, understand tasks, and plan actions.

For example, self-driving cars are a type of autonomous robot that use AI to navigate roads and traffic, detect objects, and make driving decisions. These cars use ML algorithms to recognize objects and patterns in the environment, such as other vehicles, pedestrians, and traffic signs, and use this information to make decisions about how to navigate. Another example of robotics in AI is in the area of industrial automation. Robots are used in manufacturing and assembly lines to perform repetitive and dangerous tasks, such as welding, painting, and packaging. These robots use computer vision and ML algorithms to identify parts, detect defects, and adjust their movements accordingly.

In addition to autonomous robots and industrial automation, AI is also used in robotics for other applications such as healthcare, agriculture, and space exploration. As AI technology continues to advance, can expect to see more sophisticated robots that can perform more complex tasks and operate in a wider range of environments.

5.2.3 Expert systems

Expert systems involve developing computer programs that can solve complex problems in a specific domain, often using a knowledge base and decision-making rules. An expert system is a type of AI system that uses knowledge and reasoning techniques to solve problems that would normally require human expertise. An expert system is designed to mimic the decision-making abilities of a human expert in a particular domain or field.

- The key components of an expert system are:
  - Knowledge base
    This is a collection of facts and rules about a specific domain, gathered from subject matter experts. The knowledge base is used to represent the expertise of the system. A knowledge base in an expert system is a collection of information that represents the expertise of a human expert in a particular field. It contains facts, rules, procedures, and other forms of knowledge that are used by the system to make decisions and provide solutions to problems. The knowledge base is created by experts in the field and is designed to capture the knowledge that is relevant to the system's domain. The knowledge base is the core of the expert system, and it is responsible for storing and organizing the information that the system uses to make decisions. It can be built using various techniques, such as rule-based systems, decision trees, neural networks, fuzzy logic, and other AI methods. The knowledge base is typically structured in a way that allows the system to access and retrieve the information quickly and efficiently. The knowledge base in an expert system is the repository of knowledge that represents the expertise of a human expert and enables the system to reason and make decisions in its domain.
  - Inference engine
    This is the reasoning component of the system that uses the knowledge base to draw conclusions and make decisions. The inference engine uses rules and algorithms to

process data and information from the knowledge base. An inference engine is a critical component of an expert system that uses the knowledge base to derive conclusions and make decisions. It is a software module that applies rules and logical reasoning to the data in the knowledge base to reach a solution or answer to a problem.

The inference engine works by applying a set of rules and facts from the knowledge base to the input data provided by the user. It examines the data, applies logical reasoning and inference techniques, and then generates an output that is based on the knowledge in the system. The output could be a solution to a problem, an explanation of a phenomenon, or a prediction of future events. The inference engine operates in a cycle, where it continuously applies rules to the data until a solution is reached or no more rules can be applied. This cycle is called the reasoning cycle, and it is the heart of the expert system's operation. The inference engine can be implemented using various algorithms and techniques, such as forward chaining, backward chaining, fuzzy logic, and neural networks. The choice of the technique depends on the nature of the problem, the complexity of the knowledge base, and the performance requirements of the system. The inference engine is a crucial component of an expert system that uses logical reasoning and rules to derive conclusions and make decisions based on the knowledge in the system.

- User interface

This is the interface that allows users to interact with the system, input data, and receive output. The user interface (UI) can be graphical or text-based. The UI in an expert system is the means by which the user interacts with the system. It is the interface between the user and the expert system, allowing the user to input information and receive output in a way that is easy to understand and use.

The UI in an expert system typically includes three components: input, processing, and output. The input component allows the user to enter information or data into the system, which is then processed by the inference engine using the rules and knowledge in the knowledge base. The output component displays the results of the processing to the user, either as text, graphics, or both. The UI should be designed to be intuitive and easy to use, with clear instructions and prompts for the user. It should also provide feedback to the user, letting them know the system's current state and progress, and indicating any errors or issues that need to be addressed.

There are several types of UIs that can be used in expert systems, including command-line interfaces, menu-driven interfaces, graphical user interfaces (GUIs), and natural language interfaces. The choice of interface depends on the system's complexity, the expertise of the user, and the application's specific needs. The UI in an expert system is the means by which the user interacts with the system, allowing them to input information, receive output, and interact with the system in a way that is easy to understand and use.

Expert systems are used in a variety of applications such as healthcare, finance, and engineering. For example, an expert system can be used to diagnose medical conditions by asking a series of questions and analyzing symptoms. In finance, an expert system can be used to analyze financial data and make investment recommendations. In engineering, an expert system can be used to design complex systems such as aircraft or industrial machinery. Expert systems are particularly useful in situations where there is a shortage of human experts or where human experts are unable to solve a problem due to the complexity or scale of the problem. Expert systems can be deployed in a variety of settings, including desktop applications, web-based applications, and mobile devices. While expert systems are not capable of replacing human experts entirely, they can assist human experts in making decisions and performing tasks more efficiently and accurately.

- Neural networks

   Neural networks involve developing computer systems that can simulate the behavior of the human brain, and can be trained to perform specific tasks such as image recognition or language translation. Expert systems are computer programs that simulate the decision-making ability of a human expert in a particular domain. Neural networks, on the other hand, are a subset of ML algorithms that can learn patterns and relationships from data.

   In the context of expert systems, neural networks can be used as a component of the system to provide intelligent decision-making capabilities. For example, a neural network can be trained on a dataset of historical data related to the domain of the expert system, and then used to make predictions or classifications based on new input data. Neural networks can also be used in conjunction with other components of an expert system, such as rule-based systems or decision trees, to provide more accurate and flexible decision-making. The output of a neural network can be combined with the output of other components to provide a final decision or recommendation. It's important to note that the use of neural networks in expert systems requires a significant amount of data and computing resources, as well as expertise in both the domain of the expert system and ML. Therefore, it may not be practical for all applications.

- Cognitive computing

   Cognitive computing involves developing computer systems that can mimic the cognitive processes of humans, such as learning, reasoning, and decision-making. Cognitive computing refers to the use of computer systems that can simulate human cognition, such as perception, reasoning, learning, and problem-solving. Expert systems, on the other hand, are computer programs designed to emulate the decision-making ability of a human expert in a specific domain. Incorporating cognitive computing capabilities into an expert system can enhance its ability to reason, learn, and make decisions. For example, a cognitive expert system can leverage NLP to better understand and process human language, allowing it to communicate more effectively with users and better understand their input. It can also incorporate ML algorithms to analyze and learn from data, which can improve the accuracy and effectiveness of the system over time. Furthermore, cognitive expert systems can incorporate various sensory inputs, such as images, sounds, and videos, to simulate human perception and enable the system to make decisions based on multimodal data. Cognitive computing can provide significant benefits to expert systems by enhancing their ability to reason, learn, and make decisions, making them more effective and useful tools for a wide range of applications.

5.3 Spectrum of artificial intelligence

The spectrum of AI is typically divided into four categories, based on the level of intelligence and autonomy that an AI system can exhibit. These categories are:

- Reactive machine
- Limited memory
- Theory of mind
- Self-aware

Fig. 5.5 shows the schematic diagram of different elements of the spectrum of AI.

5.3.1 Reactive machines

These AI systems are the simplest form of AI and operate based on a predefined set of rules. They can only respond to specific situations and do not have the ability to learn or adapt to new situations. Examples of reactive machines include traditional chess-playing computers and automated teller machines.

A reactive machine is a type of AI that operates purely on the basis of its immediate inputs and outputs, without any memory or ability to learn from past experiences. Reactive machines are typically designed to perform specific tasks or functions, and they do so by responding to sensory inputs in a pre-programmed way. For example, a simple reactive machine might be programmed to turn on a light when it detects a certain level of darkness, and turn it off when the light level reaches a certain threshold. The machine doesn't "learn" anything over time, but simply responds to the same inputs in the same

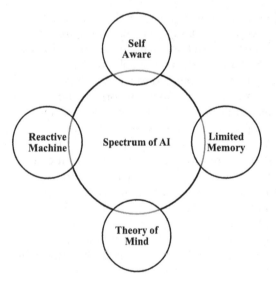

FIGURE 5.5   Spectrum of artificial intelligence.

way every time. While reactive machines are limited in their ability to adapt to changing circumstances or learn from experience, they can be useful in certain applications where consistent, reliable performance is more important than flexibility or adaptability. For example, reactive machines are often used in industrial automation, where they can perform repetitive tasks with high precision and accuracy.

5.3.2 Limited memory

These AI systems can make decisions based on past experiences and information stored in their memory. They can learn and improve their performance over time, but their knowledge is limited to specific tasks and situations. Examples of limited memory AI systems include voice assistants like Siri and Alexa, and self-driving cars.

Limited memory is a characteristic of certain types of AI systems that are designed to operate with a finite amount of memory or storage capacity. This can be contrasted with systems that have unlimited memory, such as modern computers, which can store vast amounts of data and information. In limited memory AI systems, the available memory may be used to store data, rules, or other information that the system needs to operate. However, the amount of memory available may be restricted by design, or by practical limitations such as the cost or size of the hardware.

One example of a limited memory AI system is a mobile device or Internet of Technology device with constrained resources. These devices may have limited memory or processing power, which means that AI algorithms running on them need to be optimized to make efficient use of available resources. Another example could be a self-driving car that has limited onboard storage and processing power. Designing AI systems with limited memory can be challenging, as the system must be able to operate effectively with a smaller amount of resources than a more powerful system. However, it can also be advantageous in certain applications, such as edge computing, where devices may need to operate in environments with limited power or connectivity.

5.3.3 Theory of mind

These AI systems have the ability to understand human emotions and mental states, and can interact with people in a more natural and intuitive way. They can also make predictions about other people's behavior and respond accordingly. Examples of theory of mind (TOM) AI systems are still largely in the research phase.

TOM refers to the ability to understand and infer mental states such as beliefs, desires, and intentions in oneself and others. In the context of AI, TOM refers to the ability of machines to understand and predict the mental states of humans. The development of TOM in AI has significant implications for human–machine interaction, as it enables machines to more accurately interpret human behavior and respond appropriately. For example, an AI system with TOM capabilities might be able to recognize when a human user is frustrated or confused and respond with appropriate assistance or feedback. There are a number of different approaches to implementing TOM in AI systems, including rule-based systems, ML, and cognitive architectures. Some researchers have also explored the use of embodied AI, which involves giving machines physical bodies and sensory inputs to help them better understand human behavior and social cues. While significant progress has been made in developing AI systems with TOM capabilities, there is still much work to be done. One challenge is that mental states are highly contextual and can be difficult to infer accurately, even for humans. As AI systems become more sophisticated and better able to interpret human behavior, they will need to be carefully designed and regulated to ensure that they are used ethically and responsibly.

5.3.4 Self-aware

These AI systems have human-like consciousness and can think, reason, and solve problems in ways that are indistinguishable from humans. They can also understand their own existence and emotions, and have a sense of self-awareness. Examples of self-aware AI systems only exist in science fiction and are not yet possible in reality.

TOM refers to the ability to understand and infer mental states such as beliefs, desires, and intentions in oneself and others. In the context of AI, TOM refers to the ability of machines to understand and predict the mental states of humans. The development of TOM in AI has significant implications for human−machine interaction, as it enables machines to more accurately interpret human behavior and respond appropriately. For example, an AI system with TOM capabilities might be able to recognize when a human user is frustrated or confused and respond with appropriate assistance or feedback. There are a number of different approaches to implementing TOM in AI systems, including rule-based systems, ML, and cognitive architectures. Some researchers have also explored the use of embodied AI, which involves giving machines physical bodies and sensory inputs to help them better understand human behavior and social cues.

While significant progress has been made in developing AI systems with TOM capabilities, there is still much work to be done. One challenge is that mental states are highly contextual and can be difficult to infer accurately, even for humans. As AI systems become more sophisticated and better able to interpret human behavior, they will need to be carefully designed and regulated to ensure that they are used ethically and responsibly.

5.4 Knowledge representation of artificial intelligence

Knowledge representation in AI refers to the process of encoding information and knowledge in a format that can be used by an AI system. Knowledge representation is a critical component of many AI systems, as it enables machines to reason about the world, make decisions, and solve problems.

There are a variety of different techniques and approaches to knowledge representation in AI, including:

5.4.1 Symbolic representation

In this approach, knowledge is represented using symbols and rules, such as logic or rule-based systems. These systems use formal languages to represent concepts and relationships, and can be used to infer new knowledge based on the rules and symbols. Table 5.1 shows the symbolic representation of AI.

5.4.2 Semantic networks

Semantic networks represent knowledge as a set of interconnected nodes, where each node represents a concept or object and the edges represent relationships between them. Fig. 5.6 shows the structure of the semantic network. Let's consider a semantic network representing relationships between different animals based on their characteristics:

TABLE 5.1 Symbolic representation of artificial intelligence.

Symbol	Description	Example
Predicate	Represents a relation between entities	Likes(x, y)
Variable	Represents a placeholder for an entity	x, y
Constant	Represents a specific entity or value	John, Apple
Function	Represents a computation or transformation	Add(x, y)
Rule	Represents a logical statement or inference	If A then B
Logic connectives	Represents logical operators	AND, OR, NOT, IMPLIES
Quantifiers	Represents a statement about a subset of entities	FORALL, EXIST
Inference	The process of deriving new knowledge from existing knowledge	Modus Ponens, Resolution
Ontology	A formal representation of knowledge about a domain	OWL, RDF, XML
Frames	Structures representing objects, attributes, and relationships	Semantic networks, frames, conceptual graphs
Semantic network	Graph-based representation of concepts and their relationships	Nodes and edges connected to represent concepts
Rules engine	Software system that applies rules to data or knowledge	Drools, Jess, Prolog
Knowledge base	Repository of knowledge and facts	Database, knowledge graph, rule base
Uncertainty	Represents uncertainty or probability associated with knowledge	Bayesian networks, fuzzy logic
Inheritance	Represents the sharing of properties or characteristics	Subclassing, taxonomy

```
+--------------+
|  Animal  |
+--------------+
|   |   |
|   +-------+
|   |   |
+-------v-----+      +-v------+
| Mammal  |      | Bird |
+-------------+      +--------+
|   |   |   |       |
|   |   +-v-----+      +--v------+
|   +----> Lion |      | Eagle |
|       +--------+      +---------+
|
|      +-------------+
+-----> Tiger   |
       +-------------+
```

FIGURE 5.6 Structure of semantic network.

In this semantic network, we have two top-level concepts: "Animal," "Mammal," and "Bird." The arrows indicate "is-a" relationships, where a subclass inherits properties from its superclass. For example:

- Lion is a mammal
- Eagle is a bird
- Tiger is a mammal

It can also represent additional relationships between concepts:

Mammals have properties such as "gives birth to live young" and "has fur."
Birds have properties such as "lays eggs" and "has feathers."

Semantic networks allow us to capture hierarchical relationships, attribute information, and other associations between concepts in a graphical and intuitive manner. They help in organizing and representing knowledge about a domain, facilitating reasoning and inference in AI systems.

- Python program for the above example of semantic network:

```python
class SemanticNetwork:
    def __init__(self):
        self.network = {}

    def add_node(self, node):
        if node not in self.network:
            self.network[node] = []
```

(cont'd)

```
def add_edge(self, node1, node2):
    if node1 in self.network and node2 in self.network:
        self.network[node1].append(node2)
        self.network[node2].append(node1)

def get_related_nodes(self, node):
    if node in self.network:
        return self.network[node]
    else:
        return []

def print_network(self):
    for node, neighbors in self.network.items():
        print(node + " is related to: " + ", ".join(neighbors))


# Create a semantic network
network = SemanticNetwork()

# Add nodes
network.add_node("Lion")
network.add_node("Mammal")
network.add_node("Eagle")
network.add_node("Bird")
network.add_node("Tiger")

# Add edges
network.add_edge("Lion", "Mammal")
network.add_edge("Eagle", "Bird")
network.add_edge("Tiger", "Mammal")

# Get related nodes
related_nodes = network.get_related_nodes("Lion")
print("Related nodes to 'Lion':", related_nodes)

# Print the semantic network
network.print_network()
```

Outcome:
Related nodes to 'Lion': ['Mammal']
Lion is related to: Mammal
Mammal is related to: Lion, Tiger
Eagle is related to: Bird
Bird is related to: Eagle
Tiger is related to: Mammal

(cont'd)

In this program, create a semantic network with nodes representing "Lion," "Mammal," "Eagle," "Bird," and "Tiger." We establish relationships between them using the add_edge method. The get_ related_nodes method returns a list of nodes related to a given node. The print_ network method prints the entire semantic network.

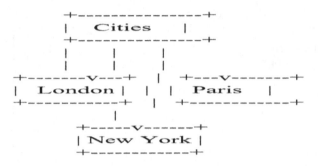

FIGURE 5.7 Semantic network for the cities.

- Consider another example for a semantic network representing relationships between different cities based on their attributes and connection. Fig. 5.7 shows the semantic networks for the cities.

In this semantic network, we have three cities: London, Paris, and New York. Each city can have various attributes and connections.

We can represent additional relationships and attributes:

- London is the capital city of England.
- Paris is the capital city of France.
- New York is a major city in the United States.

We can also capture connections between cities:

London and Paris are connected by the Eurostar train.
London and New York are connected by flights.

Semantic networks allow us to represent and organize knowledge about cities, their attributes, and connections. By representing these relationships and attributes, AI systems can reason about cities, answer questions, and perform various tasks related to city information and navigation.

- Python program for the above example of cities:

```python
class SemanticNetwork:
    def __init__(self):
        self.network = {}

    def add_node(self, node):
        if node not in self.network:
            self.network[node] = []

    def add_edge(self, node1, node2):
        if node1 in self.network and node2 in self.network:
            self.network[node1].append(node2)
            self.network[node2].append(node1)

    def get_related_nodes(self, node):
        if node in self.network:
            return self.network[node]
        else:
            return []

    def print_network(self):
        for node, neighbors in self.network.items():
            print(node + " is related to: " + ", ".join(neighbors))


# Create a semantic network
network = SemanticNetwork()

# Add nodes
network.add_node("London")
network.add_node("capital city")
network.add_node("England")
network.add_node("Paris")
network.add_node("France")
network.add_node("New York")
network.add_node("major city")
network.add_node("United States")

# Add edges
network.add_edge("London", "capital city")
network.add_edge("capital city", "England")
network.add_edge("Paris", "capital city")

network.add_edge("capital city", "France")
network.add_edge("New York", "major city")
network.add_edge("major city", "United States")

# Add additional connections
network.add_edge("London", "Paris")
network.add_edge("London", "New York")

# Get related nodes
related_nodes = network.get_related_nodes("London")
print("Related nodes to 'London':", related_nodes)

# Print the semantic network
network.print_network()
```

(cont'd)
_____

Outcome:
Related nodes to 'London': ['capital city', 'Paris', 'New York']
London is related to: capital city, Paris, New York
capital city is related to: London, England, Paris, France
England is related to: capital city
Paris is related to: capital city
France is related to: capital city
New York is related to: major city, London
major city is related to: New York, United States
United States is related to: major city

In this program, we create a semantic network with nodes representing "London," "capital city," "England," "Paris," "France," "New York," "major city," and "United States." We establish relationships between them using the add_edge method. Additionally, we add connections between cities using the same method.

5.4.3 Frames

Frames are a way of organizing knowledge into hierarchical structures, with each level representing a different aspect of the object or concept being represented. Fig. 5.8 shows the framing concept of car through the semantic network. Consider a frame representing information about a car:

In this frame, we have a concept called "Car," and it has various slots representing different attributes of a car.

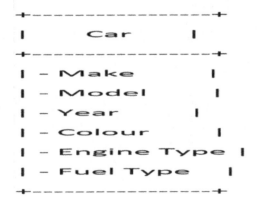

FIGURE 5.8   Framing concept of car through the semantic network.

For example:

- Make: Represents the brand or manufacturer of the car (e.g., Toyota, Ford, BMW).
- Model: Represents the specific model of the car (e.g., Camry, Mustang, X5).
- Year: Represents the manufacturing year of the car (e.g., 2015, 2020).
- Color: Represents the color of the car (e.g., red, blue, silver).
- Engine type: Represents the type of engine the car has (e.g., gasoline, diesel, electric).
- Fuel type: Represents the type of fuel the car uses (e.g., petrol, diesel, hybrid).

Frames allow us to organize and represent knowledge about objects or concepts in a structured manner. They capture attributes, relationships, and behaviors associated with the concept. By filling in the slots with specific values, it can represent individual instances of the concept, such as a particular car with its specific make, model, year, color, engine type, and fuel type. Frames facilitate reasoning, querying, and inference about objects in various AI applications.

Another example of frame, it has a concept called "Driverless Car," and it has several slots representing different attributes of a driverless car.

For example:

- Make: Represents the brand or manufacturer of the driverless car (e.g., Tesla, Waymo, Uber).
- Model: Represents the specific model of the driverless car (e.g., Model S, Waymo One, Uber self-driving car).
- Year: Represents the manufacturing year of the driverless car (e.g., 2022, 2023).
- Color: Represents the color of the driverless car (e.g., black, white, silver).
- Sensors: Represents the various sensors installed on the car for perception and navigation (e.g., LiDAR, radar, cameras).
- Autonomous system: Represents the autonomous driving system used by the car (e.g., Waymo's self-driving technology, Tesla Autopilot).

- Python program for the frames of the car information:

```
class CarFrame:
    def __init__(self):
        self.frame = {}

    def set_attribute(self, attribute, value):
        self.frame[attribute] = value

    def get_attribute(self, attribute):
        if attribute in self.frame:
            return self.frame[attribute]
        else:
            return None

    def print_frame(self):
        for attribute, value in self.frame.items():
            print(attribute + ": " + str(value))


# Create a car frame
car = CarFrame()

# Set attributes
car.set_attribute("make", "Toyota")
car.set_attribute("model", "Camry")
car.set_attribute("year", 2022)
car.set_attribute("color", "Silver")

# Get attribute values
make = car.get_attribute("make")
model = car.get_attribute("model")
year = car.get_attribute("year")
color = car.get_attribute("color")

# Print the car frame
car.print_frame()

Outcome:
make: Toyota
model: Camry
year: 2022
color: Silver
```

In this program, we define a CarFrame class that represents the frame of information for a car. The set_attribute method allows setting an attribute and its corresponding value in the car frame. The get_attribute method retrieves the value of a specified attribute from the frame. The print_frame method prints all the attributes and their values in the car frame.

In the example above, we create a car frame and set attributes such as "make," "model," "year," and "color." We then retrieve attribute values using the get_attribute method. Finally, we print the car frame using the print_frame method.

5.4.4 Ontologies

Ontologies are formal descriptions of the concepts and relationships within a particular domain of knowledge. They typically involve a set of definitions and rules that govern how the concepts can be used and related to one another. Ontologies play a crucial role in knowledge representation in AI. They provide a formal and structured way to represent knowledge about a specific domain, enabling machines to understand and reason about that domain. Following are the explanation of the concept of ontologies:

Definition: An ontology is a formal representation of knowledge that describes concepts, entities, relationships, and properties within a specific domain. It defines the vocabulary and rules for representing and organizing knowledge in a structured manner.

- Concepts and classes: Ontologies define concepts or classes that represent categories of entities or objects within a domain. These concepts can have hierarchical relationships, with more general concepts at the top and more specific concepts as subcategories.
- Relationships: Ontologies capture relationships between concepts, specifying how they are related to one another. Common relationship types include "is-a" (inheritance or subclassing), "part-of" (composition or aggregation), "has-a" (association), and "related-to" (general relationship).
- Properties: Ontologies define properties or attributes associated with concepts. Properties describe characteristics or features of entities within the domain. For example, a car concept may have properties like "make," "model," "year," and "color."
- Constraints and rules: Ontologies can include constraints and rules that define restrictions or logical statements within the domain. These constraints ensure consistency and enable reasoning capabilities within the ontology.
- Formal languages: Ontologies are often represented using formal languages, such as the Web Ontology Language (OWL) or the Resource Description Framework (RDF). These languages provide syntax and semantics for expressing ontological concepts and relationships.
- Knowledge sharing and interoperability: Ontologies facilitate knowledge sharing and interoperability among different AI systems. By using a standardized ontology, different systems can understand and exchange information in a consistent and machine-interpretable manner.
- Reasoning and inference: Ontologies enable automated reasoning and inference in AI systems. By leveraging the defined concepts, relationships, and rules within an ontology, machines can infer new knowledge, make deductions, perform consistency checks, and answer complex queries.

Consider an ontology representing knowledge about the animal kingdom:
Concepts:

- Animal: Top-level concept representing all animals.
  - Mammal: Subclass of animal representing mammals.
  - Bird: Subclass of animal representing birds.
  - Fish: Subclass of animal representing fish.

Relationships:

- "is-a" relationship:
- Mammal is-an animal.
- Bird is-an animal.
- Fish is-an animal.
- "has-a" relationship:
  - Mammal has-a habitat.
  - Bird has-a beak type.
  - Fish has-a habitat.

Properties:

- Habitat: Describes the natural habitat of animals.
- Beak type: Describes the shape or type of beak in birds.

In this ontology, have concepts such as "Animal," "Mammal," "Bird," and "Fish." The "is-a" relationship establishes hierarchical connections between these concepts. For example, "Lion" is a specific instance of the "Mammal" concept, and "Eagle" is a specific instance of the "Bird" concept.

Additionally, we have "has-a" relationships that capture specific properties of the concepts. For instance, "Mammal" has the "Habitat" property to describe its natural habitat, and "Bird" has the "Beak Type" property to describe the shape or type of its beak. By utilizing ontologies, AI systems can represent and reason about the animal kingdom. They can infer properties of specific animals based on their concepts and relationships, answer queries about the characteristics of different animals, and perform intelligent tasks within the domain.

- Python program for the ontologies of the above program:

Python program that represents the ontologies you provided using the rdflib library, which is a widely used library for working with RDF (Resource Description Framework) and ontologies:

```python
from rdflib import Graph, RDF, RDFS

# Create an RDF graph
g = Graph()

# Define namespaces
ns = {
    "": "http://example.org/",
    "rdfs": RDFS,
    "rdf": RDF
}
```

(cont'd)

```
# Add ontologies
g.add((ns["Animal"], RDF.type, RDFS.Class))
g.add((ns["Mammal"], RDF.type, RDFS.Class))
g.add((ns["Bird"], RDF.type, RDFS.Class))
g.add((ns["Fish"], RDF.type, RDFS.Class))

# Define subclass relationships
g.add((ns["Mammal"], RDFS.subClassOf, ns["Animal"]))
g.add((ns["Bird"], RDFS.subClassOf, ns["Animal"]))
g.add((ns["Fish"], RDFS.subClassOf, ns["Animal"]))

# Query the ontologies
query = """
   PREFIX rdfs: <http://www.w3.org/2000/01/rdf-schema#>
   SELECT ?subclass ?superclass
   WHERE {
      ?subclass rdfs:subClassOf ?superclass .
   }
"""

results = g.query(query)

# Print the results
print("Subclass\tSuperclass")
for row in results:
   subclass = row["subclass"].split("#")[-1]
   superclass = row["superclass"].split("#")[-1]
   print(subclass + "\t\t" + superclass)
```

Outcome:

```
Subclass   Superclass
Bird       Animal
Fish       Animal
Mammal     Animal
```

In this program, we use the rdflib library to create an RDF graph and define namespaces for our ontologies. We add the ontologies as triples to the graph, specifying the class relationships using RDF and RDFS vocabulary terms. Finally, we query the ontologies to retrieve the subclass and superclass relationships, and print the results.

- Ontologies with driverless car:

  Ontology concepts:

- Driverless car: Top-level concept representing a car capable of autonomous driving.
- Car manufacturer: Represents the brand or manufacturer of the driverless car.
- Car model: Represents the specific model of the driverless car.
- Sensor: Represents the different types of sensors used in the driverless car.
- Autonomous system: Represents the autonomous driving system implemented in the car.
- Software version: Represents the version of the software running the autonomous system.

  Ontology relationships:

- "is-a" relationship:
  - Car manufacturer is-a driverless car.
  - Car model is-a driverless car.
  - Sensor is-a driverless car.
  - Autonomous system is-a driverless car.
- "has-a" relationship:
  - Driverless car has-a car manufacturer.
  - Driverless car has-a car model.
  - Driverless car has-a sensor.
  - Driverless car has-an autonomous system.
  - Autonomous system has-a software version.
- Ontology properties:
  - Car manufacturer: Describes the brand or manufacturer of the driverless car.
  - Car model: Describes the specific model of the driverless car.
  - Sensor: Describes the different types of sensors used in the driverless car.
  - Autonomous system: Describes the autonomous driving system implemented in the car.
  - Software version: Describes the version of the software running the autonomous system.

    In this example, the ontology represents a driverless car and its associated attributes. The ontology captures the relationships between concepts like car manufacturer, car model, sensor, autonomous system, and their relationships with the top-level concept, driverless car.

    By utilizing this ontology, AI systems can represent and reason about driverless cars. They can retrieve information about the car's manufacturer, model, sensors, and the version of the autonomous system. Additionally, they can perform intelligent tasks such as comparing different driverless car models, identifying compatible sensors, and analyzing software updates for the autonomous system.

- Python program for the ontologies of the driverless car:

```python
from rdflib import Graph, RDF, RDFS

# Create an RDF graph
g = Graph()

# Define namespaces
ns = {
    "": "http://example.org/",
    "rdfs": RDFS,
    "rdf": RDF
}

# Add ontologies
g.add((ns["DriverlessCar"], RDF.type, RDFS.Class))
g.add((ns["AutonomousVehicle"], RDF.type, RDFS.Class))
g.add((ns["Sensors"], RDF.type, RDFS.Class))
g.add((ns["ComputerVision"], RDF.type, RDFS.Class))
g.add((ns["Lidar"], RDF.type, RDFS.Class))
g.add((ns["GPS"], RDF.type, RDFS.Class))

# Define subclass relationships
g.add((ns["AutonomousVehicle"], RDFS.subClassOf, ns["DriverlessCar"]))
g.add((ns["Sensors"], RDFS.subClassOf, ns["DriverlessCar"]))
g.add((ns["ComputerVision"], RDFS.subClassOf, ns["Sensors"]))
g.add((ns["Lidar"], RDFS.subClassOf, ns["Sensors"]))
g.add((ns["GPS"], RDFS.subClassOf, ns["Sensors"]))

# Query the ontologies
query = """
    PREFIX rdfs: <http://www.w3.org/2000/01/rdf-schema#>
    SELECT ?subclass ?superclass
    WHERE {
        ?subclass rdfs:subClassOf ?superclass .
    }
"""

results = g.query(query)

# Print the results
print("Subclass\tSuperclass")
for row in results:
    subclass = row["subclass"].split("#")[-1]
    superclass = row["superclass"].split("#")[-1]
    print(subclass + "\t\t" + superclass)
```

Outcome:

Subclass	Superclass
Computer Vision	Sensors
Lidar	Sensors
GPS	Sensors
Sensors	Driverless Car
Autonomous Vehicle	Driverless Car

5.4.5 Types of knowledge

In the AI, knowledge representation refers to the process of encoding and organizing knowledge in a way that can be effectively utilized by intelligent systems. There are several types of knowledge representation techniques used in AI, each suited to different problem domains and requirements. Fig. 5.9 shows the types of knowledge representation. Following are the some commonly used types:

5.4.5.1 Declarative knowledge

Declarative knowledge is a type of knowledge that describes facts or information about the world. In knowledge representation, declarative knowledge is represented in the form of statements or propositions that are true or false. These statements can be represented using various forms, such as logic-based languages, semantic networks, frames, or rules. For example, in a logic-based language, a statement can be represented as a logical formula, such as "All birds can fly," which can be expressed using first-order logic as "For all x, if x is a bird, then x can fly." Declarative knowledge can also be classified as either general or specific. General knowledge describes information that is true for a broad range of situations, while specific knowledge describes information that is true for a particular situation. Declarative knowledge is an important aspect of knowledge representation as it allows us to store and reason about the facts and information we know about the world in a structured and organized way.

Following are the example of declarative knowledge about driverless cars in AI:

- Definition:
  - A driverless car is a vehicle that can operate autonomously without human intervention.

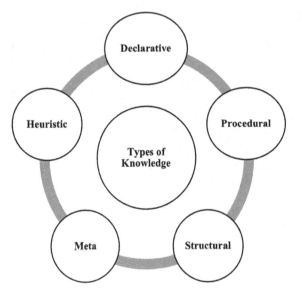

FIGURE 5.9 Types of knowledge representation.

- Sensors:
  - Driverless cars use various sensors such as LiDAR, radar, cameras, and ultrasonic sensors to perceive the surrounding environment.
  - These sensors provide information about nearby objects, traffic, pedestrians, and road conditions.
- Mapping and localization:
  - Driverless cars utilize mapping and localization techniques to understand their position and navigate accurately.
  - They use GPS, mapping data, and localization algorithms to determine their location on the map.
- Autonomous control:
  - Driverless cars employ advanced control systems to make decisions and control their movements.
  - They utilize algorithms for path planning, obstacle avoidance, and traffic rules adherence.
- Communication:
  - Driverless cars can communicate with other vehicles, infrastructure, and central systems.
  - Vehicle-to-vehicle and vehicle-to-infrastructure communication enable cooperative driving and enhance safety.
- Regulations and safety:
  - Driverless cars must comply with legal and safety regulations.
  - They should meet specific standards for safety, cybersecurity, and reliability.
- ML and AI:
  - Driverless cars leverage ML and AI techniques to improve their performance over time.
  - They learn from data, adapt to changing environments, and enhance their decision-making capabilities.

In this example, we have declarative knowledge about driverless cars, including their definition, the use of sensors for perception, mapping and localization techniques, autonomous control systems, communication capabilities, regulatory considerations, and the role of ML and AI. This knowledge describes the characteristics and capabilities of driverless cars without specifying how these tasks are implemented. Declarative knowledge in AI allows systems to understand and reason about driverless cars, facilitate decision-making, and support the development of intelligent autonomous driving technologies.

5.4.5.2 *Heuristic knowledge*

Heuristic knowledge, also known as procedural knowledge, refers to knowledge that is based on experience and is used to solve problems or perform tasks. Unlike declarative knowledge, which describes facts or information about the world, heuristic knowledge describes how to do something or how to solve a particular problem.

In knowledge representation, heuristic knowledge can be represented in the form of rules, procedures, or algorithms. These representations allow us to capture the expertise of human experts and use it to develop intelligent systems that can solve problems or perform tasks in a similar way. Heuristic knowledge can be divided into two main types:

domain-specific and domain-general. Domain-specific heuristic knowledge is knowledge that is specific to a particular domain, such as medicine, engineering, or law. Domain-general heuristic knowledge, on the other hand, is knowledge that can be applied to a wide range of domains, such as problem-solving strategies, decision-making techniques, or cognitive heuristics. Heuristic knowledge plays an important role in knowledge representation as it allows us to model human expertise and use it to develop intelligent systems that can perform complex tasks and solve difficult problems.

Heuristic knowledge refers to domain-specific rules or strategies that guide problem-solving and decision-making in AI.

Following are the example of heuristic knowledge related to driverless cars:

Lane following:

- Heuristic: Stay within the designated lane while driving.
- Strategy: Use lane detection algorithms to identify and track lane markings. Adjust steering to maintain the vehicle's position within the lane.

Safe distance:

- Heuristic: Maintain a safe distance from the vehicle ahead.
- Strategy: Utilize sensors such as radar or LiDAR to measure the distance to the preceding vehicle. Adjust speed and braking to maintain a safe following distance.

Obstacle avoidance:

- Heuristic: Detect and avoid obstacles in the environment.
- Strategy: Use sensor data to identify potential obstacles such as vehicles, pedestrians, or stationary objects. Plan alternative routes or apply braking and steering maneuvers to avoid collisions.

Traffic sign recognition:

- Heuristic: Recognize and respond to traffic signs.
- Strategy: Utilize computer vision techniques to detect and classify traffic signs. Interpret their meanings and adjust the vehicle's behavior accordingly, such as stopping at a stop sign or yielding at a yield sign.

Decision-making at intersections:

- Heuristic: Safely navigate intersections.
- Strategy: Analyze traffic signals, sensor inputs, and other vehicles' movements to make decisions such as when to proceed, yield, or stop at intersections.

Emergency situations:

- Heuristic: Respond appropriately in emergency scenarios.
- Strategy: Use predefined rules for emergency situations like sudden braking, evasive maneuvers, or prioritizing pedestrian safety.

Energy efficiency:

- Heuristic: Optimize energy usage.
- Strategy: Consider factors such as road conditions, traffic, and battery level to optimize acceleration, deceleration, and route planning for energy efficiency.

Heuristic knowledge provides rules of thumb or strategies based on expert knowledge and experience in the domain of driverless cars. These heuristics guide decision-making and problem-solving in real-time situations, allowing the autonomous vehicle to navigate safely, follow traffic rules, and respond appropriately to dynamic environments.

5.4.5.3 *Procedural knowledge*

Procedural knowledge, also known as skill or know-how, refers to knowledge about how to perform a specific task or procedure. In knowledge representation, procedural knowledge is represented as a series of steps or instructions that can be followed to accomplish a particular task. Procedural knowledge is often used in conjunction with declarative knowledge, which describes the facts or information that underlie a particular task. For example, in order to solve a mathematical problem, an individual must have both declarative knowledge about the mathematical concepts involved and procedural knowledge about how to apply those concepts to solve the problem. In knowledge representation, procedural knowledge can be represented using various techniques such as decision trees, algorithms, or flowcharts. These representations allow individuals or intelligent systems to perform complex tasks by breaking them down into a series of smaller, more manageable steps.

Procedural knowledge is an important aspect of knowledge representation because it allows individuals and intelligent systems to perform tasks and solve problems in a systematic and efficient manner. By representing procedural knowledge in a structured and organized way, we can ensure that tasks are performed correctly and consistently, regardless of who is performing them. Procedural knowledge related to driverless cars in AI encompasses the specific instructions and processes involved in the operation, decision-making, and navigation of autonomous vehicles. Following are some key areas of procedural knowledge for driverless cars:

- Sensing and perception: Autonomous vehicles use various sensors such as cameras, LiDAR, radar, and ultrasonic sensors to perceive their environment. Procedural knowledge includes the techniques for processing sensor data, detecting and tracking objects, recognizing traffic signs, and interpreting road conditions.
- Localization and mapping: Driverless cars rely on simultaneous localization and mapping (SLAM) algorithms to determine their precise location and create a map of the surrounding environment. Procedural knowledge includes the use of sensor fusion techniques, probabilistic algorithms, and map matching to accurately localize the vehicle.
- Path planning and control: Procedural knowledge encompasses the algorithms and techniques for determining the optimal path and trajectory for the vehicle to follow.

This includes methods for obstacle avoidance, lane keeping, lane changing, and intersection handling. Procedural knowledge also covers control systems that regulate the vehicle's acceleration, braking, and steering to execute the planned path.

- Decision-making and behavior planning: Autonomous vehicles need to make decisions in real-time based on their perception of the environment. Procedural knowledge involves decision-making algorithms that prioritize safety, follow traffic rules, handle complex scenarios, and interact with other road users, such as pedestrians and cyclists.
- Sensor fusion and data integration: Driverless cars often integrate data from multiple sensors to obtain a comprehensive understanding of the environment. Procedural knowledge includes techniques for fusing sensor data, such as object tracking, data association, and probabilistic filtering, to create a coherent representation of the surroundings.
- ML and deep learning: Procedural knowledge encompasses the use of ML and deep learning techniques for various tasks in autonomous driving. This includes training models for object detection and recognition, semantic segmentation, behavior prediction, and other perception and decision-making tasks.
- Safety and fault tolerance: Procedural knowledge covers the design principles and techniques for ensuring the safety and reliability of autonomous vehicles. This includes redundant systems, error detection and recovery mechanisms, fail-safe strategies, and robust testing and validation procedures.
- Human–machine interaction: Procedural knowledge involves the development of interfaces and communication methods that allow human operators or passengers to interact with autonomous vehicles effectively. This includes visual displays, voice commands, and other forms of feedback and communication.

It's important to note that procedural knowledge in the field of driverless cars is constantly evolving as research and technological advancements continue to progress. New techniques and algorithms are being developed to improve the capabilities and performance of autonomous vehicles.

5.4.5.4 *Structural knowledge*

Structural knowledge, also known as relational knowledge, refers to knowledge about the relationships between different objects or concepts. In knowledge representation, structural knowledge is represented using various techniques such as semantic networks, frames, or ontologies. In a semantic network, objects or concepts are represented as nodes, and the relationships between them are represented as links or edges. For example, in a semantic network about animals, the node representing "cat" might be linked to the node representing "mammal" with an edge labeled "is-a," indicating that a cat is a type of mammal.

In a frame-based system, objects or concepts are represented as frames or templates that include information about their attributes and relationships to other frames. For example, a frame representing a "car" might include information about its make, model, and color, as well as its relationship to other frames such as "engine" or "driver."

Ontologies are a more formal way of representing structural knowledge, using a set of concepts and the relationships between them to create a hierarchical structure. Ontologies are often used in AI and knowledge management systems to provide a common vocabulary and structure for organizing and sharing knowledge. Structural knowledge is an important aspect of knowledge representation as it allows us to model the relationships between different objects or concepts in a systematic and organized way. By representing structural knowledge in a structured and standardized format, can ensure that knowledge is easily shared and reused across different applications and domains. Structural knowledge refers to the underlying architecture, components, and subsystems that constitute a driverless car in the context of AI. Following are some key elements of structural knowledge related to driverless cars:

- Perception system: This system includes various sensors such as cameras, LiDAR, radar, and ultrasonic sensors that collect data about the vehicle's surroundings. The structural knowledge involves the physical placement of sensors, their specifications, and their integration into the vehicle's architecture.
- Central processing unit (CPU): The CPU is responsible for processing sensor data, running algorithms, and making real-time decisions. Structural knowledge encompasses the selection and configuration of high-performance CPUs capable of handling the computational requirements of autonomous driving tasks.
- Control and actuation system: This system translates the decisions made by the autonomous driving algorithms into actions. It includes components such as electronic control units (ECUs), actuators, and brakes. Structural knowledge involves designing and integrating these components to ensure precise and reliable control of the vehicle.
- Communication system: Driverless cars often require communication with external systems, such as traffic infrastructure or other vehicles. Structural knowledge encompasses the integration of wireless communication modules, antennas, and protocols to enable vehicle-to-vehicle and vehicle-to-infrastructure communication.
- Mapping and localization system: Autonomous vehicles rely on mapping and localization to understand their position and navigate the environment. Structural knowledge includes the integration of GPS modules, inertial measurement units (IMUs), and map databases, as well as the integration of localization algorithms and map matching techniques.
- High-definition mapping: Driverless cars often utilize high-definition maps that provide detailed information about road geometry, lane markings, traffic signs, and other relevant features. Structural knowledge involves the creation and maintenance of these maps, as well as the integration of map data into the autonomous driving system.
- Redundancy and safety systems: Autonomous vehicles require redundant systems and safety mechanisms to ensure reliable operation and handle unexpected situations. Structural knowledge includes the design and integration of backup sensors, redundant computing units, and fail-safe mechanisms to enhance safety and minimize the risk of failures.
- Data storage and processing: Driverless cars generate a significant amount of data from various sensors and systems. Structural knowledge involves designing the architecture for data storage and processing, including onboard storage devices, data buses, and interfaces for transferring data to external servers for further analysis and improvement of autonomous driving algorithms.
- Human—machine interface: Structural knowledge includes the design and integration of UIs and displays that enable human operators or passengers to interact with the

autonomous vehicle effectively. This may include touchscreens, voice commands, or augmented reality interfaces.

It's important to note that the specific architectural design and components of driverless cars can vary among manufacturers and research organizations, and the field is continuously evolving as new technologies and advancements emerge.

5.4.5.5 Meta knowledge

Meta knowledge, also known as meta knowledge or knowledge about knowledge, refers to knowledge that describes the characteristics, properties, and use of other types of knowledge. In knowledge representation, meta knowledge is used to describe how other types of knowledge are organized, stored, and used. Meta knowledge provides a higher-level perspective on the field of driverless cars, guiding researchers, developers, and policymakers in making informed decisions and shaping the future development and deployment of autonomous vehicles.

5.4.6 Knowledge cycle of artificial intelligence

The AI knowledge cycle is a cyclical process that involves gathering data, analyzing it, using the insights gained to make decisions, and evaluating the outcomes. The cycle involves the following stages:

- Data collection: This stage involves collecting data from various sources such as databases, sensors, or input devices. The data can be structured or unstructured.
- Data preparation: The collected data needs to be cleaned, transformed, and structured into a suitable format for analysis. This stage involves data cleaning, data integration, and data transformation.
- Data analysis: This stage involves using various AI techniques such as ML, statistical methods, or NLP to extract insights and knowledge from the data.
- Decision making: The insights gained from data analysis are used to make informed decisions or take actions.
- Implementation: The decisions or actions taken based on the insights gained from data analysis are implemented.
- Evaluation: The effectiveness of the decisions or actions taken is evaluated, and areas for improvement are identified.
- Feedback: The insights gained from evaluation are used to update and improve the AI system, data collection, or data analysis processes.

  The AI knowledge cycle is iterative, meaning that the results of the evaluation and feedback stages influence future data collection, analysis, and decision-making processes. This iterative process allows AI systems to learn from experience and improve their performance over time.

An example of the knowledge cycle in the context of an autonomous vehicle's perception system:

- Data collection: The autonomous vehicle collects data from its various sensors, such as cameras, LiDAR, and radar. The sensors capture information about the vehicle's surroundings, including other vehicles, pedestrians, and traffic signs.
- Data preprocessing: The collected sensor data undergoes preprocessing to clean, filter, and normalize the data. This step involves removing noise, correcting for sensor biases, and ensuring the data is in a suitable format for further processing.
- Data representation and feature extraction: The preprocessed data is then transformed into a suitable representation for AI algorithms. For example, the images captured by the cameras may undergo image processing techniques to extract features such as edges, colors, or object keypoints. This step helps to reduce the dimensionality of the data and extract relevant information.
- Training and learning: The transformed data is used to train AI models. In this example, the perception system's AI models are trained to recognize objects, such as cars, pedestrians, and traffic signs, from the processed sensor data. Training involves feeding the data into the models, adjusting the model's parameters iteratively, and optimizing the model's performance using techniques like supervised or unsupervised learning.
- Knowledge representation: The trained AI models capture the learned knowledge. The models represent the acquired information about objects, their characteristics, and their relationships in the environment. This knowledge is stored within the model's parameters, weights, and biases.
- Inference and decision-making: When the autonomous vehicle operates in real-time, it utilizes the trained models to make inferences and decisions based on the current sensor data. The perception system processes the incoming data from the sensors and uses the knowledge encoded in the models to recognize objects, estimate their positions, and make decisions related to navigation, object avoidance, and interaction with the environment.
- Feedback and continuous learning: The decisions made by the autonomous vehicle are evaluated, and feedback is provided to refine and improve the AI models. If the perception system misidentifies an object or fails to make appropriate decisions, the feedback loop triggers a retraining process. The misclassified or erroneous instances are used to update the models, enabling them to learn from mistakes and improve their performance over time.
- Knowledge update and adaptation: As new data is collected and the perception system encounters novel situations or changes in the environment, the AI models are updated and adapted. This can involve retraining the models with new data, fine-tuning the existing models, or incorporating additional knowledge or domain-specific rules into the perception system.

The knowledge cycle in this example involves a continuous loop of data collection, preprocessing, learning, representation, inference, feedback, and adaptation. Through this iterative process, the perception system of the autonomous vehicle improves its ability to perceive and understand the environment, enabling safer and more reliable autonomous driving.

5.5 Constraint satisfaction problem

Constraint satisfaction problems (CSPs) are a class of problems in AI where the goal is to find a solution that satisfies a set of constraints. CSPs are used in a wide range of applications, including planning, scheduling, optimization, and decision making.

In a CSP, the problem is defined by a set of variables and a set of constraints that limit the possible values that each variable can take. The goal is to find an assignment of values to the variables that satisfies all of the constraints.

- Basic Python program for the CSP:

Python program that demonstrates a basic implementation of the CSP using the Python-constraint library:

```python
from constraint import Problem

# Define the CSP problem
problem = Problem()

# Define variables
problem.addVariable('A', [1, 2, 3])  # Example variable A with domain [1, 2, 3]
problem.addVariable('B', [4, 5, 6])  # Example variable B with domain [4, 5, 6]

# Define constraints
def constraint_function(a, b):
    # Example constraint: a and b must be different
    return a != b

# Add constraint to the problem
problem.addConstraint(constraint_function, ['A', 'B'])

# Solve the problem
solutions = problem.getSolutions()

# Print the solutions
for solution in solutions:
    print(solution)
```

In this program, we utilize the Python-constraint library to define and solve a CSP. We start by creating a Problem object. Next, we add variables and their domains to the problem using the add Variable method. In this example, we have two variables "A" and "B" with their respective domains. Then, we define a constraint function that specifies the conditions that the variables must satisfy. In this case, the constraint function ensures that "A" and "B" must have different values. Finally, we add the constraint to the problem using the addConstraint method. We then solve the problem using the getSolutions method, which returns a list of all valid solutions.

When executed, the program will print all the valid solutions that satisfy the constraints.

CSPs can be represented using a variety of techniques, including graphs, matrices, and logical formulas. They can be solved using a variety of algorithms, including backtracking search, constraint propagation, and local search. One of the key challenges in solving CSPs is finding an efficient algorithm that can solve the problem in a reasonable amount of time. This is because the number of possible solutions to a CSP can grow exponentially with the number of variables and constraints. To address this challenge, researchers have developed a number of techniques for solving CSPs, including heuristics that can guide the search for a solution, and algorithms that can exploit the structure of the problem to reduce the search space. CSPs are a powerful tool for solving a wide range of AI problems, and they continue to be an active area of research in the field.

In the field of AI, a CSP consists of three components, "X," "Y," and "Z," where

X is the set of variables, $\{X1, \ldots \ldots, Xn\}$
Y is the set of domains, $\{Y1, \ldots \ldots, Yn\}$
Z is the set of constraints that specify allowable combinations of the different parameters.

Each domain Yi consists of a set of allowable values $\{u1, \ldots \ldots, uk\}$ for variable Xi. Each constraint Zi consists of a pair (scope, rel), where "scope" is a tuple of variables that participate in the constraint and "rel" is a relation that defines the value that those variables take on. A relation can be represented as an explicit list of all tuples of values that satisfy the constraint, or as an abstract relation that supports two operations: testing if a tuple is a member of the relation and enumerating the members of the relation.

For example, if $X1$ and $X2$ both have the domain $\{A, B\}$, then the constraint saying the two variable must have different values can be written as:

$$\{(X1, X2), [(A, B), (B, A)]\} \text{ or as } \{(X1, X2), X1 \neq X2\}$$

To solve a CSP, we need to define a state space and the notion of a solution. Each state in a CSP is defined by an "assignment" of values to some or all of the variables. An assignment that does not violate any constraints is called a consistent or legal assignment. Consistent assignment in CSP refers to an assignment of values to variables that does not violate any of the given constraints. In other words, a consistent assignment is one in which all the variables are assigned values that satisfy all the constraints.

For example, consider a CSP with three variables, X, Y, and Z, where X can take values from $\{1, 2\}$, Y can take values from $\{2, 3\}$, and Z can take values from $\{1, 3\}$. Let us say that there are two constraints: $X < Y$ and $Y < Z$.

If we assign $X = 1$, $Y = 2$, and $Z = 3$, then this assignment satisfies both the constraints and is therefore a consistent assignment. On the other hand, if we assign $X = 2$, $Y = 2$, and $Z = 1$, then this assignment violates the constraint $Y < Z$, and is therefore an inconsistent assignment. Finding a consistent assignment is an important step in solving a CSP. In some cases, it may not be possible to find a consistent assignment, indicating that the problem has no solution that satisfies all the constraints.

A complete assignment is one in which every variable is assigned and a solution to a CSP is a consistent, complete assignment. A complete assignment in CSP refers to an assignment of values to all the variables in the problem such that all the constraints are satisfied. In other words, a complete assignment is one in which every variable in the problem is assigned a value that satisfies all the constraints. For example, consider a CSP with three variables, X, Y, and Z, where X can take values from {1, 2}, Y can take values from {2, 3}, and Z can take values from {1, 3}. Let us say that there are two constraints: X < Y and Y < Z.

If we find an assignment that satisfies both constraints, say $X = 1$, $Y = 2$, and $Z = 3$, then this is a complete assignment because all three variables have been assigned values and all the constraints have been satisfied. On the other hand, if we find an assignment that satisfies only one of the constraints, say $X = 2$, $Y = 3$, and $Z = 1$, then this is not a complete assignment because one of the constraints has been violated. Finding a complete assignment is the goal of solving a CSP. In some cases, it may not be possible to find a complete assignment, indicating that the problem has no solution that satisfies all the constraints.

A partial assignment is one that assigns values to only some of the variables. A partial assignment in CSP refers to an assignment of values to some, but not all, of the variables in the problem. In other words, a partial assignment is one in which only some of the variables in the problem have been assigned values.

For example, consider a CSP with three variables, X, Y, and Z, where X can take values from {1, 2}, Y can take values from {2, 3}, and Z can take values from {1, 3}. Let us say that there are two constraints: X < Y and Y < Z. If we assign $X = 1$ and $Y = 2$, but do not assign a value to Z, then this is a partial assignment because only two of the three variables have been assigned values. On the other hand, if we assign all three variables $X = 1$, $Y = 2$, and $Z = 3$, then this is a complete assignment. Partial assignments are useful in solving CSPs because they can help to reduce the search space and narrow down the possible solutions. For example, if we find a partial assignment that satisfies some of the constraints, we can use this information to guide the search for a complete assignment that satisfies all the constraints.

5.5.1 Map coloring with constraint satisfaction problems

Map coloring is a classic example of a CSP. The goal of the problem is to color the regions of a map in such a way that no two adjacent regions have the same color. The problem can be modeled as a CSP by defining variables for each region and their corresponding domains as the set of available colors, and constraints that enforce that adjacent regions have different colors.

For example, consider a map of four regions (Fig. 5.10) A, B, C, and D, where A and B are adjacent, as are B and C, and C and D. Suppose there are three colors available: red, blue, and green. We can model this problem as follows:

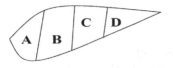

FIGURE 5.10   Map of four region.

Variables:

A: {red, blue, green}
B: {red, blue, green}
C: {red, blue, green}
D: {red, blue, green}

Constraints:

A! = B(A and B are adjacent)
B! = C(B and C are adjacent)
C! = D(C and D are adjacent)

The goal is to find an assignment of colors to each region that satisfies all the constraints. There may be multiple solutions to the problem, but any valid solution must satisfy the constraints.

To solve this problem, we can use various constraint satisfaction algorithms such as backtracking, forward checking, or constraint propagation. These algorithms systematically search through the possible combinations of color assignments until a valid solution is found. If no solution is found, the problem is deemed unsolvable given the given constraints and available colors.

- Python program for the map coloring with CSPs:

A Python program that demonstrates the map coloring problem using CSP with the Python-constraint library:

```
from constraint import Problem
```

 # Define the CSP problem
```
problem = Problem()
```

 # Define variables (Map regions)
```
regions = ['WA', 'NT', 'SA', 'Q', 'NSW', 'V', 'T']
colors = ['Red', 'Green', 'Blue']
```

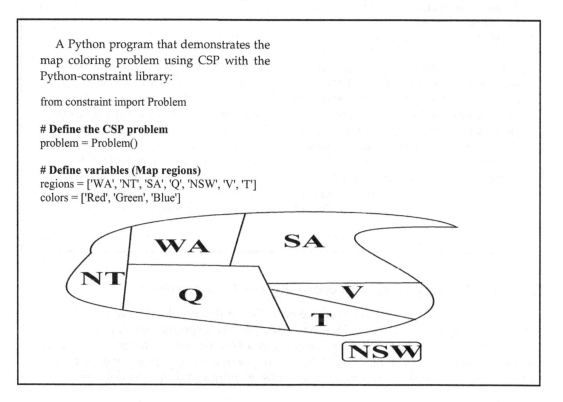

(cont'd)

```
# Add variables and their domains to the problem
for region in regions:
    problem.addVariable(region, colors)


# Define constraints
def constraint_function(region1, color1, region2, color2):
    # Example constraint: Regions with a shared border cannot have the same color
    return color1 != color2


# Add constraint to the problem for adjacent regions
problem.addConstraint(constraint_function, ('WA', 'NT', 'WA', 'SA'))
problem.addConstraint(constraint_function, ('WA', 'NT', 'NT', 'SA'))
problem.addConstraint(constraint_function, ('NT', 'SA', 'NT', 'Q'))
problem.addConstraint(constraint_function, ('NT', 'SA', 'SA', 'Q'))
problem.addConstraint(constraint_function, ('SA', 'Q', 'SA', 'NSW'))
problem.addConstraint(constraint_function, ('SA', 'Q', 'SA', 'V'))
problem.addConstraint(constraint_function, ('SA', 'NSW', 'NSW', 'V'))


# Solve the problem
solutions = problem.getSolutions()


# Print the solutions
for solution in solutions:
    print(solution)
```

In this program, we use the Python-constraint library to define and solve the map coloring problem. We start by creating a problem object. Next, we define the variables, which represent the regions of a map, and their domains (colors) using the addVariable method. In this example, the regions are "WA," "NT," "SA," "Q," "NSW," "V," and "T," and the colors are "Red," "Green," and "Blue."

Then, we define a constraint function that specifies the conditions that neighboring regions must satisfy. In this case, the constraint function ensures that neighboring regions cannot have the same color. We add these constraints to the problem using the addConstraint method. Finally, we solve the problem using the getSolutions method, which returns a list of all valid solutions.

5.5.2 Job shop scheduling with constraint satisfaction problem

Job shop scheduling is another example of a CSP. In this problem, there are a set of jobs to be performed on a set of machines, and each job has a specific sequence of operations that must be performed on different machines in a specific order. The goal is to schedule the operations on the machines in such a way that each job is completed without conflicts, and the total time taken to complete all jobs is minimized. To model the job shop scheduling problem as a CSP, it can define variables to represent the start time of each operation on each machine, and the corresponding domains as the set of possible start times. The constraints can then be defined to enforce that the operations are performed in the correct order and that no two operations conflict with each other.

For example, consider a job shop scheduling problem with three jobs and three machines. Each job requires two operations, and the order in which the operations must be performed on the machines is given in Table 5.2.

It can model this problem as follows:
Variables:

A11: {0, 1, 2, ..., T} (start time of operation A on machine 1)
B31: {0, 1, 2, ..., T} (start time of operation B on machine 3)
A33: {0, 1, 2, ..., T} (start time of operation A on machine 3)
B22: {0, 1, 2, ..., T} (start time of operation B on machine 2)
A21: {0, 1, 2, ..., T} (start time of operation A on machine 2)
B13: {0, 1, 2, ..., T} (start time of operation B on machine 1)

Constraints:

A11 + d1 < = A33 (operation A1 on machine 1 must be completed before operation A3 on machine 3 can begin)
A33 + d3 < = B22 (operation A3 on machine 3 must be completed before operation B2 on machine 2 can begin)
A21 + d2 < = B13 (operation A2 on machine 2 must be completed before operation B1 on machine 1 can begin)
B13 + d1 < = A11 + T (operation B1 on machine 1 must be completed before operation A1 on machine 1 can begin again)
B22 + d2 < = A21 + T (operation B2 on machine 2 must be completed before operation A2 on machine 2 can begin again)
B31 + d2 < = A33 + T (operation B3 on machine 3 must be completed before operation A3 on machine 3 can begin again)
A11 + d1 < = B31 + T (operation A1 on machine 1 must be completed before operation B3 on machine 3 can begin again)

TABLE 5.2 Dataset of job scheduling problem.

Job	Operation	Machine	Order
1	A	1	1
1	B	3	2
2	A	3	1
2	B	2	2
3	A	2	1
3	B	1	2

A21 + d2 < = B22 + T (operation A2 on machine 2 must be completed before operation B2 on machine 2 can begin again)

B13 + d1 < = A11 + T (operation B1 on machine)

5.5.3 Crypt arithmetic

Crypt arithmetic is a type of mathematical puzzle in which the digits in a mathematical expression are replaced with letters of the alphabet. The goal is to find the numerical value of each letter so that the equation is correct.

Here's an example of a crypt arithmetic problem:

SEND
+
MORE
=
MONEY

In this puzzle, each letter represents a unique digit, and the task is to determine what digit each letter represents so that the equation is true.

To solve the puzzle, you would start by looking at the rightmost column, which is where the ones place digits are added together. In this case, the only way to get a sum of zero in the ones place is if E + R = 10. Since each letter represents a unique digit, we know that E and R must be either 4 and 6 or 5 and 5. Next, we can look at the second column from the right, which is where the tens place digits are added together. If we assume that E and R are 5 and 5, then we would have S + O = 9 (since we carry the 1 from the ones place), which means that S and O must be 4 and 5 in some order.

Continuing in this way, we can solve the puzzle by systematically working our way from right to left, using the constraints that arise from each column to determine the possible values for each letter.

In this case, the solution is:

9 5 6 7 1
S E N D
M O R E
M O N E Y
So, SEND + MORE = MONEY, where S = 9, E = 5, N = 6, D = 7, M = 1, O = 0, Y = 2.
CRYPTARITHMATIC:

5.5.4 The Wumpus world

The Wumpus world is a classic AI problem where an agent navigates a grid-based world containing a Wumpus (a dangerous creature), pits (fatal to fall into), gold (a valuable reward), and arrows (to shoot the Wumpus). Let's walk through a solved example:

- *Initial state*: The agent starts in a random cell of the grid. The agent has limited knowledge about the environment and must explore and gather information to make decisions.
- *Perception and sensing*: The agent perceives its current cell and uses its senses to gather information about nearby cells. It can sense breeze if there is a pit in an adjacent cell and stench if the Wumpus is nearby. Initially, the agent has no information about the nearby cells.
- *Exploration and safe moves*: The agent explores adjacent cells one by one while marking visited cells. It moves cautiously to avoid falling into pits. If it senses a breeze, it deduces that there might be a pit nearby and marks the adjacent cells as potentially dangerous.
- *Shooting the Wumpus*: If the agent perceives a stench and has arrows, it may decide to shoot in the direction of the stench to kill the Wumpus. If the arrow hits the Wumpus, the agent eliminates the threat. If the arrow misses, the agent loses the arrow but knows that the Wumpus is not in that direction.
- *Updating knowledge*: As the agent explores and gathers information, it updates its knowledge base. It records the presence of pits and the Wumpus, marking safe cells and dangerous areas accordingly. The agent also notes when it finds the gold.
- *Retrieving the gold*: If the agent finds the gold, it can decide to grab it. However, grabbing the gold may introduce additional risks, such as triggering a collapse of nearby cells due to the agent's weight. The agent must carefully assess the situation before retrieving the gold.
- *Path planning and backtracking*: Once the agent has gathered the gold or decided not to retrieve it, it plans a path to exit the Wumpus World safely. It may use algorithms like A* search or depth-first search to find the shortest path back to the initial starting position.
- *Exiting and goal achievement*: The agent follows the planned path, avoiding hazards and navigating towards the exit point. Once the agent reaches the initial starting position, it exits the Wumpus World successfully. Fig. 5.11 shows the schematic diagram of the Wumpus world.

Throughout the process, the agent updates its knowledge base, avoids pits and the Wumpus, collects the gold if feasible, and safely exits the environment. The solved example demonstrates the agent's decision-making, exploration, and knowledge updating based on perception and sensory information to achieve its goals in the Wumpus world.

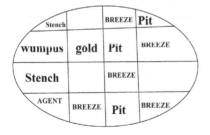

FIGURE 5.11   Schematic diagram of Wumpus world.

- Python program for the Wumpus world:

```python
import random

class WumpusWorld:
    def __init__(self, size):
        self.size = size
        self.grid = [[' ' for _ in range(size)] for _ in range(size)]
        self.player_pos = (0, 0)
        self.wumpus_pos = self.generate_random_pos()
        self.gold_pos = self.generate_random_pos()
        self.pit_pos = [self.generate_random_pos() for _ in range(size)]

    def generate_random_pos(self):
        return random.randint(0, self.size-1), random.randint(0, self.size-1)

    def display(self):
        for row in self.grid:
            print(' | '.join(row))
            print('-'*(self.size*4 - 1))

    def is_valid_position(self, pos):
        x, y = pos
        return 0 <= x < self.size and 0 <= y < self.size

    def move(self, direction):
        x, y = self.player_pos
        if direction == 'up':
            new_pos = (x-1, y)
        elif direction == 'down':
            new_pos = (x+1, y)
        elif direction == 'left':
            new_pos = (x, y-1)
        elif direction == 'right':
            new_pos = (x, y+1)
        else:
            return

        if self.is_valid_position(new_pos):
            self.player_pos = new_pos
            self.check_encounter()
```

(cont'd)

```
def check_encounter(self):
    x, y = self.player_pos
    if self.player_pos == self.wumpus_pos:
        print("You were eaten by the Wumpus! Game Over!")
        exit()
    elif self.player_pos == self.gold_pos:
        print("Congratulations! You found the gold! You win!")
        exit()
    elif self.player_pos in self.pit_pos:
        print("You fell into a pit! Game Over!")
        exit()
    else:
        self.grid[x][y] = 'P'

def run_game(self):
    while True:
        self.display()
        direction = input("Enter your move (up/down/left/right): ")
        self.move(direction)

# Create a Wumpus World instance with a size of 4x4
world = WumpusWorld(4)
world.run_game()
```

The player's position is denoted by "P," the Wumpus' position is randomly generated, and the gold and pit positions are also randomly generated. The player can move up, down, left, or right within the grid by entering the corresponding direction. The game checks for encounters with the Wumpus, gold, or pits after each move. If the player encounters the Wumpus, the game ends in defeat. If the player finds the gold, the game ends in victory. If the player falls into a pit, the game ends in defeat.

5.6 Cognitive analysis with artificial intelligence

Cognitive analysis with AI is a field of study that combines the principles of cognitive psychology with the power of AI algorithms to understand and analyze human thought processes. Cognitive psychology is the scientific study of mental processes such as attention, perception, memory, problem-solving, and decision-making. The goal of cognitive analysis with AI is to replicate some of these mental processes using algorithms and computational models.

Cognitive analysis with AI can be used in a variety of applications, such as NLP, sentiment analysis, and image recognition. For example, NLP algorithms can be trained to understand and analyze human language, including syntax, semantics, and context. This technology is used in applications such as chatbots, virtual assistants, and automated customer service systems. Sentiment analysis is another application of cognitive analysis with AI. This technology can be used to analyze the emotional tone of written or spoken language, including social media posts, reviews, and customer feedback. This information can be used by businesses to improve customer satisfaction, product development, and marketing strategies. In image recognition, cognitive analysis with AI algorithms can be used to analyze and classify visual data, such as photographs and videos. This technology is used in applications such as self-driving cars, security cameras, and medical imaging. Cognitive analysis with AI has the potential to revolutionize many fields, including healthcare, education, finance, and marketing. However, there are also concerns about the ethical implications of this technology, including privacy concerns and the potential for AI systems to perpetuate bias and discrimination.

Let's consider a solved example of cognitive analytics using AI:

- *Problem statement*: A retail company wants to analyze customer feedback to understand customer sentiment and identify areas for improvement. They have a large volume of customer reviews in text format, and they want to extract meaningful insights from this unstructured data.
- *Data collection*: The company gathers customer reviews from various sources, such as online review platforms, social media, and customer surveys. The data consists of text comments provided by customers, along with associated metadata like ratings and timestamps.
- *Text preprocessing*: The collected text data undergoes preprocessing to clean and prepare it for analysis. This involves removing irrelevant characters, converting text to lowercase, removing stopwords (common words like "the," "is," etc.), and applying techniques like stemming or lemmatization to reduce words to their base form.
- *Sentiment analysis*: The preprocessed text data is fed into a sentiment analysis model, which is an AI algorithm trained to classify text into positive, negative, or neutral sentiment categories. The sentiment analysis model assigns sentiment scores to each customer review, indicating the overall sentiment expressed by the customer.
- *Topic modeling*: The preprocessed text data is further analyzed using topic modeling techniques, such as latent Dirichlet allocation. Topic modeling identifies latent topics within the customer reviews and assigns probabilities of topic presence to each review. This helps in uncovering the key themes and subjects discussed by customers.
- *Named entity recognition*: The company employs named entity recognition (NER) algorithms to identify and extract relevant entities mentioned in the customer reviews. This includes extracting entities like product names, brand names, locations, or specific features or aspects of the business that customers are referring to in their feedback.
- *Insight generation*: By combining sentiment analysis, topic modeling, and NER results, the company generates actionable insights. For example, they may find that customers express positive sentiment about the company's product quality but negative sentiment about customer service. They may also identify specific product features that customers frequently mention and associate sentiment with.
- *Visualization and reporting*: The insights derived from the cognitive analytics process are visualized and reported in a meaningful way. This can include interactive dashboards, charts, graphs, and summary reports that provide a clear understanding of the overall customer sentiment, prevalent topics, and identified areas for improvement.

- *Decision-making and action*: Based on the insights generated, the retail company can make informed decisions to improve their products, services, or customer experience. They may decide to address the identified issues, prioritize specific improvements, or take targeted actions based on the feedback provided by customers.
- *Continuous improvement*: The company continues to collect customer feedback and applies cognitive analytics iteratively to gain ongoing insights. By monitoring customer sentiment and feedback over time, they can track the impact of their actions and make further improvements as necessary.

In this example, cognitive analytics using AI helps the retail company analyze unstructured customer feedback, extract sentiment, identify topics, and generate actionable insights. By leveraging AI techniques, the company gains a deeper understanding of customer sentiment and can make data-driven decisions to enhance their products and services.

5.7 Conclusion

In conclusion, the application of AI and ML in data analysis holds tremendous potential for unlocking valuable insights from vast amounts of data. By employing suitable techniques for knowledge representation, following the AI cycle, and incorporating cognitive science principles, researchers and practitioners can harness the power of AI and ML to extract meaningful patterns, make accurate predictions, and support decision-making processes in various domains. Continued advancements in AI and ML will undoubtedly lead to further innovations and advancements in the field of data analysis, opening up new possibilities for solving complex problems and driving data-driven decision-making to new heights.

5.8 Case study

5.8.1 Case study: knowledge representation in artificial intelligence— healthcare diagnosis

5.8.1.1 Introduction

In the field of healthcare, accurate and timely diagnosis is crucial for effective treatment and patient outcomes. AI plays a vital role in assisting healthcare professionals in diagnosing diseases. This case study explores the knowledge representation techniques employed in AI systems for healthcare diagnosis.

5.8.1.2 Problem statement

A hospital aims to develop an AI system that can assist doctors in diagnosing a specific medical condition. The condition exhibits a wide range of symptoms and requires a comprehensive understanding of various factors, including patient history, symptoms, lab results, and medical literature.

5.8.1.3 Knowledge representation approach

To represent the knowledge required for healthcare diagnosis, the AI system utilizes a combination of rule-based systems, probabilistic models, and ontologies.

5.8.1.4 Rule-based systems

The AI system incorporates a set of rules that encode medical knowledge and diagnostic guidelines. These rules are derived from expert physicians and medical literature. For instance, if a patient exhibits symptom A, symptom B, and lab result C, the system can infer a specific diagnosis based on predefined rules.

5.8.1.5 Probabilistic models

To handle uncertainty and varying degrees of confidence in diagnosis, the AI system employs probabilistic models, such as Bayesian networks or Markov models. These models capture the relationships between symptoms, medical history, test results, and the likelihood of different diagnoses. By considering the probabilities of different diagnoses, the system provides a ranked list of likely conditions.

5.8.1.6 Ontologies

The AI system utilizes ontologies, which are formal representations of domain knowledge, to capture and organize medical concepts, relationships, and terminologies. The system employs standardized medical ontologies, such as SNOMED-CT or UMLS, to ensure consistency and interoperability in knowledge representation. This allows for efficient querying and retrieval of relevant medical knowledge.

5.8.1.7 Knowledge graphs

The AI system constructs a knowledge graph that represents medical knowledge as a network of interconnected entities and relationships. The graph integrates structured data (e.g., lab results, patient history) with unstructured data (e.g., medical literature, clinical guidelines) to provide a comprehensive knowledge base. The system employs graph-based algorithms to traverse the knowledge graph, infer relationships, and make accurate diagnoses.

5.8.1.8 Case-based reasoning

The AI system incorporates a case-based reasoning approach, where past cases with similar symptoms and diagnoses are stored and utilized for future diagnosis. The system retrieves relevant cases from the database, compares them with the current patient's information, and adapts the diagnosis based on similarities and differences.

5.8.1.9 Benefits and outcomes

By employing the aforementioned knowledge representation techniques, the AI system offers several benefits:

Enhanced diagnostic accuracy: The system combines explicit medical knowledge, probabilistic reasoning, and contextual information to provide accurate and personalized diagnoses, minimizing misdiagnoses and improving patient outcomes.

Knowledge integration: By leveraging ontologies and knowledge graphs, the system integrates vast amounts of medical knowledge from diverse sources, including clinical guidelines, research papers, and patient data. This enables a comprehensive understanding of the disease and its associated factors.

Decision support: The AI system serves as a powerful decision support tool for healthcare professionals. It provides them with evidence-based recommendations, alternative diagnoses, and explanations for the diagnostic process, empowering them to make informed decisions.

Continuous learning: The system can learn from new patient cases and incorporate emerging medical knowledge. By continuously updating its knowledge base, it improves its diagnostic capabilities over time and adapts to evolving medical practices.

5.8.1.10 Conclusion

Effective knowledge representation is essential for AI systems in healthcare diagnosis. By combining rule-based systems, probabilistic models, ontologies, knowledge graphs, and case-based reasoning, AI systems can capture and utilize medical knowledge to support accurate and personalized diagnoses. These techniques empower healthcare professionals to make informed decisions and improve patient outcomes in the complex field of healthcare.

5.8.2 Case study: constraint satisfaction problems in artificial intelligence— employee scheduling

5.8.2.1 Introduction

CSPs are widely used in AI to solve problems where variables must be assigned values while satisfying a set of constraints. This case study explores the application of CSPs in employee scheduling, specifically for a retail company with complex shift scheduling requirements.

5.8.2.2 Problem statement

A retail company operates multiple stores with various departments and requires efficient scheduling of employees for different shifts. The company needs to create schedules that satisfy several constraints, such as employee availability, department requirements, shift preferences, and fairness considerations.

5.8.2.3 Constraint satisfaction approach

To solve the employee scheduling problem, the company employs a constraint satisfaction approach using CSP techniques.

5.8.2.4 Variable definition

The variables in the CSP represent the shifts that need to be assigned to employees. Each variable represents a specific shift, such as morning, afternoon, or evening, for a particular day in a specific department. The values for each variable represent the eligible employees who can be assigned to that shift.

5.8.2.5 Domain definition

The domain for each variable consists of the eligible employees who can work in the respective shift. The domain considers various factors such as employee availability, skills, preferences, and labor regulations.

Constraints: Several constraints are defined to ensure that the employee scheduling meets specific requirements:

a. *Availability constraint*: Employees' availability is taken into account, ensuring that they are not assigned to shifts when they are unavailable due to other commitments or time-off requests.
b. *Skill constraint*: Certain shifts may require specific skills or certifications. The constraints ensure that only employees with the required skills are assigned to those shifts.
c. *Preference constraint*: Employees may have preferences for certain shifts or specific days off. The scheduling system considers these preferences while assigning shifts, prioritizing employees' preferences whenever possible.
d. *Department constraint*: Each department may have specific requirements for the number of employees needed during different shifts. Constraints are defined to ensure that the number of assigned employees satisfies the department's requirements.
e. *Fairness constraint*: Constraints are defined to ensure fairness in scheduling, such as equal distribution of desirable and undesirable shifts among employees or rotation of shifts to prevent employees from being assigned to the same shift repeatedly.

Constraint propagation: To solve the CSP, constraint propagation techniques are employed. These techniques involve applying constraints iteratively to reduce the search space and prune inconsistent assignments. Techniques like forward checking and arc consistency are used to ensure that constraints are consistently satisfied during the assignment process.

Backtracking search: To find a valid solution, a backtracking search algorithm is employed. The algorithm iteratively assigns values to variables while considering constraints. When a constraint violation occurs, the algorithm backtracks and makes alternative assignments until a valid solution is found or all possibilities are exhausted.

5.8.2.5.1 Benefits and outcomes

The application of CSPs in employee scheduling offers several benefits for the retail company:

Efficient scheduling: CSP techniques enable the generation of efficient and optimized employee schedules that satisfy various constraints. The company can schedule the right employees at the right time, considering availability, skills, preferences, and department requirements.

Improved employee satisfaction: By considering employee preferences, the scheduling system enhances employee satisfaction and engagement. Employees are more likely to be assigned to shifts they prefer or have requested off, leading to improved work-life balance and morale.

Compliance with labor regulations: The CSP approach ensures compliance with labor regulations, such as maximum working hours, rest periods, and fair distribution of shifts among employees. This helps the company avoid penalties and maintain a positive relationship with employees.

Time and resource savings: The automated CSP-based scheduling system saves time and resources for the company. It reduces the manual effort required to create schedules and minimizes the likelihood of errors or conflicts in the scheduling process.

5.9 Exercise

5.9.1 Objective type question

1. Which knowledge representation technique organizes information in a network of interconnected nodes representing concepts or objects, along with labeled links or edges?
   a. Semantic networks
   b. Predicate logic
   c. Frames
   d. Bayesian networks

2. Which knowledge representation technique focuses on describing facts or statements about the world and uses logical predicates, variables, and quantifiers?
   a. Semantic networks
   b. Fuzzy logic
   c. Predicate logic
   d. Conceptual graphs

3. Which phase of the AI cycle involves developing and training AI and machine learning models using appropriate algorithms and techniques?
   a. Data acquisition
   b. Preprocessing
   c. Modeling
   d. Evaluation

4. Which phase of the AI cycle involves assessing the performance of AI models and making necessary refinements?
   a. Data acquisition
   b. Preprocessing
   c. Modeling
   d. Evaluation

5. Which of the following best describes ontologies in AI?
   a. Techniques for representing procedural knowledge
   b. Graphical models used for capturing knowledge about uncertainty
   c. Formal and explicit representations of knowledge within a specific domain
   d. Rules used to govern the behavior of other rules

6. Cognitive science contributes to AI by:
   a. Providing rules to govern the behavior of AI systems.
   b. Enabling natural language processing capabilities in AI.
   c. Training neural networks using large datasets.
   d. Studying human cognition to develop more human-like intelligent systems.

7. In a constraint satisfaction problem (CSP), the constraints represent:
   a. Variables that need to be assigned values.
   b. The desired assignments for each variable.
   c. The relationships or conditions that must be satisfied between variables.
   d. The search algorithms used to solve the problem.

8. The main goal in a constraint satisfaction problem (CSP) is to:
   a. Find the optimal solution that maximizes the objective function.
   b. Find the first feasible solution that satisfies all the constraints.
   c. Find a solution that satisfies as many constraints as possible.
   d. Find a solution that satisfies all the constraints.

9. Backtracking is a common technique used to solve constraint satisfaction problems. It works by:
   a. Randomly assigning values to variables and checking if they satisfy the constraints.
   b. Iteratively assigning values to variables and backtracking when a constraint violation is encountered.
   c. Assigning values to variables based on a priority order and backtracking when an optimal solution is found.
   d. Evaluating all possible combinations of variable assignments to find the optimal solution.

10. The arc-consistency algorithm is used in Constraint Satisfaction Problems to:
    a. Determine the optimal solution by examining the consistency of all variables.
    b. Enforce local consistency by propagating constraints between neighboring variables.
    c. Randomly assign values to variables and check if they satisfy the constraints.
    d. Perform a depth-first search to find a feasible solution.

11. Which knowledge representation technique is based on a graphical structure of interconnected nodes representing concepts or objects?
    a. Semantic networks
    b. Predicate logic
    c. Frames
    d. Bayesian networks

12. Which knowledge representation technique is suitable for representing facts and rules using logical symbols, predicates, and operators?
    a. Semantic networks
    b. Predicate logic
    c. Frames
    d. Bayesian networks

13. Which knowledge representation technique allows for representing complex object structures with slots representing attributes and their corresponding values?
    a. Semantic networks
    b. Predicate logic
    c. Frames
    d. Bayesian networks

14. Which knowledge representation technique uses probabilistic graphical models to capture relationships between variables and support probabilistic inference?
    a. Semantic networks
    b. Predicate logic
    c. Frames
    d. Bayesian networks

15. Which knowledge representation technique is commonly used for representing uncertainty and imprecision using fuzzy sets and fuzzy rules?
    a. Semantic networks
    b. Predicate logic
    c. Frames
    d. Fuzzy logic

5.9.2 Descriptive type question

1. How does knowledge representation in AI facilitate effective data analysis?
2. Explain the concept of the AI cycle and its relevance in the context of data analysis.
3. What are the key steps involved in the AI cycle when applied to data analysis?
4. How does knowledge representation play a role in different phases of the AI cycle in data analysis?
5. Describe the various techniques used for knowledge representation in AI.
6. How do semantic networks contribute to knowledge representation in data analysis?
7. Explain the role of frames in knowledge representation within the context of data analysis.
8. How do ontologies contribute to knowledge representation in AI-based data analysis?
9. What are the benefits of using neural networks for knowledge representation in data analysis?
10. Describe the application of Bayesian networks in knowledge representation for data analysis.
11. How does the AI cycle ensure the quality and effectiveness of data analysis processes?
12. Discuss the significance of data acquisition in the AI cycle for data analysis.
13. What preprocessing techniques are commonly employed in the AI cycle for data analysis?
14. Explain the process of modeling in the AI cycle and its impact on data analysis.
15. How is the evaluation phase of the AI cycle used to assess the performance of AI models in data analysis?
16. Discuss the importance of cognitive science in the context of AI and data analysis.
17. How does cognitive science contribute to the development of more human-like intelligent systems for data analysis?
18. Explain the role of NLP in the intersection of cognitive science with AI in data analysis.
19. How can insights from cognitive science be applied to enhance pattern recognition in data analysis using AI?
20. Discuss the potential future advancements and challenges in the integration of cognitive science with AI for data analysis.

Further reading

B. Ahmed, A. Ali, Usage of traditional Chinese medicine, western medicine, and integrated Chinese-western medicine for the treatment of allergic rhinitis, SPR 1 (1) (2021) 1—11. Available from: https://doi.org/10.52152/spr/2021.101.

Y. Cao, Research on the application of digital media art in modern exhibition design based on computer information technology, J. Phys.: Conf. Ser. 1648 (3) (2020).

S.Y. Chen, P.H. Lin, W.C. Chien, Children's digital art ability training system based on AI-assisted learning: a case study of drawing color perception, Front. Psychol. 13 (2022) 823078.

D. Degand, Stereotypes vs. strategies for digital media artists: the case for culturally relevant media production, Theory Into Pract. 58 (4) (2019) 368—376.

F. Fang, A discussion on developing students' communicative competence in college teaching in China, J. Lang. Teach. Res. 1 (2) (2010) 111—116. Available from: https://doi.org/10.4304/jltr.1.2.111-116.

R. Jiang, L. Wang, S.B. Tsai, An empirical study on digital media technology in film and television animation design, Math. Probl. Eng. (2022). Available from: https://doi.org/10.1155/2022/5905117.

Z. Li, Treatment and technology of domestic sewage for improvement of the rural environment in China-Jiangsu: a research, SPR 2 (2) (2022) 466—475.

F. Liang, AI-powered digital media platform and its applications, Proceedings of the 2020 Conference on Artificial Intelligence and Healthcare (CAIH2020), Association for Computing Machinery, New York, NY, USA, 2020, pp. 121—126.

Y. Lin, Research on the innovation of art design products based on the concept of "AI" boundary, J. Phys.: Conf. Ser. 1574 (1) (2020).

S. Lin, Influence of digital technology on ideological and political education in colleges and universities under 5G era, Sci. Program. (2022) 1—12.

G. Liu, Influence of digital media technology on animation design, J. Phys.: Conf. Ser. 1533 (4) (2020).

Y. Liu, S. Wu, Q. Xu, H. Liu, Holographic projection technology in the field of digital media art, Wirel. Commun. Mob. Comput. (2021) 1—12.

R.N. Mody, A.R. Bhoosreddy, Multiple odontogenic keratocyst: a case report, Anna Dent. 54 (1—2) (1995) 41—43.

A. Momohshaibu, S.O. Salihu, Z. Iyya, Assessment of physicochemical parameters and organochlorine pesticide residues in selected vegetable farmlands soil in Zamfara state, Nigeria, SPR 2 (2) (2022) 491—498.

C. Panciroli, A. Macauda, V. Russo, Educating about art by augmented reality: new didactic mediation perspectives at school and in museums, Proceedings 1 (9) (2018) 1107. Available from: https://doi.org/10.3390/proceedings1091107.

Y. Ren, Research on impact of digital media art on animation design-take film and television animation application as example, 2016 International Conference on Education, Sports, Arts and Management Engineering, Atlantis Press, Paris, 2016, pp. 902—905.

A. Shahabaz, M. Afzal, Implementation of high dose rate brachytherapy in cancer treatment, SPR 1 (3) (2021) 77—106.

X. Wang, Y. Zhang, The application of art design thinking in visual works from the perspective of digital media, J. Phys.: Conf. Ser. 1634 (1) (2020).

P.N. Whatmough, C. Zhou, P. Hansen, S.K. Venkataramanaiah, J.S. Seo, M. Mattina, Fixynn: efficient hardware for mobile computer vision via transfer learning, arXiv Prepr. arXiv (2020) 1902.11128.

H. Wu, G. Li, Visual communication design elements of an Internet of Things based on cloud computing applied in graffiti art schema, Soft Comput. 24 (11) (2020) 8077—8086.

X. Xu, D. Li, M. Sun, S. Yang, S. Yu, G. Manogaran, et al., Research on key technologies of smart campus teaching platform based on 5G network, IEEE Access. 7 (2019) 20664—20675.

B. Yang, Innovation and development analysis of visual communication design based on digital media art context, 2021 International Conference on Computer Technology and Media Convergence Design (CTMCD), IEEE, 2021, pp. 192—195.

F. Ye, Y. Liang, Art experience innovation design in digital media era, 2021 IEEE Sixth International Conference on Data Science in Cyberspace (DSC), IEEE, 2021, pp. 454—457.

Data analysis applications and methodology

Abbreviations

CRISP-DM	cross-industry standard process for data mining
SEMMA	sample, explore, modify, model, and assess
AI	artificial Intelligence
ML	machine Learning
EHR	electronic health records
DL	deep Learning
CNN	convolutional neural networks
RPN	region proposal network

6.1 Introduction

Data analysis is the process of inspecting, cleaning, transforming, and modeling data with the goal of discovering useful information, suggesting conclusions, and supporting decision-making. There are many applications of data analysis across various industries and fields, including finance, healthcare, marketing, and social sciences. In today's digital age, businesses and organizations are increasingly turning to data-driven approaches to improve their decision-making processes and gain a competitive advantage. To achieve this goal, various methodologies have been developed to guide organizations in their data analysis journey. Two such popular methodologies are CRISP-DM and SEMMA. CRISP-DM (Cross-Industry Standard Process for Data Mining) is a comprehensive and widely used methodology for data mining and analytics. It consists of six phases: business understanding, data understanding, data preparation, modeling, evaluation, and deployment. This methodology provides a structured approach to tackle complex data mining problems and ensures that all relevant aspects of the business problem are considered. Similarly, SEMMA (Sample, Explore, Modify, Model, and Assess) is a methodology developed by SAS for data analysis and predictive modeling. This methodology emphasizes the importance of iterative exploration and modification of data to uncover patterns and relationships that can be used for modeling and prediction. In recent years, the field of artificial intelligence (AI) has made significant advancements, leading to the development of various AI techniques and applications. AI is transforming the way organizations approach data analysis and decision-making

Cognitive Science, Computational Intelligence, and Data Analytics
DOI: https://doi.org/10.1016/B978-0-443-16078-3.00006-X
© 2024 Elsevier Inc. All rights reserved, including those for text and data mining, AI training, and similar technologies.

by providing powerful tools for data processing, analysis, and automation. One such application of AI is object detection, which involves identifying and localizing objects within an image or video. Object detection has numerous applications, including surveillance, autonomous vehicles, and facial recognition systems. In this chapter, will explore the CRISP-DM methodology, SEMMA methodology, and their applications in data analysis. It will also discuss the role of AI in data analysis, specifically in the context of object detection models.

6.2 CRISP-DM methodology

CRISP-DM (Cross-Industry Standard Process for Data Mining) is a widely used methodology for data mining and machine learning (ML) projects. It provides a structured approach to guide the project from the initial problem understanding to the deployment of the final model. Fig. 6.1 shows the steps of CRISP-DM methodology. The CRISP-DM methodology consists of six phases, which are as follows:

Business Understanding: The first phase involves understanding the problem statement and defining the project objectives. The aim is to understand the business requirements and constraints, and how the project can help address them. During the Business Understanding phase, the data mining team works closely with the business stakeholders to define the problem to be solved, identify the data sources that will be used, and determine the success criteria for the project. This may involve conducting interviews, analyzing business processes, and reviewing relevant documentation. The Business Understanding phase is critical to the success of the data mining project, as it helps to ensure that the analysis is focused on the most important business objectives and that the results are relevant and actionable. It lays the foundation for the rest of the data mining process, including data preparation, modeling, evaluation, and deployment.

Data Understanding: In this phase, the data is collected and analyzed to gain insights into its quality, completeness, and usefulness for the project. This includes data exploration, data cleaning, and data preprocessing. During the Data Understanding phase, the data mining team collects and examines the data to identify any issues or anomalies that may impact the analysis. This may include checking for missing values, outliers, or inconsistencies in the data. The team

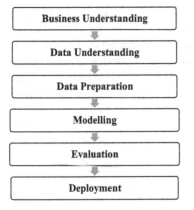

FIGURE 6.1 Steps of the CRISP-DM methodology.

also explores the relationships between variables to identify any potential patterns or trends. The Data Understanding phase helps to ensure that the data is suitable for the analysis and that any issues or anomalies are identified and addressed. It also helps to guide the selection of appropriate modeling techniques for the analysis, based on the characteristics of the data and the business objectives of the project.

The Data Understanding phase is critical to the success of the data mining project, as it ensures that the analysis is based on a comprehensive understanding of the data and its underlying structure. It lays the foundation for the rest of the data mining process, including data preparation, modeling, evaluation, and deployment.

Data Preparation: In this phase, the data is prepared for modeling. This involves feature engineering, data transformation, and data selection. During the Data Preparation phase, the data mining team selects the relevant data for analysis, eliminates any irrelevant or redundant data, and deals with missing values, outliers, and inconsistencies in the data. The team also transforms the data into a format suitable for modeling, which may involve scaling, normalization, and encoding categorical variables. The Data Preparation phase is critical to the success of the data mining project, as the accuracy and effectiveness of the modeling and analysis depend on the quality of the data. The Data Preparation phase is often the most time-consuming and resource-intensive phase of the data mining process, but it is essential for ensuring that the analysis produces accurate and meaningful results.

The Data Preparation phase lays the foundation for the modeling phase, where the data is used to build models that can predict future outcomes or identify patterns and trends in the data. By ensuring that the data is clean, complete, and in the right format, the Data Preparation phase helps to ensure that the modeling phase is accurate and effective.

Modeling: In this phase, various ML algorithms are used to build the models that solve the problem statement. The models are evaluated, and the best model is selected. During the Modeling phase, the data mining team selects the appropriate modeling technique based on the business objectives and the characteristics of the data. The team then trains and tests the model using the prepared data, and adjusts the model as necessary to improve its accuracy and effectiveness. The Modeling phase is where the insights and predictions generated by the analysis are developed. It is the phase where the data mining team applies the techniques and algorithms to the prepared data and uses them to develop a predictive or descriptive model that can provide insights into the business problem or opportunity. The Modeling phase is critical to the success of the data mining project, as it is where the insights and predictions generated by the analysis are developed. The modeling technique used must be appropriate for the data and the business problem, and the model must be tested and validated to ensure its accuracy and effectiveness. The Modeling phase lays the foundation for the Evaluation phase, where the model is evaluated for its effectiveness and suitability for the business problem or opportunity. If necessary, the model may be adjusted or refined to improve its accuracy or effectiveness.

Evaluation: In this phase, the performance of the model is evaluated against the project objectives. The model is tested on new data to assess its accuracy and effectiveness. During the Evaluation phase, the data mining team tests the model against new, unseen data to determine its accuracy and effectiveness. The team also assesses the model's suitability for the business problem, including its ability to meet the success criteria defined during the Business Understanding phase. The Evaluation phase helps to ensure that the model developed during the Modeling phase is effective and appropriate for the business problem or opportunity. The team may need to adjust or refine the model based on the results of the evaluation, or they may decide that the model is not suitable and return to an earlier phase of the process.

The Evaluation phase is critical to the success of the data mining project, as it determines whether the analysis has produced results that are relevant and actionable for the business. It also helps to guide the deployment phase, where the model is implemented and integrated into the business processes. The Evaluation phase is not necessarily the final phase of the data mining process, as the model may need to be adjusted or refined based on ongoing feedback and monitoring. However, it is a critical component of the process for ensuring that the analysis produces meaningful and actionable results.

Deployment: In the final phase, the model is deployed into the production environment, and the results are monitored. This involves documenting the model, creating user guides, and integrating the model into the business process. During the Deployment phase, the data mining team works with the business stakeholders to deploy the model into production, which may involve integrating it into existing systems, developing new software applications, or creating reports or dashboards that incorporate the model's predictions or insights. The Deployment phase also includes developing a plan for monitoring and maintaining the model to ensure its ongoing effectiveness and relevance. This may involve setting up alerts or notifications to detect any changes in the data or the business environment that could impact the model's performance. The Deployment phase is critical to the success of the data mining project, as it determines whether the insights and predictions generated by the model can be effectively used to drive business decisions and improve performance. The team must work closely with the business stakeholders to ensure that the model is integrated into the business processes in a way that is meaningful and actionable. The Deployment phase is not necessarily the end of the data mining process, as the model may need to be adjusted or refined based on ongoing feedback and monitoring. However, it represents a significant milestone in the process, as it marks the transition from the analysis and development of the model to its implementation and use in the business.

The CRISP-DM methodology is an iterative process, and each phase may be revisited as needed. It provides a flexible and adaptable framework that can be used in a variety of industries and applications.

6.3 SEMMA methodology

SEMMA is an acronym for Sample, Explore, Modify, Model, and Assess, which is a data mining methodology developed by SAS Institute Inc. SEMMA provides a structured approach for data analysis and modeling in order to derive insights and make predictions from large volumes of data. Fig. 6.2 shows the steps of SEMMA methodology.

The five stages of SEMMA are as follows:

Sample: In this stage, a representative sample of data is selected from the entire dataset. This is done to reduce the amount of data that needs to be analyzed, as well as to ensure that the sample is statistically representative of the larger dataset. During the Sample step, the data mining team selects a subset of the data that is representative of the larger dataset and is appropriate for the business problem at hand. The team may use various sampling techniques, such as random sampling or stratified sampling, to ensure that the sample

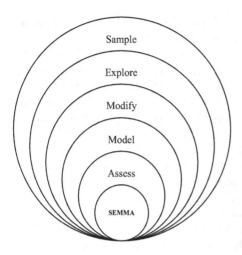

FIGURE 6.2 Steps of SEMMA methodology.

accurately reflects the larger dataset. The Sample step is critical to the success of the data mining project, as the accuracy and effectiveness of the predictive models developed later in the process depend on the quality of the sample data. If the sample is not representative of the larger dataset or is biased in some way, the resulting models may not accurately reflect the patterns and relationships in the data.

The Sample step is followed by the Explore, Modify, Model, and Assess steps, which involve further analysis and refinement of the data, development of predictive models, and evaluation of their effectiveness.

Explore: In this stage, the data is explored and visualized to gain a better understanding of the relationships and patterns within the data. This can involve basic statistical analysis such as calculating mean, median, and standard deviation, as well as more advanced techniques such as correlation analysis and cluster analysis. During the Explore step, the data mining team examines the sample data to identify trends, patterns, and relationships between variables. This may involve using statistical techniques, such as correlation analysis or regression analysis, to explore the relationships between different variables in the data. It may also involve visualizing the data using charts or graphs to identify trends or anomalies.

The Explore step is critical to the success of the data mining project, as it allows the team to gain a deeper understanding of the data and identify potential predictors or factors that may be relevant to the business problem at hand. The insights gained during this step may inform the development of predictive models and help to identify new opportunities for the business.

Modify: In this stage, the data is cleaned, transformed, and manipulated to prepare it for modeling. This can involve tasks such as removing outliers, filling in missing values, and scaling or normalizing the data. During the Modify step, the data mining team cleans and pre-processes the data to ensure that it is ready for modeling. This may involve filling in missing values, removing outliers, correcting inconsistent formatting, or transforming variables to make them more suitable for modeling. The Modify step is critical to the success of the data mining project, as the accuracy and effectiveness of the predictive models developed later in the process depend on the quality of the data. If the data is not properly prepared, the resulting models may not accurately reflect the patterns and relationships in the data.

Model: In this stage, predictive models are developed based on the cleaned and transformed data. This can involve a variety of modeling techniques such as linear regression, logistic regression, decision trees, and neural networks. The goal of the Model step is to develop a model that accurately predicts the outcome variable or variables of interest, based on the predictors or input variables. The model is typically evaluated using performance metrics such as accuracy, precision, recall, and F1-score. The Model step is critical to the success of the data mining project, as it allows the team to develop predictive models that can be used to make informed decisions or predictions based on the data. The insights gained during this step may inform the development of new strategies or approaches for the business.

Assess: In this final stage, the performance of the models is evaluated using validation techniques such as cross-validation, holdout validation, and bootstrap validation. The best-performing model is selected and deployed for use in making predictions on new data. The goal of the Assess step is to ensure that the predictive models are accurate, reliable, and effective in predicting the outcome variable or variables of interest. The team may also assess the impact of the predictive models on the business and evaluate the return on investment of the data mining project.

The insights gained during the Assess step may inform the development of new strategies or approaches for the business, and may also provide insights for future data mining projects.

At the end, the SEMMA methodology provides a structured approach for data analysis and modeling that can help to ensure that the insights and predictions derived from data are accurate and reliable.

6.4 Real life work with artificial intelligence, machine learning, and deep learning

6.4.1 Application of artificial intelligence

AI has a wide range of applications in various industries. Fig. 6.3 shows the application of artificial intelligence.

6.4.1.1 Artificial intelligence in healthcare industry

AI is used for medical diagnosis and treatment planning, drug discovery, personalized medicine, and patient monitoring. AI is being increasingly used in the healthcare industry to improve patient outcomes, increase efficiency, and reduce costs. Here are some of the ways AI is being used in healthcare:

- *Medical image analysis*: AI algorithms can analyze medical images, such as X-rays, MRI scans, and CT scans, to help detect diseases and conditions. For example, AI-powered algorithms can help detect tumors, identify fractures, and diagnose conditions like Alzheimer's disease.
- *Clinical decision support*: AI can help doctors and healthcare providers make more informed decisions by providing real-time recommendations based on patient data. This can help reduce errors and improve outcomes.
- *Electronic health records*: AI algorithms can analyze electronic health records (EHRs) to identify patterns and insights that can inform treatment decisions. For example, AI can

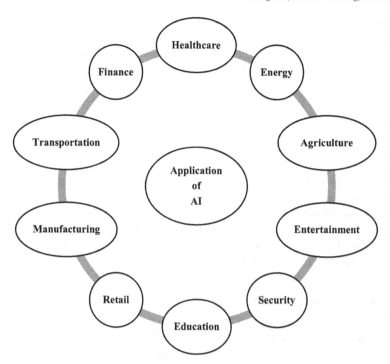

FIGURE 6.3   Application of artificial intelligence.

help identify patients who are at risk of developing chronic conditions, and provide personalized treatment plans.

- *Drug discovery and development*: AI can be used to identify new drugs and speed up the drug development process. By analyzing large amounts of data, AI can help identify potential drug candidates and predict their efficacy and side effects.
- *Virtual assistants and chatbots*: AI-powered virtual assistants and chatbots can help patients manage their health and access information. For example, chatbots can help patients schedule appointments, answer common questions, and provide guidance on managing chronic conditions.
- *Robotics*: AI-powered robots can assist in surgeries, provide companionship for patients, and perform other tasks in healthcare settings. For example, robots can be used to deliver medications, monitor vital signs, and help with physical therapy exercises.

6.4.1.2 Artificial intelligence in finance

AI is used for fraud detection, credit scoring, trading, and risk management. AI is being increasingly used in the finance industry to improve customer experience, increase efficiency, and reduce costs. Here are some of the ways AI is being used in finance:

- *Fraud detection and prevention*: AI algorithms can analyze large amounts of data to identify patterns and detect fraudulent activity. This can help prevent financial losses and protect customers' sensitive information.

- *Credit scoring and risk assessment*: AI can be used to assess creditworthiness and calculate risk. By analyzing data such as credit scores, financial history, and social media activity, AI algorithms can provide more accurate and personalized credit scores and risk assessments.
- *Trading and portfolio management*: AI-powered algorithms can analyze market data and make predictions about future performance. This can help investors make more informed decisions about buying and selling securities, and help portfolio managers optimize their portfolios.
- *Customer service and support*: AI-powered chatbots and virtual assistants can provide 24/7 customer support, answer common questions, and help customers with basic transactions. This can improve customer satisfaction and reduce the need for human support agents.
- *Personalized financial advice*: AI algorithms can analyze a customer's financial history, goals, and risk tolerance to provide personalized financial advice. This can help customers make better decisions about investing, saving, and managing their finances.
- *Risk management and compliance*: AI can help financial institutions identify and mitigate risks related to regulatory compliance, cybersecurity, and other threats. This can help prevent financial losses and protect customer data.

6.4.1.3 Artificial intelligence in transportation

AI is used for autonomous driving, route optimization, and predictive maintenance. AI is playing an increasingly important role in transportation, and its potential benefits are vast. Here are some of the ways AI is being used in transportation:

- *Autonomous vehicles*: AI is a key technology for developing self-driving cars, trucks, and other vehicles. These vehicles use sensors, cameras, and ML algorithms to navigate roads, avoid obstacles, and make decisions.
- *Traffic management*: AI can be used to optimize traffic flow by analyzing data from sensors, cameras, and other sources. This information can be used to adjust traffic signals, reroute vehicles, and improve overall traffic efficiency.
- *Predictive maintenance*: AI can be used to monitor the health of vehicles and predict when maintenance is needed. This can help reduce downtime and prevent breakdowns on the road.
- *Intelligent transportation systems*: AI can be used to create intelligent transportation systems that integrate data from various sources to provide real-time information to drivers, passengers, and transportation officials. This can include information about traffic, weather, and public transit schedules.
- *Supply chain optimization*: AI can be used to optimize supply chains by analyzing data on shipping routes, inventory levels, and delivery times. This can help reduce costs and improve efficiency.

6.4.1.4 Artificial intelligence in manufacturing

AI is used for quality control, predictive maintenance, and supply chain management. AI is transforming the manufacturing industry by enabling greater efficiency, flexibility, and productivity. Fig. 6.3 shows the different application of AI. Here are some ways AI is being used in manufacturing:

- *Predictive maintenance*: AI can help predict when equipment will need maintenance, reducing downtime and increasing overall equipment effectiveness.
- *Quality control*: AI can be used to detect defects in products, reducing waste and improving product quality.
- *Production optimization*: AI can optimize production schedules, reducing the time needed for changeovers and improving throughput.
- *Supply chain optimization*: AI can optimize the supply chain by forecasting demand and optimizing inventory levels, reducing waste and improving efficiency.
- *Process automation*: AI can automate routine tasks, such as data entry, freeing up employees to focus on more complex tasks.
- *Predictive analytics*: AI can analyze data from sensors and other sources to predict product quality, identify process improvements, and optimize production.

6.4.1.5 Artificial intelligence in retail

AI is used for personalized marketing, inventory management, and demand forecasting. AI is playing an increasingly important role in the retail industry, from supply chain management to customer experience. Here are some ways AI is transforming retail management:

- *Personalized customer experience*: AI algorithms can analyze customer data to provide personalized recommendations, offers, and shopping experiences. Retailers can use AI-powered chatbots to interact with customers in a personalized manner, provide assistance, and answer their queries.
- *Inventory management*: Retailers can use AI to optimize inventory management and demand forecasting. By analyzing sales data, AI algorithms can predict demand and optimize inventory levels, ensuring that products are available when customers want them.
- *Price optimization*: AI can help retailers optimize pricing strategies based on real-time demand, competitor pricing, and other factors. AI algorithms can analyze data to identify price elasticity, predict demand, and recommend pricing strategies.
- *Fraud detection*: Retailers can use AI to detect fraud and prevent losses. AI algorithms can analyze transactions, identify suspicious behavior, and flag potential fraudulent activity.
- *Supply chain management*: AI can help retailers optimize their supply chain operations by predicting demand, optimizing inventory, and streamlining logistics. By analyzing data from various sources, including suppliers, warehouses, and transportation, AI can optimize the entire supply chain process.

6.4.1.6 Artificial intelligence in agriculture

AI is used for crop monitoring, yield prediction, and precision farming. AI is playing an increasingly important role in agriculture, from optimizing crop production to improving supply chain management. Here are some ways AI is transforming agriculture:

- *Precision farming*: AI can help farmers optimize crop production by analyzing data on soil conditions, weather patterns, and plant growth. By using sensors and drones to collect data, AI algorithms can provide farmers with insights on when and where to plant, water, and fertilize crops.

- *Crop monitoring*: AI can help farmers monitor crop health and detect pests and diseases. By analyzing data from drones and satellites, AI algorithms can identify areas of crops that need attention, allowing farmers to take corrective action before a problem spreads.
- *Yield prediction*: AI can help farmers predict crop yields based on weather conditions, soil health, and other factors. By using predictive analytics, AI algorithms can forecast crop yields and help farmers make informed decisions about when to harvest and how much to plant.
- *Supply chain management*: AI can help improve the efficiency of the agricultural supply chain by optimizing logistics, reducing waste, and improving traceability. By using blockchain technology, AI can provide farmers, processors, and retailers with real-time visibility into the status of crops and products.
- *Farm management*: AI can help farmers manage their operations more efficiently by automating tasks, such as irrigation and fertilization. By using robotics and automation, AI can help farmers reduce labor costs, increase productivity, and improve safety.

6.4.1.7 Artificial intelligence in education

AI is used for personalized learning, intelligent tutoring, and plagiarism detection. AI is transforming the education system by providing new ways to deliver personalized and adaptive learning experiences. Here are some ways AI is changing education:

- *Personalized learning*: AI algorithms can analyze student data, such as learning style, pace, and preferences, to provide personalized learning experiences. By using ML, AI can adapt learning content to each student's needs and provide real-time feedback.
- *Intelligent tutoring*: AI can act as an intelligent tutor, providing personalized guidance and feedback to students. By using natural language processing, AI can interact with students in a conversational manner, answering their questions and providing support.
- *Automated grading*: AI can automate the grading of assignments, quizzes, and exams, freeing up teachers' time for more valuable tasks, such as providing feedback and guidance to students. By using ML, AI can also learn from previous grading patterns and adjust its grading accordingly.
- *Predictive analytics*: AI can use predictive analytics to identify students who are at risk of falling behind or dropping out. By analyzing student data, such as attendance, grades, and behavior, AI can alert teachers to intervene and provide support before it's too late.
- *Curriculum design*: AI can help teachers and curriculum designers create more effective learning content. By using natural language processing and ML, AI can analyze large amounts of data, such as textbooks and articles, to identify key concepts and recommend content.

6.4.1.8 Artificial intelligence in entertainment

AI is used for content recommendation, speech recognition, and natural language processing. AI is transforming the entertainment industry by providing new ways to create, distribute, and personalize content. Here are some ways AI is changing the entertainment industry:

- *Content creation*: AI can help content creators generate new ideas and develop content more efficiently. By using ML to analyze audience preferences, AI can identify trends and patterns that can inform content creation.
- *Content distribution*: AI can help entertainment companies distribute content more effectively by analyzing data on user behavior and preferences. By using

recommendation engines, AI can personalize content delivery, making it more likely that users will engage with it.

- *Content personalization*: AI can help personalize content for individual users based on their preferences and behavior. By using ML, AI can analyze data on user behavior and preferences to create personalized recommendations, offers, and experiences.
- *Visual effects*: AI can help create more realistic and sophisticated visual effects in movies and video games. By using deep learning (DL) algorithms, AI can generate realistic images and animations, and even create new virtual worlds.
- *Music composition*: AI can help compose music for movies, video games, and other media. By using ML, AI can analyze large amounts of music data to generate new compositions and create soundscapes that complement the visuals.

6.4.1.9 Artificial intelligence in energy

AI is used for smart grid management, energy optimization, and predictive maintenance. AI has the potential to transform the energy sector in numerous ways. Some of the key areas where AI is being applied include:

- *Energy management*: AI can be used to optimize energy generation, distribution, and consumption by analyzing data on energy usage patterns, weather conditions, and other relevant factors. This can lead to more efficient and cost-effective energy management, reducing energy waste and lowering costs for consumers.
- *Predictive maintenance*: AI can help predict when equipment will fail, allowing for preventative maintenance to be carried out before it becomes a major issue. This can improve the reliability of energy infrastructure and reduce downtime, leading to increased efficiency and cost savings.
- *Renewable energy*: AI can be used to improve the efficiency of renewable energy sources such as wind and solar power, by predicting weather patterns and adjusting energy generation accordingly. This can help increase the reliability and competitiveness of renewable energy sources.
- *Grid management*: AI can be used to optimize the management of energy grids, by analyzing data on energy flows, identifying potential bottlenecks, and adjusting energy distribution accordingly. This can help improve grid stability, reduce the risk of blackouts, and increase the resilience of energy infrastructure.

6.4.1.10 Artificial intelligence in security

AI is used for video surveillance, facial recognition, and threat detection. AI has the potential to revolutionize the security industry by providing new tools and capabilities to enhance the safety and security of people, organizations, and assets. Some of the key roles of AI in security systems are:

- *Threat detection*: AI can analyze vast amounts of data from various sources and identify potential security threats in real-time. This can include detecting suspicious behavior, identifying weapons or dangerous objects, and recognizing known criminals.
- *Surveillance*: AI can enhance video surveillance by analyzing video feeds and identifying potential security breaches, suspicious activities, or anomalies in behavior. This can help reduce false alarms and enable a more proactive approach to security.

- *Access control*: AI can provide advanced access control systems that use facial recognition, biometric data, and other technologies to verify the identity of individuals entering a secured area. This can help reduce the risk of unauthorized access and improve overall security.
- *Cybersecurity*: AI can be used to detect and respond to cyber threats in real-time by analyzing network traffic, identifying anomalies, and responding to potential attacks before they can cause damage.
- *Security automation*: AI can automate security tasks such as threat analysis, incident response, and vulnerability management, enabling security teams to focus on more complex tasks and reducing the risk of human error.

6.4.2 Application of machine learning

ML is a powerful tool that is being increasingly used in many industries to automate, optimize, and improve various processes. Some examples of real-life work with ML include:

Image and object recognition: ML is used in computer vision applications for image classification, object detection, and face recognition. For example, ML algorithms can be trained to detect and identify objects in security camera footage or medical images.

Natural language processing: ML is used in language processing applications to perform tasks such as sentiment analysis, text classification, and language translation. For example, ML algorithms can be trained to understand and respond to customer queries in customer service chatbots.

Recommender systems: ML is used in recommender systems that provide personalized recommendations for products, services, or content. For example, ML algorithms can be trained to recommend movies, music, or books to users based on their past behavior.

Fraud detection: ML is used in fraud detection applications to identify and prevent fraudulent activities such as credit card fraud or insurance fraud. For example, ML algorithms can be trained to analyze transaction data and detect patterns that are indicative of fraudulent behavior.

Predictive maintenance: ML is used in predictive maintenance applications to identify potential issues in machinery and equipment before they occur, reducing downtime and maintenance costs. For example, ML algorithms can be trained to analyze sensor data and predict when a machine is likely to fail.

Autonomous vehicles: ML is used in self-driving cars and autonomous drones to detect and avoid obstacles, recognize traffic signs, and make decisions in real-time. For example, ML algorithms can be trained to identify pedestrians and vehicles in real-time and adjust the vehicle's trajectory accordingly.

These are just a few examples of the many real-life applications of ML, and the list is growing rapidly as ML technology advances and becomes more widely adopted.

6.4.3 Application of deep learning

DL is a subset of ML that uses neural networks with multiple layers to learn from data and make predictions or decisions. Some examples of real-life work with DL include:

Image and speech recognition: DL is used for image classification, object detection, and speech recognition. For example, DL models can be trained to recognize objects in images, identify individual speakers in a noisy environment, and transcribe speech to text with high accuracy.

Natural language processing: DL is used for natural language processing applications such as sentiment analysis, language translation, and chatbots. For example, DL models can be trained to understand the context of language and generate responses that mimic human-like conversation.

Autonomous vehicles: DL is used in self-driving cars and autonomous drones to detect and avoid obstacles, recognize traffic signs, and make decisions in real-time. For example, DL models can be trained to analyze sensor data and identify objects in real-time, enabling autonomous vehicles to navigate safely on the road.

Medical diagnosis: DL is used in medical diagnosis and treatment planning. For example, DL models can be trained to identify patterns in medical images such as X-rays or MRI scans, enabling doctors to detect diseases such as cancer at an early stage.

Video analysis: DL is used for video analysis, such as video surveillance, facial recognition, and gesture recognition. For example, DL models can be trained to analyze video data and identify suspicious behavior, track individuals or objects, or recognize facial expressions.

Gaming: DL is used in gaming for tasks such as player behavior prediction, game recommendation, and character control. For example, DL models can be trained to predict the behavior of players in a game, identify the most suitable game for a player, or control the movement of characters in a game based on the player's input.

These are just a few examples of the many real-life applications of DL, and the list is growing rapidly as DL technology advances and becomes more widely adopted.

6.5 Object detection models

Object detection models are computer vision models that identify and locate objects within an image or a video stream. An object detection model is a DL algorithm that can automatically detect the presence of objects in an image or video, and classify them into predefined categories. Object detection models typically use convolutional neural networks (CNNs) to extract features from images and then use these features to identify and localize objects. They work by dividing the input image into a grid of small regions, and then predicting the probability of an object being present in each region. These models also predict the bounding box coordinates of the detected objects to localize them accurately.

Object detection models are significant because they enable computers to recognize and understand the visual world around them, which has a wide range of practical applications. Some of the key benefits of object detection models include:

- *Improved efficiency*: Object detection models can automate tasks that would otherwise require human intervention, which can significantly improve efficiency in a variety of industries. For example, they can be used to automatically detect defects in manufacturing processes, reducing the need for manual inspections.
- *Enhanced safety*: Object detection models can be used in various safety-critical applications such as surveillance, traffic monitoring, and autonomous driving. They

enable computers to detect and respond to potential hazards in real-time, which can help prevent accidents and save lives.

- *Increased accuracy*: Object detection models are trained on large datasets and can learn to recognize objects with high accuracy, even in complex and cluttered environments. This makes them ideal for applications such as medical imaging, where accuracy is critical.
- *Personalization*: Object detection models can be customized to recognize specific objects or features, which can be useful in applications such as retail, where they can be used to identify customer preferences and make personalized recommendations.

These models are widely used in various applications, such as self-driving cars, surveillance systems, and image search engines.

- Object detection versus image segmentation:

Segmentation is a way of defining the pixels of an object class within images or video frames in computer vision datasets. With semantic image segmentation, every pixel belonging to a tag or label will be identified. However, this approach won't define the boundaries of the objects in an image. Object detection, sometimes known as object recognition, won't segment objects based on pixels. But it will pinpoint the location of objects or object instances within boxes. Fig. 6.4 shows the difference between object classification, object detection, and image segmentation.

There are several object detection models, including:

6.5.1 Faster R-CNN

Faster R-CNN, which stands for Faster Region CNN, is a popular object detection algorithm introduced by Shaoqing Ren, Kaiming He, Ross Girshick, and Jian Sun in 2015. It is an improvement over the earlier R-CNN (region-based convolutional neural network) and Fast R-CNN models. Faster R-CNN is designed to address the speed limitations of previous object detection methods. It achieves this by introducing a region proposal network (RPN) that shares convolutional layers with the detection network, resulting in a unified architecture. The key idea behind

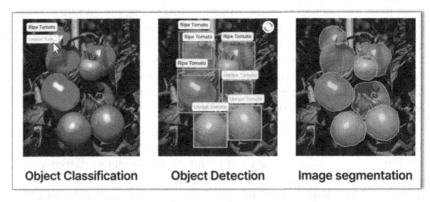

FIGURE 6.4 Object classification, object detection, and image segmentation. Source: *Full Guide to Automated Data Annotation | Encord.*

Faster R-CNN is to replace the selective search algorithm used in R-CNN with the RPN, which is fully trainable and capable of generating region proposals for potential object locations. Fig. 6.5 shows the cross section of an input volume of input image.

Following are the high-level overview of the faster R-CNN architecture:

1. *Input image*: The faster R-CNN algorithm starts with an input image on which object detection will be performed.
2. *CNN*: The input image is passed through a CNN, such as a pre-trained network like VGG16 or ResNet, to extract convolutional feature maps. Let's consider a simple CNN with a single convolutional layer followed by a fully connected layer. Following are the mathematical formulation:
   - Convolutional layer
     Input: Let's denote the input to the convolutional layer as X, which is a 3D tensor representing the input image. X has dimensions (W, H, C), where W and H are the width and height of the image, and C represents the number of channels (e.g., red, green, blue).
     Convolutional filters: We have F number of convolutional filters, each with dimensions (K, K, C), where K is the spatial extent of the filter. The filters are represented by a set of weight matrices W, with W_i denoting the weights of the i-th filter.
     Stride and padding: The convolutional operation is performed with a certain stride (S) and padding (P), which control the amount of spatial displacement and the amount of zero-padding applied to the input, respectively.
     Convolution operation: The convolutional operation is defined as follows:
     For each filter i, the filter is convolved with the input X, resulting in an intermediate feature map Z_i.
     The output of the convolutional layer, denoted as A, is obtained by applying an activation function (e.g., ReLU) to the sum of the intermediate feature maps plus a bias term

$$b_i : A_i = \text{activation}(Z_i + b_i)$$

   - Pooling layer
     After the convolutional layer, a pooling layer is often applied to reduce spatial dimensionality and extract dominant features.
     Pooling operation: Max pooling is a commonly used pooling operation. It partitions the input feature maps into non-overlapping regions of size (P, P) and outputs the

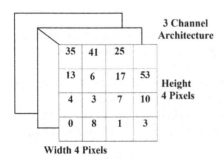

3 Channel Architecture

Height 4 Pixels

Width 4 Pixels

FIGURE 6.5 The cross-section of an input volume of size: $4 \times 4 \times 3$ for input image.

maximum value within each region. The pooling operation is applied independently to each feature map A_i, resulting in pooled feature maps P_i.

- Fully connected layer

  Flattening: The pooled feature maps P_i are flattened into a 1D vector to be processed by the fully connected layer.

  Weights and biases: The fully connected layer has weight matrices W_{fc} and bias term b_{fc}.

  Output: The output of the fully connected layer, denoted as Y, is obtained by multiplying the flattened input with the weight matrices and adding the bias term:

$$Y = \text{activation}(W_{fc} \cdot P + W_{fc})$$

The activation function used in both the convolutional and fully connected layers can vary, but popular choices include ReLU (rectified linear unit), sigmoid, or tanh.

This formulation represents a simplified version of a CNN architecture. In practice, CNNs often consist of multiple convolutional and pooling layers, followed by several fully connected layers and additional components like normalization, dropout, and more complex activation functions.

3. *RPN*: The RPN takes the feature maps from the CNN as input and generates region proposals. These proposals are potential bounding boxes that may contain objects. The RPN is trained to classify whether each anchor box (a set of pre-defined boxes at different scales and aspect ratios) contains an object or not and to refine the bounding box coordinates.

Following are the mathematical formulation of the RPN:

- Input

  Feature maps: Let's denote the input feature maps to the RPN as F, which is obtained from the shared convolutional layers of the CNN. F has dimensions (W, H, C), where W and H represent the width and height of the feature maps, and C denotes the number of channels.

  Anchor boxes: The RPN uses a set of pre-defined anchor boxes at different scales and aspect ratios to propose potential object locations. Let's denote the set of anchor boxes as A, and each anchor box is represented by its center coordinates (x, y), width (w), and height (h).

- Convolutional layer

  Convolutional operation: The RPN applies a 3×3 convolutional filter to the input feature maps F to extract features for each spatial location. This operation is represented as:

$$H = \text{convolution}(F)$$

- Anchor classification

  Objectness score: For each anchor box, the RPN predicts an objectness score, which indicates the likelihood of an anchor box containing an object. Let's denote the objectness score for an anchor box a_i as S_i.

  Classification layer: The RPN applies a convolutional layer with $2k$ filters, where k is the number of anchor boxes, to obtain a feature map of shape $(W, H, 2k)$.

  Softmax activation: The objectness scores S_i for each anchor box are obtained by applying a softmax activation function to the corresponding slice of the feature map.

- Bounding box regression

  Bounding box offsets: In addition to the objectness scores, the RPN also predicts the bounding box offsets for each anchor box. These offsets refine the coordinates of the anchor boxes to precisely localize the objects. Let's denote the bounding box offsets for an anchor box a_i as $(\Delta x_i, \Delta y_i, \Delta w_i, \Delta h_i)$.

Regression layer: The RPN applies a convolutional layer with $4k$ filters, where k is the number of anchor boxes, to obtain a feature map of shape $(W, H, 4k)$.

Bounding box regression: The predicted bounding box offsets are obtained by applying appropriate activation functions (e.g., sigmoid or linear) to the corresponding slices of the feature map.

The RPN generates objectness scores and bounding box offsets for each anchor box based on the feature maps obtained from the convolutional layers. These outputs are used to filter out anchor boxes and select the most relevant region proposals for further processing in the Faster R-CNN framework.

4. *Region of interest (ROI) pooling*: The proposed regions from the RPN are passed to the ROI pooling layer. This layer warps the features inside each region proposal to a fixed size, typically a small spatial resolution, while maintaining their spatial alignment.

Following are the mathematical formulation of the ROI:

- Input

  Feature maps: Let's denote the input feature maps to the ROI Pooling operation as F, which is obtained from the convolutional layers of the network. F has dimensions (W, H, C), where W and H represent the width and height of the feature maps, and C denotes the number of channels.

  Region proposals: The ROI pooling operation takes as input a set of region proposals, denoted as R. Each region proposal r_i is represented by its coordinates (x_i, y_i, w_i, h_i), where (x_i, y_i) represents the top-left corner coordinates of the region, and w_i and h_i represent its width and height, respectively.

- ROI pooling

  Spatial subdivision: The ROI pooling operation subdivides each region proposal r_i into a fixed number of spatial bins or cells.

  Pooling operation: For each spatial bin, the ROI pooling operation applies a pooling operation to the corresponding region of the input feature maps F. The pooling operation aggregates information within each bin to obtain a fixed-sized output feature map.

  Commonly used pooling operations include max pooling or average pooling.

  The size of the output feature map is determined by the number of spatial bins and is typically uniform across all region proposals.

- Output

  Output feature maps: The output of the ROI pooling operation is a set of fixed-sized feature maps corresponding to each region proposal. The dimensions of the output feature maps are the same for all region proposals, regardless of the original size or aspect ratio of the regions.

  The ROI pooling operation ensures that feature representations extracted from region proposals have a consistent size, which enables subsequent layers to process them uniformly. This operation helps in efficiently handling regions of various sizes and aspect ratios, allowing the Faster R-CNN algorithm to handle object detection and localization tasks effectively.

5. *Classification and localization*: The ROI-pooled features are fed into fully connected layers, which perform object classification and bounding box regression. The

classification branch predicts the probability of each ROI belonging to different object classes, while the regression branch refines the coordinates of the bounding boxes.

6. *Non-maximum suppression (NMS)*: After obtaining the final set of proposed regions along with their class probabilities and bounding box coordinates, NMS is applied to filter out overlapping and redundant detections. This process ensures that only the most confident and non-overlapping detections are retained. NMS is a post-processing step used in object detection algorithms, including faster R-CNN, to filter out redundant and overlapping bounding box detections. Although NMS is not an inherent part of faster R-CNN itself, it is commonly applied after the object proposals are generated. Here's a mathematical formulation of the NMS algorithm:

- Input

  Bounding boxes: Let's denote the set of bounding boxes detected by the model as B. Each bounding box b_i is represented by its coordinates (x_i, y_i, w_i, h_i), where (x_i, y_i) represents the top-left corner coordinates, and w_i and h_i represent the width and height, respectively.

  Confidence scores: Each bounding box b_i is associated with a confidence score c_i, representing the probability or confidence level that the bounding box contains an object of interest.

- NMS algorithm

  Sort bounding boxes: Sort the bounding boxes B based on their confidence scores c_i in descending order. Denote the sorted bounding boxes as B_{sorted}. Initialize the selected bounding boxes list, S, as an empty list. While B_{sorted} is not empty: select the bounding box with the highest confidence score from B_{sorted} and denote it as b_max. Add b_max to S, as it is currently the most confident detection. Calculate the intersection over union (IoU) of b_{max} with all remaining bounding boxes in B_{sorted}.

  Remove any bounding boxes from B_{sorted} that have an IoU with b_{max} above a specified threshold (e.g., 0.5). This removes redundant detections that significantly overlap with the selected bounding box.

- Output

  The selected bounding boxes in S represent the final NMS output, where redundant and overlapping detections have been filtered out. The NMS algorithm iteratively selects bounding boxes with the highest confidence scores and removes overlapping detections based on their IoU. By discarding redundant bounding boxes, NMS ensures that only the most relevant and non-overlapping detections are retained.

  At the end faster R-CNN combines the advantages of DL -based feature extraction, efficient region proposal generation, and accurate object classification and localization. It has been widely adopted in various computer vision tasks, including object detection, instance segmentation, and even video object detection.

6.5.2 YOLO (you only look once)

YOLO is a real-time object detection system that uses a single neural network to predict bounding boxes and class probabilities for multiple objects in an image. YOLO (you only look once) is an object detection algorithm that was introduced in 2016. It is a popular DL model used for real-time object detection in images and videos. YOLO is based on a single neural network that takes an entire image as input and outputs a set of bounding boxes and class probabilities for the objects detected in the image. The YOLO algorithm works by dividing the input image into a grid of cells and predicting bounding boxes, class probabilities, and abjectness scores for each cell. The abjectness score determines whether an object is present in the cell or not, while the class probabilities indicate the class of the object (e.g., car, person, dog, etc.). The image is partitioned into a grid of size $S \times S$ using this architecture. If the center of the object's bounding box falls within a particular grid, that grid is assigned the responsibility of detecting that object. Each grid predicts its own bounding boxes, along with a confidence score that indicates the accuracy and precision of the predicted bounding box coordinates relative to the ground truth. Fig. 6.6 shows the Yolo image in the $s \times s$ grid.

One of the main advantages of YOLO is its speed. Because it processes the entire image in a single forward pass, it is much faster than other object detection algorithms that require multiple passes over the image.

Following are the mathematical formulation of the YOLO algorithm:

- Input
  Image: Let's denote the input image as I, with dimensions (W, H, C), where W and H represent the width and height of the image, and C denotes the number of channels (e.g., red, green, blue).
- YOLO algorithm
  Grid division: Divide the input image into an $S \times S$ grid of cells, where each cell represents a spatial region of the image. The grid cells have dimensions $(W/S, H/S)$.
- Bounding box predictions
  For each grid cell, predict B bounding boxes. Each bounding box is represented by its coordinates (x, y, w, h), where (x, y) represents the center coordinates of the bounding box relative to the cell, and w and h represent the width and height of the bounding box relative to the cell size. Each bounding box has associated confidence scores indicating the probability that the box contains an object, denoted as confidence_c. Additionally, class probabilities are predicted for each bounding box, denoted as class_probabilities.
- Class prediction
  For each grid cell, predict C class probabilities, representing the likelihood of different object classes being present within the cell.

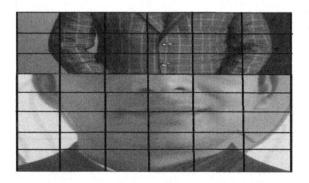

FIGURE 6.6 Yolo image ($S \times S$ grid).

- Output

    Bounding box output: The algorithm outputs a set of bounding boxes along with their associated confidence scores and class probabilities. Bounding box coordinates are transformed from relative values to absolute values in the image. NMS can be applied to remove redundant and overlapping bounding box detections, similar to the NMS algorithm described earlier.

    The YOLO algorithm operates by directly predicting bounding boxes and class probabilities within each grid cell, eliminating the need for region proposals or sliding windows. This approach allows for real-time object detection and has gained popularity due to its efficiency and accuracy.

- Python program for "You Only Look Once"

    Implementing YOLO algorithm in Python requires DL libraries like TensorFlow or PyTorch, as well as a trained YOLO model. Here is an example of using the YOLOv3 model to detect objects in an image using Tensor Flow:

```python
import cv2
import numpy as np
import tensorflow as tf

# Load the pre-trained YOLOv3 model
model = tf.keras.models.load_model('yolov3.h5')

# Define the classes that the model can detect
classes = ["person", "car", "motorbike", "bus", "truck", "traffic light", "stop sign"]

# Load the image to be detected
image = cv2.imread('test_image.jpg')

# Preprocess the image for the YOLOv3 model
image = cv2.resize(image, (416, 416))
image = image.astype('float32') / 255.0
image = np.expand_dims(image, axis=0)

# Run the YOLOv3 model on the input image
boxes, scores, classes, num_detections = model.predict(image)

# Print the results
for i in range(int(num_detections[0])):
    if scores[0][i] >= 0.5:
        class_name = classes[int(classes[0][i])]
        print("Detected", class_name, "with", scores[0][i]*100, "% confidence.")
```

This code loads the YOLOv3 model, which has been pre-trained on the COCO dataset, and uses it to detect objects in an image. The classes that the model can detect are defined, and the image is preprocessed to match the input format expected by the model. The model is then run on the input image, and the results are printed to the console.

Note that this is a simplified example, and there are many additional parameters and options that can be configured when using the YOLO algorithm for object detection.

6.5.3 Single shot multibox detector

Single shot multibox detector (SSD) is another real-time object detection model that uses a single neural network to predict object locations and class probabilities. It uses a set of default boxes of various aspect ratios to improve accuracy. The SSD is a popular object detection algorithm that was introduced in 2016. Like YOLO, it is a DL model that performs object detection in real-time, but it uses a different approach to achieve this goal. SSD is based on a CNN that is designed to predict a set of bounding boxes and class probabilities for each object in an input image. However, unlike YOLO, SSD uses multiple feature maps of different scales to detect objects of different sizes. This allows SSD to detect small objects more accurately than YOLO.

The SSD algorithm works by first generating a set of default bounding boxes of different sizes and aspect ratios. These default boxes are then refined using information from the feature maps to better match the objects in the image. The final output of the algorithm is a set of bounding boxes and class probabilities for the objects detected in the image. One of the advantages of SSD is its flexibility. It can be trained to detect objects in a wide range of categories and can be easily adapted to new object detection tasks. Additionally, it has a relatively simple architecture, which makes it easy to implement and train. In summary, SSD is a DL -based object detection algorithm that uses multiple feature maps of different scales to detect objects of different sizes. It is known for its flexibility and accuracy in detecting small objects.

Simplified overview of the SSD process:

Base convolutional network: SSD starts with a base convolutional network, such as VGG or ResNet, that processes the input image and extracts a set of feature maps at different spatial resolutions.

Multi-scale feature maps: SSD applies a series of convolutional layers to the feature maps obtained from the base network, gradually decreasing their spatial dimensions while increasing the number of channels. This allows the detector to capture object information at multiple scales.

Convolutional predictions: At each scale, SSD uses a set of convolutional layers to make predictions for both class labels and bounding box offsets. These predictions are made for each position in the feature maps using small receptive fields.

Default anchor boxes: SSD generates default anchor boxes with different aspect ratios and scales for each position in the feature maps. The aspect ratios and scales are pre-defined based on the characteristics of the dataset.

Predictions: For each anchor box, SSD predicts the class probabilities for different object categories and the offsets required to match the corresponding ground truth boxes.

Matching and loss: During training, SSD matches the predicted boxes to the ground truth boxes based on their overlap. This is done using a matching strategy that assigns positive and negative labels to anchor boxes. The model is trained using a combination of classification loss (e.g., softmax loss) and localization loss (e.g., smooth L1 loss).

By using multiple layers with different receptive fields and anchor boxes, SSD is capable of detecting objects at different scales and aspect ratios. This allows it to handle objects of varying sizes within an image efficiently. The final output of SSD is a set of bounding boxes, along with their corresponding class labels, indicating the detected objects within the image.

- Python program for SSD:

Implementing a SSD algorithm in python requires DL libraries like TensorFlow or PyTorch, as well as a trained SSD model. Following are an example of using the SSD300 model to detect objects in an image using Tensor Flow:

```python
import cv2
import numpy as np
import tensorflow as tf

# Load the pre-trained SSD300 model
model = tf.keras.models.load_model('ssd300.h5')

# Define the classes that the model can detect
classes = ["background", "person", "car", "motorbike", "bus", "truck", "traffic light", "stop
sign"]

# Load the image to be detected
image = cv2.imread('test_image.jpg')

# Preprocess the image for the SSD model
image = cv2.resize(image, (300, 300))
image = image.astype('float32') / 255.0
image = np.expand_dims(image, axis=0)

# Run the SSD model on the input image
predictions = model.predict(image)

# Decode the predictions
num_detections = int(predictions[0][0])
for i in range(num_detections):
    class_index = int(predictions[0][1][i])
    class_name = classes[class_index]
    confidence = predictions[0][2][i]
    box = predictions[0][3][i]
    print("Detected", class_name, "with", confidence*100, "% confidence.")
    print("Bounding box coordinates:", box)
```

This code loads the SSD300 model, which has been pre-trained on the COCO dataset, and uses it to detect objects in an image. The classes that the model can detect are defined, and the image is preprocessed to match the input format expected by the model. The model is then run on the input image, and the results are decoded and printed to the console. Note that this is a simplified example, and there are many additional parameters and options that can be configured when using the SSD algorithm for object detection.

6.5.4 RetinaNet

RetinaNet is a variant of the faster R-CNN model that addresses the problem of class imbalance by introducing a new loss function that focuses on hard examples. RetinaNet is a type of object detection algorithm used in computer vision that was introduced in a paper published by researchers at Facebook AI Research in 2017. The algorithm is designed to address the problem of detecting objects at multiple scales and with varying levels of detail in an image. RetinaNet uses a feature pyramid network to detect objects at different scales in an image. The feature pyramid is generated by applying a CNN to the input image at multiple scales. The output of the network at each scale is then used to generate a set of feature maps, which are then fused together to create a feature pyramid.

RetinaNet also uses a novel focal loss function, which is designed to address the problem of class imbalance in object detection. In traditional object detection algorithms, the majority of image regions do not contain any objects, leading to a class imbalance problem where the network can become biased towards the negative class. The focal loss function helps to mitigate this problem by down-weighting the loss assigned to well-classified examples, which are often the majority of examples.

- Python program for RetinaNet:

Implementing RetinaNet in python requires DL libraries like TensorFlow or PyTorch, as well as a trained RetinaNet model. Here is an example of using the RetinaNet model to detect objects in an image using TensorFlow:

```
import cv2
import numpy as np
import tensorflow as tf

# Load the pre-trained RetinaNet model
model = tf.keras.models.load_model('retinanet.h5')

# Define the classes that the model can detect
classes = ["person", "car", "motorbike", "bus", "truck", "traffic light", "stop sign"]
```

(cont'd)

```
# Load the image to be detected
image = cv2.imread('test_image.jpg')

# Preprocess the image for the RetinaNet model
image = cv2.resize(image, (800, 800))
image = image.astype('float32') / 255.0
image = np.expand_dims(image, axis=0)

# Run the RetinaNet model on the input image
predictions = model.predict(image)

# Decode the predictions
for i in range(len(predictions)):
    scores = predictions[i][4:]
    class_index = np.argmax(scores)
    class_name = classes[class_index]
    confidence = scores[class_index]
    box = predictions[i][:4]
    print("Detected", class_name, "with", confidence*100, "% confidence.")
    print("Bounding box coordinates:", box)
```

This code loads the RetinaNet model, which has been pre-trained on the COCO dataset, and uses it to detect objects in an image. The classes that the model can detect are defined, and the image is preprocessed to match the input format expected by the model. The model is then run on the input image, and the results are decoded and printed to the console.

Note that this is a simplified example, and there are many additional parameters and options that can be configured when using the RetinaNet algorithm for object detection.

6.5.5 Mask R-CNN

Mask R-CNN is an extension of the faster R-CNN model that adds a branch for predicting object masks in addition to the bounding box and class probabilities. It is commonly used for instance segmentation, which involves identifying and segmenting individual objects within an image. Mask R-CNN is a type of object detection algorithm that can also perform instance segmentation, which means it can detect and segment each instance of an object in an image. It was introduced in a paper published by researchers at Facebook AI Research in 2018 and is an extension of the Faster R-CNN algorithm.

The Mask R-CNN algorithm uses a two-stage detection pipeline. The first stage generates a set of region proposals, which are potential objects, using a RPN. The second stage uses a fully connected network to classify the proposals and refine their bounding boxes to generate the final object detections. In addition to object detection, Mask R-CNN also predicts a binary mask for each detected object instance, indicating the pixel-wise segmentation of the object in the image. This is done by adding an additional branch to the network that generates a binary mask for each object instance, based on the features learned from the second stage of the network. Mask R-CNN is widely used in computer vision applications, including autonomous vehicles, robotics, and medical imaging. It has achieved state-of-the-art results on several benchmark datasets and is considered one of the most powerful object detection and instance segmentation algorithms available.

These models vary in their accuracy, speed, and complexity, and their choice depends on the specific application and the available computing resources.

- Python program of Mask R-CNN

Implementing Mask R-CNN in Python requires DL libraries like TensorFlow or PyTorch, as well as a trained Mask R-CNN model. Here is an example of using the Mask R-CNN model to detect and segment objects in an image using TensorFlow:

```python
import cv2
import numpy as np
import tensorflow as tf
from mrcnn import model as modellib, utils

# Load the pre-trained Mask R-CNN model
model_dir = "/path/to/mask_rcnn/model/"
config = modellib.Config()
model = modellib.MaskRCNN(mode="inference", config=config, model_dir=model_dir)
model.load_weights('mask_rcnn_coco.h5', by_name=True)

# Define the classes that the model can detect
classes = ["person", "car", "motorbike", "bus", "truck", "traffic light", "stop sign"]

# Load the image to be detected and segmented
image = cv2.imread('test_image.jpg')

# Preprocess the image for the Mask R-CNN model
image = cv2.cvtColor(image, cv2.COLOR_BGR2RGB)
image, _, _, _ = utils.resize_image(image, min_dim=config.IMAGE_MIN_DIM,
max_dim=config.IMAGE_MAX_DIM)
image = image.astype(np.float32) / 255.0
image = np.expand_dims(image, 0)

# Run the Mask R-CNN model on the input image
results = model.detect(image)
```

(cont'd)

```
# Decode the predictions
r = results[0]
for i in range(r['rois'].shape[0]):
    class_id = r['class_ids'][i]
    class_name = classes[class_id]
    score = r['scores'][i]
    bbox = r['rois'][i]
    mask = r['masks'][:,:,i]
    print("Detected", class_name, "with", score*100, "% confidence.")
    print("Bounding box coordinates:", bbox)
    print("Mask shape:", mask.shape)
```

6.6 Conclusion

In conclusion, the chapter highlights the significance of data mining methodologies such as CRISP-DM and SEMMA in guiding data mining projects. These methodologies provide a structured approach to project management, enabling organizations to achieve their data mining objectives efficiently and effectively. Furthermore, the chapter emphasizes the growing importance of AI and ML in object detection. CNNs such as YOLO are capable of detecting objects in real-time with high accuracy, making them suitable for a variety of applications. The case study presented in the chapter demonstrates the practical application of these methodologies and technologies in a real-world project.

6.7 Case study

6.7.1 Case study-CRISP-DM methodology in health care industry

One real-life example of the CRISP-DM methodology being applied is in the healthcare industry, where data mining is used to improve patient outcomes and reduce healthcare costs. Let's consider a case study of using CRISP-DM in the healthcare industry.

Business understanding: The business objective is to reduce hospital readmissions among heart failure patients, which is a major contributor to healthcare costs.

Data understanding: The data sources include EHRs containing patient demographics, medical history, medications, and diagnostic test results.

Data preparation: The data is cleaned and prepared for analysis, with missing values imputed, outliers identified and treated, and categorical variables transformed.

Modeling: Several predictive models are developed and tested, including logistic regression, decision trees, and random forest models. The goal is to predict which patients are at highest risk of readmission, so that interventions can be targeted at those patients.

Evaluation: The models are evaluated using metrics such as accuracy, sensitivity, and specificity. The best-performing model is selected for deployment.

Deployment: The model is deployed into the clinical workflow, where it is integrated into the EHR system. Clinicians are alerted to patients at high risk of readmission, and targeted interventions such as medication adjustments and home health visits are implemented.

By using the CRISP-DM methodology, this healthcare organization was able to identify patients at high risk of readmission and intervene early, resulting in a reduction in hospital readmissions and associated healthcare costs. This is just one example of how the CRISP-DM methodology can be applied in real-life scenarios to improve business outcomes and drive success.

6.7.2 Case study: SEMMA methodology in health care industry

The SEMMA methodology can be applied to various industries, including the healthcare industry. Let's consider an example of how SEMMA could be applied in the healthcare industry to improve patient outcomes.

Sample: In the first stage, a sample of patient data is selected from the EHR system. The sample should be representative of the larger population of patients and should include relevant data such as demographic information, medical history, and treatment outcomes.

Explore: In the second stage, the data is explored to identify trends and patterns that could be useful in improving patient outcomes. This can involve basic statistical analysis such as calculating mean, median, and standard deviation, as well as more advanced techniques such as correlation analysis and clustering.

Modify: In the third stage, the data is cleaned and transformed to prepare it for modeling. This can involve tasks such as removing missing values, dealing with outliers, and scaling or normalizing the data.

Model: In the fourth stage, predictive models are developed based on the cleaned and transformed data. For instance, we could build a model to predict which patients are at high risk of readmission, based on their previous medical history and demographic data.

Assess: In the final stage, the performance of the models is evaluated using validation techniques such as cross-validation, holdout validation, and bootstrap validation. The best-performing model is selected and deployed for use in making predictions on new patient data.

Using SEMMA methodology in the healthcare industry can help to identify patients who are at risk of poor health outcomes, such as readmission to the hospital, and intervene early to improve their outcomes. For example, the predictive model developed in stage 4 could be used to identify high-risk patients and assign care coordinators to work with them on care coordination and disease management, leading to better health outcomes and reduced healthcare costs.

6.7.3 Case study on the object detection model

Objective: A retail company wants to improve the efficiency of its inventory management system by automating the process of tracking the movement of products in and out of its warehouses. The company wants to build an object detection model that can accurately detect and identify products in images and videos, and track their movements in real-time.

Data collection: The retail company collects a large dataset of images and videos of its products in various locations, including warehouses, stores, and distribution centers. The images and videos are captured using CCTV cameras and smartphones, and are annotated with bounding boxes around the products of interest.

Data preparation: The data is pre-processed and cleaned to ensure that it is suitable for training the object detection model. The images and videos are resized and normalized, and the annotations are converted into a format that can be used by the object detection algorithm.

Model development: The object detection model is developed using a DL approach, specifically the faster R-CNN algorithm. The model is trained on the annotated dataset using a GPU cluster to accelerate the training process. The model is optimized for accuracy, precision, and recall, and is tested on a validation set to ensure that it generalizes well to new data.

Model deployment: The trained object detection model is deployed in the retail company's warehouses and stores, where it is used to track the movement of products in real-time. The model is integrated with the company's inventory management system, which receives real-time updates on the location and quantity of products.

Model evaluation: The performance of the object detection model is evaluated on a regular basis, using metrics such as accuracy, precision, recall, and F1-score. The model is also tested on new data to ensure that it continues to perform effectively over time.

Results: The object detection model improves the efficiency and accuracy of the retail company's inventory management system. The model accurately detects and tracks products in real-time, reducing the need for manual tracking and minimizing the risk of errors or discrepancies in inventory records. The company is able to optimize its supply chain and improve customer satisfaction by ensuring that products are always in stock and available for purchase.

Conclusion: The object detection model is a valuable tool for the retail company, enabling it to automate and optimize its inventory management system. The model can be further improved by incorporating additional data sources and refining the annotation process to improve the accuracy of the model.

6.8 Exercise

6.8.1 Objective type question

1. What does CRISP-DM stand for?
   a. Croxss-industry standard process for data mining
   b. Creative research and innovation in statistical process
   c. Comprehensive risk identification and statistical process

2. How many phases are there in CRISP-DM methodology?
   a. 4
   b. 5
   c. 6

3. Which phase of CRISP-DM methodology involves identifying the data sources and collecting the relevant data?
   a. Data understanding
   b. Data preparation
   c. Modeling

4. Which phase of CRISP-DM methodology involves selecting the appropriate data mining techniques and developing the predictive models?
   a. Modeling
   b. Deployment
   c. Evaluation

5. Which phase of CRISP-DM methodology involves transforming the data into a format that can be used by the data mining algorithms?
   a. Data understanding
   b. Data preparation
   c. Modeling

6. What does SEMMA stand for?
   a. Sampling, Evaluation, Modeling, Modification, Assessment
   b. Sample, Explore, Modify, Model, Assess
   c. Statistical Evaluation, Model development, Model assessment

7. Which phase of SEMMA methodology involves selecting a representative sample of the data for analysis?
   a. Sample
   b. Explore
   c. Modify

8. Which phase of SEMMA methodology involves evaluating the effectiveness of the predictive model and selecting the best model for deployment?
   a. Model
   b. Assess
   c. Modify

9. Which phase of SEMMA methodology involves assessing the performance of the model in the real-world environment?
   a. Assess
   b. Modify
   c. Model

10. Which phase of SEMMA methodology involves transforming the data to prepare it for modeling?
    a. Sample
    b. Explore

    c. Modify
11. Which of the following is an example of an AI application in the healthcare industry?
    a. Autonomous vehicles
    b. Social media analysis
    c. Medical diagnosis

12. Which of the following is an example of an AI application in the finance industry?
    a. Speech recognition
    b. Recommendation systems
    c. Fraud detection

13. Which of the following is an example of an AI application in the transportation industry?
    a. Virtual assistants
    b. Predictive maintenance
    c. Inventory management

14. Which of the following is an example of an AI application in the retail industry?
    a. Natural language processing
    b. Facial recognition
    c. Personalized recommendations

15. Which of the following is an example of an AI application in the manufacturing industry?
    a. Sentiment analysis
    b. Quality control
    c. Social network analysis

16. Which of the following is an example of an AI application in the education industry?
    a. Autonomous vehicles
    b. Adaptive learning
    c. Speech recognition

17. Which of the following is an example of an AI application in the entertainment industry?
    a. Virtual assistants
    b. Recommendation systems
    c. Facial recognition

18. Which of the following is an example of an AI application in the agriculture industry?
    a. Inventory management
    b. Crop management
    c. Speech recognition

19. Which of the following is an approach to object detection that involves generating a set of bounding boxes and using a classifier to determine the presence of an object in each box?
    a. YOLO
    b. SSD
    c. Faster R-CNN

20. Which of the following is an approach to object detection that involves directly predicting the coordinates of the bounding box for each object?
    a. YOLO
    b. R-CNN
    c. Faster R-CNN

6.8.2 Descriptive type question

1. Describe the six phases of the CRISP-DM methodology.
2. Explain the SEMMA methodology and its application in data mining.
3. Discuss the various applications of artificial intelligence in different industries.
4. Describe the working of an object detection model, and explain the various approaches used in object detection.
5. Discuss the challenges associated with the development and deployment of an object detection model, and explain how these challenges can be addressed.

Further reading

P. Cato. Einflüsse auf den Implementierungserfolg von Big Data Systemen. Ergebnisse einer inhalts- und kausalanalytischen Untersuchung. Dissertation. Friedrich-Alexander-Universität Erlangen-Nürnberg (2016).

N.W. Grady, J.A. Payne, H. Parker. "Agile Big Data Analytics. AnalyticsOps for Data Science." IEEE International Conference on Big Data (BIGDATA) (2017) (17), 2331–2339.

J. Ivančáková, F. Babič, P. Butka. Comparison of different machine learning methods on Wisconsin dataset. 2018 IEEE 16th World Symposium on Applied Machine Intelligence and Informatics (SAMI), 2018, pp. 173–178.

M. Kebede, D.T. Zegeye, B.M. Zeleke, Predicting CD4 count changes among patients on antiretroviral treatment: application of data mining techniques, Computer Methods Prog. Biomedicine 152 (2017) 149–157.

Data science & big data analytics, in: C. Long, K. Talbot (Eds.), Discovering, Analyzing, Visualizing and Presenting Data, John Wiley & Sons, Indianapolis, IN, 2015.

D. Oliveira, F. Portela, M. Santos, F. Rua. "Towards an Intelligent Systems to Predict Nosocomial Infections in Intensive Care." 2017 5th International Conference on Future Internet of Things and Cloud Workshops (FiCloudW), 2017, pp. 150–155.

J. Saltz, I. Shamshurin, K. Crowston. "Comparing Data Science Project Management Methodologies via a Controlled Experiment." Hawaii International Conference on System Sciences 2017 (HICSS-50). Hilton Waikoloa Village, Hawaii, January 4–7, 2017.

J. Saltz, N. Hotz, D. Wild, K. Stirling. "Exploring Project Management Methodologies Used Within Data Science Teams Orleans, LA, USA, August 16–18, 2018." 24th Americas Conference on Information Systems, AMCIS 2018, New Orleans, LA, USA, August 16–18, 2018: Association for Information Systems.

J.S. Saltz, I. Shamshurin. "Big data team process methodologies: A literature review and the identification of key factors for a project's success." IEEE International Conference on Big Data (Big Data) (2016), pp. 2872–2879.

J. Schnell, C. Nentwich, F. Endres, A. Kollenda, F. Distel, T. Knoche, et al., "Data mining in lithium-ion battery cell production, J. Power Sources 413 (2019) 360–366.

J. Silva, N. Varela, L.A.B. López, R.H.R. Millán, Association rules extraction for customer segmentation in the SMEs sector using the Apriori algorithm, Procedia Computer Sci. 151 (2019) 1207–1212.

R. Wirth, J. Hipp. "CRISP-DM: Towards a Standard Process Model for Data Mining." Proceedings of the 4th international conference on the practical applications of knowledge discovery and data mining (4) (2000), pp. 29–39.

Glossary

A   **Analogies**: A comparison between two things that shows a way in which they are similar

Analytics: Analytics serves as the transformative process that converts conventional information into intelligent data, which can then be utilized in diverse decision-making processes

Anthropology: The genesis and development of human civilizations and cultures are the subject of anthropology

Artificial Intelligence: Artificial intelligence is a broader field encompassing the development of computer systems or machines that can perform tasks typically requiring human intelligence

Augmented Reality: Augmented Reality is a technology that overlays digital information, such as images, videos, or 3D models, onto the real-world environment in real-time.

B   **Big Data**: Big data refers to extremely large and complex datasets that exceed the capabilities of traditional data processing tools and methods

Binary Data: Binary data is expressed numerically as a mix of zeros and ones

Blockchain: Blockchain is a distributed and decentralized digital ledger technology that records transactions across a network of computers in a secure and transparent manner

Business Analytics: Business analytics is a subset of business intelligence and a data management solution that focuses on the use of methodologies for data-driven business decisions

Bounce Rate: The percentage of visitors to website that leave after only reading one page is known as the "bounce rate."

C   **Cognitive Science**: Cognitive science is the study of how the mind works, including processes such as attention, memory, problem-solving, and language

Computational Neuroscience: Computational neuroscience focuses on developing mathematical models of the brain's information processing and functional organization

Concepts: Concepts are mental images, or entities "in the head," with a structure that reflects the outside world

Connectionism: An approach to studying human cognition known as connectionism makes use of mathematical models called connectionist networks or artificial neural networks

Cerebrum: Cerebrum is the largest part of the brain and is responsible for conscious thought, learning, memory, and voluntary movement

Cerebellum: The cerebellum, sometimes known as the "little brain," is a fist-sized section of the brain situated in the rear of the head, above the brainstem and below the temporal and occipital lobes

Cranial System: The cranial system, also known as the skull, is the bony structure that encloses and protects the brain

Creative Linguistics: Creative linguistics is a subscience of linguistics that studies creative aspects of language/speech and language aspects of creativity

Continuous data: Continuous data is a type of quantitative data that can take any value within a certain range or interval

Conjoint Analysis: Conjoint analysis is a sophisticated method of market research that is frequently used to examine how people choose between options

Causal Analysis: It determines why something happens and its effect on other variables

Cluster Analytics: Cluster analysis is a statistical technique used to group similar observations into clusters or segments

Constraint Satisfaction Problem: Constraint satisfaction problems (CSPs) are a class of problems in artificial intelligence where the goal is to find a solution that satisfies a set of constraints

CRISP-DM: CRISP-DM (Cross-Industry Standard Process for Data Mining) is a widely used methodology for data mining and machine learning projects

Crypt Arithmetic: Crypt arithmetic is a type of mathematical puzzle in which the digits in a mathematical expression are replaced with letters of the alphabet.

D   **Data Aggregation**: It is the process of gathering, organizing, and cleaning up data so it can be evaluated. Analytics require a strong data management strategy and a current data warehouse

Data Mining: Data mining sifts through sizable databases, analyzes data from various perspectives, and discovers trends, patterns, and linkages that were not before recognized

Data Security: Data security, also known as information security or cybersecurity, refers to the practice of protecting digital data from unauthorized access, disclosure, alteration, or destruction

Data Cleaning: Data cleaning, also known as data cleansing or data scrubbing, is the process of identifying and correcting errors, inconsistencies, and inaccuracies in a dataset

Data Processing: Data processing refers to the manipulation and transformation of data to convert it into a more usable and informative format

Data Visualization: Data visualization is the use of graphical representations to present data in a visually accessible and understandable way

Diagnostic Analytics: Diagnostic analytics provides an explanation for why something occurred or "why did it happen"

Descriptive Analytics: Descriptive analytics is a branch of analytics that focuses on describing and summarizing historical data to gain insights and understand patterns, trends, and characteristics of a given dataset

Deep Learning: Deep learning is a subfield of machine learning that focuses on neural networks with multiple layers (hence, the term "deep")

Data as a Whole: Data as a whole refers to all of the information that has been collected, stored, and analyzed in a particular context

Deductive Approach: The deductive method entails examining qualitative data in accordance with a specified structure

Discrete Data: Discrete data is a kind of quantitative information that contains countable statistics and nondivisible numbers

Discriminant Analysis: Discriminant analysis is used to classify observations into predefined groups based on their measured characteristics

Declarative Knowledge: Declarative knowledge is a type of knowledge that describes facts or information about the world.

E   **Epistemology**: An epistemologist might investigate the reliability of science and the veracity of our senses

Exploratory Data Analysis: Exploratory Data Analysis is a process of examining and understanding the structure and characteristics of a dataset.

F   **Formal logic**: The study of logical truths or deductively sound inferences is known as formal logic

Frontal lobe: The frontal lobe, the largest part of the brain, controls personality traits, judgment, and movement. It is situated in the front of the head

Factor Analytics: Factor analysis is a statistical technique used to identify underlying factors or dimensions that explain the pattern of correlations among a set of observed variables

Frames: Frames are a way of organizing knowledge into hierarchical structures, with each level representing a different aspect of the object or concept being represented

Faster R-CNN: Faster R-CNN, which stands for Faster Region Convolutional Neural Network, is a popular object detection algorithm introduced by Shaoqing Ren, Kaiming He, Ross Girshick, and Jian Sun in 2015.

H   **Hadoop**: Hadoop is an Apache open-source platform used to store, process, and analyze extraordinarily large volumes of data

HBase: Built on Hadoop, HBase is an open-source database with sorted map data. It is scalable horizontally and column-oriented

Hive: Hive is a data warehouse system used for structured data analysis. It is constructed on the top of Hadoop.

I   **Internet of Things**: The Internet of Things refers to a network of physical objects (devices, vehicles, appliances, and so on) that are embedded with sensors, software, and connectivity capabilities, allowing them to collect and exchange data with each other and with central systems over the Internet

Inbound Logistics: Activities related to receiving, warehousing, and inventory management of source materials and components

Outbound logistics: Activities related to distribution, including packaging, sorting, and shipping

Inductive Approach: Contrarily, the inductive approach does not rely on preconceived guidelines or a predefined framework

Interval Aata: Interval data, also called an integer, is defined as a data type which is measured along a scale, in which each point is placed at equal distance from one another

Inferential Analysis: It studies the relationship between different variables or makes predictions for the whole population

Inference Engine: This is the reasoning component of the system that uses the knowledge base to draw conclusions and make decisions.

K **K-Means**: K-Means clustering intends to partition n objects into k clusters in which each object belongs to the cluster with the nearest mean.

L **Logic**: Logicians research both sound and flawed justifications, as well as formal symbolic languages used to represent premises, phrases, and arguments

Linguistics: The systematic examination of the features of both specific languages and of language in general is the main goal of linguistics, which is the scientific study of language

Long-Term Memory: As long-term memory may store memories from the past to be recalled at a later time, it is believed to have an infinite amount of space

Linear Regression Analysis: Linear regression analysis is a statistical technique used to study the relationship between two continuous variables

Limited memory: Limited memory is a characteristic of certain types of artificial intelligence systems that are designed to operate with a finite amount of memory or storage capacity.

M **Machine Learning**: Machine learning is a subset of artificial intelligence (AI) that focuses on developing algorithms and models that enable computers to learn from and make predictions or decisions based on data

Metaphysics: The types of entities that exist, the nature of the universe and its elements, and the relationships between things or events are all topics of study for metaphysicians

Mail Questionnaire: A mail questionnaire enables the researcher to reach a variety of audiences by mailing the survey to a large portion of the sample population

Median: The median is the middle score for a set of data that has been arranged in order of magnitude

Mode: The mode is the most frequent score in our dataset

Multivariate Regression Analysis: Multivariate regression analysis extends the concept of simple linear regression to multiple predictor variables

Meta Knowledge: Meta knowledge, also known as meta knowledge or knowledge about knowledge, refers to knowledge that describes the characteristics, properties, and use of other types of knowledge.

N **Natural Language Processing**: NLP stands for natural language processing, which is a subfield of artificial intelligence (AI) and linguistics that focuses on the interaction between computers and human language

Neuroscience: The scientific study of the nervous system's functioning and diseases includes the study of the brain, spinal cord, and peripheral nervous system

Nominal Data: Nominal data is any sort of data that is used to label something without assigning it a number value

Neural networks: Neural networks involve developing computer systems that can simulate the behavior of the human brain and can be trained to perform specific tasks such as image recognition or language translation.

O **Occipital lobe**: The back portion of the brain that controls vision is called the occipital lobe

Ordinal Data: Ordinal data is qualitative data that has been ranked or scaled in a certain way

Ontologies: Ontologies are formal descriptions of the concepts and relationships within a particular domain of knowledge.

P **Page views**: Page views represent the total amount of times a page on website has been visited

Philosophy: The systematic study of broad and fundamental issues, such as those pertaining to existence, reason, knowledge, values, the mind, and language, is known as philosophy

Predictive Analytics: The question "What is likely to happen in the future?" is answered by predictive analytics

Prescriptive Snalytics: Using prescriptive analytics, we can determine "what course of action to pursue"

Python: Python is a high-level, interpreted programming language known for its simplicity, readability, and versatility. It was created by Guido van Rossum and first released in 1991

Procurement: Activities related to the sourcing of raw materials, components, equipment, and services

Psychology: The scientific study of the mind and behavior is called psychology

Probability Sampling: Probability sampling is a sampling technique that involves random selection to gather data from the target audience, allowing researchers to obtain a probability statement

Percentile: Percentiles are values that separate the data into 100 equal parts

Principal Component Analytics: Principal component analysis (PCA) is a statistical technique used to reduce the dimensionality of a dataset by identifying the most important underlying patterns of variation

Procedural Knowledge: Procedural knowledge, also known as skill or know-how, refers to knowledge about how to perform a specific task or procedure.

Q   **Qualitative Data**: Qualitative data is the term used to describe information that cannot be expressed in numerical or quantitative terms

Quantitative Data: Quantitative data is information that is expressed as counts or numbers, each of which has a specific numerical value

Quartiles: Quartiles are values that separate the data into four equal parts.

R   **Returning Visitors**: The quantity of people who have previously visited on the website is referred to as returning visitors (or users)

Reinforcement Learning: Reinforcement learning (RL) is a subfield of machine learning concerned with how an agent can learn to make sequential decisions in an environment to maximize a notion of cumulative reward

Robotics: Robotics involves developing machines that can perform physical tasks and interact with the environment, often using sensors and machine vision

Reactive Machine: A reactive machine is a type of artificial intelligence that operates purely on the basis of its immediate inputs and outputs, without any memory or ability to learn from past experiences.

S   **Sqoop**: Sqoop is a command-line interface application for transferring data between relational databases and Hadoop

Sessions: A session is a collection of activities that happen on website over a specific period of time, such as page views, CTA clicks, and events

SEMMA Methodology: SEMMA is an acronym for Sample, Explore, Modify, Model, and Assess, which is a data mining methodology developed by SAS Institute Inc.

Segmentation: Segmentation is a way of defining the pixels of an object class within images or video frames in computer vision datasets

Spark: Apache Spark is an open-source cluster computing framework. Its primary purpose is to handle the real-time generated data

Short-Term Memory: Short-term memory can only store information for about 30 seconds

Structured Data: Structured data is data that follows a preestablished data model and is easy to analyze

Semistructured Data: Data that has some structure but does not adhere to a data model is referred to as semistructured data

Standard Deviation: In statistics, the standard deviation is a measure of the amount of variation or dispersion of a set of values

Supervised Learning: Supervised learning is a subfield of machine learning where an algorithm learns from labeled training data to make predictions or take actions

Semantic networks: Semantic networks represent knowledge as a set of interconnected nodes, where each node represents a concept or object and the edges represent relationships between them

SSD (Single Shot MultiBox Detector): SSD is another real-time object detection model that uses a single neural network to predict object locations and class probabilities

Structural Knowledge: Structural knowledge, also known as relational knowledge, refers to knowledge about the relationships between different objects or concepts.

T   **Text Mining**: Text mining, also known as text analytics or natural language processing (NLP), is the process of extracting valuable information and insights from unstructured text data

      Trend analysis: A common method for analyzing interval data is trend analysis, which is used to identify patterns and insights in survey data across time

      TURF Analysis: A marketer might use the TURF analysis method, which stands for Totally Unduplicated Reach and Frequency analysis, to assess the potential of market research for a variety of goods and services.

U   **Unstructured Data**: Unstructured data is any data that deviates from a data model and lacks a clearly defined structure, making it difficult for computer programs to use

      Unsupervised Learning: Unsupervised learning is a subfield of machine learning where the algorithm learns patterns and structures in unlabeled data without any specific target or output variable to guide the learning process

      User Interface: This is the interface that allows users to interact with the system, input data, and receive output.

V   **Volume**: The size of the datasets that an organization has gathered for analysis and processing is referred to as the volume of data

      Velocity: Data velocity refers to the speed in which data is generated, distributed and collected

      Variety: Structured, unstructured, and semistructured data that is compiled from various sources is referred to as "variety of big data"

      Value Chain Analytics: Value chain analytics is a method for visually examining a company's operations to determine how the company might gain a competitive edge

      Variance is the measure of how notably a collection of data is spread out.

W   **Web Analytics**: The gathering, monitoring, and evaluating website data is referred to as web analytics

      Web Scrapping: Web scraping is a computerized technique for gathering copious volumes of data from websites.

Y   **YOLO**: YOLO (You Only Look Once) is a real-time object detection system that uses a single neural network to predict bounding boxes and class probabilities for multiple objects in an image.

Z   **Z-Score**: Z-score is a statistical measurement that describes a value's relationship to the mean of a group of values.

Index

Note: Page numbers followed by "*f*" and "*t*" refer to figures and tables, respectively.

Printed in the United States
by Baker & Taylor Publisher Services

Printed in the United States
by Baker & Taylor Publisher Services